Materials and Procedures for Residential Construction

Materials and Procedures for Residential Construction

Alonzo Wass

Gordon A. Sanders

Reston Publishing Company, Inc.
A Prentice-Hall Company
Reston, Virginia

Library of Congress Cataloging in Publication Data

Wass, Alonzo.
  Materials and procedures for residential
construction.

  Includes index.
  1. House construction.   2. Building materials.
I. Sanders, Gordon A., joint author.   II. Title.
TH4811.W359   690'.837   80-27471
ISBN 0-8359-4284-8

10 9 8 7 6 5 4 3 2 1

Printed in the United States of America

Contents

PREFACE   **xv**

1   THE BUSINESS OF BUILDING   1

1.1   Business Capital, 2
1.2   Making a District Market Survey for a Building Lot, 2
1.3   Inspecting and Surveying the Building Site, 3
1.4   Legal Considerations, 3
1.5   Land Purchase, 3
1.6   Land Registry Office, 4
1.7   Title Deeds and Easement, 5
1.8   Sanitary Fill, 5
1.9   Building Permits, 5
1.10   Land Appraisal, 6
1.11   Drawings and Specifications, 6
1.12   Preliminary Building Operations, 7
1.13   Partnerships, Limited Partnerships, and Corporations, 8
1.14   Bankruptcy, 11
1.15   Class Research, 11

2   **PRELIMINARY BUSINESS: PRIOR TO BUILDING LAND
        PURCHASE**   **15**

2.1 *Municipal Planning Department, 15*
2.2 *Building License, 16*
2.3 *Zone Classification, 17*
2.4 *Guide List of General Overhead Expenses, 18*
2.5 *Guide List of Overhead Expenses Chargeable to Each Individual
         Job, 19*

3   **LAND TITLES**   **23**

3.1 *Land Titles, 23*

4   **DEPRECIATION**   **33**

4.1 *Outline of Depreciation, 33*
4.2 *Straight Line Method of Depreciation, 34*
4.3 *Declining Balance Method of Depreciation, 35*
4.4 *Sum-of-the-Years-Digits Method of Depreciation, 36*
4.5 *Equipment: Schedules and Maintenance, 38*
4.6 *Industrial Equipment, 38*
4.7 *Leasing Contractor's Equipment, 39*

5   **FINAL INSPECTION OF NEW BUILDINGS**   **41**

5.1 *The Final Inspection, 41*
5.2 *Advertising and Selling the Final Product, 43*
5.3 *Facts to Ascertain Before Drawing Contract of Sale, 44*

6   **AN INTRODUCTION TO THE CRITICAL PATH METHOD**   **47**

6.1 *Terms, 47*

6.2　*Using the CPM Chart, 50*
6.3　*Computing CPM Time, 50*

7　PRELIMINARY BUILDING OPERATIONS　　　　　53

7.1　*Single and Multiple Residential Units, 53*
7.2　*The Commitment to Build, 54*
7.3　*Inspecting the Building Site, 54*
7.4　*Datum and Benchmarks, 54*
7.5　*Underground Conditions and Dewatering, 55*
7.6　*Subsurface Exploration, 56*
7.7　*Building Inspectors, 56*
7.8　*Building in Frigid Conditions, 56*

8　AN INTRODUCTION TO LAND GRADING　　　　59

8.1　*A Glossary of Land Grading Terms, 59*
8.2　*Swell Percentage of Cut Earth, 60*
8.3　*Benchmark or Data, 60*
8.4　*Volumes: Imperial and Metric, 61*
8.5　*Estimating Cut, 61*

9　FOUNDATIONS LAYOUT: BATTER BOARDS, AND STORY RODS　　　　69

9.1　*The Right-angle Triangle, 69*
9.2　*The Builder's Foundation Layout Square, 70*
9.3　*Grading: Building Lines and Foundation Layout, 70*
9.4　*Batter Boards, 75*
9.5　*Story Rods for Carpenters, 77*
9.6　*Story Rods for Masons, 78*
9.7　*Carpenter's Door Strap, 78*
9.8　*Kitchen Cabinet Rod, 78*
9.9　*Excavation Story Rod Exercise, 79*

10 FOUNDATION, CHIMNEYS, AND SLAB ON GRADE 83

10.1 *Underpinning, 83*
10.2 *Pier Pads, 84*
10.3 *Chimney Foundations, 84*
10.4 *Estimating the Number of Bricks in Chimneys, 84*
10.5 *Average Weight of Solid Brick Walls, 87*
10.6 *Wall Footings, 89*
10.7 *Reinforcing-steel Contractor's Specifications, 89*
10.8 *Combined Slab and Foundation, 90*
10.9 *Step Footings, 90*
10.10 *Piles and Ground Beams, 90*
10.11 *Slab on Grade Floor Panel Heating, 91*
10.12 *Mesh: Steel-welded Reinforcing, 92*
10.13 *Installation for Floor Panel Heating, 92*

11 FORMWORK AND CONCRETE 97

11.1 *Concrete Formwork: Basement Walls, 98*
11.2 *Design Mix by Weight, 98*
11.3 *Weight of Concrete, 99*
11.4 *Ready-mixed Concrete, 99*
11.5 *Storage of Cement for On-the-job Mixing, 100*
11.6 *Water-Cement Ratio, 100*
11.7 *Surface Area of Aggregate, 101*
11.8 *Manufactured Aggregates: Crushed Rock, 102*
11.9 *Bank or Pit-Run Aggregates, 103*
11.10 *Estimating Quantities of Dry Materials for One Cubic Yard of Wet Concrete, 103*
11.11 *Concrete Floor Specification and Problem, 104*
11.12 *American and Canadian Gallon, 104*
11.13 *Runways and Ramps, 105*
11.14 *Machine Mixing Time, 105*
11.15 *Sizes of Concrete Mixers, 105*
11.16 *Dry Materials and Water per Batch, 105*
11.17 *Estimating Quantities of Dry Materials for a Concrete Floor, 106*
11.18 *Wood Bucks, 106*
11.19 *Curing, 110*

Contents   ix

12   **TYPICAL WALL SECTIONS, AND MATERIALS GUIDE LIST   113**

12.1   Wall Sections, 113
12.2   Platform or Western Framing, 113
12.3   Balloon Framing, 116
12.4   Post and Beam Framing, 116
12.5   Post and Beam Framing Combined with Conventional Framing, 116
12.6   Brick Veneer 4", 120
12.7   Thin Brick Veneer or Ceramic Tile, 120
12.8   Brick Veneer with 1" Air Space, 120
12.9   Typical Wall Section with Brick Veneer, 121
12.10 Brick Veneered Frame, 121
12.11 A Guide List for Residential Construction, 122

13   **BASEMENT WALLS, COLUMNS, AND FIRST FLOOR ASSEMBLY 129**

13.1   A Glossary of Underpinning Member Terms, 130
13.2   Insulation Requirements for Concrete Floor Slabs on Ground, 131
13.3   Ground Slab Reinforcing Grade Beams and Foundation Walls, 135
13.4   Joist Ends Embedded in Concrete; Balloon Framing Sill, 135
13.5   Types of Centrally Located Supports for Floor Assemblies, 136
13.6   Bridging for Floor Joists, 139
13.7   Joist Supports over Wood Beams, 141
13.8   In-line Joist System and Floor Framing, 141
13.9   Joist Layout, 16" on Centers, 143
13.10 Framing Floor Openings, 145

14   **CONCRETE FORMS, PLYWOOD, AND HARDWARE   149**

14.1   The Advantages of Plywood for Concrete Forming, 149
14.2   Release Agents for Plywood Concrete Forms, 152
14.3   Hardware for Plywood Concrete Forms, 153
14.4   Framed Forms, 153
14.5   Design of Plywood Formwork, 157
14.6   Certification Marks on COFI Plywood, 158

15   WALL FRAMING, ANCHORS, AND FASTENERS   161

15.1   *Conventional Wall Framing, 161*
15.2   *The Carpenter's Traditional Framing Square, 165*
15.3   *Rough Openings for Doors and Windows, 166*
15.4   *Prefabrication and Semi-prefabrication, 166*
15.5   *Wood Backing for Subtrades, 170*
15.6   *Structural Wood Fasteners, 171*
15.7   *Case Study of a Housing Development, 182*
15.8   *Steel Floor Joists and Studs, 185*

16   SCAFFOLDING   191

16.1   *Half-horse Scaffold, 191*
16.2   *Double-pole Scaffold, 193*
16.3   *Single-pole Scaffold, 193*
16.4   *Metal Scaffolding, 193*
16.5   *Scaffold Maintenance, 194*

17   POST AND BEAM CONSTRUCTION   197

17.1   *Posts and Beams, 197*
17.2   *Curtain Walls in Post and Beam Construction, 198*
17.3   *Post and Beam: Description and Design Factors, 202*
17.4   *Advantages of Post and Beam, 204*

18   CEILINGS AND FLAT ROOFS   207

18.1   *Ceiling Framing, 207*
18.2   *Tiled Ceilings, 212*
18.3   *Tongue and Groove Softwood Plywood Roof Decks, 213*

18.4 *Floors, 215*
18.5 *Roofs, 215*
18.6 *Metric Nomenclature for Surfaced Softwood Lumber Products, 216*

19   PITCH ROOFS   221

19.1 *Types of Roofs, 221*
19.2 *Definitions of Roof Terms, 223*
19.3 *The Carpenter's Traditional Framing Square, 225*
19.4 *Layout of a Common Rafter for a One-third Pitch Roof, 226*
19.5 *A Regular Hip Roof, 231*
19.6 *Layout of the Hip Rafter, 232*
19.7 *Hip Rafter Original Level Line at the Birdsmouth, 233*
19.8 *Shortening of the Hip Rafter, 233*
19.9 *Side Cuts (Cheek Cuts) of the Hip Rafter, 234*
19.10 *Backing (Beveling) of the Hip Rafter, 234*
19.11 *Dropping the Hip Rafter, 236*
19.12 *Review of the LL of the Tail of the Common Rafter, 237*
19.13 *The LL of the Tail of the Hip Rafter, 237*
19.14 *Check the LL of the Hip Rafter by the Step Off Method, 237*
19.15 *The Tail End Side Cuts of the Hip Rafter, 238*
19.16 *Jack Rafters for a Regular Hip Roof, 241*
19.17 *Layout of Jack Rafters, 241*
19.18 *Wood Roof Trusses, 243*
19.19 *Metric Roof Framing, 244*

20   WALL CLADDING, FIBER BOARDS, INSULATION, AND VAPOR
           BARRIERS   249

20.1 *Wall Cladding and Fiber Boards, 249*
20.2 *Basic Patterns, 251*
20.3 *Nailing Techniques, 252*
20.4 *Basic Wall Construction, 253*
20.5 *Types of Nails, 254*
20.6 *Basic Patterns and Application, 255*
20.7 *Applications and Estimating, 256*
20.8 *Requirements for Sound Control, 257*
20.9 *Insulation and Vapor Barriers, 261*
20.10 *Conduction (Metric Measurements of Heat Transfer), 261*

21   SUBTRADES AND JOB SAFETY   273

21.1 *The Proposal to Build, 274*
21.2 *The Appraiser, 274*
21.3 *Responsibilities of the General Contractor to the Subcontractor, 275*
21.4 *The Excavator, 276*
21.5 *Concrete Subcontractors, 276*
21.6 *A Guide List of Subtrades, 277*
21.7 *Workers' Compensation Agencies, 278*
21.8 *Insurances, 280*
21.9 *Experience Rating, 283*

22   STAIRS, FIREPLACES, AND INTERIOR TRIM   285

22.1 *A Glossary of Stair Building Terms, 285*
22.2 *Risers and Treads, 287*
22.3 *Finding the Line of Flight for a Stairway, 289*
22.4 *Ratio of Rise to Tread, 290*
22.5 *Chimneys and Fireplaces, 291*
22.6 *A Glossary of Chimney and Fireplace Terms, 294*
22.7 *Chimney Illustrations, 296*
22.8 *The Metric "Standard" Brick Format, 296*
22.9 *Interior Trim, 296*

23   MASONRY UNITS, GLASS BLOCKS, AND GLIDING DOORS   301

23.1 *Introduction to Masonry Units, 301*
23.2 *Adjustable Wall Ties, Reinforcing, and Control Joints, 302*
23.3 *Glazed Masonry Walls, 302*
23.4 *Glass Blocks and Glass Block Panel Construction, 302*
23.5 *Masonry Unit Lintels, 314*
23.6 *Gliding Doors, 315*
23.7 *Metric Masonry Blocks, 322*

24 PAINTING, DECORATING, FLOOR FINISHING, AND EXTRUDED METAL FINISHING PIECES 325

24.1 *Painting, 325*
24.2 *Wallpaper, Mirrors, and Chandeliers, 326*
24.3 *Resilient Floor Coverings, 327*
24.4 *Carpeted Floors, 327*
24.5 *Wood Flooring, 327*
24.6 *Abrasive Safety Stair and Walking Products, 331*

25 LANDSCAPING, FINAL INSPECTION, NOTARIZATION OF DOCUMENTS, AND PROPERTY SALE 333

25.1 *Driveways, Paths, and Outside Concrete Steps, 333*
25.2 *Types of Driveways, 334*
25.3 *Landscaping, 335*
25.4 *The Final Inspection, 335*
25.5 *Maintenance, 336*
25.6 *Land Title, 336*
25.7 *Facts to Ascertain Before Drawing Contract of Sale, 336*
25.8 *Advertising and Selling the Final Product, 338*

APPENDIXES
A Glossary of Common Building Terms, 341
Metric Conversion Tables, 351

INDEX 357

Preface

This book is designed for ambitious and mature tradesmen; for instructors and students at technical colleges and vocational schools; and for on-the-job persons who intend to enter the residential construction industry as a career. It is a natural sequel to the two editions of METHODS AND MATERIALS OF RESIDENTIAL CONSTRUCTION, published by Reston Publishing Company, Inc., and written by Alonzo Wass.

This new book has been developed with the collaboration of its coauthor, Mr. Gordon A. Sanders, who brought to it his long educational experience with the very type of person for whom the book is designed. New material includes metric conversion tables, easily referred to in Appendix B.

For those offering courses, the book offers wide scope for student research in the areas described in Section 1.15. CLASS RESEARCH. Student committees may conduct research studies in specific areas, bringing to the class the results of their findings. In this manner, the course becomes a simulated on-the-job sequence of events. Furthermore, as a result, all students will have acquired files of up-to-date construction literature, and some may have discovered for themselves challenging jobs in industry.

For persons in industry and for students, the book emphasizes through content organization the very important relationship of preliminary and actual building operations. It suggests the need for the reader to obtain general knowledge of the building process before becoming a builder, a contractor, a subcontractor, or one of many types of construction specialists. The idea of a systematic approach or systems approach to building is implied by both content assembly and selection of topics.

The authors extend sincere thanks to Cindi Arden for her typing and re-typing; to Mrs. R.G. Cox for her reading and re-reading of the text; and to our respective wives for their help, support, and patience with us during the writing of the manuscript.

A.W.
G.A.S.

1

The Business of Building

This chapter is designed to help an entrant into the business of residential construction become aware of the procedures of doing limited market research for buying a parcel of building land and for forming a partnership.

Many young businesses fail because the operators, who may know a lot about building, know little about business procedures. To enter into the residential construction field there are some five basic requirements. The would-be entrepreneur must:

1. Be physically fit, competent in a trade, and confident in himself/herself.

2. Know the procedures for purchasing a parcel (piece) of building land and know if a house built on such a parcel would have sales appeal. *A parcel of land is an area held as one unit under one ownership.*

3. Be prepared to pay cash for, and have a clear title to, the land upon which to build. This means that there are no legally registered liens nor indebtedness against the land.

4. If necessary, be prepared to work for others, earning a weekly wage packet while working spare time for himself/herself.

5. Know the advantages and disadvantages of going into business on his/her own account, or in partnership, or in forming a corporation.

1.1 BUSINESS CAPITAL

The first thing to know about business capital is that lending institutions do not lend money to anyone to commence a business. Once a business is well started, they will loan money for business expansion, but they will want possession of the land title certificate as collateral security. That is a pledge, and in case of default on payment on the loan, they could foreclose on the land.

1.2 MAKING A DISTRICT MARKET SURVEY FOR A BUILDING LOT

The object of speculation building is to erect the right type of house in the right place to suit the purse and aesthetic taste of a certain group of people. **Remember that it costs just as much to build an expensive house on a poor lot as it does to build a similar house on an appropriate and appealing good lot.**

Here are some points that should be carefully considered before building residential units:

1. General location

2. Cost of the land

3. Topographical features of the land. Will it have to be cut and filled (landscaped), or is it reclaimed land? (If the land is purchased from the local au-

thority, the county, or a city, they may know its history.) Has the land been sanitary filled?

4. Drainage. Is the area subject to extremes of rain, snow, freezing temperatures, flooding, or wind?

5. Removal of trees or existing buildings. At what cost?

6. Kind of water available. Is it city, rural, spring, or well water? What about the sewage system? Will you have to put in a septic field yourself? Will a well have to be drilled? How do these things affect the end price of your product?

7. Availability of power, natural gas, telephone, and transportation.

8. Distance to existing or projected schools, shopping centers, libraries, parks, hospitals, churches, mail boxes, and post offices. Are there postal delivery, police, and fire department services?

9. Other residential construction being built in the area. What is the price range? Are there vacant units? What types are vacant?

10. Places people will work. Are there any projected industries near this area? (Contact the state agencies for commerce, for economic development, for economic opportunity, and for housing.)

11. Zoning laws. (Contact the municipality for a copy.)

12. Number of rooms (the number of square feet or square meters)

13. Price range of the unit

14. Probable taxes on the completed building. (You may get an assessment from the local authority, county, state, city, or municipality.)

1.3 INSPECTING AND SURVEYING THE BUILDING SITE

Before purchasing a lot for building a residence or before submitting a bid to erect a residential building, it is important to identify and thoroughly inspect the proposed site. Some local authorities may, for a charge, officially survey land. Where this is not done, and there is the slightest doubt about the location of the original survey stakes, hire a registered surveyor.

While you are reading this chapter, someone is having a partly (or completely) finished house demolished or removed from one building lot to a correctly located one. In one case, a contractor was well advanced on the building of a city home. His operations were on an open, staked, new subdivision, and he believed that he was working on 15th Street and 18th Avenue N.W. of a certain city. There were no other houses in the area at that time. The building inspector arrived at the correct lot to make his first inspection and discovered a vacant lot. Immediately due north, he saw a house in the course of construction and ready for its first inspection. This was situated due north on 15th Street and 19th Avenue N.W. The building inspector informed the builder of his mistaken site operations. Imagine the critical blow that this could have been to the contractor. In this case, the rightful owner very graciously consented to exchange lots— with the provision that the contractor bear the total cost of conveyance of the two properties.

Occasionally, even the surveyor can make a mistake, but he or she is bonded against such an eventuality, so you are protected. The advice, therefore, is to employ a registered surveyor who will correctly locate your lot, put up the batter boards, and establish your levels. When this is done professionally, you can begin to build with every confidence as to location and to levels.

1.4 LEGAL CONSIDERATIONS

It is important that the builder consult an attorney before, not after, signing any legal documents. The fee should be considered as an overhead expense, like that of the surveyor, and it can be reflected in the end price of the product. The builder must be aware of many points of law. As an example of one such point, the definition of *foreclosure* is given below.

> FORECLOSURE is a legal proceeding by which the equity of redemption of a mortgagor in and to a mortgaged property is extinguished. Foreclosure is in order when a mortgagor fails to pay principal and interest monies as stipulated, or to comply otherwise with the conditions of mortgage, such as paying taxes and insurance on mortgaged property, etc. In the event of foreclosure sale, the mortgagor is entitled to receive any excess funds produced, by the sale, over the amount due to the mortgagee and over the legal costs and expenses. In many States, and in Provinces of Canada, the method is to enter a foreclosure suit in court. The sheriff advertises and sells the mortgaged property.

Methods may differ in other jurisdictions. It is important to remember that the courts require a complete statement of all monies paid by the mortgagor to the mortgagee. Keep good records!

1.5 LAND PURCHASE

The land in North America is owned either by the government or by private parties. The title to all parcels of land is recorded in the land registry office of the area in which the land is located.

Assume you want to purchase a small parcel of vacant land within the municipal jurisdiction and that you do not know the owner. Take the following steps:

1. Obtain a map of the area from the local authority (county, state, municipality, or city) and identify the land and its address in relation to the adjoining property.

2. Inquire at the local taxation department for the name of the person paying the taxes—the owner.

3. Obtain from the local taxation department the official description of the property. This bears no relation to the postal address. It may be something like: LOT 7 OF BLOCK 14 CITY OF_____ AP 2816.

4. Proceed to the local planning department and check for zoning restrictions on the property.

5. Using the official description of the property, go to the land registry office (or have your agent go for you) and search the title.

6. Write to the owners of the property asking if they wish to sell the land. They may live miles away, possibly even abroad.

1.6 LAND REGISTRY OFFICE

In every state and province there is a land registry office where all the land in that particular registration district is registered according to ownership on documents called titles. All the land in North America is registered by individual parties or by the government.

It is important to become familiar with the system of land registry and of the searching of titles in your district; there are differences between some states and some provinces.

For a very nominal fee any citizen, or his lawyer or agent, may scrutinize any title to any land registered in any particular office. This is called "searching the title." The prospective purchaser of a parcel of land may wish to search the title with a view to having any encumbrance removed from it. If there are no encumbrances registered on the title, the property is said to have a "clear title."

Some of the encumbrances registered on the title may be as follows:

1. A *reservation* by any party or the government for the mineral rights on the property.

2. A *first, second, or third mortgage*, or more mortgages, registered against the property.

3. A *mechanics lien*. This is a statement of claim registered against the property for work alleged to have been done on the property for which the mechanic has not been paid. Such liens must be registered by the individual who did the work within a certain number of days of completion.

4. *Power of Attorney*. This entry on a title shows that the title owner has given another party the authority to act for him in any dealings in connection with the land specified. These powers are very sweeping and are usually given to highly reputable law firms, but the power of attorney may be given to almost anyone over the age of twenty-one. This instrument is useful where the owner is living at a great distance from his holding.

5. *Writ or Judgment.* This is a recorded statement on the title deeds showing that, at a certain time and place, a judgment was handed down by a court of law to the effect that the party in whose name the title stands was indebted at that time to another party for some services or goods that were not paid for. These services or goods could even be indebtedness to multiple stores, garages, and so on.

6. *Caveat.* This instrument is a *"notice to beware"* that the party who has filed the caveat has an interest in this property; this interest must be taken into account before any change in ownership is made.

1.7 TITLE DEEDS AND EASEMENT

A **title deed** for land is a legal document on which is recorded the legal description of a parcel (piece) of land and the registered owners thereof. A title is also a certificate constituting legal evidence of ownership of a thing other than land. An **easement** is the right of one party to enjoy some privilege on the land of another. Easements are often registered (after an agreed compensation to the owner or owners of a parcel of land for such things as sewer, gas, power, and telephone lines); the owners have the right to enter the property for the maintenance of such lines.

Sometimes a contractor while building in a metropolitan area may negotiate with the owner of a vacant lot for a temporary easement to enable him to use it for his field office, storage sheds, and to park his equipment so as to be near his job. Thus the contractor for a negotiated fee (and after the easement has been legally registered) will

have the right, under law, to use such property for the agreed purposes for the legally agreed length of time. Inquire at your local land office for the location of the land titles office of your area and *visit it!*

1.8 SANITARY FILL

Many authorities bring low-lying land to a desired grade by sanitary filling the depression. First, the topsoil is stockpiled on the site; then household refuse is compacted in the depression to a depth of several feet (meters). This is followed with several feet (meters) of clean gravel or other approved clean compacted fill. Sandwiching is continued until the replaced topsoil brings the whole area to the desired grade.

Within a few years, the area is perfectly sanitary and ready for building or recreational uses. Records of reclaimed land under their jurisdiction are maintained by local authorities and are available for study.

The importance of the builder (contractor) making his own subsurface exploration cannot be overemphasized—even though the architect/engineer supplies soil data in contract documents. There is always a risk of adverse ground conditions—from rock to water.

With the exception of incorrectly locating the building according to local ordinances, there is more money lost through subsurface hazards than any other facet of building construction.

1.9 BUILDING PERMITS

A proposal for a new building permit must first be submitted to the municipal planning department, which examines the plans and specifications to determine whether they will conform to the planned pattern of the area in which the building is proposed to be erected.

When approved by the planning department, the application is passed to the municipal engineers for structural examinations. If they approve, a building permit is issued upon payment of a scaled fee, depending on the type of building. This building permit must be prominently displayed at the new building site.

Other permits may include water, street closing, permission to use city water hydrants, and connections to city sewer line.

1.10 LAND APPRAISAL

The American Institute of Real Estate Appraisers was founded in 1932, and the Society of Real Estate Appraisers was founded 1935. Both organizations are international, and there are smaller organizations in localized areas.

A member of the Institute or the Society may be retained if an appraisal of a parcel of land is required. An appraisal may be needed for:

1. The purchase or sale of a property;

2. Financing a mortgage;

3. Assessing municipal taxes;

4. Insurance, such as fire, or other perils;

5. Disposition of property between beneficiaries under a will;

6. Take-over by government by right of Eminent Domain. Such a take-over would be made for the public good, say to incorporate the land into a public park, or to build a swimming pool, or to erect a library. Eminent Domain is the right of government to take private prop-

erty for public benefit, provided that it serves a necessary public use and gives fair compensation to the owner.

The following appraisal methods are typical of those used by small loan associations.

1. Appraisal by comparative values of recent sales of similar property in the same district;

2. Appraisal by adjusted values against trends of the environment in the district, and;

3. Appraisal by intended future development in the district by the municipality. The appraiser should be a very experienced realtor who knows the district intimately.

1.11 DRAWINGS AND SPECIFICATIONS

The best house designs are prepared by architects who specialize in this field. Their duties fall under four main divisions: preliminary sketches; working drawings and specifications; obtaining and letting contracts; and supervision of the structure. Such a home will be designed to suit: soil conditions; lot; view; compass points; prevailing wind; and all to the satisfaction of the local building code and the needs and purse of the owner.

Government Sponsored Drawings and Specifications are available through the state and also manufacturers' associations. The U.S. Department of Agriculture Forest Service, Forest Products Laboratory, Madison, Wisconsin, is an excellent source for obtaining drawings and specifications for inexpensive homes. They will supply drawings and specifications at little cost. The Canadian Government sponsors a nonprofit Canada Mortgage and Housing Corporation from whom may be obtained many free publications about housing, together with a publication depicting hundreds of architect-designed homes. Three sets of drawings for any of these homes may be purchased for less than $20.00. These drawings are acceptable across the country by all local authorities. You may want to build speculatively one or two of these homes, or you could recommend this publication to a prospective customer. Many of these drawings lend themselves to enlargement, but any alterations must have the approval of the issuing body and of the local building engineering department.

Real Estate Companies usually have a great number of house drawings from which you can select the type of home you or your prospect would like to build. A great advantage here is that you may go to see an occupied home built to the design and specifications which interest you. The owners may let you look through their home. This could be a very profitable visit. You may find out not only what the owners like about it but also how they would improve on it if they were building another similar home. *It is most important that you build the type of home that people want at the price they can afford to pay.*

Distribution of Copies of Drawings and Specifications are as follows:

1. The owner.
2. The authority having jurisdiction. That copy will be the Master Copy on which the authority will enface any corrections

or special requirements to be complied with. (Such amendments should be neatly copied onto all other copies.)
3. The lending organization. (This organization may also make periodic inspections.)
4. The builder.

1.12 PRELIMINARY BUILDING OPERATIONS

1. Have an official survey made of the building lot.
2. Make a grid of the building lot showing the contours.
3. Submit to the local authority a copy of the drawings and specifications.
4. Obtain a building permit from the local authority engineers and display it on the building site.
5. Get a profile of the street sewer system from the local engineers.
6. Note carefully the present and future grade of the property.
7. Check test pits for the soil conditions upon which you propose to build.
8. If blasting will be necessary, consult the local experts.
9. Decide what type of temporary office, store sheds, and facilities are necessary. It may be cheaper to run a half-ton truck from an off-site locaton.
10. Contact local authorities for power, light, and water services, both temporary and permanent.
11. Clear the property of such things as existing buildings and fences, and check whether or not existing mains to the property have to be removed.

12. Decide where on the property the top-soil is to be stockpiled ready for final landscaping.

13. Know where you may legally dump excess excavated material.

14. Erect advertising signs.

15. Order reinforcing and contact the local concrete manufacturer for a tentative date to deliver concrete. Determine the proper amount.

16. Order lumber and nails.

17. Check that men and machines will be available when required.

18. Check financial arrangements.

19. Prepare a progress report.

20. Check all insurances including workmen's compensation.

21. Order weeping tiles for outside of footings.

22. Have the surveyor erect the batter boards.

1.13 INDIVIDUAL PROPRIETORSHIP, PARTNERSHIPS, LIMITED PARTNERSHIPS, AND CORPORATIONS

Individual Proprietorship

With individual ownership, the total operation of the business is conducted by one person (frequently with the help of the family or employees). Legally, only one person is responsible for the indebtedness or profits of the business.

Some of the advantages and disadvantages of owning your own business are:

Advantages

1. The profits and business expansion are yours.

2. As your own boss, you direct your own policy.

3. There are no complications with others about responsibilities and rewards.

4. You do not have to meet in committee to formulate policy.

5. You set your own working days and hours.

6. You may cut overhead expenses by operating the business from your own home.

Disadvantages

1. Your liabilities include your *business* and *personal assets*.

2. In case of business failure, your personal and business assets are subject to seizure and sale.

3. Assets that you may acquire from the time of your declaration of bankruptcy to the time of discharge are also subject to seizure.

4. The liability of married men is restricted to their own personal property; that which is listed in the wife's name cannot be touched: *Married persons entering business in the Province of Quebec must go through legal proceedings to determine to what extent the property of the one is separate and distinct from the other.*

5. The business is usually small in size and will have to compete with large organizations with specialists in every field.

6. You cannot purchase materials in the same bulk with the same discounts available to larger companies.

7. After your death, the administrators of your estate may carry on the business under letters of administration until the estate is settled and the business is handed over to your heirs. The business may suffer as a consequence, but you may purchase Key-Man Insurance.

If you wish to add "and Company" to your name or to use an entirely different name from your own, such a business name must be registered in the state or province in which you are conducting business. This is understandable since the public must always be protected by having access to the correct name of any organization with which any person wishes to do business or present claims.

Partnerships

In a partnership, at least two people pool their resources and abilities to conduct a particular business enterprise. A partnership is created by entering into a contract that has two main points: (1) it states the contribution to be made to the business by each partner; and (2) it specifies the manner in which earnings of the enterprise are to be shared by the partners. Note carefully that, upon the demise of a partner, the partnership does not exist.

General Partnerships

In general partnerships, the members are jointly and severally (individually) liable for the debts of the entire business. That is to say, if creditors cannot get satisfaction from the business, they can enforce their claims against any partner(s).

It has been said that partnerships are the easiest things to get into and the most difficult from which to withdraw. Any partnership agreement should be given most serious thought. It should be drawn up and registered by an attorney who is acquainted with your type of business. *Consult an attorney before (not after) you enter into partnership.*

Limited Partnerships

In a limited partnership, one or more partners operate the business, and one or more invest cash only. Liability is limited to creditors' claims only to the amount of cash invested in the business; no claim may be made against their personal assets.

Individuals considering entering into a limited partnership should itemize those points they wish to have included in the agreement. They should meet in committee once or twice and present a rough draft in legal terminology. The participants should again meet in committee and then present the final draft to the attorney for final drafting and notarization.

Partnership Agreements

A partnership agreement should contain a number of details. Among them are:

1. The purpose of the agreement.
2. The name and permanent address of the firm and of each partner.
3. The commencement date of the partnership.
4. The duration of the partnership.
5. The manner in which the partnership is to be terminated.
6. The name and address of the bankers.

7. The name and address of the attorney.

8. The procedure for continuing the agreement.

9. The amount of capital to be invested by each partner, with a statement as to whether or not the amount or part of it is to be paid in property, and if in property, a full description thereof.

10. The starting date of the fiscal year.

11. The amount of interest, if any, that is to be paid on capital.

12. The powers and duties of the partners.

13. Whether or not the partners are to devote full, normal business hours to the partnership.

14. Whether or not partners are allowed to enter into any other business that is in any way connected with the building industry.

15. The manner in which profits or losses of the business are to be divided.

16. The name of the person who will keep the books of the business to which all members will have access at any reasonable time.

17. The percentage division of partnership assets at dissolution.

18. The method of continuing the partnership in the event of the death or incompetence of any partner.

19. In case of dispute, all differences in regard to the partnership affairs shall be referred to the arbitration of a single arbiter, if the parties agree upon one; otherwise to five arbiters, two to be appointed by each party, and the fifth to be chosen by the four first named before they enter upon the business or arbitration. The award and determination of such arbiters, or any three of such arbiters, shall be binding upon the parties hereto and their respective executors, administrators, and assigns, always providing that the recommendation of the board shall not preclude any party the right of access to a court for a law ruling.

It is very important that you know that in the absence of express agreement the law provides that the profits shall be equally divided, regardless of the ratio of the partners' respective investments.

The foregoing list is not exhaustive.

Advantages of Partnerships

1. Partners can specialize in their own fields.

2. Each can direct workmen in his own area.

3. There may be more collective working capital.

4. The company may obtain better trade discounts.

5. The company may operate on a larger scale than an individual enterprise.

6. The company can maintain and keep operating more equipment.

7. The company may more easily undertake projects in different places at the same time.

8. Partners pay income tax on net profits. Net profits are those remaining after all operating expenses have been deducted, and are subject to personal income tax **whether or not the proceeds are taken out of, or remain in the business.**

Disadvantages of Partnerships

1. The partnership is not a tangible entity for the person who enters it.

2. Each general partner is individually responsible for the whole business.

3. If creditors cannot get satisfaction from the business partnership, they may press the total claim against any partner having private assets.

4. A partner may be dishonest.

5. A partner may be incompetent.

6. A partner may have a moral lapse.

7. A partner may neglect the business.

8. A partner may repeatedly exercise bad judgment.

9. The partnership ceases to exist if a partner severs his connection with the business or if a partner dies, but this potential loss may be mitigated by taking out Key-Man Insurance.

Corporations

A corporation is an association of three or more persons that are able legally to act as one entity under a common name. A corporation continues to exist even though its membership may change. It may engage in business or it may be a charitable enterprise or social/religious association. It can own property, can be sued, and can sue. The extent of its activities are shown in a charter that is given by federal, state, or provincial governments. (A charter is a document granting certain rights to a person, group of persons, or a corporation.)

1.14 BANKRUPTCY

Bankruptcy may be defined as the adjudication of a debtor's inability to pay his debts. Bankruptcy proceedings are of two kinds: voluntary and involuntary; that is, instituted either by the insolvent debtor or by his creditors. Two of the main purposes of these proceedings are to secure equitable division among creditors of the bankrupt's available assets, and to release or discharge the bankrupt from his obligations if he has complied with the law.

Bankruptcy Cases Filed and Pending. A bankruptcy case is a proceeding in a U.S. District Court under the National Bankruptcy Act. "Filed" means the commencement of a proceeding through the presentation of a petition to the clerk of the court; "pending" is a proceeding in which the administration has not been complete.

It is an offense for a person to continue to trade after he knows that he is insolvent. *As soon as he believes himself to be insolvent he should see an attorney for advice.* Sometimes the official receiver (person appointed by a court to manage property in controversy, especially in bankruptcy) may retrieve a situation in small building construction by managing the business until all properties are completed and sold.

The duties of a bankrupt include submitting to an examination, attending on creditors at the first meeting, fully disclosing all assets, and assisting in every way in the official administration of the estate. Punishable offences include failing to comply with a bankrupt's duties, fraudulently disposing of property, concealing or falsifying books or documents relating to the business, refusing to answer fully and truthfully any question asked at an examination, and obtaining credit or property by false representation after or within twelve months preceding bankruptcy.

1.15 CLASS RESEARCH

For those offering courses and using this book, it is suggested that consideration be given to apportioning chapters among the students for research, and having them make an oral report to the class, and then giving a typed paper of their findings to each student and to the instructor. As an example, one or more students may be assigned to make a comprehensive study of the advances made in adopting the metric system in the building industry; another student committee may make an in-depth study of Chapter two, and so on throughout the whole book.

Students should list the name, address, and telephone number of each organization that they visit, and return to class with sufficient copies of any acquired literature to give copies to each student and to the instructor. They should arrange to have a speaker from the workers' compensation agency address the class and show films on safety. They should also arrange for other speakers from, say, an insurance company specializing in builders' bonds and insurances; and a representative from one of the house builder's associations, and from a successful builder. After the students have given a short oral report to the class, they should follow this with a question and answer period.

Students should visit building projects; architects and engineers on large house building projects; relevant city departments; and building contractors. They should get a local building inspector to address the class and get a copy of a title deed to land, preferably one that includes some registered encumbrances.

It is suggested that this method be followed throughout all chapters and that every student be involved. Students will not only be exposed to current methods, materials, and philosophy of residential construction, they will also be attracted to specialize in particular aspects of construction that appeal to them. Many will be offered jobs.

At the end of the course, they will have been exposed to lectures by practicing professionals in the industry and have questioned each other and the instructor; in short they will have sufficient knowledge to enter the construction industry with confidence, competence, and to make a profit.

The class should have available to them a copy of the latest building code, and students should be made aware of the value of consulting "Sweet's Architectural Catalog File," which comprises twelve volumes, 17,000 pages, and is represented by 1,500 manufacturers of building materials. There is also a Canadian version of this catalog in which many papers are published in both English and French.

A number of pertinent review questions are presented at the end of each chapter of this book.

Review

1. List four desirable qualities one should have entering the housebuilding profession.

2. Clarify the term *business capital*.

3. List 10 points that should be considered before building residential units.

4. What services will a licensed surveyor perform (for a fee) for a residential construction contractor?

5. Define *foreclosure of land.*

6. Give the address of the nearest land titles office in your area.

7. Define the term *sanitary fill.*

8. What is the main function of a government land registry office?

9. What is meant by "searching a title"?

10. Define *power of attorney.*

2

Preliminary Business: Prior to Building Land Purchase

Zoning restrictions and opportunities and two types of overhead expenses are presented in this chapter.

2.1 MUNICIPAL PLANNING DEPARTMENT

Before purchasing building land, the contractor should visit the planning department. Here may be seen the proposed plans for the future development of the area showing future freeways, expressways, airport developments, bridges, recreation grounds, suburban development for residential construction, schools, shopping centers, churches, libraries, hotels, and motels. Also shown will be the very important zoning regulations, such as districts for single dwelling units, two units, three units, and multiple dwelling units such as apartment blocks. In some areas the heights and floor areas of buildings will be restricted. In the better-class districts, residential areas may have all the powerlines buried and have very decorative standard street lighting. These services will be reflected in the taxes.

Future industrial developments will also be shown with road and railway trackage and available services.

Some housing project promoters purchase large areas of land which they develop with roads and utilities. They divide the land into individual building lots, erect modern houses, and sell them to the public. All this development must conform and be approved by the engineers' department and the planning department. An advantage to both the vendor and the purchaser of such units is that the utilities—that is, roads, sidewalks, boulevards, gas, power, water, telephone, and cable television—are included in the original cost of the property. The purchaser is only responsible for making payments to one person each month.

When a smaller housebuilder offers a new home for sale, it is quite usual that the purchaser pays to the vendor each month a certain sum to cover the mortgage interest and repayment plus a separate annual tax bill. In many instances, however, the purchaser may have to wait a long period of time before all the utility amenities are installed.

It is from the planning department that a contractor might want to seek to have a parcel of land re-zoned from a single-dwelling-unit area to a multiple-dwelling area for the erection of an apartment block. *You must visit your planning department. The officers there will be very happy to show you through and answer your questions.* From the information given and a further talk with the taxation department, you may get a fair assessment of future property taxes in the area in which you wish to build.

Trouble Calls

Some departments provide twenty-four-hour service. These include: electric light and power, gas, sewer, garbage, streets, fire, police, and ambulance.

You as a builder may want at any time one or more of these services. Their telephone numbers should be kept in a ready file. Assume that your street has caved in because of a flash flood. What are you going to do about it?

2.2 BUILDING LICENSE

A proposal for a new building permit must first be submitted to the planning department, which examines the plans and specifications to determine whether they will conform to the planned pattern of the area in which the building is proposed to be erected.

When approved by the planning department, the application is passed to the engineers for structural examinations. If they approve, a building permit is issued upon payment of a scaled fee, depending on the type of building. This building permit must be prominently displayed at the new building site.

Other permits may include water, street closing, permission to use city water hydrants, and connections to sewer line, and so on.

In many areas before a person starts to operate as a builder, it is necessary that he/she obtain a builder's license from local authorities. There is a different fee for builders living and contracting within the area and for builders living outside the area. There is also a difference in fees for subcontractors. The purchase of a builder's license is not an indication that the purchaser is a good builder. His work has to stand up to progressive inspection by the building inspectors during all phases of construction.

The builder's license will enable the holder to make building material purchases at normal trade discounts. In business there are several different discounts which apply, depending upon the number of days within which payment for delivered goods must be made. The differences are considerable, and you should make very careful inquiries from the merchants. A license holder may also, upon nomination, be accepted into the local and national construction associations.

The contractor and all subcontractors shall comply with all local, state, provincial, or national government rules, regulations, and ordinances. They will prepare and file all necessary documents or information, pay for and obtain all licenses, permits, and certificates of inspection as may be specified or required.

Wherever municipal bylaws or state or provincial legislation require higher standards than those set forth in the drawings and specifications, such higher standards shall govern.

Note: *Assume there is some peculiar subsoil condition in a certain area. It is fair to assume that the local authority, knowing the conditions, may require special precautions to be taken which are more stringent than those set forth in the specifications. In all cases, the highest building standards shall prevail.*

2.3 ZONE CLASSIFICATION

The following zone classifications are typical of many of those pertaining to cities in North America.

- R-1 Zone Comprising all Single-family Dwelling Districts, including R-1A and R-1B, General Single-family Dwelling District.
- R-1C Zone Extended Use Single-family Dwelling District.
- R-2 Zone Comprising all Two-family Dwelling Districts.

R-3 Zone Multiple Dwelling Districts.

R-3H Zone High-density Multiple Dwelling Districts.

R-3S Zone Special Multiple Dwelling Districts.

R-3G Zone Garden Apartment Districts.

R-3B Zone Bonus Multiple Dwelling Districts.

C-1 Zone Limited Commercial Districts.

C-1S Zone Limited Commercial Service Station Districts.

C-1SC Zone Limited Commercial— Shopping Center Districts.

C-1AS Zone Limited Commercial—Automotive Service Center Districts.

C-1CR Zone Commercial-residential Districts.

C-2 Zone Commercial Districts.

C-2S Zone Comprising all General Commercial—Service Station Districts.

T-1 Zone Limited Transient Accommodation Districts.

M-1 Zone Limited Light Industrial Districts.

M-2 Zone Light Industrial Districts.

M-3 Zone Heavy Industrial Districts.

M-3T Zone Tank Farm Districts.

S-2 Zone Special Districts.

The R-3H High-density Dwelling District permits single-family and two-family dwellings, subject to compliance with provisions of the R-1B and R-2 sections of the bylaw, and allows high-density multiple dwellings up to specific maximum and minimum heights.

Maximum building height
120 ft
Minimum building height
70 ft
Minimum site area
30,000 ft²

Maximum site coverage
    19 percent (down to 14 percent)
Maximum floor space ratio
    1.68 to 1 (12 or more stories)
Landscaping minimum
    40 percent
Parking
    120 percent of the number of
    dwelling units
Setback from street
    50 ft minimum
Setback from other boundaries
    1/2 height of buildings (i.e., minimum of 35 ft)

These typical zone classifications, although not an exhaustive list, indicate the complexities of zoning. The would-be builder is advised to thoroughly study the local classifications and the implications of each, to the point of being aware of the current political climate(s) with respect to the potential building sites.

Knowledge of zoning restrictions and opportunities relevant to a specific area are high priority considerations for the builder. Of equal importance is the general knowledge of overhead expenses associated with building.

2.4 GUIDE LIST OF GENERAL OVERHEAD EXPENSES

There are two types of overhead expenses, i.e., those that are constant, irrespective of the amount of building being done at any one time, and those that are chargeable specifically to each individual job. An example of the former is as follows. A contractor completed four separate jobs in one year which were valued as follows: (a) $116,000; (b) $146,000; (c) $36,000; and (d) $52,000 respectively. He had therefore completed

$350,000 worth of construction in one year. The percentage proportion of general overhead expenses chargeable to each of the jobs would be as follows:

$$\text{(a)} \ \frac{116,000 \times 100}{350,000} = 33\%;$$

$$\text{(b)} \ \frac{146,000 \times 100}{350,000} = 42\%;$$

$$\text{(c)} \ \frac{36,000 \times 100}{350,000} = 10\%; \text{ and}$$

$$\text{(d)} \ \frac{52,000 \times 100}{350,000} = 15\%$$

These percentages of the total cost of all general expenses would be apportioned to each of the four jobs respectively. Note the following general overhead expenses:

General Office: Rent or interest on invested capital; depreciation of office building and contents; fuel; light; telephone; stationery; postal services; business machines; furnishings; fire and public liability insurance; property tax; heat; telex; office supplies; business machines; office furnishings

Staff Salaries: Executives; accountant; estimators; draftsmen; stenographers; clerks; janitors; staff traveling expenses

Advertising: Radio; television; magazines and journals; daily newspapers; club association dues; billboards

Literature: Trade magazines; trade journals; trade reports; company library (new publications); association dues

Tools and Equipment: Purchases; maintenance; depreciation. *Note: There is a fixed*

table of allowances; see *Inland Revenue Department* for details.

Legal Retention Fees: Attorneys, barristers, and lawyers

Professional Services: Architects; engineers; surveyors; certified public accountant; auditors

The overhead expenses totally chargeable to each individual job are as follows:

Salaries: Superintendent; job sponsor (usually an assistant to the superintendent); foreman, carpenter, mason, and others; timekeeper and storeman; watchman; cleanup man

Temporary Buildings: Field office; toolshed; store sheds; workshops; toilet facilities; fencing; hoardings; job signs; roads and trackage; ramps; platforms; temporary doors and stairs; barricades; protecting new and adjoining properties; job billboards for advertising

Legal: Public liability insurance; workmen's compensation; fire insurance; bonds—performance, and so on; attorneys and lawyers (barristers and solicitors); social security benefits; accountants and auditors; real estate fees

Building Permits: Town; out of town; special permits for roads; sewer connections; excavating sidewalks and roads

Utilities: Temporary light and power; poles and meters; temporary heat; temporary water meter and taxes; digging of well, haulage of water by tanker; temporary telephone

Testing: Soil compaction; concrete; decibel readings

Progress Reports: Written; photographs; progress diary.

Out of Town Jobs: Traveling; premium rates for staff and workmen; room and board; freight and trucking of own or rented/leased materials and equipment

Professional Services: Survey; engineers; accountant; attorney; engineers/architects

Protection of Work: Curing, covering, water-spraying, or keeping concrete ice-free; protecting finished work such as wood floors and staircases

Attending on Other Trades: Cut away and make good; breaking and repairing sidewalks and streets

Plant: Own equipment; concrete mixers; wheelbarrows, buggies, hoses, cutoff saws; hired equipment; pumps; maintenance and haulage of equipment; company transport

Completion Dates: Penalties or rewards

Final Cleanup: Replace and clean all damaged glass; janitor service

Computer Services: Estimate annual expenses

Landscape and Lawn: Shrubs

Notarization Costs

2.5 GUIDE LIST OF OVERHEAD EXPENSES CHARGEABLE TO EACH INDIVIDUAL JOB

Salaries
Superintendent
Foreman, carpenter, mason, and others

Job sponsor
Timekeeper and storeman
Watchman
Clean up man

Temporary Buildings
Office
Tool shed
Store sheds
Workshops
Toilet facilities
Fencing
Hoardings
Job signs
Roads and trackage
Ramps
Platforms
Temporary doors and stairs
Barricades
Protecting new and adjoining proper-
ties
Job billboards for advertising

Legal
Surveyor's Fees
Public Liability Insurance
Workmen's Compensation
Fire Insurance
Bonds Performance, and so on
Barristers and Solicitors
Social Security benefits
Accountants and Auditors
Real Estate Fees

Building Permits
Town
Out of town
Special permits for roads, and so on
Sewer connections
Excavating sidewalks and roads

Utilities
Temporary light and power: Poles and
meters

Temporary heat: electric, gas or sala-
manders
Temporary water: meter and taxes
Digging of well, haulage by tanker
Temporary telephone

Testing
Concrete
Soil compaction
Decibel readings

Progress Reports
Written
Photographs
Progress diary

Out-of-Town Jobs
Traveling
Premium rates for staff and workmen
Room and board
Freight and trucking of own or hired
materials and equipment

Professional Services
Survey
Engineers
Accountant
Attorney
Engineers/Architects

Protection of Work
Curing, covering, water-spraying, or
keeping concrete ice-free
Protecting finished work such as wood
floors and staircases

Attending On Other Trades
Cut away and make good
Breaking and repairing sidewalks and
streets

Plant
Own equipment
Concrete mixers, wheelbarrows, bug-
gies, hoses, cutoff saws

Hired equipment
Pumps
Maintenance and haulage of equipment
Company transport

Final Cleanup
Replace and clean all damaged glass
Janitor service

Completion Dates
Penalties or rewards

Computer Services
Estimate annual expenses

Review

1. Prepare a list, giving names and telephone numbers, of five local authorities that provide 24-hour service to projects of builders.

2. Prepare a set of reasons why a housebuilder should visit a local authority planning department.

3. State the difference between a building license and a builder's license.

4. Define the term *zoning*. Obtain a document which clearly indicates the zone classification for the area in which you live. State in your own words the restrictions and the opportunities for building in that area.

3

Land Titles

3.1 LAND TITLES

The following material has been excerpted from the book *Real Estate Principles and Practices,* 8th edition, by Alfred A. Ring and Jerome Dasso, published by Prentice-Hall, Inc., and is here reproduced with the permission of the copyright holders.

Protection of Title. As landed property became more valuable and ownership of real estate more diverse, it became increasingly important to provide safeguards to protect the true owner from loss of title by claim, error, or fraud. With cooperative aid of public and private agencies, transfer of title by the rightful and true owner and continued, though absentee, ownership were safeguarded by one or more of the following methods of title assurance: (1) recording acts and examination of title, (2) title insurance by private companies, (3) land title registration by public agencies in accordance with legislative enactments.

Recording of Conveyances. Possession of property is notice to the world that the possessor claims or has some interest in the property. An owner in possession under a valid deed may be discovered to the actual knowledge of anyone who goes to the property. However, it is not always practicable for the owner actually to be in possession. He may own many buildings, or the structure may be an office or factory building or vacant land. One might go to the premises many times and not find the owner. Some method of *constructive* notice of ownership had to be devised as a substitute for *actual* knowledge, to protect the owner by relieving him of the necessity of remaining constantly in possession and to protect persons who, desiring to deal with the property, would wish to ascertain the real owner. Otherwise A, an owner, might sell his land to B, giving him a deed; and if B did not take possession, A might turn about and sell it to C. Or he might give a mortgage to D to secure a loan after he had sold to B. To prevent such frauds, recording acts have been enacted in all states. These provide that all instruments affecting real property may, when properly proved, be recorded in a certain public office in the county where the property is located. All such instruments are copied on the records and indexed. When so recorded, they are notice to the world with exactly the same effect as if the owner were actually in possession.

Constructive notice is just as good as actual notice. Consequently, one dealing with real estate is bound by all recorded instruments. Suppose A sells a piece of land to B and B fails to record his deed; A then sells it again to C, who knows nothing of the prior sale to B, and records his deed before B's deed is recorded. Under the theory of notice, C's right to the property is ahead of B's because B was not in possession and the records at the time C bought the property showed title in A. B should have pro-

tected himself by recording his deed as soon as he received it. Constructive notice is, however, no better than actual knowledge. If C, in the case above, had known of B's purchase, he could not obtain any right superior to B by recording his deed first.

Proof of Execution. No instrument may be recorded unless proved as required by the law of the state. Proof varies in the several states. Some require a subscribing witness; others an acknowledgment; others both. The following are the officials who are authorized to take acknowledgments: notaries public, commissioners of deeds, justices of the peace, judges of courts of record, mayors of cities, ambassadors and ministers residing abroad, consular agents, and commissioners of deeds appointed by the governors of states to take acknowledgments in other states. Each of these officials has definite limits of authority. He cannot act outside the area of his authority. Within his area of authority he may take an acknowledgment of an instrument to be recorded elsewhere. When he does this, the instrument cannot be recorded elsewhere without a certificate attached from the clerk of the court of the county or city in which the official is qualified to act, stating that the official is qualified to take acknowledgments of instruments intended to be recorded in that state, that the signature of the official is known to the clerk, and that the signature affixed to the certificate of acknowledgment is genuine.

Examination of Records. It is readily seen that one who contemplates a real estate transaction not only must inspect the realty involved but also must procure a thorough examination of the records to ascertain the owner and the condition of the title and all instruments concerning which the law presumes everyone to have notice. The examination reveals the entire history of the title from the earliest record to the present time and shows the chain of deeds, wills, and actions by which the property has passed from owner to owner, as well as mortgages, leases, restrictive and other agreements, and instruments encumbering or affecting the title or use of the property. The examiner first *abstracts* all the instruments conveying the title; that is, he makes a separate digest of each. This gives him what is known as a chain of title. He may find his chain very simple, consisting perhaps of a grant from the state to A and successive deeds from A to B, B to C, C to D, D to E, and E to F, F being the present owner. Usually, however, someone in the chain has died owning the property. In that event he may find deeds from A to B and B to C and no deed from C, although F claims ownership. The probability is that C died owning the property. In that case his will (if he left one) was probated and is on record in the court. If he left no will, it is usually found that an administrator of his personal property had been appointed, and the papers on file for that purpose state the names of his heirs. The examiner accordingly turns to the records of deaths and wills to fill the gap and finds the will or record of death of C. This supplies him with the names of C's devisees or heirs, and he then resumes his search by locating the deed from them to D, and so continues his chain. The chain is often broken by some legal action, such as foreclosure. Some person in the chain may have mortgaged the property so that the chain of title stops in D. A search of the records of legal actions shows that D was cut off in a foreclosure suit. Examination of the judgment in the action reveals the name of the official who sold and gave a deed of the property. Search against him will show his deed, and the chain is re-

sumed. After the chain of title is completed, separate search is made against each owner for the period he owned the property to ascertain what encumbrances he may have placed upon the property.

The examiner's completed works is an *abstract of title*. In many states the abstract passes with each sale of the property, being kept up to date by the addition of a memorandum of each new transfer. It is deemed so valuable that in some states it is customary to provide in the contract of sale that the seller shall deliver the abstract of title at or before the delivery of the deed.

The Title Examiner. The law of real property is complicated and technical. The average person dealing in real estate has no knowledge of these rules, nor has he time to examine the title. He usually employs counsel or a conveyancer to do this work for him—someone who is familiar with the records, their location, indexes, and, more important, the law applicable to the various situations in the title which the examination might reveal. The responsibility of the examiner to his employer should be noted. He does not guarantee the result of his search. He simply asserts (1) that he has sufficient knowledge and experience to be a competent examiner of titles and (2) that he will use his knowledge honestly and diligently in accordance with the appropriate rules of law. His report of title is only his opinion, backed, to be sure, by his legal training and a careful scrutiny of the records. The records are copies of instruments; he is not responsible if the signature on some deed in the chain later proves to be a forgery. C may have died intestate owning the property. X and Y thereafter conveyed the property by deed, reciting that they were the only heirs of C. Z may thereafter claim to have been an heir as well. The examiner is not to blame. He may pass upon some situation in the title in accordance with the law as then in force. Later a court may reverse the decision upon which the examiner based his opinion. For none of these things is the examiner liable, yet his employer may lose large sums as a result.

As the records in the county and other offices grow in size and complexity, it is safe to have searches made only by someone familiar with them. Specialists in this field of work are at every county seat. Customs and the volume of work will regulate their type and methods of conducting business. To a large extent in the rural counties and even in the cities, a great deal of title searching is done by lawyers or conveyancers. In some places the searching is customarily done by men who make a specialty of making up abstracts and who supply them to lawyers on order. The lawyer then reads the abstract and certifies the title.

In more active counties, abstract companies do this work. Every abstract company has a force of employees, who duplicate and offer additional records, maps, and surveys, and supply complete and accurate abstracts.

Title Insurance. No system of title searching is perfect. As previously indicated, errors may creep in, or forgeries and other things that cannot be guarded against may cause loss. To remedy this situation, title insurance has come into use in the larger cities. It is a direct growth of the abstract company. Many of these companies, years ago, devised the idea of insuring not only their abstracts but going a step beyond, and for an additional fee, reading and insuring the title as well. Like all other insurance, title insurance is a distribution of loss among all insured. Title companies are organizations authorized by law to examine and insure titles. They charge a fee or premium for their service. The amount of the premium is usually based upon the value of the property and covers not only the expense of the examination and abstract, but also an additional amount that is placed in a general fund to cover the losses insured against. The company makes a careful examination of the title. If it is satisfied that there are no apparent defects in the title, it insures against any loss. Should there later be a loss, by reason of forgery or any other defect arising prior to the insurance, the title company pays the loss. This, in brief, is the theory of title insurance.

In seeking title insurance, the person about to acquire the title or some interest in the real property first applies to the title company. He agrees to pay a certain fee for examination of the title. The title company on its part obligates itself to make an examination of the title and to insure against undiscovered defects. It does not, however, agree to insure against defects and encumbrances that may appear from the examination.

After the examination is completed, the applicant should therefore insist on being given a *report of title,* which is a statement setting forth a description of the property, the name of the record owner, and a detailed list of all objections to the title, that is, encumbrances and defects found upon the records. The reason for having this report is simple: it enables the applicant to know the exact condition of the title. If he is a purchaser, his contract stipulates that he shall take title subject to certain encumbrances. The report sets forth all the encumbrances found on the records. The purchaser demands that the seller dispose of all those not agreed upon in the contract before delivering a deed. If the applicant has agreed to make a mortgage loan, he insists that the owner render his title free and clear before the loan is made. After the objections not agreed upon have been removed, the title is closed and the instruments passing title are delivered and recorded. The title company now prepares to issue its policy of the title insurance. There may, of course, still be encumbrances on the property which have been agreed upon. For example, the transaction may be a sale of the property subject to one or more mortgages. The policy should be carefully examined to see that the property is properly insured without any exceptions other than those agreed upon.

Title Insurance Policy. The usual form of title insurance policy contains four parts:

1. Agreement of insurance
2. A schedule describing the subject matter of insurance
3. A schedule of exceptions
4. Conditions of the policy

The agreement of insurance usually reads as follows:

[The company] in consideration of the payment of its charges for the examination of this title to it paid doth hereby insure and covenant that it will keep harmless and indemnify. . . . (hereafter termed the assured) and all other persons to whom this policy may be transferred with the assent of this company, testified by the signature of the proper officer of this company, endorsed on this policy, against all loss or damage not exceeding. . . . dollars which the said assured shall sustain by reason of defects, or unmarketability of the title of the assured to the estate, mortgage, or interest described in Schedule A hereto annexed, or because of liens or encumbrances charging the same at the date of this policy. *Excepting* judgments against the

assured and estates, defects, objections, liens, or encumbrances created by the act or with the privity of the assured, or mentioned in Schedule B or excepted by the conditions of this policy hereto annexed and hereby incorporated into this contract, *the loss* and the amount to be ascertained in the manner provided in the annexed conditions and to be payable upon compliance by the assured with the stipulations of said conditions and not otherwise.

This agreement is dated and executed by the proper officers of the company under its corporate seal.

The company's charge is a fixed rate based usually on the amount of insurance named. Unlike other insurance, it is a flat fee, paid but once. Customarily the company insists that the property be insured for at least its full value. The insured also should want the property insured for its full value, since the company is in no case obligated to pay more than the amount set forth in the policy. The insured may, if he contemplates improving the property, have his title insured for a sum greater than its value at the time of transfer. The date of the policy is very important. The company insures only against loss to the insured arising from some defect at or prior to the date of the policy. The insured should insist that the policy be dated at or after the time title is closed. Because the policy is issued under seal, the time to sue upon it does not begin to run until a loss is sustained. The statute of limitations may be twenty years. The loss might not occur until fifteen years after the policy was issued. In such cases the right to sue on the policy would not expire until thirty-five years after the date of the policy.

The schedule describing the subject matter of insurance usually follows the agreement of insurance. It is divided into three parts. First it states the estate or title of the insured. Next comes a brief description of the premises covered by the policy. This description should be sufficiently detailed so that the property may be easily identified. The policy covers not only the land but all buildings and fixtures thereon. It does not cover personalty. The insured should see to it that the description is clear.

The schedule of exceptions is virtually the most important part of the policy. It sets forth a detailed list of all encumbrances and defects against which the company does not insure. No loss arising from any of these exceptions is covered by the policy. The insured should insist that only such encumbrances as he has agreed to shall be inserted in the schedule. Much trouble has arisen on this point, and many companies insist, before the closing of title, that the insured consent in writing to such objections to the title as have not been removed. Nearly all companies refuse to insure against the rights of tenants and persons in possession of the property; therefore those rights usually appear in the schedule. All encumbering facts shown by a survey are excepted, or if there be no survey, the policy will except "any state of facts an accurate survey may show."

The last part of the policy is a statement of the conditions of the policy. These conditions are seldom read but are very important. They specify the terms of the company's liability and the relations between the company and the insured. First it is stipulated that the company will, at its own cost, defend the insured in all actions founded on a claim of title or encumbrance prior to the date of the policy and thereby insured against. This stipulation not only assures the insured against loss but saves him the inconvenience and expense of litigation.

Should the insured contract to sell the property and the purchaser reject the title for some defect not excepted in the policy, the company reserves the option of either paying the loss or maintaining at its own expense an action to test the validity of the defect. In such a case the company is not liable under the policy until the termination of the litigation.

If the policy is issued to a mortgagee, the company's responsibility arises only in the event that the mortgage, upon foreclosure, is adjudged to be a lien upon the property of an inferior quality to that described in the policy, or in the event that the purchaser at the foreclosure sale is relieved by the court of completing his purchase by reason of some defect not excepted in the policy.

The conditions of the policy also provide for arbitration, in certain cases, of disputes as to the validity of objections to the title insured. The policy covers the insured even after he has sold the property, should he be sued upon the convenants in his deed.

The policy is not transferable, except that if it insures a mortgagee and he sells the mortgage, his rights under the policy may be passed to his assignee. But even then the company's consent must be obtained.

Should there be a loss under the policy, the company, having settled the claim, acquires all the rights and claims of the insured against any other person who is responsible for the loss. This right is based upon the legal doctrine of subrogation. The title company may be able to collect all or part of the loss from the person who caused the loss.

In any case, if the company has paid a loss totaling the amount of the policy, it reserves the right to take over the property from the insured at a fair valuation. There is a very good reason for this provision. In some instances the title is defective but can, with time and effort, be cured. The company in such cases pays the fair value to the insured, receiving a deed from him. It then owns the property and at its pleasure can take such action as may be necessary to remove the defects in the title.

Encroachments on Others. The building on the lot may cover more land than is within the lot lines. The municipality either owns the street or has an easement to use the street for public purposes. In either event no one has a right to encroach upon it, except by legal permission. Such an encroachment by a permanent structure may render the title unmarketable. Likewise, if the building encroaches upon a neighbor's land without his consent, the neightbor may be able either to recover damages for the encroachment or to compel the removal of so much of the building as encroaches on his land. A purchaser could not be compelled to accept a title under such conditions. The survey should indicate party walls, and it should also be examined with reference to any restriction upon the property and as to whether or not such restrictions are violated by the building. The effect of such conditions could be determined only by one familiar with the law applicable in each case.

Encroachments by Others. The entire building may stand upon the proper lot, and a nieghbor's building may encroach. The title to the portion of the lot that is not encroached upon is marketable, but it may be doubtful whether or not the encroachment affects the marketability of the lot as a whole. This is a question not so much of law as of commercial utility, and the courts consider it to be the latter. If the court finds the encroachment does not substantially lessen the value and extent of the property, it will compel a purchaser to accept

it. If the encroachment does substantially lessen the value and extent of the land, the purchaser may refuse to take it, or he may take it and be given an allowance for the land lost by the encroachment.

Use of Title Policy. Of course, the insured seldom needs to resort to his policy to recover a loss, but he should always refer to it in subsequent transactions with reference to the property. It tells him at once just what property he owns and what are the encumbrances on it. If he later enters into a contract to sell the property, he should use the description in the policy and undertake to give a title subject to just those encumbrances stated as exceptions in the policy.

Land Title and Registration. Throughout the history of title recording, means and ways have been sought to make transfer of real property as simple and safe as the transfer of other property, doing away, if possible, with the repeated search and examination of titles. The search for some permanent form of title registration is still prompted by the tedious and often difficult and cumbersome method by which title changes and, in addition, by the ever-present fear that ownership in farm or home, despite title insurance, may be invalidated by court order because of faulty or illegal property transfer somewhere in the chain of title grantors. Although the development and perfection of title insurance has speeded the search and transfer of title, particularly in urban areas, the necessity to reestablish and recheck the chain of ownership and title encumbrances every time a sale takes place still impedes the use of realty as a readily transferable, liquid asset or form of investment.

Under present operation of the recording acts, deeds and other instruments affecting rights or property in realty are placed on public record. These records are generally maintained in the office of the registrar by the clerk of the county in which the property is located. They are notice to the world as to constructive ownership in realty, and an examination of all recorded instruments affecting the property in question is necessary to determine the validity and condition of title. In early days, far fewer instruments were on record; it was therefore possible to examine a title with fair speed and consequent reasonable time and expense. Now, the more active counties have such voluminous records that the operation is slow, time consuming, and expensive, and, in addition, this condition is becoming worse as time passes and more and more instruments are recorded. Yet, theoretically, it is necessary for each title examination to go back to the date of conquest by war or revolution, or to the date of original gift or sale by a sovereign ruler; some states—Illinois, Indiana, Iowa, Massachusetts, Michigan, Wisconsin, and others—have established by statute a maximum period of time varying from thirty to fifty years beyond which an otherwise valid title need not be searched to prove ownership good and marketable. These laws do not estop an individual, however, who claims an interest in the property arising from events antedating the statute of title limitation from filing an affidavit of claim and from recording such claim for all to know and heed. Obvious interests that are evident by physical inspection, such as easements or party walls, need not be recorded to be protected in these states against title search statutes of limitations. In most states, however, there is still no legal date that can be fixed beyond which there is no need of going back to search a title. The lack of such a basic date, in

brief, is the problem faced by title searchers.

In actual practice, title and abstract companies usually "assume title good at some fairly early date." There is nevertheless an irritating duplication of work on successive title examinations. And some meticulous attorneys are not satisfied unless the examination is carried back to the earliest date, as witness the following story:

In a legal transaction involving transfer of property in New Orleans, a firm of New York lawyers retained a New Orleans attorney to search the title and perform other related duties. The New Orleans attorney sent his findings, back to the year 1803. The New York lawyers examined his opinion and wrote again to the New Orleans lawyer, saying in effect that the opinion rendered by him was all very well, as far as it went, but that title to the property prior to 1803 had not been satisfactorily answered.

The New Orleans attorney replied to the New York firm as follows:

I acknowledge your letter inquiring as to the state of the title of the Canal Street property prior to the year 1803.

Please be advised that in the year 1803 the United States of America acquired the territory of Louisiana from the Republic of France by purchase. The Republic of France acquired title from the Spanish Crown by conquest. The Spanish Crown had originally acquired title by virtue of the discoveries of one Christopher Columbus, sailor, who had been duly authorized to embark upon the voyage of discovery by Isabella, Queen of Spain. Isabella, before granting such authority, had obtained the sanction of His Holiness, the Pope; the Pope is the Vicar on Earth of Jesus Christ; Jesus Christ is the Son and Heir Apparent of God. God made Louisiana.

A number of suggestions have been made to remedy this date situation. All of them hinge on some method of registering title and stem from the system first suggested by Sir Robert Torrens of Australia.

Review

1. Obtain for study a copy of a current title deed to a piece of property. Write in your own words what the document says.

2. With respect to that title deed:

   How was ownership safeguarded?
   In which county is the deed recorded?
   How was the document proved?
   Is the document an abstract of the title?
   Is there a lien on the property?
   How would you determine whether there has been encroachment by others? How much would it cost to find out?

3. Find out from the land titles office how a historical search of title for a piece of property is conducted and how much it would cost for a search, or a limited search, say to the first owner.

4
Depreciation

4.1 OUTLINE OF DEPRECIATION

In accounting for contractors' equipment, the depreciation of an asset represents a loss in its worth from its last *assessed book value*. The book value of an asset is not necessarily the actual worth of said asset on the market. Equipment such as woodworking machines, tubular scaffolding, trucks, tractors, and so on, are all subject to allowable depreciation for income tax purposes. It should be noted that there is a difference between "depreciation" and "depletion"; the latter refers to wasting an asset through dissipation, such as a mine or an oil well which is worked to complete exhaustion.

There are several acceptable methods used to evaluate depreciation, and each year governments make tax guides available outlining such methods. However, it must be remembered that *tax laws may be changed at any time by an Act of Congress in America, or an Act of Parliament in Canada.* You may obtain a copy of "Depreciation Guidelines and Rules" from the Superintendent of Documents, U.S. Government Printing Office,

Washington, D.C. 20402, for a small fee. Since section 521 of the Tax Reform Act of 1969 made changes in U.S. law relating to depreciation with respect to taxable years ending after 24 July 1969, a copy of Public Law 91-172 may be obtained from the same source, also for a small fee.

The Canadian Government issues a General Tax Guide (free) that may be obtained from any federal taxation office. For more details see one of the revenue department officials of the country concerned.

There are different taxation schedules showing the life expectancy for different kinds of assets. Certain equipment may have a life expectancy of five years *or less*. On the other hand, a building may have an allowable lifetime of fifty years. Using the "straight line method of depreciation" the former allows for a 20 percent per annum depreciation (over a period of five years) of the original cost less the salvage value. The latter allows for a 2 percent depreciation (over a period of fifty years) from the original cost less the salvage value.

In all cases the salvage value of an asset is not allowed "by law" to fall below a reasonable value. In case of doubt as to what is meant by a "reasonable value", contact an Internal Revenue Department official.

In cases where major repairs and/or modifications have been made to an asset which has increased its value and utility, the remaining book value at the end of the year may be more than its value at the previous year end. The improvement then becomes a further capital cost and the asset *appreciates* in the year end value.

In unusual cases, depreciation can result from an asset becoming obsolete. Assume that a new piece of machinery could outperform older, existing equipment in quality, quantity of work performed, relative prime cost, and maintenance expenses. The older machine may be declared obsolete because the owner could not possibly compete on equal terms with the owners of new equipment. However, a very convincing argument would have to be presented before the officials of the Internal Revenue Department would accept it.

The basic premise for depreciation allowances arises from the fact that, in using a piece of equipment to achieve a desired end, such equipment is subject to wear, tear, and cost of maintenance, and that such costs are recoverable by the owner from the revenue of the work performed. Thus the owner recovers the depreciated value of the equipment for the period of time during which it is operated.

Depreciation may be stipulated in terms of a year, a month, a day, or even an hour. Assume that the installed cost of a piece of equipment is $9,250.00, with a salvage value of $750.00 over a five-year life. Using the "straight line method of depreciation" (which follows), the asset would depreciate at the rate of 20 percent per annum from its original cost less salvage value. Thus, in five years $8,750.00 ÷ 5 = $1,750.00 per annum depreciation. Further, suppose the working time for the equipment to be 2,000 working hours per annum. Then the actual depreciation of the equipment would be $1,750.00 ÷ 2,000 = $0.88 per hour. Estimators use this method when pricing certain jobs.

4.2 STRAIGHT LINE METHOD OF DEPRECIATION

Given the following charges for the purchase and installation of a new piece of equipment: original cost $8,450.00; taxes $173.00; transportation charges from point of ownership between vendor and purchaser $272.00; unloading $150.00; and cost of assembly and installation $205.00. The total cost would be $9,250.00. Note that all the above costs would be incurred legitimately by the purchaser before he could start to earn money from his investment. Assuming the life expectancy of the asset to be five years, and allowing for a final salvage value of, say, $750.00, the straight line method of depreciation would be as follows.

Step 1: List and find the total cost of the equipment to be depreciated.

Purchase price	$8,450.00
Taxes	173.00
Transportation	272.00
Unloading	150.00
Installation	205.00
	$9,250.00

Step 2: Deduct from the total cost the final salvage value of the asset, say $750.00; then $9,250 − 750 = $8,500.00.

Step 3: Divide the cost of the asset less its salvage value by the number of years over which the equipment is to be depreciated. Thus $8,500.00 over a life expectancy of five years would be $8,500 ÷ 5 = $1,700.00 depreciation per annum. This is the straight line method of depreciation.

Step 4: Lay out a table as follows:
Original total gross cost of the asset $9,250.00, salvage value $750.00, life expectancy, five years.

Year	Depreciation per Annum	Cumulative Depreciation	Year End Value
0	$1,700	$ 0	$8,500
1	1,700	1,700	6,800
2	1,700	3,400	5,100
3	1,700	5,100	3,400
4	1,700	6,800	1,700
5	1,700	8,500	0

Cumulative depreciation	$8,500.00
Salvage value	750.00
Original cost	$9,250.00

Summary: The straight line method of depreciation may be adopted where a regular flow of business is expected and where recovery of the cost of the asset is made in annual equal amounts during the life of the equipment.

4.3 DECLINING BALANCE METHOD OF DEPRECIATION

This method differs from the straight line method of depreciation in that, instead of depreciating the value of the asset by a fixed-dollar value each year, the depreciation is made by a fixed annual percentage reduction of the year-end value of the asset. Using the same cost and condition of installing a piece of equipment as in part 4.2, the declining balance method of depreciation is as follows.

Step 1: Find the rate percentage that you would use on the same asset by the straight line method of depreciation. This was 20 percent per annum of the original installed cost (less salvage value) spread over a period of five years.

Step 2: Double that rate. In this case, 20 percent becomes 40 percent.

Step 3: Depreciate each *year end book value* of the asset by 40 percent.

Step 4: Using this method, *the salvage value of the asset is not immediately taken into account,* but the balance remaining at the end of the fifth year will represent the salvage value with this qualification: The Internal Revenue Department says that you are never allowed to depreciate the value of an asset below a reasonable salvage value. The term "reasonable value" may have to be determined through an interview with an official from the taxation department.

Step 5: Using the total cost and life expectancy of the asset as being the same as that shown in the straight line method, the following table would result.

Original total gross cost of the asset is $9,250.00. Salvage value equals the remaining balance at the end of five years of depreciation.

Analysis: Depreciation for the first year, 40 percent of $9,250.00 taken without any deduction at this time for salvage value of the asset, is $3,700.00. Deduct this amount from the original cost of the asset as shown in column 4, leaving $5,550.00 as the book value of the asset at the end of the first year.

The second year depreciation, 40 percent of $5,550.00, is $2,220. Deduct this amount from the year-end book value of the asset as shown at the end of the second year column 4, leaving $3,330.00.

The cumulative depreciation for the first two years is $3,700.00 plus $2,220.00 which equals $5,920.00 as shown for the second year in column 3, and so on until there is a final year-end value of the asset (salvage) remaining of $719.00 as shown at the fifth year column 4.

Summary: The declining balance method of depreciation may be adopted when a contractor wishes to take the greatest amount of depreciation during his early years of ownership of the asset, to compensate for high annual profits during that projected period.

4.4 SUM-OF-THE-YEARS-DIGITS METHOD OF DEPRECIATION

This method yields high rates of depreciation during the early years of the asset's life. Use the same equipment and conditions as follows.

Step 1: Find the sum of the digits of the years of life expectancy of the asset.

Step 2: The sum of the years digits = 1 + 2 + 3 + 4 + 5 = 15 digits.

Step 3: After deducting the salvage value of the asset, the depreciation is calculated by

Year	Depreciation per Annum from Year End Book Value (40%)	Cumulative Depreciation to Salvage Value	Year End Value of Asset
0			$9,250
1	$3,700	$3,700	5,550
2	2,220	5,920	3,330
3	1,332	7,252	1,998
4	799	8,052	1,198
5	479	8,531	719

Cumulative depreciation from column 3 $8,531.00
Salvage value remaining column 4   719.00
Original Cost $9,250.00

deducting the following fractional amounts each year.

First year:	⁵/₁₅ of the original cost of the asset
Second year:	⁴/₁₅ of the original cost of the asset
Third year:	³/₁₅ of the original cost of the asset
Fourth year:	²/₁₅ of the original cost of the asset
Fifth year:	¹/₁₅ of the original cost of the asset
Total digits:	¹⁵/₁₅

Step 4: Lay out the table as follows.

Original total gross cost of the asset $9,250.00; salvage value $750.00; life expectancy of five years.

Year	Depreciation per Annum	Cumulative Depreciation	Year End Book Value
0			$8,500
1	$2,833	$2,833	5,677
2	2,267	5,100	3,400
3	1,700	6,800	1,700
4	1,133	7,933	565
5	567	8,500	0

Cumulative depreciation	$8,500.00
Salvage value	750.00
Original cost of asset	$9,250.00

Summary: Using the sum-of-the-years-digits method of depreciation, the greatest recovery is made during the early years of the life of the asset. This method may be adopted when the contractor wishes to take advantage of prospective high earnings during the first few years of the life of the asset (and thus save in income tax charges).

Comparative Depreciation Table

The following comparative depreciation table shows the relative amounts that may be depreciated for the same equipment for the same period of time as outlined in all the previous articles in this chapter.

Comparative Depreciation Table

Year	Straight Line Method 20%	Declining Balance Method 40%	Sum-of-the-Years-Digits Method
1	$1,700	$3,700	$2,833
2	1,700	2,220	2,267
3	1,700	1,332	1,700
4	1,700	799	1,133
5	1,700	479	567
Salvage	750	719	750
	$9,250	$9,250	$9,250

Analysis: Depreciation for the first two and last two years of the asset is as follows.

Straight line (20%)	$3,400	$3,400
Declining balance (40%)	$5,920	$1,278
Sum-of-the-years-digits	$5,100	$1,700

Summary: The highest depreciation occurs during the first two years (of a five year period) on the declining balance method, and the same method also shows the lowest depreciation for the last two years. Where earnings are expected to be high during the early life of an asset, either the declining balance method or the sum-of-the-years-digits method would be advantageous from a tax point of view. Where a steady turnover is expected, a regular straight line method may be adopted.

4.5 EQUIPMENT: SCHEDULES AND MAINTENANCE

Many general contractors have large investments in construction equipment which must always be kept in first class working order; the equipment, also, must be rigidly accounted for on the jobs on which it is used. As with all schedules, there are various ways of making and keeping them up-to-date. The following is offered as a guide.

The head of the maintenance department would be responsible for the filing of all owners' maintenance manuals issued by the manufacturer of each piece of equipment. He would keep on file a case history of each machine, the date it was bought, whether new or used, the latest book value, what major repairs have been done to it and when. He would determine the regular oiling, greasing, and maintenance done in the field and the shop.

Over the life expectancy of equipment, maintenance costs will run from one to two times the initial cost of the equipment. The equipment must be kept in good condition whether in use or not, and it must always be ready for the owner's use, leasing, or for sale. The timing of major repairs, for years of high income, may lessen the tax charges against the company for such years. Maintenance costs tend to increase as a company ages and needs more maintenance crews and technicians. Large companies may set up a separate company to handle all major equipment; they may also operate a rental service to others.

The head of the maintenance department would maintain a filing system showing the dates that each piece of equipment is "charged out" to each job. This means that each individual job "overhead expense account" would be charged a daily rate for each piece of equipment detained on the job, whether in use or not. The job superintendent would show in his daily job report each piece of equipment on his temporary charge; it would be in his interest to return the equipment as soon as possible and thus keep his overhead expenses at a minimum.

Some large contractors engage the services of the equipment dealers to service and maintain their products. The dealers provide continual supervision of their products. They maintain a 24-hour service, and it is claimed by some that they can keep equipment in working order for more hours per year than could the construction contractor himself. Remember that depreciation goes on whether or not the machines are in use. Management must decide whether to concentrate its undivided attention on construction contracting only, or on construction, plus servicing and maintenance of its own equipment and the possibility of leasing some of its own equipment to others. In short, in what business or businesses does the contractor wish to operate.

When large (international) construction contractors bid on large jobs, the unsuccessful bidders often lease their equipment and crews to the successful bidder. No company can afford to have millions of dollars worth of equipment kept idle for any length of time waiting for a successful bid.

4.6 INDUSTRIAL EQUIPMENT

To remain competitive, a contractor must keep his industrial equipment up-to-date: by wise and discriminate purchases; by assurance of available parts servicing agencies; by efficient maintenance; and by a knowledge of methods of depreciating equipment (see the local federal taxation department for this information).

Before making a purchase, a contractor should see a demonstration of the piece of equipment in action, doing the type of job for which he would use it. Further, he should see a demonstration of a similar piece of equipment from a competitor doing the same work on similar terrain to the first. It pays to shop around!

Remember that depreciation commences from the moment of transfer of ownership.

A further important point is to determine at what geographical place the transfer of ownership will occur. It once came to notice that an expensive piece of equipment had been lost (through horseplay) in the bottom of a deep lake. The equipment was insured, and replacement was made at the stated contracted place according to the terms of the insurance contract, but the contracted place was more than 1,000 miles from the scene of the loss. Be careful!

As an alternative to the purchase of heavy equipment, a contractor may consider leasing or renting equipment, with the advantage of little or no responsibility for its maintenance or for the cost of accounting, except for initial fees.

4.7 LEASING CONTRACTOR'S EQUIPMENT

There are many advantages to a contractor leasing major items of equipment. Some of them are as follows:

1. Leasing, instead of purchasing, frees more funds for working capital.

2. It virtually eliminates maintenance crews and is known in the industry as "saving another headache."

3. It reduces accountancy entries, and the contractor knows exactly what his charges will be in one statement.

4. It reduces the time in keeping track of insurance and depreciation.

5. It may be easier to lease than to find financing for new equipment.

6. There is little idle time with leased equipment.

7. The time saved may be used for the purchase of new equipment or disposing of the old.

8. Estimators can accurately price the cost for the use of heavy equipment on any specific job.

9. Working the machines overtime may reduce overall costs of hiring instead of owning.

10. The owner of leased equipment must keep up-to-date with all the latest models to remain competitive.

11. Renewal of leasing the same equipment may be cheaper to the contractor.

12. The leasing of automobiles can only be assessed against the anticipated annual mileage; the greater the mileage, the more advantageous the leasing.

Review

1. Obtain specifications and a price list for one piece of equipment, such as a back-hoe. With current information gathered from the manufacturer

and from a government taxation office, prepare a data table of comparative depreciation schedules.

2. In terms of life expectancy of the machine, which method of calculating depreciation would you select for annual reporting to the government? Give your reasons for the selection.

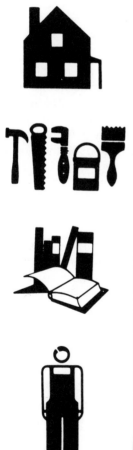

5

Final Inspection of New Buildings

The material in section 5.1 has been excerpted from a publication of the Canada Mortgage and Housing Corporation, Ottawa, and is reproduced with permission of the copyright holder.

5.1 THE FINAL INSPECTION

The final inspection, the maintenance of the completed building for a stated time, and the method of final payments to the contractor are all part of the general conditions of the contract set forth in the original specifications and contract documents. The following extract of specifications presents typical clauses covering the final handover of the building to the owner, the final payments to the contractor, and the maintenance of liability of the contractor.

Extract of Specifications

Payments. On the twentieth of each month, the contractor shall submit to the architect an estimate on all work done and material supplied onto the job. Contractor shall attach to his progress estimate receipted accounts and wage sheets covering the items entering into his estimate. Upon this total the Board will allow 10 percent (10%) to cover the Contractor's overhead and operational expenses. When approved by the Architect, the Board shall pay to the Contractor eighty-five percent (85%) of the amount of his estimate. The final payment of balance shall be paid to the Contractor forty days after completion and acceptance of the building, provided satisfactory evidence is shown that all accounts for material and labor have been satisfied.

Correction of Work After Final Payment. (a) Neither the final certificate of payment nor any provisions of the Contract documents shall relieve the Contractor from responsibility for faulty materials or workmanship which shall appear within a period of one year from the date of the completion of the work, and he shall remedy any defects, and pay for any damage to other work resulting therefrom which shall appear within such period of two years, but beyond that the Contractor shall not be liable.

(b) No certificate, payment, partial or entire use of the building or its equipment by the Owner shall be construed as an acceptance of defective work or material.

General Contractor's Inspection

A short time before the final inspection it is usual for the general contractor, in company with the superintendent and the foreman, to make a careful inspection of the whole work, at which time notations are made of all details to be completed and a time set for these to be done. It is most likely that some broken glass will have to be replaced, door locks adjusted, paint work retouched, and so on.

Architect's Final Inspection

When the general contractor is quite sure that the building is completed, he will notify the architect in writing and request a date and time for the final inspection.

The final inspection is made by the architect with the clerk of the works, the owner, and the general contractor and his superintendent.

Any adjustments are noted and corrected, and the building is then ready for handing over, provided there are no liens or other legal encumbrances against the property.

Sidewalk and Landscaping

When concrete sidewalks are not placed in the late fall because of extremely cold weather, the architect may retain a holdback of cash sufficient to do that work in the spring. Landscaping is usually an entirely separate contract outside the scope of the general contractor's work.

Window Cleaning

On a large job, this is a subtrade; for smaller jobs the contractor's own men may do the work, but in either case it must be allowed for in the estimates. Upper story windows should be reversibly hinged so that outside surfaces may be cleaned inside the room.

Janitor Services

Some jobs will require the services of janitors to clean thoroughly the whole building. Many specifications state that all fingerprints shall be removed from all paint and polished work and that the building shall be left ready for immediate occupation. This may also be a subtrade.

5.2 ADVERTISING AND SELLING THE FINAL PRODUCT

Part of the cost of a speculatively built home, warehouse, office block, or other structure is for advertising. Some of the methods of bringing and keeping the builder's name and product before the public, and by which most people find the home they purchase are as follows:

1. Most people locate the home they want by driving around in the family car and by hearing of a reliable builder.

2. Model homes (especially if furnished) attract many visitors who are potential buyers.

3. Newspapers are a good source of advertising, especially if portraying a finished home ready for occupation.

4. Friends often recommend a builder, a district, and type of home.

5. People look for accessibility to schools, shopping, public utilities, transportation, churches, and an acceptable district.

6. Company trucks, cars, and mobile field offices should prominently display the builder's name.

7. Billboards on the building site, listing the names of the builder and subcontractors, attract attention.

8. Radio and TV keep the public informed.

9. Real estate companies are experienced in introducing prospective buyers. They can explain the different means of financing and draw up necessary papers and notarize them.

It is important that the builder realize all of his investment of cash, wages, and a minimum of 10% profit, in the sale of a house. Financiers advance money on first mortgages up to about 60% of the assessed value of the property; this leaves a balance of much more than many people can afford as a down payment. There is a temptation for some builders to hold a second mortgage in the sum of say 20 to 25%, making it easier for the prospective purchaser to buy the property.

A builder must be very circumspect before leaving part or all of his salary and profit in the property by way of a second mortgage. It must be remembered that he will not only have to pay income tax on the salary and profit that he leaves in the house, but he will become more pressed for working capital for his future operations. *The builder must remain in the construction business; not enter the financial business.*

Let us assume that a house is listed to sell for $70,000.00 which includes the real estate agent's fee of 5%. There is to be a first mortgage of 60% of the assessed value and the builder agrees to hold a second mortgage in the sum of 20% of the assessed value.

The position would be as follows:

Listed price of the property		$70,000.00
Real estate fee of 5%	$ 3,500.00	
First mortgage of 60%	42,000.00	
Second mortgage of 20% held by the builder	14,000.00	
Down payment of purchaser	10,500.00	
	$70,000.00	$70,000.00

It can be seen from the above record that a builder would only have to repeat this type of transaction five times, to have more than $70,000.00 of his own funds tied up in real estate mortgages. Mortgages can be discounted, but the percentage is considerable, especially on second mortgages. It is common for second mortgages to be discounted from 20 to 40%. Assume that a second mortgage from $14,000.00 (as shown) was discounted at a rate of 30%; this would yield to the builder $9,800.00, the discount being $4,200.00 on $14,000.00.

Speculatively built homes must be of the right type, erected in a district compatible with price value, and aimed at the class of people that can afford the amount of down payment required to close each deal.

To maintain a good public image, the speculative builder must make good any legitimate complaints by purchasers for a short time after occupation.

5.3 FACTS TO ASCERTAIN BEFORE DRAWING CONTRACT OF SALE

1. Date of contract.
2. Name and address of seller.
3. Is seller a citizen, of full age, and competent?
4. Name of seller's wife and whether she is of full age.
5. Name and residence of purchaser.
6. Description of the property.
7. The purchase price:
    a. Amount to be paid on signing contract;
    b. Amount to be paid on delivery of deed;
    c. Existing mortgage or mortgages and details thereof;
    d. Purchase money mortgage, if any, and details thereof.
8. What kind of deed is to be delivered: full covenant, quit claim, or bargain and sale?
9. What agreement has been made with reference to any specific personal property, i.e., gas ranges, heaters, machinery, partitions, fixtures, coal, wood, window shades, screens, carpets, rugs, and hangings?
10. Is purchaser to assume the mortgage or take the property subject to it?
11. Are any exceptions or reservations to be inserted?
12. Are any special clauses to be inserted?
13. Stipulations and agreements with reference to tenancies and rights of persons in possession, including compliance with any governmental regulations in force.
14. Stipulations and agreements, if any, to be inserted with reference to the state of facts a survey would show: i.e., party walls, encroachments, easements, and so forth.
15. What items are to be adjusted on the closing of title?
16. Name of the broker who brought about the sale, his address, the amount of his commission and who is to pay it, and whether or not a clause covering the foregoing facts is to be inserted in the contract.
17. Are any alterations or changes being made, or have they been made, in street lines, name, or grade?

18. Are condemnations or assessment proceedings contemplated or pending, or has an award been made?

19. Who is to draw the purchase money mortgage and who is to pay the expense thereof?

20. Are there any convenants, restrictions, and consents affecting the title?

21. What stipulation or agreement is to be made with reference to Tenement Building Department and other violations?

22. The place and date on which the title is to be closed.

23. Is time to be of the essence in the contract?

24. Are any alterations to be made in the premises between the date of the contract and the date of the closing?

25. Amount of fire and hazard insurance, payment of premium, and rights and obligations of parties in case of fire or damage to premises from other causes during the contract period.

Upon the Closing of Title, the Seller Should Be Prepared with the Following

1. Seller's copy of the contract.

2. The latest tax, water, and assessment receipted bills.

3. Latest possible meter reading of water, gas, or electric utilities.

4. Receipts for last payment of interest on mortgages.

5. Originals and certificates of all fire, liability, and other insurance policies.

6. Estoppel certificates from the holder of any mortgage that has been reduced, showing the amount due and the date to which interest is paid.

7. Any subordination agreements that may be called for in the contract.

8. Satisfaction pieces of mechanics liens, chattel mortgages, judgments, or mortgages that are to be paid at, or prior to, the closing.

Review

1. What are the respective areas of responsibility of those persons who accompany an architect when making a final inspection of a newly completed building? From a local newspaper, clip typical job descriptions for such persons.

2. Describe briefly the making of progress payments to the builder for completed work and building materials on the ground.

3. Obtain a copy of an architect's certificate of completed work as forwarded to an owner. Examine it and then write in point form what in effect it says.

4. Clip from trade magazines or newspapers examples of six different methods of advertising for the sale of a speculatively built house. Explain how the methods differ.

6

An Introduction to the Critical Path Method

6.1 TERMS

Part of a dictionary definition of the word *critical* is "quick to find fault." The Critical Path Method (CPM) was devised for the construction industry for assessing the minimum time required to erect a structure and for planning the critical consecutive jobs to be done to accomplish this end. See the Critical Path Flow Chart on page 49.

Observe how the arrowed flow indicates the progress of the units of work which follow each other, such as: preliminary operations, hoarding, fencing, delivery of lumber (these activities should be going on at the same time); then land grading, and so on. Note that the glazing and painting may be going on from the readiness of the second floor until the job is finished. Those items are critical that have to be completed before other items may be started; and when such items are given a time limit for completion, we are *quick to find fault* if they fall behind schedule.

The term **project** denotes the whole project. The term **activity** denotes any identifiable job that takes time to complete within the project. Every activity occurs before, after, or at the same time as another activity or activities. Study the chart and note that, when the formwork is being made and erected, it is an identifiable activity; it occurs after the layout but before the activity of placing concrete footings. It also occurs at the same time that reinforcing is being set in the formwork; furthermore, while the forms are being made, excavating may proceed. The critical activity in the above operations is formwork because other activities cannot proceed until it is finished. This is an activity that must be carefully watched so that it may be completed in the time schedule.

It is suggested that, to make up a simple CPM flow chart, you proceed as follows:

Step 1: Type a list of all identifiable activities for the project. Examine the example as a guide.

Step 2: Cut out all typed activities and place them in a single straight line on a flat surface.

Step 3: Arrange the activities in sequential operational order using the following reasoning:

a.   This activity occurs before that. (See cut and fill and layout.)

b.   That occurs after this. (See backfill after concrete walls.)

c.   This happens at the same time as that. (See footing forms, wall forms, excavating, and ditching.)

d.   This occurs at the same time as all these things. (See glazing and plumbing, which occur during lots of other activities.)

Rearrange all activities until you have satisfied yourself that they are in sequential order of events. The term **event** denotes a point in time between the finish of one activity and the start of another.

Step 4: On a long piece of paper (a good quality piece of kitchen shelving paper will do) make a freehand arrowed flow chart similar to the one shown. *Note carefully that the length of the arrows is immaterial* and they may be straight, bent, or curved. Arrange all activities that may be worked on at the same time, such as hoarding, fencing, delivery of lumber. *(See the flow chart.)*

Step 5: Underline each activity and underneath it write the duration of time required to complete it. The term **duration** is an experienced judgment of the time required to complete an activity.

Step 6: When you are completely satisfied that all the activities (together with their durations) are in correct order, make a final CPM chart. *Be aware that the making of a CPM chart takes time and patience and can only be attempted against the background of your experience in the field.*

You will notice the dotted lines on the chart between first, second, and third floors, and the following partitions. These lines indicate that some of the carpenters will leave the floor framing to start working on the partitions before the whole floor assembly is completed. You will find the experience of making a CPM chart interesting and rewarding, and it will fix in your own mind the best order of operations; you will also be better able to communicate with others about the job.

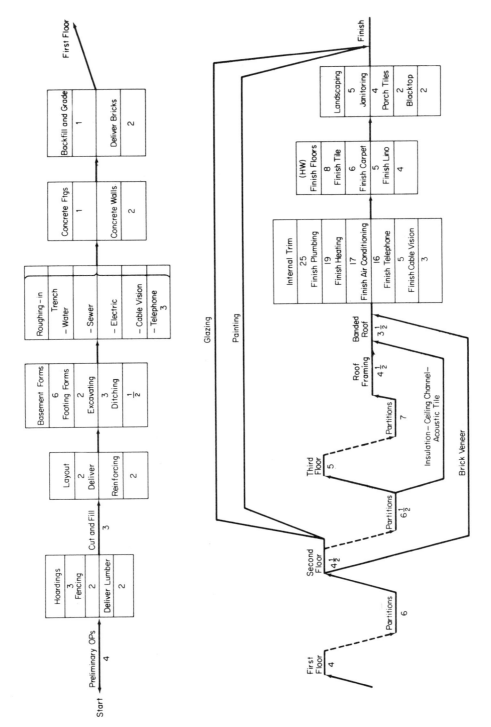

Fig. 6.1

6.2 USING THE CPM CHART

Step 1: To find the total duration of the project, add together the number of days required for all activities that appear on the top arrowed paths. See the CPM Analysis Chart—column (a).

Step 2: Add up all the days required for all activities appearing on the arrowed path, but including the second-row arrows instead of the first—column (b).

Step 3: Add up all the days required for activities appearing on the arrowed path, but including the third-row arrows instead of the first—column (c).

Step 4: Add up all the days required for all activities appearing on the arrowed path, but including the fourth-row arrows instead of the first—column (d).

Step 5: Compare the total times for each arrowed path in columns (a), (b), (c), and (d). *The longest path is the critical path.* Anything that can speed any of the activities on this path will shorten the total time required for the project. Assuming that by using more men and equipment, or by working overtime, the longest critical path was shortened to fewer days than the second-longest path, then the next-longest path would become critical, and an endeavor would be made to speed it. This is how we examine the CPM chart for critical events. Where more men, machines, or equipment are used to shorten a critical path, it reflects itself in direct costs; but indirect costs will go down by completing the project in a shorter period of time.

6.3 COMPUTING CPM TIME

Time is measured by a five-day week, excluding holidays. If a building takes 75 working days to complete, this is $75 \div 5 = 15$ weeks plus public holidays. This could mean as much as 100 calendar days in all.

To calculate on the CPM chart when brickwork will commence we make what is termed a **forward pass.** This is done by adding together all the preceding time activities and relating this total to a calendar date (allowing for public holidays), which yields the date for the bricklaying to commence. The subtrades must know when they are to arrive on the job, and they must know quite definitely when they must have finished their part. A delay in any subtrade can very seriously affect the whole course of the progress of the project. *You will notice that on the* CPM *chart the delivery of bricks is shown at the time of backfill.* It is important to show delivery times for important items, including mechanical items.

To calculate on the CPM chart when the carpet layer should commence work, we make what is termed a **backward pass.** This is done by adding together all the timed activities (including that of the carpet layer), starting with his allotted duration time until the finish of the project, and subtracting this number of days from the total number of working days for the whole project. Remember to transcribe this total of working days into calendar dates.

For housing units and small jobs, you may make a CPM chart yourself, but for large, complex jobs you may, *according to the terms in the specifications,* have to make a computerized CPM chart.

The creation of a computer program can be very expensive. It might be much better to go "shopping" for prepared pro-

Analysis Chart CPM

Item	(a)		(b)		(c)		(d)	
		Activity		Activity		Activity		Activity
1	4	Preliminary ops	4	Preliminary ops	4	Preliminary ops	4	Preliminary ops
2	2	Deliver lumber	2	Deliver lumber	2	Deliver lumber	2	Deliver lumber
3	3	Hoardings	2	Fencing	2	Fencing	2	Fencing
4	3	Cut and fill	3	Cut and fill	3	Cut and fill	3	Cut and fill
5	2	Layout	2	Layout	2	Layout	2	Layout
6	2	Deliver reinforcing	2	Deliver rein	2	Deliver rein	2	Deliver rein
7	6	Basement forms	6	Footing forms	3	Excavating	½	Ditching
8	3	Roughing-in	3	Roughing-in	3	Roughing-in	3	Roughing-in
9	1	Concrete ftgs	2	Concrete walls	2	Concrete walls	2	Concrete walls
10	1	Backfill	1	Backfill	1	Backfill	1	Backfill
11	3	Deliver bricks	3	Deliver bricks	3	Deliver bricks	3	Deliver bricks
12	4	First floor	4	First floor	4	First floor	4	First floor
13	6	Partitions	6	Partitions	6	Partitions	6	Partitions
14	4½	Second floor	4½	Second floor	4½	Second floor	4½	Second floor
15	6½	Partitions	6½	Partitions	6½	Partitions	6½	Partitions
16	5	Third floor	5	Third floor	5	Third floor	5	Third floor
17	7	Partitions	7	Partitions	7	Partitions	7	Partitions
18	4½	Roof framing	4½	Roof framing	4½	Roof framing	4½	Roof framing
19	3½	Bonded roof	3½	Bonded roof	3½	Bonded roof	3½	Bonded roof
20	25	Interior trim	19	Finish plumbing	19	Finish heating	17	Finish telephone
21	8	Finish floors	6	Finish tile	6	Finish carpet	5	Finish lino
22	5	Landscaping	5	Janitoring	4	Porch tiles	4	Blacktop
	Days:	109	Days:	96	Days:	92	Days:	76½

Note: Items 12–16 have similar activities for each floor level; the extra time is taken up by the raising of material and placing at progressively greater heights.

51

grams which may be used for relatively small fees.

Knowing how to relate to the data processing field, without neccessarily being a specialist, is important to the modern builder.

Review

1. Define the following terms as used in the Critical Path Method:

    (a) project

    (b) activity

    (c) event

    (d) duration

    (e) forward pass

    (f) backward pass.

2. Observe the building of a house. Keep notes and develop a Critical Path Method Chart which you might use at a later date.

7

Preliminary Building Operations

This chapter presents a discussion of important business procedures that are necessary before actual building operations begin.

7.1 SINGLE AND MULTIPLE RESIDENTIAL UNITS

The decision to build certain types of homes will be influenced by local appeal—single dwellings with basements or single dwellings without. The former are particularly recommended where severe weather conditions prevail, the basement being useful for children's game rooms, for storage, and especially for the installation of heating units for the home.

Consideration may be given to the building of side by side, two story duplexes with or without basements or to the building of apartments. The advantage of this type of construction (where it is acceptable according to the local building code) is that only one foundation or basement has to be dug; only one set of service lines installed; the workmen are under one roof for a longer

period of time; there is less moving of equipment and temporary buildings.

It is important to remember that actual building costs are the same for similar residences on expensive or cheap poor lots. It is a good policy to produce homes to complement building lots and patterns of existing homes.

7.2 THE COMMITMENT TO BUILD

Once a determination has been made either to sign a contract to build a residence, or to build on speculation of selling, immediate consideration must be given to the labor force and from where it will be recruited; who will run the job; what kind of equipment will be needed.

Some stationary equipment will have to be assembled such as: cut-off saws; hand electric saws; electric drills; ladders; scaffold; picks; shovels; wheelbarrows; wrecking bars.

Temporary Buildings will have to be provided and they may include some mobile units for offices and first-aid rooms. Remember that if a mobile unit costs $4,000 and is used forty times, the actual cost per usage is only $100 plus its maintenance and haulage from job to job. Information is available on depreciation of equipment and leasing.

General Conditions of Contract always embrace the following:

1. The contractor and all subcontractors shall comply with all local, state, provincial, or government rules, regulations and ordinances. They will prepare and file all necessary documents and information, pay for and obtain all licenses, permits and certificates of inspection as may be specified or required.

2. By executing the contract documents for the contract for construction, the contractor represents that he has personally visited the site, familiarized himself with the local conditions under which the work is to be performed, and correlated his observations with the requirements of the contract documents and the local building code.

7.3 INSPECTING THE BUILDING SITE

Before purchasing a lot for building residences, or before submitting a bid to erect a residential building, it is important to identify, and inspect thoroughly, the proposed site.

Incorrectly Located Buildings are daily being either torn down or removed from an incorrect lot to a correct one, or are being relocated properly on the correct lot. Be careful and employ the services of a registered surveyor if you have any doubts on these matters.

Demolition or Removal of Existing Buildings must be authorized by the local authority. In addition, all service lines below and above ground from the city mains to such buildings must be completely removed from the property by the contractor. That is to say that water, sewer, power, telephone and cable vision lines must be detached from the building, unearthed and removed back to the city mains. This is understandable; otherwise disused underground lines over a long period of time would become confusing and could lead to accidents.

7.4 DATUM AND BENCH MARKS

A very important post held by one of the officials at the city engineers department is the "official grade striker." There is probably more grief over incorrect grades in building construction than in any other phase of the operation. After the survey of the land, but before the contractor builds, the bench mark or datum must be established.

The official grade striker will come to the land and set up a peg showing the depth of the sewer line and another peg showing the height of the city sidewalk curb. This is assuming that you are building on virgin ground. If you set your house too low in the ground, you may have difficulty in getting a fall to the sewer line of the city. If your house is built too high, you may find later that the city will cut a road and leave your house far too high, making it difficult to drive onto your lot.

A building line is the prescribed minimum distance set back from the street or avenue fronting the lot; it is illegal to build between that line and the street. It is also the prescribed minimum distance that the structure must be kept from other buildings or boundaries of the property. A house that is built infringing on these regulations may have to be moved to its correct place on the lot. *Be careful; this is very important!* A builder may recover from all sorts of mistakes, but an avoidable error of this nature may force a builder out of business immediately if it occurs.

7.5 UNDERGROUND CONDITIONS AND DEWATERING

Sometimes, due to unpredictable underground conditions, either natural ones, or, in older cities, pre-existing man made structures, such as sewer mains, city utilities, or underground cables, it is not uncommon for the successful bidder for work to be performed above ground to be awarded a contract on a cost plus basis for work to be

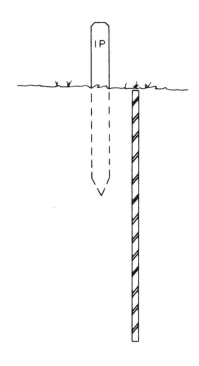

Fig. 7.1. Wooden stake indicating official survey metal pin.

performed below ground. Cost plus is the actual cost of the work plus overhead expenses, plus a percentage for the contractor's fee, say, ten percent,

There are more hazards and unpredictables in excavating and in the underpinning of buildings than in any other feature of the construction industry. While the contractor can be reasonably sure of all operations above ground, there is never any certainty about conditions below ground.

When it is necessary to excavate below the natural water level (unless tremie concrete is to be placed), the basic methods of water control are reducing the flow by diversion—thus keeping the water out of the excavated area—or designing a system of well points and pumps. Apart from being an accident hazard to workmen, seepage of water into excavated areas may cause sloughing of the walls of the excavation, the heaving of the bottoms, and unstable underpinning.

Where foundation work must be carried out in the "dry" (on firm, unyielding foundations), it may be necessary to engage the services of a professional engineer for the dewatering of the area of operations. This will involve an evaluation of field conditions. Some of the considerations to be taken into account are:

1. The size and depth of the excavation.

2. The length of time that the area must be kept dewatered.

3. The conditions necessary for the completion of the structure.

4. A careful survey of the subsurface geological conditions.

5. The proximity and sources of water.

6. The variation in the water table; artesian pressures caused by seasonal conditions and variations in rivers, lakes, tides, and freezing conditions; the influence of these conditions on the sides and bottoms of excavated areas.

7.6 SUBSURFACE EXPLORATION

There are a number of methods that may be used for making an inspection of subsurface conditions. The method adopted will depend upon the depth to which the test is to be made, the probable nature of the soil and the weight of the structure to be imposed upon the earth. Methods include sounding rods, augers, wash borings, rock drillings, and test pits.

Test Pits: These are expensive since they are often dug by hand. They usually measure about 4'0" square and 9'0" deep. In the case of wet soil, sheet piling is driven in advance of pit excavation. This, in itself, would be indicative to the contractor that sheet piling may have to be provided over some or all of the area for mass excavations. Some of the advantages of test pits are that visual inspection may be made of the soil layers; compactness and water content of the layers may be checked; undisturbed samples may be taken for laboratory investigation; load tests may be made on any of the soil at any depth desired. For deep test pits, machine excavating would have to be resorted to.

7.7 BUILDING INSPECTORS

It is in the public interest that progressive official inspections be made of new structures; for example, faulty plumbing could be a severe public hazard. It is obligatory for contractors to request that inspections be made at prescribed times. All work—such as on the sewer line or electric circuits—must be left open until an official certificate of approval has been given by the building inspector.

Building inspectors specialize in their own fields. You must be aware that inspections have to be arranged ahead of time so that the work schedule will not be delayed.

7.8 BUILDING IN FRIGID CONDITIONS

In some areas, especially in Canada, special consideration will have to be given to maintaining continuous work under frigid working conditions by using winter enclosures.

Review

1. Where conditions allow, what are five advantages for building houses with basements?

2. Which pieces of equipment must be on site before starting to build a house?

3. Prepare your reference list, complete with names, addresses, and telephone numbers, of agencies from which drawings and specifications for houses may be obtained.

4. List the persons/agencies (giving names, addresses and telephone numbers) who will require copies of drawings and specifications before building operations commence.

5. What should be done to ensure that a new house will be correctly placed on its correct lot, at its correct height on the lot?

6. Locate an official survey metal pin. Record and explain the markings.

8

An Introduction to Land Grading

In this chapter, we present a discussion on land grading terms, swell percentage of cut earth, benchmarks, measurements, and a simple method of estimating cut.

8.1 A GLOSSARY OF LAND GRADING TERMS

Cut: Land that has to be cut (usually with heavy machinery) to a lower level (grade) and the cut earth (burrow) either to be hauled from the site and **legally dumped,** or compacted in a low lying area of the same parcel of land.

Parcel of Land: Any area of land registered as one unit such as a building lot. It could be several acres which may later be divided (and registered) into smaller parcels.

Fill: Land that has to be brought to a higher level (grade) by filling with earth from cut areas, or by hauling loose fill from other parcels of land to the job site.

Grade: The existing grade (level) of land. For a proposed new building, the future grade of the sidewalk and/or the center of the proposed new road may be obtained from the city engineers department.

Grade Line: A predetermined line indicating the proposed elevation of the ground for an area such as: a parking lot or the area around a new building and so on.

Grade Striker: The title given by some authorities to the person whose duty it is to place **official stakes** on the city property adjoining a new building project and indicating the depth of the sewer below the existing grade and the future grade of the sidewalk and the center of the road.

Test Holes: Holes drilled or dug on a proposed building site to determine the nature of the subsoil.

Topsoil: Organic earth which will sustain vegetation.

Soil: Subsoil or the inert earth beneath the top soil such as cobbles, boulders, gravel, fine sand, soil and clay.

Interstices: The voids between pieces of cut rock (or grains of sugar and so on). The larger the volumes of the pieces of rock, the greater the collective volume of voids between the lumps.

Grid: Baselines intersecting at right angles as used on survey maps. (*See Fig. 8.8.*)

Station: A point from which an observation is taken as at the corners of a parcel of land (*See Fig. 8.1.*)

Interpolate: To determine an intermediate (average) term between two stations, such as 112.7' and 105.1'. The intermediate reading is the difference between the elevations of the two stations

divided by two; thus: 112.7'—105.1' divided by two is 3.8' average. Notice that, in the imperial system of measurement, survey readings are given in feet and decimal fractions of feet.

8.2 SWELL PERCENTAGE OF CUT EARTH

The actual amount of swell for any given cut is determined by soil tests or by studying the soil reports given in the specifications. Soil means earth. Topsoil is expensive and is estimated separately for either buying or selling.

Type of Earth Cut	Swell Percentage
Sand and gravel	6 to 20%
Loam and clay	20 to 25%
Rock	30 to 50%

8.3 BENCHMARK OR DATA

The grade to which land has to be cut and/or filled is taken from a benchmark having this symbol: 🔨. The center of the horizontal bar is the benchmark level or datum line. For small jobs, this symbol is usually cut onto a stout stake which is erected near the perimeter of the site and fenced around for protection during operations. The center of the bar is identified as 100.0'; for example, 112.2' equals 12.2' of cut and 89.2' means the land is 100.0'—89.2' and requires 10.8' of fill.

Many bridges and large public buildings bear a benchmark showing their height above sea level; other levels may be taken from these to determine sewer levels, street drainage, and so on. A manhole cover in the center of a road could be taken as an initial reference. Internationally, the sea level is recognized as a datum.

8.4 VOLUMES: IMPERIAL AND METRIC

In this chapter, most land measurements are given in feet and decimals of a foot. An introduction is given to land dimensions in the metric system.

Imperial Measurements (Conversions)

Inches	Feet	Inches	Feet
1	0.083	7	0.583
2	0.1667	8	0.667
3	0.25	9	0.75
4	0.333	10	0.833
5	0.417	11	0.917
6	0.5	12	1.0

Metric Measurements. The cubic meter is used to measure volumes such as cuts or excavations. The symbol for cubic meter is m^3.

$1 m^3 = 1 m \times 1 m \times 1 m$ (one cubic meter)

The dimensions of an excavation may be given in millimeters:

2400 mm $\times$ 4500 mm $\times$ 7300 mm = 78 840 000 000 mm³

The volume expressed in this form is cum-bersome. A better way is to convert measurements in millimeters to meters:

2.4 m $\times$ 4.5 m $\times$ 7.3 m = 78.84 m³

Remember that, when estimating quantities, computations are not worked out to mathematical exactitudes.

8.5 ESTIMATING CUT

Problem 1. Estimate the number of cu yds of cut to be removed from a square parcel of land 50.0′ × 50.0′ as shown in Fig. 8.1. The land is to be graded to 100.0′ as shown on the benchmark. As an example station (a) is shown as 107.1′ which is 7.1′ higher than the benchmark.

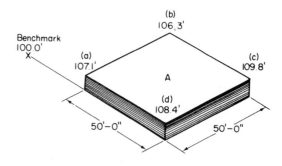

Fig. 8.1

Step 1: From the given benchmark of 100.0′, estimate the average height of the four stations (a) (b) (c) and (d)

$$\frac{7.1 + 6.3 + 9.8 + 8.4}{4} = 7.9 \text{ average height}$$

Step 2: Multiply the area of the land in sq ft by the average height of the stations in ft:

2500 × 7.9 = 19,750 cu ft. Since excavating is reckoned in cu yds, the estimate would be 731 cu yds.

Using graph paper (or draw to scale) a section of the land on line (d) (c). See Fig. 8.2.

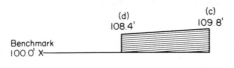

Fig. 8.2

Problem 2. From the given benchmark, estimate the number of cu yds of earth to be cut and hauled from two separate parcels of land dimensioned as shown in Fig. 8.3.

Note that, in the previous example, *A* has already been estimated as 731 cu yds, as in Step 2, Example 1.

The average height of the stations in lot **B** is 7.0' and the estimated cu yds is 648. The total cut of lots *A* and *B* is 731 + 648 = 1379 cu yds. The total number of stations

taken into consideration for the two lots is eight, four for each lot.

Remember that estimating *is* estimating and does not necessarily require mathematical exactitude.

Examine Fig. 8.4, where both lots are placed end-on-end. It will be seen that the adjoining lot stations—that is 6.3 and 9.8—were taken twice; once for parcel *A* and once for parcel *B*. Since eight stations must be taken into account, set out the work as follows:

Station Readings	Times Taken	Totals
7.1	1	7.1
6.3	2	12.6
4.4	1	4.4
7.5	1	7.5
9.8	2	19.6
8.4	1	8.4
	8	59.6

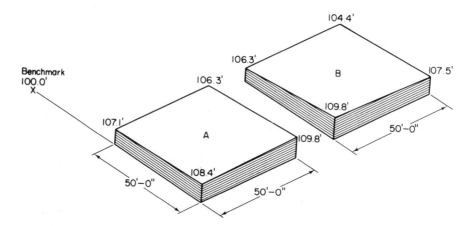

Fig. 8.3

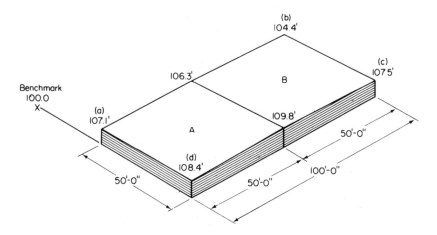

Fig. 8.4

Average cut is $\dfrac{59.6}{8}$

$$= 7.45 \text{ and } \dfrac{7.45 \times 5000}{27} = 1379$$

cu yds. The figure 5,000 is the area of the two lots together.

From the given benchmark, using six station elevations only, make a calculation of the cut required for the land shown in Fig. 8.4. Subtract the result of calculations using six elevations from the result of calculations using eight elevations. Satisfy yourself that it is more accurate to take into account eight elevations than six. Remember this is a very small parcel of land on an even plane.

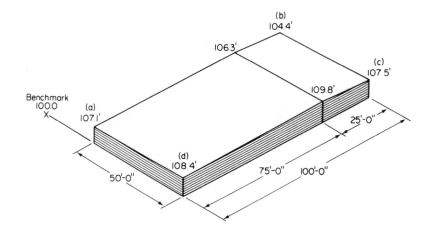

Fig. 8.5

No Scale

Fig. 8.6

Be sure to always check the number of elevations taken into account.

Rule: Take the number of station elevations in adjoining grids which have the same shape and perimeter and multiply by the number of grids. This equals the number of elevations to be taken into account.

Problem 3. From the given benchmark, estimate the number of cu yds of cut on a parcel of land with the dimensions and stations as shown in Fig. 8.5. Read the rule

again. Note that the area of Fig. 8.5 is the same as in Fig. 8.4. The station elevations are the same, the benchmark is the same, *but the grids are not the same dimensions.* Take each grid estimate separately, add them together, and then subtract the differences of cuts for Figs. 8.4 and 8.5.

Make a scaled sectional drawing on line *d–c*, Fig. 8.4. Impose on this section a section in colored ink of line *d–c* of Fig. 8.5 (see Fig. 8.6).

Satisfy yourself on the validity of the rule.

Problem 4. Estimate the number of cu yds of earth to be cut from a parcel of land with the dimensions, stations, and benchmark as shown in Fig. 8.7.

Re-read the rule and set out your work as shown in Problem 2 on page 62. How

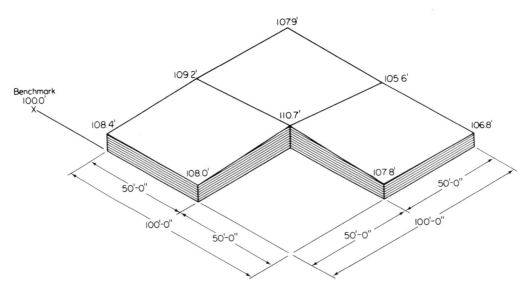

Fig. 8.7

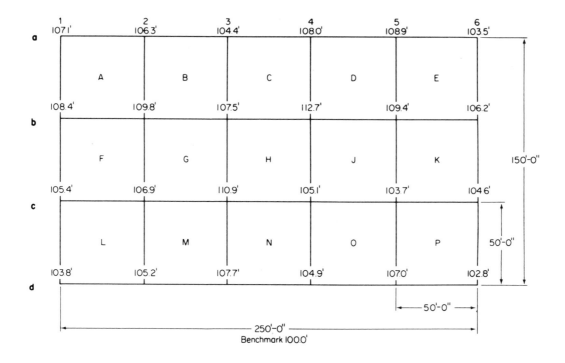

Fig. 8.8

many times are you going to take station reading 110.7?

Problem 5.

(a) Estimate the number of cu yds of earth to be cut from a piece of land with the dimensions, stations, and benchmark as shown in Fig. 8.8. Re-read the rule. There are fifteen equal area grids and four station elevations to each grid. There are 60 stations to be reckoned, thus:

Stations

(i) The four outside-corner stations are reckoned once: $4 \times 1 =$ 4

(ii) The outside adjoining equal area and perimeter grid stations are reckoned twice: $12 \times 2 =$ 24

(iii) The internal adjoining equal area and perimeter grid stations are reckoned four times: $8 \times 4 =$ 32
                                                                                    ————
                                                                                      60

For this problem, set out your work on a cut and fill sheet similar to the one shown in Fig. 8.9.

John Doe Construction Company Ltd
Cut and Fill Estimating Sheet

Job Apartment Block at........................   Date 9 September

1	2	3	4	5	6	7
	Cut				Fill	
Grid	Area Sq Ft	Average Cut	Volume Cu Yds	Area	Average Fill	Volume Cu Yds
a	2500	17.5	1620			
B	2401	8.2	730	99	1.67	6
C						
D						
E						
F						
G						
H						
I						
K						
	TOTAL CUT				TOTAL FILL	
Note: This is an Example of Cut and Fill Sheet Only.						

Fig. 8.9

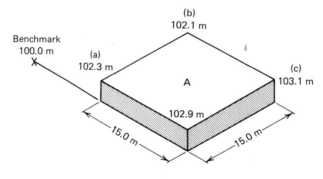

Fig. 8.10

(b) Allowing for a swell of 15 percent for cut earth, how many 8-cu-yd truckloads of burrow (cut earth) will have to be hauled from the site?

Problem 6. Estimate the number of cubic meters of cut to be removed from a square parcel of land 15.0 m × 15.0 m as shown in Fig. 8.10. The land is to be graded to 100.0 m as shown on the benchmark.

Step 1: From the given benchmark of 100.0 m estimate the average height of the four stations (a) (b) (c) and (d).

$$\frac{2.3 \text{ m} + 2.1 \text{ m} + 3.1 \text{ m} + 2.9 \text{ m}}{4} = 2.6 \text{ m}$$

Step 2: Multiply the area of land in square meters by the average height of the stations in meters:

$$15 \text{ m} \times 15 \text{ m} \times 2.6 \text{ m} = 585.0 \text{ m}^3$$

Review

1. List ten land grading terms.

2. Why does the swell percentage of cut earth swell more for rock than for sand? Use a sketch to help explain.

3. The dimensions shown in Fig. 8.7 are in feet and decimal fractions of feet. Study Fig. 8.7. Then, using the conversion tables in the back of the book, convert all dimensions in Fig. 8.7 to the metric system.

9

Foundations Layout: Batter Boards, and Story Rods

In this chapter we present: how to use the right-angle triangle in building construction; building lines; batter boards; and the builder's square and story rods.

9.1 THE RIGHT-ANGLE TRIANGLE

Let us refresh our memories of school days when we were taught that: *The square on the base plus the square on the height equals the square on the hypotenuse.*

It will be seen that the squares on the base (3 × 3 = 9) added to the squares on the height (4 × 4 = 16) equals the square on the hypotenuse (5 × 5 = 25). See Fig. 9.1.

Any convenient multiple of these basic unit measures is equally valid as the following examples show:

Set 1 - General

Base	Height	Hypotenuse
3	4	5
6	8	10
9	12	15
15	20	25
30	40	50

Set 2 - Metric

300 mm	400 mm	500 mm
600 mm	800 mm	1000 mm

3.0 m	4.0 m	5.0 m
6.0 m	8.0 m	10.0 m
9.0m	12.0 m	15.0 m
12.0 m	16.0 m	20.0 m
15.0 m	20.0 m	25.0 m
18.0 m	24.0 m	30.0 m
30.0 m	40.0 m	50.0 m
		and so on

The larger the units of measure used, the more exact the layout. As an example (if it is not windy) you could use 60'-0", 80'-0" and 100'-0", or in restricted areas you could use 15'-0", 20'-0" and 25'-0". For metric measurements, use 18 m, 24 m, and 30 m or 6.0 m, 8.0 m and 10.0 m.

9.2 THE BUILDER'S FOUNDATION LAYOUT SQUARE

For convenience you may make and use a large wooden square for some foundation layouts. See Fig. 9.3.

To make the square take the following steps:

Step 1: Take three lengths of straight parallel edged pieces of 1 × 4 pine, or better still take three pieces of trued 1 × 4 rippings of ¾" plywood.

Step 2: Cut them into **exact** squared-end lengths of 9'-0", 12'-0" and 15'-0" respectively.

Step 3: Using one nail, temporarily secure the 9'-0" length to the 12'-0" length as in -A-, Fig. 9.3.

Step 4: Nail the ends of the 15'-0" member (the hypotenuse) to the ends of the other two members.

Step 5: Recheck the square for its exactness as a 90° angle; then well nail and clench at the three corners. Nail in place an intermediate brace to stiffen the frame. Trim off the corners from the hypotenuse member and fix the stiffening brace—the foundation square is ready for use.

The number of times that such a square may be used would depend on the finish and care of the instrument. It may be painted red so that anyone seeing it would respect it as being an important tool. Such a square has many uses for small insets and offsets in the layout of housing units. A similar square of smaller dimensions (say 3'-0", 4'-0" and 5'-0") is used extensively in the building trade.

9.3 GRADING: BUILDING LINES AND FOUNDATION LAYOUT

Before any layout is undertaken the builder must assure himself that he has:

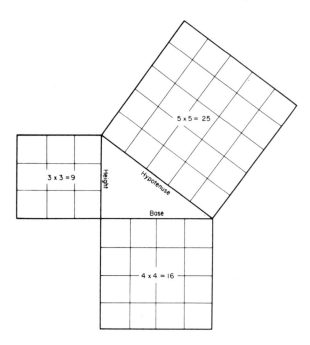

Fig. 9.1. Right-angle triangle.

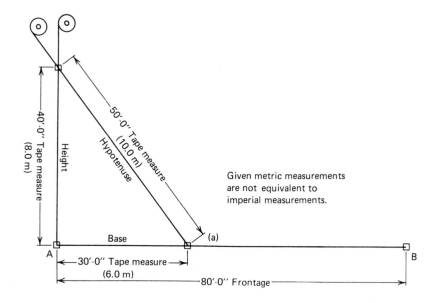

Fig. 9.2. Foundation layout.

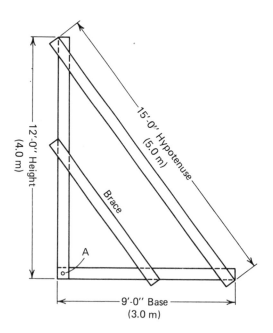

Fig. 9.3. Builder's wooden layout square.

1. Checked the soil conditions, depth of frost penetration which will affect the depth of foundations and service lines, height of present or future centers of public roads and sidewalks, street furniture requirements (decorative street lighting, buried electric power, cable television lines, and so on) and special treatment for sidewalks and curbs.

2. Checked for zoning restrictions, such as single or multiple housing area, maximum permitted height of the building, minimum floor area requirement for the area, minimum setbacks for building lines from adjoining roads and boundaries of the lot.

3. Checked the grading restrictions which may impose minimum and maximum

gradients for property walks, driveways, and swales (low places).

For all the above information see the local planning authority for the area in which you propose to build. Remember that, once the correct location of the site and the correct location for the residence on the site have been established, and the foregoing checks have been made, the builder is off to an excellent start for a profitable job. The following steps may then be taken.

Let us assume that the irregular shaped lot as in Fig. 9.4, A-B-C-D, **has surveyed stakes at each corner,** that it is situated on the corner of a main and side road, that the building lines are to be 20'-0" from the main road and 12'-0" from the minor road. See Fig. 9.4.

To establish the building lines from the known information, take the following steps:

Step 1: Clear the topsoil and stockpile it ready for dispersing on the site for landscaping.

Step 2: Reduce the lot to the correct grade and remember that the land should fall away from the residence on all sides for drainage.

Step 3: String a taut mason's line between (nail spotted) points A-B-C. See Fig. 9.4, south and east sides of the lot.

Step 4: On line B-C, from -B- measure 20'-0" (for the frontage setback to the building line) and drive a peg and spot a nail on the top of the peg to mark the **exact** measurement as at -b-.

Step 5: Using A-B as a base line, place the base of the builder's wooden square (as described in art. 9.2) as shown in Fig. 9.4.

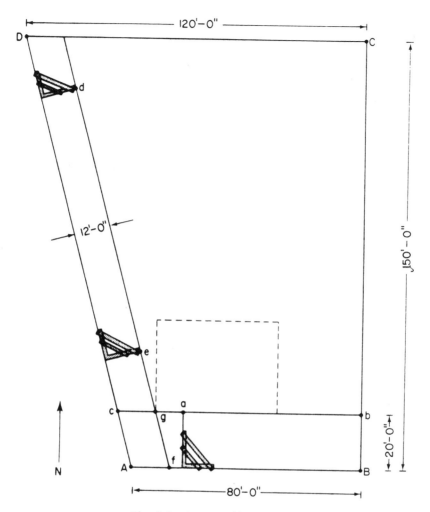

Fig. 9.4. Layout of building lines.

Draw a steel tape tight and parallel to the blade (long side) of the square and measure 20'-0" setback. Drive a stake, and spot a nail to mark the **exact** measurement as at -a-.

Step 6: String a taut mason's line from stake -b- over the spotted nail of stake -a-, and continue the line to a new peg to be placed at -c-.

Step 7: Using A-D as a base line, place the base of the wooden square at a convenient place near the stake -D- (northwesterly) as shown at Fig. 9.4, and drive stake -d- and spot the **exact** point with a nail.

Step 8: Using A-D as a base line, place the base of the wooden square at a convenient place from stake -c-, and set stake -e-.

Step 9: String a taut line from -d- over stake -e- to a new stake -f- on the frontage line.

Step 10: At the **exact** intersection of the two building lines, drive the last stake -g- and spot the exact position with a nail. This last stake -g- is the critical focal point for the layout of the rectangular residence shown in broken lines.

To get the most out of this exercise, get a piece of paper and draw freehand the irregular shaped lot; then follow the text (imagine that you are out in the field) and do the layout step by step.

Once a proposed building has been correctly located for its place and elevation

on its legal lot, the building is off to a good start.

Metric Substitute Measurements for Article 9.3 and Figure 9.4

Imperial	Metric Substitute*
12'-0"	4.0 m (see Fig. 9.3 for reference to wooden square.)
20'-0"	6.0 m
80'-0"	24.0 m
120'-0"	36.0 m
150'-0"	45.0 m

*Not equivalent measurements

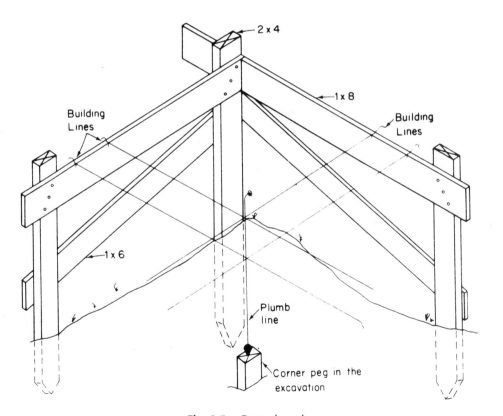

Fig. 9.5. Batter boards.

9.4 BATTER BOARDS

Batter boards are frames placed adjacent to (but on the outside corners of) proposed excavations over which a taut mason's line (or wire for larger jobs) is strung for delineating building lines when excavations are completed. See Fig. 9.5.

Let us assume that we have established the front building line stakes for a residence having a rectangular plan of 30'-0" × 48'-0" (for metric use 15.0 m × 10.0 m). See Fig. 9.6. Note carefully that, for small offsets from an otherwise rectangular plan, the wooden square may be used as described in Fig. 9.2.

To lay out the batter boards, proceed as follows:

Step 1: Using the methods of triangulation described in the foregoing articles, lay out the four corner stakes for the above mentioned residence as in Fig. 9.6.

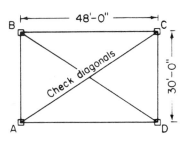

Fig. 9.6.

Step 2: Remember the importance of checking by steel tape all diagonals in field layout. They should be equal.

It once came to my notice that the building lines for a rectangular house 30'-0" × 90'-0" were 2'-0" out of square. The layout had been done using a transit level, but the diagonals were not checked for equality of length (diagonals must always be checked). The error was not discovered until the carpenters tried to lay the subfloor with 4'-0" × 8'-0" sheets of plywood. *Be careful! Be very careful!* You cannot rush this kind of work.

Step 3: With two men working together, one may sight over stakes A and B to align stake -b- which the second man will place about 3'-0" (1.0 m) from stake B. See Fig. 9.7.

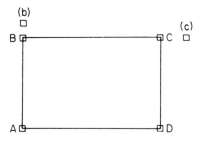

Fig. 9.7.

Step 4: This operation may be repeated with one man now sighting, over stakes B and C, while the other places stake -c- (about 3'-0" or 1.0 m from C), and so on, until two stakes have been placed adjacent to each original corner stake. See Fig. 9.8.

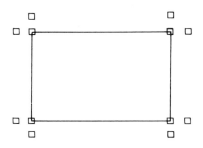

Fig. 9.8.

Step 5: The original stakes A-B-C and D may now be removed leaving the area free for the excavator. Some small jobs may be accomplished using stakes only. See Fig. 9.9 which shows the original corner stakes removed and the mason's lines drawn over the outer stakes. Remove the lines for excavating, then replace them, dropping a plumb line from each of their intersections to reestablish the stakes in the bottom of the excavation. See Fig. 9.5.

boards are placed 3'-0" (1.0 m) clear from the proposed excavation, the arms must be at least 4'-0" (1.25 m) in length.

Step 7: Set the arms of the first batter board with its top edges level to each other, and placed at a determined height, say, the top of the basement wall. The three other batter boards must be placed and leveled to the first.

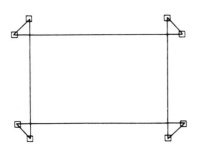

Fig. 9.9.

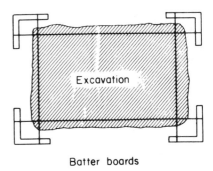

Batter boards

Fig. 9.10. Checking building layout.

Step 6: It will be seen from Fig. 9.10 that a more durable job of establishing the building lines may be made by using batter boards on the outside corners of proposed excavations. Remember that the further away that batter boards are placed from an excavation, the longer the arms must be. If the batter

Step 8: To level from one batter board to another, use a long straightedge of wood (say, 14'-0" or 4.25 m in length) and a spirit level, the longer the better. See Fig. 9.11. Place one end of the straightedge on the first batter board; level the straightedge with the spirit level as shown in Fig. 9.11; and set a

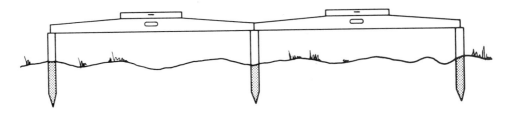

Use straightedge and spirit level for levelling

Fig. 9.11.

stake, at the other end of the straightedge, exactly level with the batter board. Turn the straightedge and spirit level, end for end, and recheck the work. The bubble of the spirit level should read the same for both ways. Then level from one stake to another until the next batter board is leveled from the first.

It is recommended that the first level be made to the center of the area to be excavated. Then from the accuracy of height of this stake, it may be used as a reference to radiate all the remaining batter boards. The less times the straightedge has to be used, the less the risk of error.

Step 9: A saw kerf may be cut into the tops of the arms of each batter board indicating the building lines. On large jobs, the footing lines and wall widths may also be cut on the arms of the batter boards.

Step 10: It is important that the excavation

be made well clear of the building lines to give room for men to work between the basement underpinning and the walls of the excavations. Some jurisdictions have stipulated minimum clearance for such working areas. Get a copy of the local building code from your local authority.

Step 11: When the area has been excavated, the building lines may be established in the excavation by dropping a plumb bob from each corner intersection of the building lines above. See Fig. 9.12, and Fig. 9.5.

9.5 STORY RODS FOR CARPENTERS

Story rods are derived from the idea of laying off on a wooden rod (lath) the heights of critical horizontal members of a wall between successive floors. They are used by carpenters to lay off the heights for concrete bucks for basement windows in the cribbing

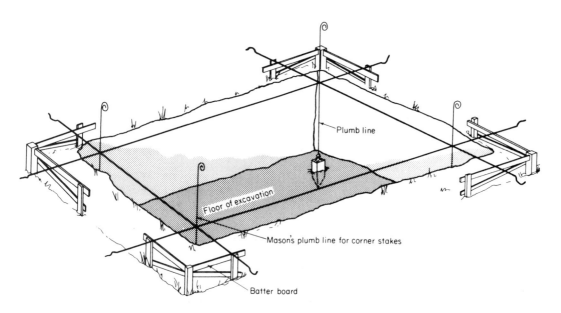

Fig. 9.12.

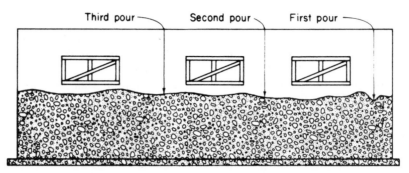

Fig. 9.13. Concrete wall with wood bucks; wet concrete must flow under each window and fill up to the underside.

forms. They are also used for establishing the levels for mud sills, and header (rim) joists. When constructing the cribbing walls, the carpenter stands the story rod on top of the concrete footings and transfers to the cribbing walls the heights that different members will be placed. In this manner, all the windows may be set at the same height. It is a handy and accurate method and saves time in measuring for each window separately. See Fig. 9.14, page 79.

9.6 STORY ROD FOR MASONS

Masons lay off on the rod the height of all courses of concrete block or bricks and their mortar joints. In this way, two masons working on the same wall may lay-up the corners and both check for uniformity of height by checking with the same story rod. Thus, they may keep all courses parallel to each other and to the top of the concrete footings. See Fig. 9.15, page 79.

9.7 CARPENTER'S DOOR STRAP

A story rod is used by carpenters when hanging a number of similar type doors (for the same side of opening). They use a thin, straight, and dry lath which they call a door strap. It is usually about ⅜" (9.25m) and is the exact length of the door. They accurately mark off on the rod the position for the hinges and the door lock. The rod is then used to transcribe the markings onto the door frames and onto the edges of the doors. Any door may then be hung in any frame and the prettiest grained doors may be placed where they will be most seen. Also, the carpenter may use one room as a temporary work place and confine his wood chippings to one area. See Fig. 9.16, page 79.

9.8 KITCHEN CABINET ROD

Kitchen cabinet makers use a rod on which they mark all heights of the cabinets. See Fig. 9.17, page 80. A similar measuring device is used for horizontal measurements of cabinets.

A rod is also used to set the height of all valances for drapes. This is important because manufacturers market drapes in standard lengths.

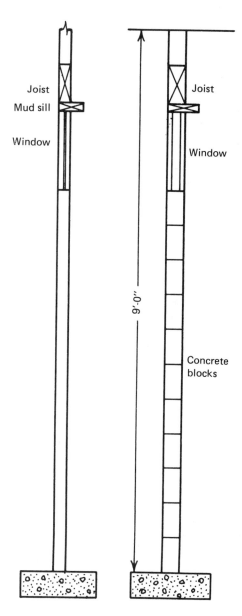

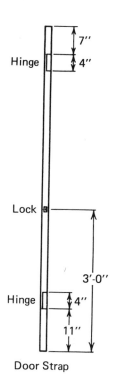

Fig. 9.16.

Story Rod

Fig. 9.14.

Story Rod

Fig. 9.15.

9.9 EXCAVATION STORY ROD EXERCISE

Complete Figure 9.18 by

1. Writing either imperial or metric measurements in the blanks, and then

2. Drawing and dimensioning an outside door buck and basement window buck in the concrete wall(s).

Assuming an existing grade as EL 99'-0" or 99.0 m, determine the depth of excavation to provide adequate drainage from the outside door sill to the edge of the building lot 30'-0" (or 10.0 m) away.

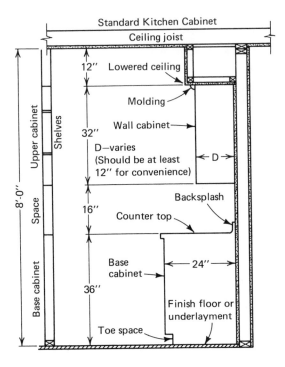

Fig. 9.17.

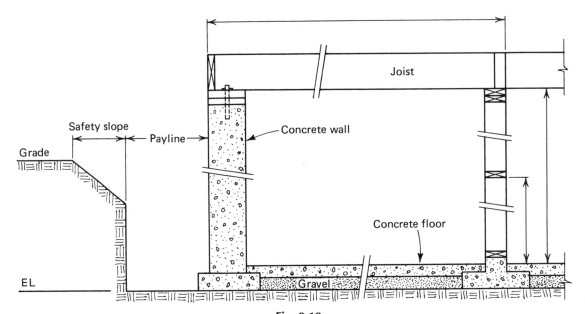

Fig. 9.18.

Record on one side of a story rod only those measurements required to determine the elevation of the underside of the footing, the depth of excavation.

Note: A straight story rod of square or rectangular section can be used to record four sets of data by marking one set on each face of the rod.

Using gathered data, draw a section of the building and lot to show how the building will be set in relation to the finished lawn and local street storm sewer drainage.

Review

1. Sketch a set of batter boards in place. Explain how and why they are used.

2. Explain, using a sketch, how to check for squareness of a building corner by using a tape measure.

Foundations, Chimneys, and Slab on Grade

In this chapter we shall discuss footings for foundation walls, pier pads, and chimney foundations; the number and weight of bricks in chimney stacks; and why step footings or piles and ground beams are used. The chapter concludes with a discussion of slab on grade panel heating.

10.1 UNDERPINNING

The stability of a building depends upon the adequacy of its foundation. In all cases excavations shall extend down to undisturbed soil unless the foundation is specifically designed for the existing soil conditions. *Study the local building code!*

Special care must be taken in designing pier pads for columns; foundations for chimneys; and foundations for pilasters (a pilaster is a column or pier forming an integral part of a wall, and partly projecting from the face of it). In each of the foregoing cases, the superimposed weight of that part of the structure to be imposed on the earth is proportionately greater than that of the main foundation footings.

10.2 PIER PADS

Pier pads at the foot of columns must be designed for surface area, depth, and types of concrete reinforcing each way (EW) in the footing. Unless an engineering design shows otherwise, footings (pier pads) supporting piers or columns should be at least four square feet in one story buildings, six square feet in two story buildings, and eight square feet in three story buildings.

Consider the weight of the superimposed weight on the pier pad, as in Fig. 10.1, where 5,000 lbs. are imposed centrally on a beam between each wall and the column. How much weight is imposed on the pier pad? Now consider the weight imposed on each pier pad, as in the plan at Fig. 10.2, where 5,000 lbs. are imposed, centrally, between the walls and the columns. How much weight is imposed on the pier pads shown on the plan?

10.3 CHIMNEY FOUNDATIONS

Foundations for chimneys must be designed for surface area; depth; types of concrete; and reinforcing EW in the footing so that it will support the weight of the masonry in the chimney without any settlement causing fractures in the stack itself, or in the adjoining walls, or in the flashing at roof level causing leaks. Remember also that a fractured chimney is a serious fire hazard. For a better appreciation of the methods of constructing, estimating quantities of materials, and estimating the weights of chimneys, study the following two articles.

10.4 ESTIMATING THE NUMBER OF BRICKS IN CHIMNEYS

The usual method for finding the number of bricks required in a chimney is to find the

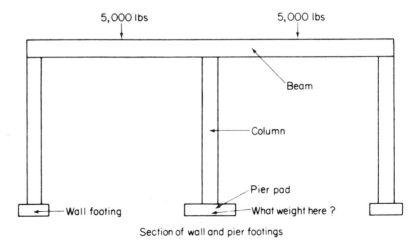

Section of wall and pier footings

Fig. 10.1

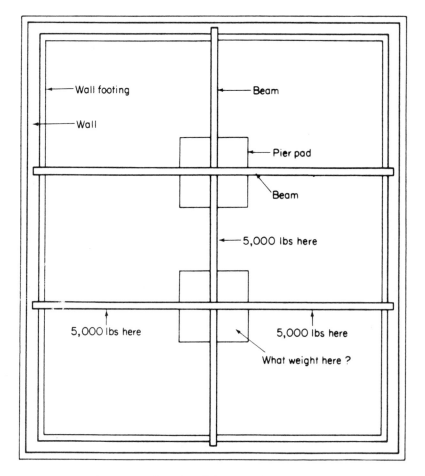

Fig. 10.2 Plan of wall footings, beams, and pier pads.

number of bricks per ft. in the height of the chimney and to multiply by the total height taken in ft.

In order to find the number of bricks required per ft. in height, we must first know how many bricks are required for *one course* in height of the chimney, and then how many courses there are in 1 ft. in height.

In Fig. 10.3 is shown various sizes of chimneys and flues and the way the bricks are bonded in each case. For each different size of flue and chimney, two layers of courses of brick are shown. This is done to show how the courses will bond. In some cases, one course will require more bricks than the other, as, for example, chimney (f). This will require 12 bricks for one course and 13 bricks for the other course. This makes an average of 12½ bricks per course.

From Fig. 10.4 we can see how many

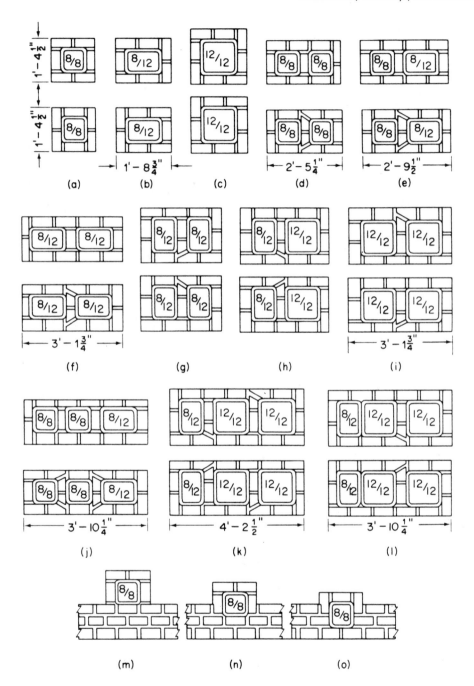

Fig. 10.3 Different sizes of chimneys and flues with their brick bonds.

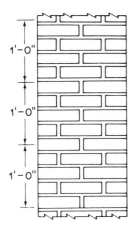

Fig. 10.4 Showing number of courses in one foot of height.

courses make up 1 ft. in height. We may also figure out how many courses make up 1 ft. in height. The standard brick is 2¼″ thick and the average joint is ½″ thick. This makes 2¾″ in height for every course. In 1 ft. or 12″ in height, there are 12 ÷ 2.75 = 4.36 courses.

Chimney (a) in Fig. 10.3 is shown to have 6 bricks to each course, which would require 6 × 4.36 = 26.16, say, 27 bricks per ft. in height. Chimney (f), which we found above to have an average of 12½ bricks per course, would require 12½ × 4.36 = 54.5 bricks per ft., say 55 bricks per ft. in height. To find the total bricks in a chimney, we must multiply the bricks per ft. in height by the total height. Thus a chimney of the type (a) requiring 27 bricks per ft. in height, if built 30 ft. high, would require 30 × 27 = 810 bricks.

Chimneys of types (m), (n), and (o), which are built as part of a wall, do not require as many extra bricks. Type (m) requires 4 extra bricks of each course. Type (n) requires only 2 extra bricks, that is, 2

more bricks for each course than would be required if the wall were built straight without the chimney.

How to Estimate Fireplaces

Fireplaces for chimneys of irregular shape that cannot be figured by lin. ft. in height are often figured by the cu.-ft. method. By this method the total cu. ft. of brickwork required is figured and the openings for the flues or ash pits are deducted.

10.5 AVERAGE WEIGHT OF SOLID BRICK WALLS

Brick assumed to weight 4½ lbs. each—½″ mortar joints

Area in Sq. Ft.	4-Inch Wall	8-Inch Wall	12-Inch Wall
1	36.782lb.	78.808 lb.	115.414 lb.
10	368	788	1,154
20	736	1,576	2,308
30	1,103	2,364	3,462
40	1,471	3,152	4,617

Estimating Firebrick

For estimating on fire-brickwork, use the following figures: From 400 to 600 pounds of high temperature cement or fire clay are enough to lay one thousand nine-inch straight brick.

> 1 square foot 4½-inch wall requires 6 nine-inch straight brick.

1 square foot 9-inch wall requires 12 brick.

1 square foot 13½-inch wall requires 18 brick.

1 cubic foot of fire-brickwork requires 17 brick.

1 cubic foot of fire-brickwork weighs 125 to 140 pounds.

1000 brick (closely stacked) occupy 56 cubic feet.

1000 brick (loosely stacked) occupy 72 cubic feet.

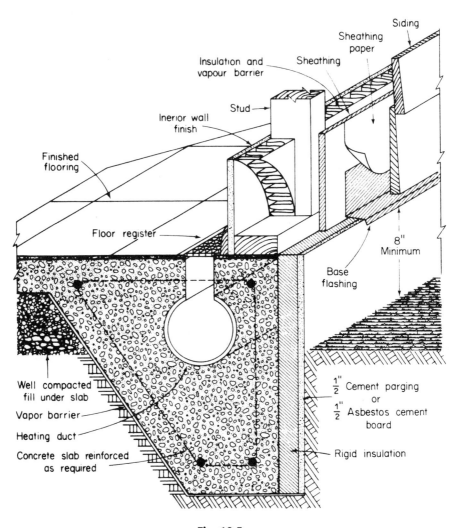

Fig. 10.5

10.6 WALL FOOTINGS

It is important to study closely with this section the footings and typical walls as shown in Chapter 12.

In some areas where the soil (ground) is firm enough, it may be permitted to dig trenches for wall footings and directly fill them with concrete without any formwork as in Fig. 10.5. When this method is used, it is recommended that stakes be driven, centrally, every 10'-0" apart in the footings, and leveled throughout. A screed may then be activated, from stake to stake, to level the whole surface area of wet concrete.

A better and cleaner job may be done by placing two-inch planks of suitable depth to edge the footings. These members are secured in place and kept level with stout stakes nailed every six feet apart; braced across the top, and supported at the sides, as shown in Figs. 10.6 and 10.7.

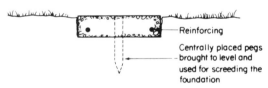

Reinforcing

Centrally placed pegs brought to level and used for screeding the foundation

Footing trench in firm ground with no edge support
no scale

Fig. 10.6

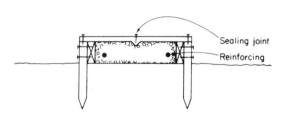

Sealing joint

Reinforcing

Fig. 10.7

10.7 REINFORCING-STEEL CONTRACTOR'S SPECIFICATIONS

The following clauses are typical extracts from the specifications for the reinforcing-steel contractor:

1. Reinforcing steel shall be stored on racks or skids to protect it from dirt and to keep its fabricated form.

2. All reinforcing steel shall be placed by experienced steel men, and shall be wired in position, and shall be approved by the architect or his representative before concrete is placed.

3. Reinforcing bars shall be of medium-grade deformed steel suitable for working stress of 20,000 psi and shall conform to meet ASTM and CESA standards. *Note that* ASTM *is American Society for Testing Materials and* CESA *is Canadian Engineering Standards Association.*

4. Reinforcing steel shall be bent cold and shaped as shown or required, accurately spaced and located in forms, and wired and secured against displacement before concrete is placed.

5. Place reinforcing so that the distance from the face of steel to the nearest face of the concrete is not less than 1 diameter nor in any case less than the following:

Footings	3"
Columns	1½"
Beams	1½"
Walls	2"
Slabs	¾"

6. Surface of bars shall be absolutely clean and free from mill scale, loose rust, oil, paint, and so on. Wire for tying shall be 18 U.S.S.G. annealed. (*Note:* U.S.S.G. *is United States Standard Gage.*)

7. Bend horizontal wall steel around corners and continue 40 diameters of the
bar. Support reinforcing on steel chairs
and space with bar spacers. Support
footing steel on brick or stone.

8. Necessary splices not shown on the
drawings shall be made by lapping and
wiring adjacent bars. Splices and adjacent bars shall be lapped at least 24 bar
diameters.

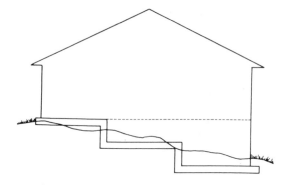

Fig. 10.8   Step footings.

10.8 COMBINED SLAB AND FOUNDATION

The following material has been excerpted
from a book titled "Canadian Wood-frame
Construction." It is recommended reading
for house builders and may be obtained from
the Canada Mortgage and Housing Corporation, Ottawa, Canada.

> **Combined Slab and Foundation.** The
> combined slab and foundation, some-
> times referred to as the thickened-edge
> floating slab, consists of a shallow pe-
> rimeter reinforced footing or beam
> placed integrally with the slab. The bot-
> tom of the footing should be at least 1
> foot below the natural gradeline and be
> supported on solid, unfilled, and well-
> drained ground. The slab is usually de-
> signed to support interior bearing parti-
> tions and a masonry chimney or fire-
> place. Anchor bolts are provided for
> securing the sill plates to the slab.

10.9 STEP FOOTINGS

To prevent the slippage of buildings erected
on sloping ground, it is mandatory that step
footings be provided, as shown in Fig. 10.8.

In solid rock, such horizontal step footings
may be cut where convenient with indeter-
minate heights of risers between adjoining
horizontal members. In other types of soils,
the rise of any step shall not exceed the
length of either of its adjoining horizontal
steps. This is an important phase of construction, and it is important to know your local
building code.

10.10 PILES AND GROUND BEAMS

In all cases foundations shall extend to solid
ground below frost line. In some cases, a
builder may wish to develop land for housing
units on ground that has previously been
filled (such land is also known as "made"
ground). City authorities, usually, have a
history of such filled land, and profiles of it
may be seen at the city engineer's office. In
such cases it may be economical to have
(engineer designed) piles and ground beams
for underpinning. Expensive houses erected
in coastal areas affording spectacular views
may also use this system. See Fig. 10.9.

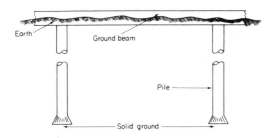

Fig. 10.9

10.11 SLAB ON GRADE FLOOR PANEL HEATING

This article is included at the suggestion of Mr. Harry A. Panton, P.E., who reviewed the outline for this book, and is presently living in a ranch style basementless house with floor panel heating which he recommended.

The following notes on the preparation of a concrete slab on grade are offered as a guide, *but builders must familiarize themselves with the local building code.*

1. The ground should gently slope away from the concrete slab on all sides, and the top of the slab should not be less than eight inches above the surrounding ground.

2. The perimeter excavation for wall footings should extend to solid ground below the frost line.

3. The footings should be reinforced with three No. 6 rods, with lappings of at least twenty-four bar diameters. It is recommended that footings and wall be monolithic (poured with concrete at one time).

4. To minimize heat loss all outside walls should be protected between the slab and the wall, and down to the footings with waterproof insulation such as: cellular-glass insulation board available in 2, 3, 4, and 5 inch thicknesses; glass fibers with plastic binder available in thicknesses of ¾", 1", and 1¼"; foamed plastic (polystyrene) and others in varying thicknesses; insulating concrete such as expanded mica aggregate in proportion of 1 part cement to 6 parts aggregate; also concrete made with lightweight aggregate of expanded slag.

5. Soil beneath the slab should be compacted, and provided with five inches of coarse clean granular material with not more than 15% by weight of material passing a #10 sieve. The fill should be compacted and brought to a level of not less than six inches from the top of the foundation wall.

6. Metal pipes passing under or through cinder or other corrosive material should be protected by a heavy coating of bitumen, or encased in concrete, or otherwise protected against corrosion. Install sewer, water, cable television, and power lines *before placing the concrete slab.*

7. A vapor barrier should separate the inert fill from the *initial* three inches of concrete slab, and this slab should be reinforced with wire fabric 6 × 6–6 × 6. A spaded finish is acceptable for the initial slab. The types of vapor barriers include: 55 lb. roll roofing or heavy asphalt laminated duplex barrier; heavy plastic film such as 6-mil polyethylene; three layers of roofing felt mopped with hot asphalt; heavy impregnated and vapor-resisting rigid sheet material with sealed joints; or other acceptable material to meet the local building code.

10.12 MESH: STEEL-WELDED REINFORCING

Mesh: Steel-Welded Reinforcing is used largely in concrete floors, driveways, and roads. It is also used in other areas of building construction as temperature reinforcing. Some of the main things that an estimator should know about this type of reinforcing are as follows:

1. It is fabricated in both square and rectangular mesh.

2. The longitudinal gage of the wire may be of a heavier gage than the transverse wire.

3. When there is any difference in the gages of the wire for any one type of mesh, the longitudinal wire is the heavier gage.

4. The style of the mesh may be described as 4″ × 4″–9 × 12 (or 44–912) which means that the area of each mesh is 4″ × 4″, and that the longitudinal gage of the wire is No. 9, and that the transverse wire is No. 12 (for a 4″ × 8″–9 × 12 or 48–912 welded steel mesh, each mesh is 4″ × 8″ and the gages of the wire are No. 9 and No. 12 respectively).

5. The smaller the number of the gage, the thicker the wire.

6. The slab should be laid out into its planned areas, and the plates secured to the initial concrete slab with concrete nails.

7. On the initial slab the heating man may now arrange the soft copper tube in a serpentine manner. See the following *Installation Details* for floor panels and Fig. 10.10.

8. After all the copper tubing is placed, it must be thoroughly pressure tested; then the final 1⅝″ concrete slab may be poured and brought to a level trowelled finish.

10.13 INSTALLATION FOR FLOOR PANEL HEATING

The following material has been excerpted from a booklet titled, *A Simplified Design Procedure For Residential Panel Heating*, prepared by the Research Department Staff and Consultants of *Revere Copper and Brass Incorporated*, 605 Third Avenue, New York, N.Y. 10016 and is reproduced here with the permission of the copyright holder.

Recommended tube spacing for floor panels is 9″ or 12″ on centers.

Coils should not be installed in cinder base concrete or on cinder fill. The tube can be fastened to reinforcing wire mesh or supported on blocking to establish the desired depth of bury.

Note that instead of the suggested location of the balancing cock and cut-off valve, they could be located near the heater, provided individual return lines from each panel are run to that point. Shown is one method of insulating a floor panel against heat loss through the foundation walls and into the ground.

These illustrations show a preferred method of insulating floor slabs in a Radiant Heating installation. Note that in this case the insulation extends under the entire panel as well as around the edge of the slab in contact with exterior foundation walls.

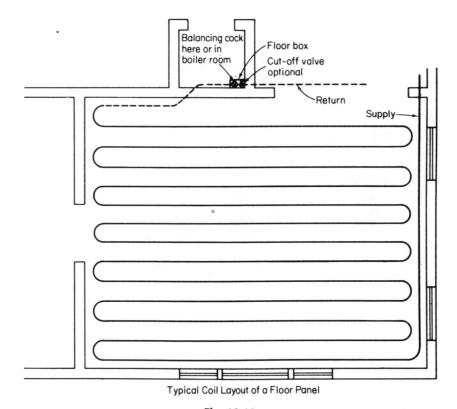

Typical Coil Layout of a Floor Panel

Fig. 10.10

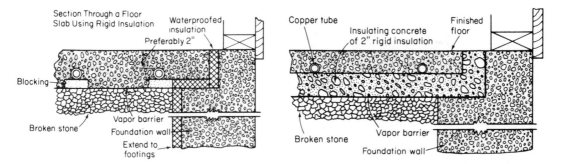

Fig. 10.11

Fig. 10.12 Section through a floor panel using insulating concrete.

Fig. 10.13

Venting, Controls, Testing, Starting, Balancing for Floor Panel Heating

Venting: The system must be properly vented so that positive circulation through all coils will be possible. Filling the system with water should be done slowly with all vents open so that the air in the system will be completely expelled. The vents should be closed as soon as water issues from them. Occasional checking of air vents and expansion tank is advisable.

Controls: In selecting the controls for a radiant heating system, the designer has a choice of several methods of control. The control of a radiant heating system is substantially the same as that of a conventional two-pipe forced circulation hot water system. Controls can be simple or relatively complex, depending in most cases on the requirements of the particular installation. Continuous circulation and modulation of the water temperature with changes in outdoor temperature conditions will produce more uniform indoor conditions. Excellent literature has been published by control manufacturers who are willing to assist designers in the proper application of their products.

Testing the System: The piping system and panel coils should be thoroughly pressure tested before any tube is embedded in the plaster ceiling or concrete floor, to make sure there are no leaks in any of the joints. This should be done before any connections are made to the boiler, circulator, or other devices so that excess pressure will not affect these parts.

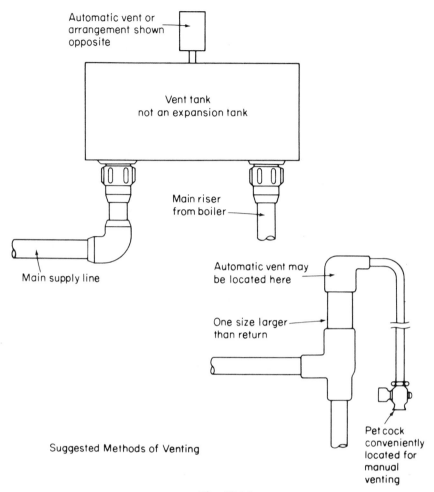

Automatic vent or arrangement shown opposite

Vent tank
not an expansion tank

Main riser from boiler

Main supply line

Automatic vent may be located here

One size larger than return

Pet cock conveniently located for manual venting

Suggested Methods of Venting

Fig. 10.14

It is suggested that the system first be tested with air at fifty pounds pressure or more. This permits any leaks that may occur to be repaired in a dry condition which facilitates the operation and eliminates the necessity of draining the system.

A second test with water at a pressure of 150 pounds per square inch can also be applied to the system for a period of 4–8 hours and all joints carefully checked for leaks.

Starting the System: The procedure in starting a radiant heating system for the first time, and in making subsequent adjustments, is similar in most respects to a two-pipe forced circulation hot water system.

Before starting the system, the plaster panels or concrete floor panels must be thoroughly dry. The drying period may extend over three or four weeks, but in no case should the radiant heating system be used to hasten the drying of the panels. It is recommended that when water is first circulated through the coils, its temperature does not exceed 90° for the first day or so, and then, increased gradually until design water temperature is reached.

All controls, circulators and other devices that are a part of the system should be installed and adjusted according to manufacturers' recommendations.

Balancing: In a radiant heating system, in an average age residence, little, if any, trouble should be experienced in balancing the flow of water through the various parts of the system. After the system has been in operation, however, it may be necessary to make some adjustments in balancing due to heat regain in the structure, exposure, or wind conditions. Balancing the system is best accomplished on a cold day.

At the start, all balancing cocks should be wide open. If the temperature conditions in any room seems to be higher than in others, the balancing cocks for those panels concerned should be adjusted so as to reduce the flow of hot water through them. Adjustments should be continued until temperature conditions in all rooms seem to be satisfactory.

Review

1. Use a sketch to explain the term *underpinning.*

2. Sketch a reinforced pier pad. Include two sectional views.

3. Sketch a regular shaped brick chimney on its footing. Prepare the estimate with respect to bricks required.

4. Sketch an irregular shaped brick chimney on its footing. Prepare the estimate with respect to bricks required.

5. Write a specification for footing steel reinforcing rods.

6. Sketch a step footing. Write an operations list for form building.

7. Explain by means of a sketch how and where welded steel reinforcing mesh is used.

11

Formwork and Concrete

In this chapter we shall discuss formwork and on-the-job quality-controlled concrete by volume mix, and how to determine the correct amount of cement, sand, gravel, and water that should be hand fed into any concrete mixer to produce a predetermined strength of concrete. It has been our experience that many technicians know a great deal about concrete, but they are often at a loss to determine the exact volumes of materials to be fed into a specific concrete mixer to produce a specified strength of concrete to conform with the local building code for residential construction. For this reason, several handwritten examples showing how to determine volume mixes are given.

There is ample literature about ready-mixed concrete which may be ordered to meet any specification. The contractor is urged to take an extension course on the design and control of quality concrete. The Portland Cement Association is constantly doing research and making authoritative publications available to engineers, contractors, and farmers in language suitable to occupation. Your personal library should be well-stocked with reference books.

11.1 CONCRETE FORMWORK: BASEMENT WALLS

There are many types of semipermanent patented forms used in concrete work. The following example is for a contractor making his own forms for reuse by his own men. The number of times that such forms may be used depends upon the organizing ability of the job superintendent. *Some men would only get five uses out of them while others would use them up to fifty times.*

Design of Forms

1. Forms should be substantial and sufficiently tight to prevent leakage of mortar. They should be properly braced and tied together so as to maintain their position and shape. If adequate foundations for shores cannot be secured, trussed supports shall be provided.

2. Snap ties should be used for internal ties so arranged that when the forms are removed no metal shall be within 1″ of any surface. Wire ties will be permitted only on light and unimportant work; they must not be used where discoloration would be objectionable.

3. Shores supporting successive lifts should be placed directly over those below, or so designed that the load will be transmitted directly to them.

4. Forms should be set to line and grade, and so constructed and fastened as to produce true lines. Special care should be taken to prevent bulging.

5. Forms should be lined with plywood for main-entrance surroundings.

Specifications

The specifications for a set of semipermanent ¾″ plywood forms frames with 2 × 4 dimension lumber are as follows:

1. 80 forms 4′-0″ × 8′-0″ S1S ¾″ plywood. (S1S means solid one side.)

2. 16 forms 2′-0″ × 8′-0″ S1S ¾″ plywood.

3. 8 forms 1′-0″ × 8′-0″ S1S ¾″ plywood.

4. Provide one top plate and one bottom plate for all forms, and space the studs 16″ OC for the 4′-0″ × 8′-0″ forms, all others to have stud spacings of 12″ OC. See Fig. 11.1.

5. Construction-grade dimension lumber shall be used.

6. Frames shall be secured with 3½″ common nails.

7. Plywood shall be secured to frames with 2½″ common nails.

8. Sheet-metal strapping shall be secured to all outside corners of forms.

11.2 DESIGN MIX BY WEIGHT

Modern concrete mixes are designed by weighing the component parts of water, cement, sand, gravel, and any other additives necessary to achieve the designed results. This is done so that a predetermined strength of concrete may be obtained. Sand and gravel are called aggregates; sand is fine aggregate (FA), and crushed rock is called coarse aggregate (CA). The final strength of concrete is known as the psi, indicating the

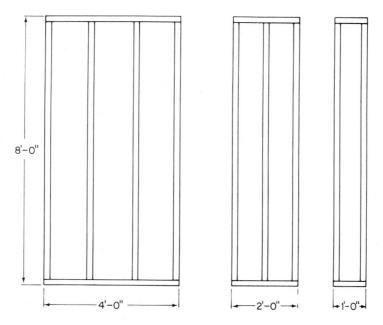

Fig. 11.1 Semipermanent forms for concrete.

number of pounds per sq. in. that a test cylinder of concrete 12″ long and 6″ in dia. will withstand (after a stated period of time in moist curing) under hydraulic pressure without fracturing.

Test specimens are taken while the concrete is being placed. The test specimens will be required by the local authority, the architect, and by the contractor for his own satisfaction.

11.3 WEIGHT OF CONCRETE

One cu. ft. of concrete weighs about 140 lbs. If the first floor of a building is 40′-0″ × 60′-0″ and is placed to a depth of 0′-6″ with concrete, the weight of supported concrete would be 168,000 lbs. or 84 tons. This does not include the weight of forms, nor of the

men, nor of the tools, nor of the loaded buggies during placing. The estimator must get the "feel" of a job when estimating, in the same way that the job superintendent must be aware of all the hazards inherent in the administration of the physical work to be performed.

No amount of careful estimating can offset the inefficient running of a job. The chief ingredient of estimating and job-running is the morale of all persons engaged. The estimator and the job superintendent should have comparable job knowledge.

11.4 READY-MIXED CONCRETE

Great progress has been made, especially during this century, in the design and mix of concrete. In all our cities, concrete manufacturers will deliver (ready-mixed) designed concrete to meet specified requirements. There is a maximum free time allowed for unloading ready-mixed concrete from the delivery vehicle. After the allowed free time has elapsed, a charge is made for each fraction of an hour delay. For small jobs and for delivery of ready-mixed concrete to ordinary householders, the merchants will deliver in units of 1 cu. yd. and to the next higher ⅓ cu. yd. They will also place and finish the concrete for an inclusive price. *Mass concrete is charged by the cu. yd., (or cubic meter) and finished concrete—as for concrete floors and sidewalks—is charged by the sq. ft. (square meter) placed and finished.*

11.5 STORAGE OF CEMENT FOR ON-THE-JOB MIXING

Since good cement is so dry and finely ground, it follows that it is very susceptible to dampness. If it goes lumpy while in storage and will not revert to its powdered form when rolled in the sack, it should be discarded. The addition of moisture sets up a chemical reaction, and once this reaction has started, the cement will not revert to its powdered form, and so should be discarded entirely. On many jobs, the inspector will insist that lumpy cement be hauled away from the building site.

Cement must be stored under very dry conditions. No amount of careful estimating can prevent a loss unless every precaution is taken to keep the cement (and indeed all building materials) secure against injurious hazards.

When it is necessary to haul cement onto the job some time before it will be used, it should be enveloped in polyethyl-ene. First a wood platform should be provided about 0'-6" above the ground level. This may consist of a few pieces of 4 × 4 common lumber supporting any rough loose boarding such as subfloor material. Then the polyethylene sheet is placed over the platform, and the stack of cement is enveloped by the sheet. *Remember, if you are using tarpaulins or polyethylene sheets, the cost will have to be allowed for on your estimate.*

11.6 WATER-CEMENT RATIO

Mixed water and cement is known as cement paste. The whole concept of concrete making is based on the relationship of gallons of water to 1 sack of cement. The ratio of 5 gals. of water to 1 sack of cement is known as a 5-gal. paste. Similarly, the ratio of 6 or 7 gals. of water to 1 sack of cement is known as 6- or 7-gal. pastes, respectively. It would follow that the thicker (stronger) the paste, the stronger and more durable the concrete; and the thicker the paste, the more expensive the concrete. With this in mind, the estimator would expect to find concrete mixed with a very strong paste to be used in the most psi (pounds per sq. in.)-demanding places on a building. The concrete specifications always state the mix of concrete to be used in each section of the building. The estimator must examine the drawings and specifications very carefully to see where different psi mixes are required, since the cost of the concrete will vary with the different psi requirements.

When the cement paste is intimately mixed with the aggregates, every particle of sand and crushed rock must be completely coated with cement paste. Some architects specify the minimum allowable time for the mixing of each batch of concrete. This time must be given careful thought—especially since the number of men in the crew and the total time required to place the concrete will be governed by the mixture time allowed per batch. Assume a specification called for a 2-min. mix for 1-cu.-yd. delivery batch mixer as against another specification calling for a 1½-min. mix for the same machine. The saving in crew time is 25 percent with the latter time factor. This part of the specifications must be given very careful study before determining the labor cost of placing concrete.

11.7 SURFACE AREA OF AGGREGATE

It will be recalled that the determining factor in the making of concrete is the water-cement ratio (cement paste). The difference in quality between, say, a 4½-gal. and a 7-gal. paste is, simply, that in the latter case the yield of cement paste is 55 percent greater than in the former, and the latter is consequently a weaker paste and only suitable for restricted uses.

The finer the aggregate, the more surface area of aggregate to be covered.

Example

Step 1: A 12″ cube has a surface area of 12 × 12 × 6 sides = 864 sq. in.

Step 2: A 6″ cube has a surface area of 6 × 6 × 6 sides = 216 sq. in.

Step 3: The cu. capacity of the 12″ cube is equal to the sum total cu. capacity of eight 6″ cubes.

Step 4: The surface area of eight 6″ cubes is

6 × 6 × 6 sides, which is 216; this times 8 cubes is a sum total surface area of 1728 sq. in. which is double the surface area of a 12″ cube.

The estimator, when making a survey of an area for sand and gravel, should keep firmly in mind that the materials must be of a rounded nature. Unless materials are rounded, the mix will require more cement per batch to cover the increased surface area; or, worse yet, the specimen tests may not stand up to the psi specifications and the work may be condemned.

Coarse aggregates contain very little moisture compared with sand, and so their effect may be disregarded.

Conclusion

Any cube cut into 8 equal parts doubles the surface area of the original cube. This situation is equally evident with any sphere remolded into 8 equal-size spheres. This will approximately double the surface area of the original sphere.

The estimator must keep in mind the enormous increase in surface area of aggregate where the amount of fines (sand and very fine gravel) is out of all proportion to the requirements of evenly graduated material. The more evenly graduated the sizes of aggregate, the greater the economy of cement paste.

In recapitulation, the estimator should try to insure:

1. That rounded aggregates are used with not more than 15 percent slivers.

2. That aggregates with not too much fine grade are used.

In both cases, if the surface area of the

aggregates is increased, the result will be that either more cement is required for a given mix, or else the design of the mix may fall below the psi requirements of the specification. The permissive amount of slivers in aggregates is about 15 percent.

11.8 MANUFACTURED AGGREGATES: CRUSHED ROCK

Clean, well-graded, hard, and rounded manufactured crushed rock, ranging in size from ¼" and up to a maximum grading limit of 1½", is known as coarse aggregate (CA). In the crushing process, too many fine particles are produced and some of these have to be eliminated to produce a well-graded aggregate.

You will have noticed that with both fine and coarse aggregates, rounded material is recommended; this is because such shaped pieces of rock have the least surface area.

Example

Examine the three solids shown in Fig. 11.2. Each has the same cubic capacity, but the shape and surface area of each is different.

The cu. capacity of (a) is 64 cu. in., and the surface area is 96 sq. in.
The cu. capacity of (b) is 64 cu. in., but the surface area is 112 sq. in.
The cu. capacity of (c) is 64 cu. in., but the surface area is 168 cu. in.

In each instance, the cu. capacity is the same but the surface area is different.

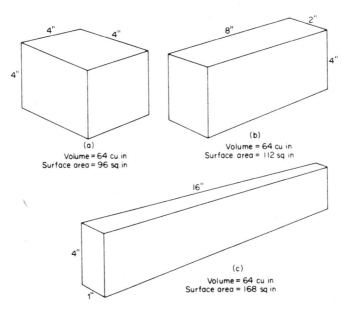

Fig. 11.2 Comparative surface area of three solids having the same cubic capacity.

Table 11.1 Estimating Materials: Quantities of Cement, Fine Aggregate, and Coarse Aggregate Required for 1 cu. yd. of Compact Mortar or Concrete

Mixtures			Quantities of Materials		
Cement	FA (Sand)	CA (Gravel or Stone)	Cement in sacks	FA, cu ft	CA, cu ft
1	2	—	12	24	—
1	3	—	9	27	—
1	1	1¾	10	10	17
1	1¾	2	8	14	16
1	2¼	3	6¼	14	19
1	2¾	4	5	14	20

Imagine the greatly increased surface area of aggregates containing many long slivers. This accounts for the specification calling for coarse aggregate from ¼" and up to 1½" that will grade to 1½" with a maximum of 15 percent slivers.

11.9 BANK OR PIT-RUN AGGREGATES

Bank or pit-dug aggregate is the natural virgin product of sand and gravel—discovered in most places by digging a pit.

The common characteristics of this class of aggregate are:

1. It usually contains far too high a ratio of fine-to-coarse aggregate (i.e., fine rock (sand), to rock over ¼ in. in size).

2. It often is dirty and unfit for use in concrete without washing.

3. It may contain organic or acidic matter.

11.10 ESTIMATING QUANTITIES OF DRY MATERIALS FOR ONE CUBIC YARD OF WET CONCRETE

The estimator must discipline himself to remember that on all estimates for volume-mix concrete he should add one-half as much more material in the dry state by volume than the capacity of the finished volume of concrete.

Note that the additions of cement and sand for two mortar-design mixes shown in the right-hand columns of Table 11.1 add up to 36 and 37 cu. ft., respectively. This is 1⅓ (plus) bulk volume of dry materials to wet placed mortar. Allow 1⁴/₉ dry for 1 wet.

Example

You are referred to the completed work-up sheets, after studying the following problem, which should be carefully followed step by step. See the problem on page 104.

11.11 CONCRETE FLOOR SPECIFICATION AND PROBLEM

A concrete floor 40'-0" × 40'-0" is to be placed with 0'-5" of finished concrete. The mix is to be by volume. Using a 3-cu.-ft.-capacity concrete mixer, a 5-gal. paste, and a 1:2¼:3 mix, estimate the following.

Read the work-up sheets on pages 107, 108, 109 with this problem.

1. The area of the floor.

2. The quantity of placed concrete required for the floor.

3. The total volume of materials in the dry state required to place the floor (allow 1½ times the volume of dry materials to place the volume of concrete required).

4. The number of sacks of cement required to place the floor.

5. The number of cu. ft. of sand required to place the floor.

6. The number of cu. ft. of gravel required to place the floor.

7. The quantity of water required to place the floor.

8. The quantity of dry cement required per batch.

9. The quantity of sand required per batch.

10. The quantity of gravel required per batch.

11. The quantity of water required per batch.

12. The number of batches required to place the floor.

13. The time it would take to place the floor, allowing 2 mins. per batch and allowing at least 1 half-hour extra for starting and cleaning up afterwards.

14. The estimated cost to place the floor, using the local prices, for example:

Materials:		
Cement	per sack	take up
Sand	per cu. yd.	to the
Gravel	per cu. yd.	next
		higher
Note: **Add for inflation.**		cu. yd.

Labor:	
1 man	per hour
4 men	per hour

In addition to these costs, an allowance must be made for lumber, screeds, and framework, and possibly for constructing a wheelbarrow ramp. Make an allowance also for depreciation of plant, maintenance, and gas. If the project is on the outskirts of a town, you may have transportation costs to meet for the crew.

11.12 AMERICAN AND CANADIAN GALLON

Note: This problem has been worked out using the standard gallon of the United States, which is the old English wine gallon containing 231 cu. in. and weighing 8.377 lbs. The Canadian imperial gallon contains 277.418 cu. in. and weighs 10 lbs. For Canadian use, in Step 8 *express 12⅚ American gals. in pounds and ounces and use the same weight of water per batch.*

Problem

How much water, cement, sand, and gravel will be required per batch of concrete when using a 5-gal. paste and a 1:2¼:3 mix in a 16-S concrete mixer?

11.13 RUNWAYS AND RAMPS

Nearly all concrete jobs require runways, ramps, lumber for screeds, and so on. Every job has its own estimating problems which may require a survey to be made of the area.

The following points should be remembered:

1. Estimate for the lumber, nails, ties, and labor to construct runways and ramps.

2. Allow material for screeds; this lumber cannot be reused.

3. Allow for scaffolds.

4. Remember that formwork must be strong enough to withstand the concrete pressures so that it will not deflect under load.

5. Floors will have to support wet concrete, power buggies, men, and tools.

6. Estimate whether or not any of the lumber used (a), (b), or (c) may be reused. Most specifications clearly state that all lumber on the job may be used for one purpose only.

11.14 MACHINE MIXING TIME

The machine mixing time is reckoned from about 1 min. per batch for a small-batch mixer up to 2 mins. per batch for a large unit. Opinions vary, but architects may specify the minimum mixing time for each batch. Study this mixing time very carefully indeed, since the whole operation of placing concrete is entirely dependent upon the delivery

time per cu. yd. from the batch mixer. The maximum allowable time for placing concrete is usually about 45 mins. after mixing.

11.15 SIZES OF CONCRETE MIXERS

Some standard types of concrete mixers follow:

Type of Mixer	Cu. Ft. of Wet Concrete Capacity
3-S	3
6-S	6
11-S	11
16-S	16

Note: 3-S means side delivery, and so on.

11.16 DRY MATERIALS AND WATER PER BATCH

Problem

Assuming a concrete foundation is to be placed, using an 11-S mixer with a specified 7-gal. paste and a 1:3:5 mix, how much water, cement, sand, and gravel will be required per batch?

Example

Step 1: An 11-cu.-ft. side-delivery concrete mixer will require 1½ times its wet delivery capacity of dry materials to be fed into it per batch.

Step 2: 11 × 1½ = 16½ cu. ft. of dry

materials to produce 11 cu. ft. of wet concrete.

Step 3: The mix is 1:3:5 with a 7-gal. paste. The total units of dry materials per batch are 9, of which cement is one.

Step 4: 16½ ÷ 9 = 1⅚ *sacks of cement per batch.*

Step 5: It will require 3 times as much sand as cement: 1⅚ × 3 = 5½ *cu. ft. of dry sand per batch.*

Step 6: It will require 5 times as much gravel as cement: 1⅚ × 5 = 9⅙ *cu. ft. of gravel per batch.*

Step 7: Check the total cu. ft. of dry volumes required per batch: 1⅚ cement, 5½ sand, and 9⅙ gravel added together equal 16½ cu. ft. of dry materials (see Step 2).

Step 8: It requires 7 gals. of water per sack of cement: 7 × 1⅚ sacks of cement equals 12⅚ gals. per batch.

11.17 ESTIMATING QUANTITIES OF DRY MATERIALS FOR A CONCRETE FLOOR

The work-up sheets on pages 107–109 provide examples of how to estimate the quantities of dry materials needed for concrete floors.

11.18 WOOD BUCKS

A wood buck is a temporary wood frame which is used in concrete work to form an opening in a wall for a door frame, window

Fig. 11.3   Section of wood window buck.

frame, or small door such as a crawl space; the latter should not be less than 2'-0" × 2'-0". The bucks have bevelled cleats nailed to their sides which remain in the concrete and afford good nailing for the final frame. Nail the cleats from the inside walls of the bucks to the cleats, with double-headed nails. See Figs. 11.3 and 11.4.

When pouring concrete into walls that have bucks, it is important to keep pouring in one place until the concrete flows under the frame and emerges at the other end after completely filling the wall with concrete to the underside of the buck. If wet concrete is poured on both sides (at or about the same time), it will form an air-lock and create a void under the sill of the frame. Should this happen, bore a few holes through the formwork at a point under the sill, release the air, and work the concrete until it fills the void. Remember that all openings in concrete

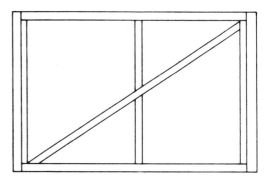

Fig. 11.4   Elevation of wood window buck with diagonal brace and center support against deflection under load of wet concrete.

WORK-UP SHEET

DATE_____

SHEET No. __1__ OF __3__

BUILDING	LOCATION	ARCHITECT	ESTIMATOR
Concrete Floor	40'-0"x42'-0"x0-5"deep	Olsen Jensen & Asso.	J. Smith
1. Area of floor	40'-0"X42'-0" 1680 sq ft 5 gal paste 1-2½-3		1680 sq ft
2. Concrete Volume: Place 0'-5" deep	1680x5 = 700 cu. ft.		700 cu. ft.
3. Total Dry Materials: Add ½ extra to fill the voids			
	700x1½ =	1050 cu. ft.	1050 cu. ft.
4. Cement:	5 gal paste and a 1-2½-3 mix		
	The total number of dry units required		
	is 1+2½+3 = 6¼		
	1050 ÷ 6¼ = 1050/25 x 4 =	168 cu.ft.	168 sacks cement.
5. Sand:	It requires 2½ times as much sand as cement		
	168x2½ = x42/x9 = 378 cu ft		378 cu ft. sand
6. Gravel:	It requires 3 times as much gravel as cement		
	168X3 =	504 cu. ft	504 cu ft gravel.
7. Water:	It requires 5 gals of water for each sack of cement		
	168 x 5 =	840 gals	840 gals water
Check the total volume of dry materials required:			
	168 cu ft (sacks of cement)		
	378 cu. ft sand		
	504 cu. ft gravel		
Total dry mix required 1050 See item No. 3 above			

WORK-UP SHEET

DATE _____

SHEET No. 2 OF 3

BUILDING	LOCATION	ARCHITECT	ESTIMATOR
Concrete Floor	40'-0" x 42'-0" x 0'-5" deep	Olsen Jensen Assoc	J. Smith

Quantities per batch.

(X) A 3 cu ft capacity mixer required 4½ cu. ft of dry materials per batch. The mix is 5 gal paste and 1-2¼-3

8 Cement: 4½ divided by the number of units in the batch = 6¼

$$4\tfrac{1}{2} \div 6\tfrac{1}{4} = \tfrac{9}{2} \times \tfrac{4}{25} = \tfrac{18}{25} \text{ cu ft} \qquad \tfrac{18}{25} \text{ cu ft cement}$$

9 Sand: It requires 2¼ times as much sand as cement $\tfrac{18}{25} \times 2\tfrac{1}{4} = \tfrac{18}{25} \times \tfrac{9}{4} = \tfrac{81}{50} = 1\tfrac{31}{50}$ cu ft $\qquad 1\tfrac{31}{50}$ cu ft sand

10. Gravel: It requires 3 times as much gravel as cement $\tfrac{18}{25} \times 3 = \tfrac{54}{25} = 2\tfrac{4}{25}$ cu ft $\qquad 2\tfrac{4}{25}$ cu ft aggregate

11. Water: It requires 5 gallons of water for one sack of cement, and it requires $\tfrac{18}{25}$ of 5 gals of water for each batch

$$\tfrac{18}{25} \times 5 = 3\tfrac{3}{5} \text{ gals of water per batch} \qquad 3\tfrac{3}{5} \text{ gals water}$$

Check the total dry materials required per batch:

$\tfrac{18}{25}$ cement plus $1\tfrac{31}{50}$ sand plus $2\tfrac{4}{25}$ gravel.

$$= \tfrac{(36+31+8)}{50} + 3 = 4\tfrac{1}{2} \text{ cu ft per batch}$$

(X) See Quantities per batch above

12 Number of batches required to place the floor: The number of batches required is equal to the total volume of the placed concrete floor divided by the wet capacity of the mixer

$700 \div 3 = 233\tfrac{1}{3}$ say 234 $\qquad$ 234 batches

WORK-UP SHEET

DATE _____

SHEET No. _3_ OF _3_

BUILDING	LOCATION	ARCHITECT	ESTIMATOR
Concrete Floor	40'-0"x42'-0"x5"deep	Olsen Jensen Assoc	J. Smith

13. Time required to place the floor:
234 batches @ 2 min per batch = 468 min

468 ÷ 60 = 7 hrs 48 min
Say 9 hrs including start and clean up   9 hours

14. The estimated cost to place the floor:
Cement: 168 sacks @ $1.50 per sack $252.00 cement

Sand: 378 cu ft   27)378 (14 cu yds
                       108

14 cu yds @ $3.40 per cu yd $47.60 $47.60 sand

Gravel: 504 cu ft 27)504 (18⅔ say 19 cu yd
                       27
                       234
                       216
                       18

19 cu yds of gravel @ $3.85 per cu yd $73.15 Gravel

Labor: 1 man @ $5.80 per hr = $5.80
4 men @ $4.40 per hr = 17.60
                        23.40

9 crew hrs @ $23.40 per hr $210.60 $210.60 Labor.

Summary: Cement   252.00
         Sand   47.60
         Gravel   73.15
                   372.75
         Labor   210.60
                  $583.35 $583.35 Cost

Note: This estimate does not cover
labor and materials for forms,
runways, equipment, traveling
time, overheads and profit.
For overheads and profit add 25%

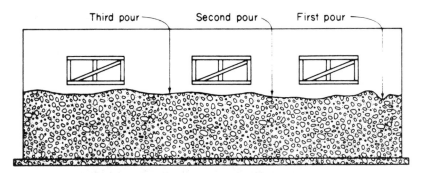

Fig. 11.5 Concrete wall with wood bucks; wet concrete must flow under each window and fill up to the underside.

walls weaken the structure unless reinforcing is introduced. Check! See Fig. 11.5.

Stripping and Reconditioning of Forms

As soon as the forms are taken from the concrete, they should be cleaned of all loose and clinging concrete, repaired, oiled, and level-stacked ready for shipping or carrying to the next job. Note carefully that no allowance is made in this exercise for shipping costs from job to job. This must be allowed for according to distances and conditions.

11.19 CURING

The object of curing is to keep the newly placed concrete from either drying out too fast or, even more important, to keep it from freezing. In the former case, it may have to be covered with polyethylene sheets; or it may be specified that it must be cured by the application of a very fine water spray on the surface for 7 to 28 days, according to the nature of the job. In the latter case, it may have to be protected with straw, burlap,

tarpaulins, and so on. In all cases it requires that both labor and materials be estimated.

Some of the agents for curing are:

1. Heat to repel freezing conditions.

2. Water-spraying for warm conditions.

3. Continuous water-saturated covering of sand.

4. Wet burlap.

5. Spraying the flat surfaces with water and covering with plywood panels.

6. Water-sprayed surfaces covered with cotton mats.

7. Water-sprayed surfaces covered with polyethylene sheets.

8. Sealing compounds.

Most specifications call for exposed surfaces of newly placed concrete to be kept moist for a minimum of 7 days; some require 14 days.

Water is applied on trowelled surfaces as soon as the concrete has set sufficiently so that the cement will not wash away. For untrowelled surfaces, water may be sprayed on as soon as the forms are removed.

The beginning contractor is strongly urged to take a course on design and control of concrete mixtures. Practical experience, on the job, is essential with respect to formwork, form hardware, and floor-joist-to-concrete wall construction.

Review

1. Make out an order for the materials required to make eighty 4'-0″ by 8'-0″ semi-permanent plywood forms using 2 by 4 material and ¾″ plywood; include the nails.

2. Define p.s.i. CA and FA as used in concrete work.

3. What is the approximate weight of one cubic foot of concrete?

4. State briefly the difference between ready-mixed and volume-mixed concrete.

5. Why is it disadvantageous to use too much fine aggregate in making quality concrete?

6. What is the difference in capacity between the standard American gallon and the Canadian imperial gallon?

7. How much water, cement, sand, and gravel would be required for each batch of a six cubic feet capacity mixer? The mix is to be 1:2¼:3 volume.

8. Why is concrete mixing time (per batch) so important to the estimator?

9. Sketch a window buck in place. From dimensions assigned, estimate the possible weight of normal concrete that the buck will carry.

12

Typical Wall Sections, and Materials Guide List

In this chapter we will examine a number of typical wall sections for residential construction as used in America and Canada.

12.1 WALL SECTIONS

Figure 12.1 illustrates a typical North American traditional house wall section. To refresh our memories, all parts of this drawing are named, and it is recommended that all components of any typical wall section be memorized.

12.2 PLATFORM OR WESTERN FRAMING

Figure 12.2 illustrates a view of a platform or what is known as western framing. The first floor framing originates with the sill plate, over which are placed the rangers (rim and header joists); then, follows the subfloor like a platform; the walls have a top plate and a cap plate. The operation is then re-

113

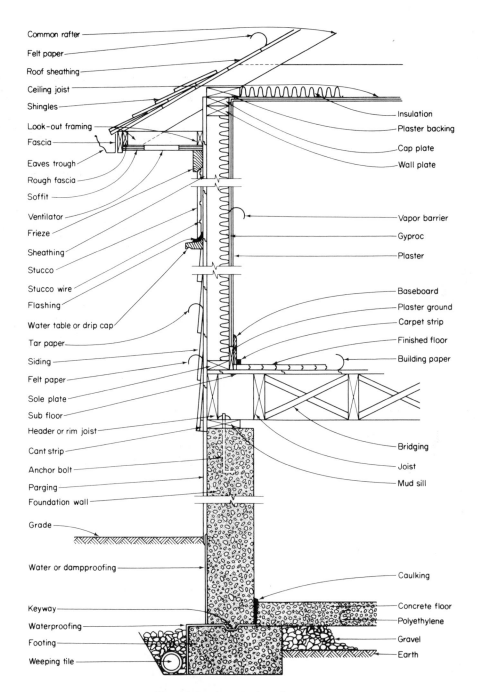

Common rafter
Felt paper
Roof sheathing
Ceiling joist
Shingles
Look-out framing
Fascia
Eaves trough
Rough fascia
Soffit
Ventilator
Frieze
Sheathing
Stucco
Stucco wire
Flashing
Water table or drip cap
Tar paper
Siding
Felt paper
Sole plate
Sub floor
Header or rim joist
Cant strip
Anchor bolt
Parging
Foundation wall
Grade
Water or dampproofing
Keyway
Waterproofing
Footing
Weeping tile

Insulation
Plaster backing
Cap plate
Wall plate
Vapor barrier
Gyproc
Plaster
Baseboard
Plaster ground
Carpet strip
Finished floor
Building paper
Bridging
Joist
Mud sill
Caulking
Concrete floor
Polyethylene
Gravel
Earth

Fig. 12.1 A typical wall section.

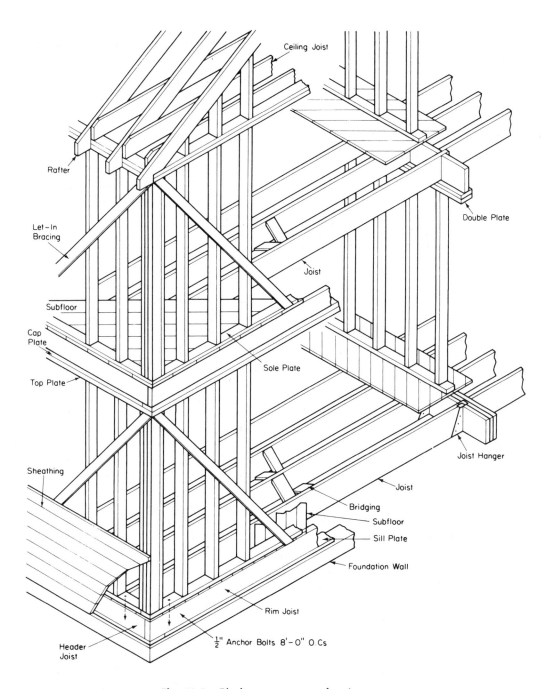

Fig. 12.2 Platform or western framing.

peated for the second floor. In some jurisdictions, not more than four stories may be built in this manner, but check locally for the bylaws. An advantage of this type of construction is the ease with which the 8'-0" walls may be raised from the floor (platform) into place. A great disadvantage lies in the fact that many longitudinal members are subject to shrinkage. Add all those members together to really appreciate the total thickness subject to shrinkage. Lengthways of the grain, the shrinkage is negligible, but where platform framing is used for a four-story apartment that must, by law, have a concrete fire wall, the difference in shrinkage between the lumber and the concrete could cause uneven floors, especially in the third and fourth floors.

12.3 BALLOON FRAMING

Figure 12.3 illustrates a view of balloon framing. The 18'-0" (plus or minus) wall studs originate on top of the sill plate. The first floor joists are spiked to the feet of the wall plates and the floor joists and extend to the wall plates and the cap plates at the ceiling level of the second floor. Note carefully that the only shrinkage possible with this construction for the two stories is in the sill plate, and in the wall plate and cap plate of the second floor at the ceiling height level. A disadvantage of this type of construction lies in the fabricating and raising of the walls.

Note how the ¾" × 6" diagonal bracings are let into the outside faces of the studs. To support the second floor joists, a ¾" × 6" ribbon is let into the inside face of the studs. The floor joists to the second floor rest upon the ribbon and are spiked to the studs. These joists also form the ceiling joists of the first floor.

12.4 POST AND BEAM FRAMING

The post and beam system is essentially a framework made up of decking, (see Fig. 12.4) beams and posts supported on a foundation. The floor and roof decks transfer loads to the beams which, in turn, carry them to posts and on down to the foundation. (p. 2 CWC Datafile WB-2)

12.5 POST AND BEAM FRAMING COMBINED WITH CONVENTIONAL FRAMING

Posts and beams are larger and spaced farther apart than studs, joists, and rafters of conventional framing. Horizontal spaces between beams are normally spanned by plank (see Fig. 12.5) decking, but conventional joist construction is sometimes used. Spaces between posts can be filled with wall panels, glass, or supplementary framing and sheathing.

In recent years, trends in architecture have separated the posts and beams from the conventional frame and made them visible as a prominent part of the construction system. This concept is used in many types of buildings. Residential, commercial, industrial, and recreational buildings are some examples where post and beam framing is used, either by itself or in combination with conventional framing. The architectural style of post and beam is both charming and impressive, but, like other systems, it should be used with discrimination.

Post and beam, though similar in style, should not be confused with heavy timber construction. In building codes, "heavy timber" is classed by itself, and calls for specific minimum sizes of beams, columns, and other components.

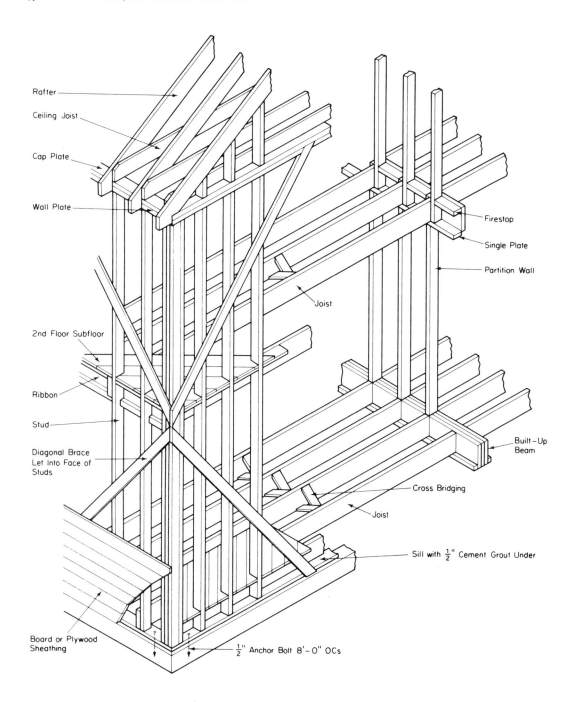

Fig. 12.3 Balloon framing.

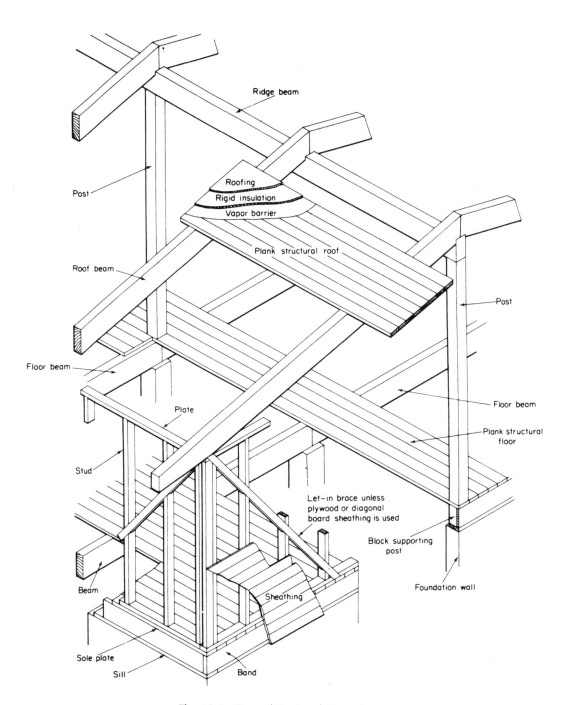

Fig. 12.4 Typical Post and Beam Framing.

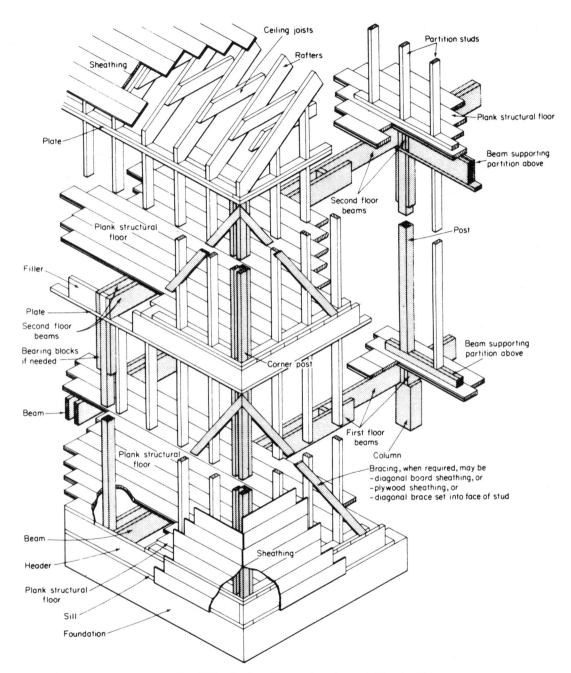

Fig. 12.5 Post and beam framing combined with conventional framing in two story house. (*Courtesy of Canadian Wood Council, Ottawa.*)

12.6 BRICK VENEER 4″

Figure 12.6 illustrates the component parts of a 4″ brick veneer finish to a wood-frame building.

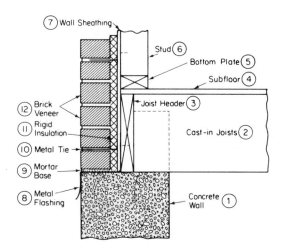

Fig. 12.6   Four-inch brick veneer.

An advantage of brick veneer construction is that the maintenance costs for brickwork are negligible. A disadvantage is that it requires the services of an additional sub-tradesman during construction. This type of building affords excellent insulation against either heat or cold penetrating or leaving the building according to the climatic conditions. It is excellent construction for all regions of North America except for the very far north.

12.7 THIN BRICK VENEER OR CERAMIC TILE

Figure 12.7 illustrates the component parts of a thin brick or ceramic tile veneer finish to a wood-frame building.

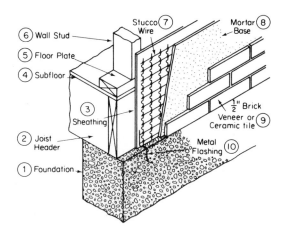

Fig. 12.7   Thin brick or ceramic veneer.

This is a somewhat similar treatment as for the 4″ brick, except that the thin brick or ceramic tile is grouted onto a mortar base which is supported by stucco wire. The tiles may also be of longer dimensions than those of the standard brick. Once installed, such a veneer is virtually maintenance free; whereas fiber boards and many other wood siding finishes require frequent maintenance.

12.8 BRICK VENEER WITH 1″ AIR SPACE

Figure 12.8 illustrates a brick veneer wall, tied to the sheathing of a wood-frame structure with corrugated metal ties spanning a 1″ space. With this type of construction the 1″ dead air space between the wood sheathing and the brick veneer acts as an insulator. Note carefully that the corrugated metal ties are placed at 4'0″ OCs both horizontally and vertically. To keep the 1″ air space free of mortar droppings, the mason uses a 1″ board suspended at each end with a cord; this he places between the sheathing and the inside of his brickwork. At every 24″

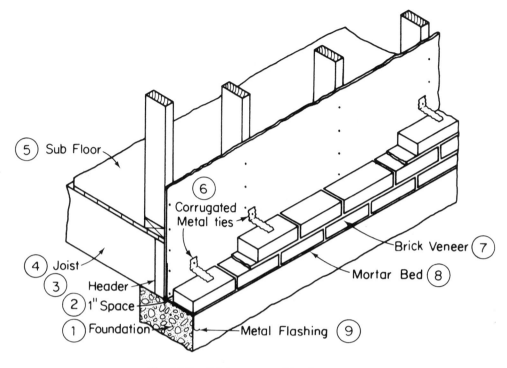

Fig. 12.8   Brick veneer with 1" air space.

in height and before, he places another row of corrugated metal strips. He then raises the board, cleans it, and replaces it again.

A weep hole should be left at 4'0" OCs on the first course of bricks. *A weep hole has no mortar in the vertical joints; this is done so that moisture may weep through these openings.*

12.9 TYPICAL WALL SECTION WITH BRICK VENEER

Figure 12.9 illustrates a typical wall section with brick veneer up to the eaves. Read the drawing together with the text and learn all the names of the parts as follows: *concrete foundation; metal flashing; floor joist header; sheathing; building paper; air space; face brick; metal tie; plancier; facia board; lookouts; rafter; ceiling joist; cap plate; wall plate; stud; interior finish; floor plate; subfloor; and floor joist.*

In addition there would be some form of insulation between the studs and a vapor barrier between the studs and the interior finish.

12.10 BRICK VENEERED FRAME

The exploded view of brick veneered construction in Fig. 12.10 is published through the courtesy of the Canada Mortgage and Housing Corporation, Ottawa. This is a clearly defined drawing with the added advantage of named parts.

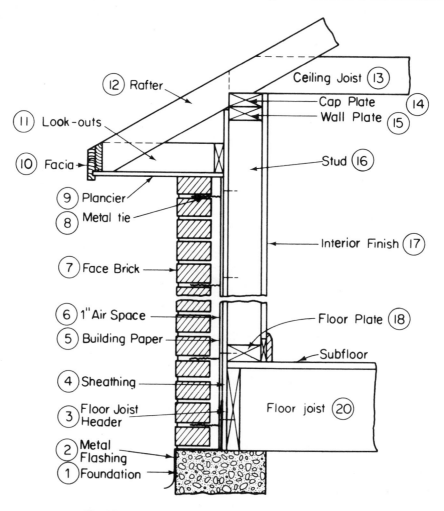

Fig. 12.9 Typical wall section with brick veneer.

12.11 A GUIDE LIST FOR RESIDENTIAL CONSTRUCTION

The guide list below (which is not exhaustive) covers, in order of building, the operations and materials required in residential construction. The list should be continually revised with new materials added and redundant matter excised. The list is offered as a check so that when originally estimating, and later when costing, nothing is overlooked. Costing means the comparing of actual job costs of every unit of completed work with its original estimate, and adjusting the pricing of such units for future estimating. It is only in this way that good pricings may be made for other competitive work. When contracting, anything forgotten on the original successful bid is a four-way loss, i.e., the cost of the material, the labor to install it,

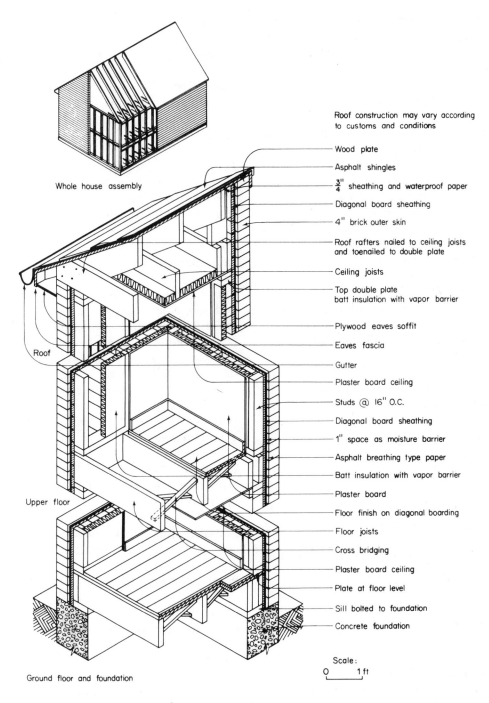

Whole house assembly

Roof construction may vary according
to customs and conditions

Wood plate

Asphalt shingles

$\frac{3}{4}''$ sheathing and waterproof paper

Diagonal board sheathing

4" brick outer skin

Roof rafters nailed to ceiling joists
and toenailed to double plate

Ceiling joists

Top double plate
batt insulation with vapor barrier

Plywood eaves soffit

Eaves fascia

Gutter

Plaster board ceiling

Studs @ 16" O.C.

Diagonal board sheathing

1" space as moisture barrier

Asphalt breathing type paper

Batt insulation with vapor barrier

Plaster board

Floor finish on diagonal boarding

Floor joists

Cross bridging

Plaster board ceiling

Plate at floor level

Sill bolted to foundation

Concrete foundation

Roof

Upper floor

Ground floor and foundation

Scale:
0   1 ft

Fig. 12.10   Brick veneered frame.

the time, and the profit. Refer to this guide in conjunction with the typical wall sections and other building methods throughout the book.

Preliminary Building Operations: Lot purchase; transfer of title; surveyor's certificate; architect/engineer's fee; locating survey pegs; location of building on site, bench mark; legal costs; real estate fees; city taxes; plans and specifications; building permits; billboard and sign permit; road closure permit; application to excavate street for installing sewer, water, gas, electric conduit, telephone, and paving; city water permit; cost of alternate water supply.

Temporary Amenities: Buildings on site; mobile office; toilet facilities; power pole and meter; light; heat; sewer application; application to erect a billboard for advertising.

Builder's Loan Charges: Bank; real estate; insurance company; credit union; other

Insurance: Bonds; public liability; workers' compensation; fire; vehicle; equipment; bonds; fringe benefits

Permanent Utilities: Heat; light; power; telephone; cable television; sewer; water

Advertising: Newspapers; trade papers; billboards; radio and TV; realtors

Supervision: Superintendence; job runner (junior estimator); foreman; transportation costs

Equipment: Machinery (own or hired); ladders; scaffold; wheelbarrows; hoses; picks; shovels; wrecking bars; sawhorses

Topographical: Clearing the site; demolitions; soil tests; establishing a benchmark; grading; lot layout; batter boards

Excavations: Remove and stockpile topsoil; cut; fill; and grade; mass excavations—basement; septic tank; soak-away area; swimming pool

Extras: *You must get signed agreements for all extra work done over and above that which is called for on the original drawings and specifications.* **This is most important.**

Trenches: Sewer; water; power; telephone; cable television; backfill; and landscaping

Concrete and Formwork: Estimate concrete and formwork together; concrete slab on grade floor heating; footings, house and garage; reinforcing; pier pads; walls (internal and external) wood or masonry units; floors; steps; sidewalks and driveways; septic tank; concrete test specimens; swimming pool

Driveways: Black-top; gravel stone flagging; concrete; other

Drain and Weeping Tile: Straight runs; elbows; tees; inspection chambers; fabric; application for connection to city drain

Waterproofing and Dampproofing: Special concrete; pargeting; emulsion

Progress Reports: Written; photographs

Underpinning for First Floor Joists: Wood posts; wood partitions; masonry walls; lally posts; masonry columns; tele-posts; steel columns; termite shield

Beams: "I" beam; wood, solid; wood, laminated; glu-lam; reinforced concrete

Rough Floor Assembly: Joists; joist hangers; headers (rangers); tail joists; bridging, wood or metal; subfloor; floor deadening material; building paper; reinforced concrete; chimney, stair and linen chute openings

Walls: Plates; studs, wood or metal; expanding metal; girths or girts; metal strapping for plumbing; concrete block and reinforcing; plumbing wall; cripples to doors and windows; headers for doors and windows, exterior and interior; fuel chute

Ceiling Joists: Blocking at wall plates; backing; bridging, wood or metal; metal hangers; hanging beams; ceiling access door

Roof Framing: Gable studs; barge boards; barge board mouldings; roof bracing members; purlins; collar ties and bracing; rafters, common—hip—jack—valley; trusses; vents; dormer window framing; hanging beam or strong-back; wall and roof flashing

Carport: Framing; posts; fire protection; footings; ceiling (see local fire regulations)

Garage: (See local fire regulations)

Roof Eaves: Look-out framing; soffit and soffit ventilators; fascia board—rough and finished; eaves troughs and downpipe

Roofing Materials: Sheathing; flashing; building paper; shingles, wood or wood shakes; concrete tile; asbestos; masonry; asphalt tile; asphalt roll roofing; underlay for roofing; corrugated metal; plastic; slate

Chimney: Concrete reinforced footing; bricks—common, decorative fireclay; mortar fireclay; flue lining; flat concrete arch; metal for arch; damper; clean-out; fuel chute; ash dump; parging—cement, lime and sand; flue lining; chimney pots; chimney cap; flashing—roof to chimney; insulation—chimney to wood through floors and roof (see local fire regulations); hearth; fireplace surrounds

Cladding Exterior: Sheathing, board, plywood, other; building paper; siding; stucco and stucco wire; brick, veneer, and wood framing; brick, solid; brick and cinder block; stone; decorative masonry units

Stairs: Wood, metal, concrete; stringers; undercarriage; treads; nosings; risers; wedges; newel posts; handrail and brackets; concrete forms and ties; stair finish—resilient material, carpet

Cladding Interior: Insulation—floor, walls and ceilings; vapor barriers—floors, walls and ceilings; grounds for doors and windows; lath and plaster; drywall and taping; decorative finish; expanding metal; corner beads

Window Units: Wood, metal and storm; basement, main floor, dormer; flywire screens; flashing to all openings; headers, wood, metal or concrete lintels

Outside Trim: Gable ends; eaves; frieze; fascia and soffit; drip cap flashing; drip cap; ventilators

Door Frames: Inside and outside; garage

Doors: Front, back, storm and screen; room; closet; linen cabinets; clothes and storage; ceiling access door

Inside Trim: Baseboard; window and door trim; window stool-apron-stop; carpet strip; closet rods and shelves; valance; decorative beams

Bathroom: Medicine cabinet; vanity; towel bars; soap and grab bar; tissue paper holder; shower-rail and curtain; wall and floor finish

Glass Block: Front entrance and patio; decorative light to stairs

Decorative Concrete Units: Bricks and metal ties; stone

Tiling: Living room; kitchen; bathroom; den; hall and other

Hardware: Form wire or ties; screws and fastening devices; door locks, hinges, checks and stops; towel rails; cabinet tracks, hinges, catches and pulls; coat hangers; handrail brackets; weather stripping; letter-drop chute; clothesline posts; glue and sandpaper; nails—common and finish, double-headed nails for formwork, roofing, galvanized, copper, aluminum or shingle, wall board

Attending on other Trades: Cutting away and making good after plumbers, electricians, heating engineers, etc. Some allowance must be made

Cabinets: Meters; storage; ironing boards; den; medicine; books; kitchen

Special Fixtures: Chandeliers; dishwasher; oven and range; refrigerator; deep freeze; garbage-disposal; hood and fan; planter boxes; mirrors; ceiling fans; ceiling decorative light fixtures; shower doors; vacuum cleaning outlets; cable television and telephone outlets; installation of vacuum cleaning service lines; door chimes; trash compactors

Subtrades: Excavator; concrete; plumber; chimney and fireplace; plasterer and drywall; electrician; heating engineer; hardwood floor layer and finisher; linoleum, tile, and carpet layer; sheet metal worker; air conditioning; telephone and cable television; painter and decorator; sidewalk and cement finishers; landscaping; swimming pool; seeding and planting; fencing, wood, metal, decorative, brick, stone or other; final clean up—windows, doors, floors, vacuum and polish; clean up of surrounds; blacktop, gravel, concrete or other

Overheads: Cancel all temporary utilities; proportion of general office expenses to each job; individual job overheads; superintendent, job runner and foreman salaries; sinking fund appropriations; builders loan fees; mortgage fees; federal taxes; remove all temporary buildings

Handover of Property: Professional fees; attorney; fixed fees for registrations; notarization fees, real estate; accountancy; accrued interest charges; maintenance clause; sign release and occupation certificate

Profit: You may be surprised to know how many bids are submitted where an allowance for profit has been forgotten. **Take care!**

Review

1. Sketch an exterior wall section of the building you are in.

2. State the advantages of using balloon framing instead of western framing.

3. State the advantages of using western framing instead of balloon framing.

4. Sketch the section of a typical brick-veneer wall. Dimension the sketch.

5. Use a sketch or sketches to describe the following roof members: plancier; look-out; wall plate; cap plate; rafter; and ceiling joist. Dimension the sections of the members.

6. Enquire with respect to current house mortgage rates. Using the information, complete the following table.

Loan	Rate percent per annum	Charges per $1000 per annum	Total Charges for Total Loan per annum
$ 9,000			
25,000			
60,000			
85,000			
100,000			

13

Basement Walls, Columns, and First Floor Assembly

In this chapter we shall discuss below ground insulation, vapor barriers, walls, and floor assemblies. The drawings shown in this chapter are not exhaustive, and continuing research by builders is necessary to keep abreast of building techniques. Two books containing rich sources of information for builders are as follows:

1. *Wood-Frame House Construction,* U.S. Department of Agriculture, Forest Service, Agriculture Handbook No. 73. This book is prepared by the Forest Products Laboratory, U.S. Department of Agriculture, Madison, Wisconsin. It is constantly being updated, and is for sale by the Superintendent of Documents, U.S. Government Printing Office, Washington, D.C. 20402.

2. *Canadian Wood-Frame House Construction,* obtainable from any Canadian Office of the Canada Mortgage and Housing Corporation. This book too is continually under revision. See the telephone directory for the address of the local office.

13.1 A GLOSSARY OF UNDERPINNING MEMBER TERMS

Anchor bolts: A steel bolt deformed at one end and embedded in concrete to secure a sole plate. Steel bolts are placed at stipulated OC's (on centers) to one another.

Basement: Has one half or more of its height above ground.

Beams: Structural members supported at two or more points, but spanning unsupported distances.

  I-beam: A steel beam with a cross section resembling the letter "I."

  wood, solid: A beam of solid wood.

  wood, built-up: A wood beam built up from smaller members spiked or glued together.

  wood, laminated: Selected wood members glued together under controlled conditions.

Brick veneer: A facing of bricks or ceramic tiles attached to a wood or masonry wall

Bridging: Wood or metal members used to stiffen wood floors.

Building paper: Used in many areas of building construction, it may form a dust trap between a hardwood floor and its subfloor.

Cant strip: A piece of wood used laterally at the base of siding to cant the first board outwards, in line with, or beyond, the rest of the siding.

Caulking: Sealing material between basement floor and wall forming a moisture barrier and termite protection.

Cavity wall: Two separate leaves of masonry units forming a wall with a space of 2" minimum between them and secured together with metal ties or bonding units. The leaves are called wythes or withes and may be of different-sized units.

Cellar: Has one half or more of its height below ground.

Column: A vertical member transmitting its load to its base.

Crawl space: Space between the lowest member of a floor and the ground beneath affording two or three feet of clearance.

Dampproofing: Material used to render a surface impervious to the passage of damp by an emulsion or with special mortar for masonry units near ground level.

Drain tile: Clay or concrete units 4" in diameter and 12" long, laid with open joints and covered with asphalt paper and placed outside footings to drain water away. See also noncorrode perforated piping in eight-foot lengths.

Fire cut: An angular cut to a wooden member that fits into masonry walls, enabling the member to fall free in case of fire without fracturing the wall. See Fig. 13.7.

Flashing: Metal or other material used to shed water or exclude termites in walls; also used in roofs.

Floor sheathing: Floor boarding, such as T & G (tongue and groove), or S.E. (Square-edged), or shiplap boards, or plywood.

Footings or Footers: The concrete base upon which a building stands.

Frost line: The depth of frost penetration below which footings and service lines should be placed.

Girths or Girts: Wood members tightly fitted between wood walls as stiffeners and as fire traps. See Fig. 13.11.

Grade: The finished level of earth around a building.

Joists: Horizontal members supporting floors. See Fig. 13.19.

  double: Two joints together (or close together) are mandatory under partitions.

  hangers: Metal devices forming stirrups into which the ends of joists are secured.

  headers: Short joists doubled and placed at right angles to common joists in floor openings for stairwells, chimneys or other floor openings.

  stringers or trimmers: Joists doubled on the long sides of openings as for stairwells.

  tail: Short joists between headers and wall or beam.

Keyway: Used in concrete footings to secure the walls against lateral pressures; when waterproofed, moisture penetration is controlled.

Mudsil: Originally it was lumber placed directly on the ground over which a building was erected. The term is used where a member is secured with anchor bolts to a masonry wall, over which a wooden sole plate is secured.

Parging or Pargetting: A coat of plaster or cement mortar applied to masonry walls and inside chimneys. Used with special mixtures to waterproof basement walls.

Pedestal: A concrete base-pad supporting a pier in house construction. The pier is secured to the pedestal with a metal dowel against lateral pressures.

Sill sealer: A waterproof material used between a mudsil and a sole plate. See Fig. 13.1.

Steel column: A vertical member transmitting its load to its base.

Steel girder: A main beam supporting minor beams or joists.

Stepped footings: Horizontal footings stepped or toothed into sloping ground.

Subfloor: The first floor applied to joists: *See floor sheathing.*

Vapor barrier: Material used to arrest the passage of vapor or moisture.

Water table: The depth at which ground is saturated with water.

Weep holes: Openings left in masonry construction to allow the leaching of water from an area; prevents accumulations of water from freezing and the fracturing of walls.

Information in the following article is provided through the courtesy of the Forest Products Laboratory, U.S. Department of Agriculture, Madison, Wisconsin.

13.2 INSULATION REQUIREMENTS FOR CONCRETE FLOOR SLABS ON GROUND

The use of perimeter insulation for slabs is necessary to prevent heat loss and cold floors during the heating season, except in warm climates. The proper locations for this insulation under several conditions are shown in Figs. 13.1, 13.2, and 13.3.

The thickness of the insulation will depend upon requirements of the climate and upon the materials used. Some insulations have more than twice the insulating

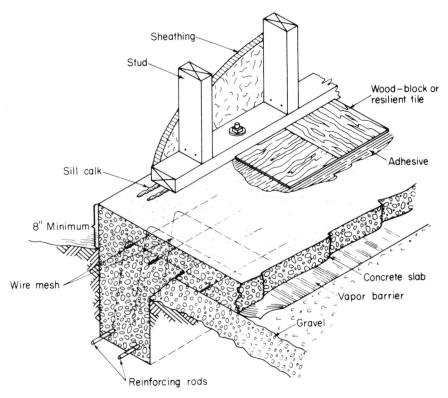

Fig. 13.1 Combined slab and foundation (thickened edge slab). *(Courtesy of the Forest Products Laboratory, U.S. Department of Agriculture.)*

values of others. The resistance (R) per inch of thickness, as well as the heating design temperature, should govern the amount required. Perhaps two good general rules to follow are:

1. For average winter low temperatures of 0°F. and higher (moderate climates), the total R should be about 2.0 and the depth of the insulation or the width under the slab not less than 1 foot.

2. For average winter low temperatures of −20°F. and lower (cold climates), the total R should be about 3.0 without floor

heating and the depth or width of insulation not less than 2 feet.

Table 13.1 shows these factors in more detail. The values shown are minimum, and any increase in insulation will result in lower heat losses.

Insulation Types

The properties desired in insulation for floor slabs are: 1. High resistance to heat transmission, 2. permanent durability when exposed to dampness and frost, and 3. high

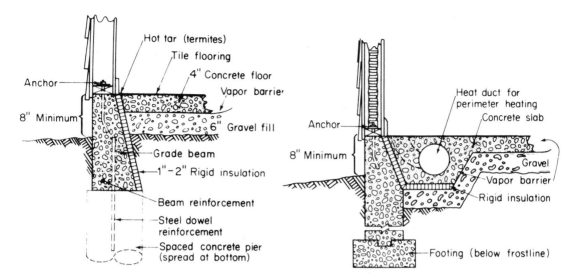

Fig. 13.2 Reinforced grade beam for concrete slab. Beam spans concrete piers located below frostline. *(Courtesy of the Forest Products Laboratory, U.S. Department of Agriculture.)*

Fig. 13.3 Full foundation wall for cold climates. Perimeter heat duct insulated to reduce heat loss. *(Courtesy of Forest Products Laboratory, U.S. Department of Agriculture.)*

resistance to crushing due to floor loads, weight of slab, or expansion forces. The slab should also be immune to fungus and insect attack, and should not absorb or retain moisture. Examples of materials considered to have these properties are:

Table 13.1   Resistance values used in determining minimum amount of edge insulation for concrete floor slabs on ground for various design temperatures

Low temperatures	Depth insulation extends below grade	Resistance (R) factor	
		No floor heating	Floor heating
°F.	Ft.		
−20	2	3.0	4.0
−20	1½	2.5	3.5
0	1	2.0	3.0
+10	1	2.0	3.0
+20	1	2.0	3.0

1. *Cellular-glass insulation board,* available in slabs 2, 3, 4, and 5 inches thick. *R* factor, or resistivity, 1.8 to 2.2 per inch of thickness. Crushing strength, approximately 150 pounds per square inch. Easily cut and worked. The surface may spall (chip or crumble away) if subjected to moisture and freezing. It should be dipped in roofing pitch or asphalt for protection. Insulation should be located above or inside the vapor barrier for protection from moisture. This type of insulation has been replaced to a large extent by the newer foamed plastics such as polystyrene and polyurethane.

2. *Glass fibers with plastic binder,* coated or uncoated, available in thicknesses of ¾, 1, 1½, and 2 inches. *R* factor, 3.3 to 3.9 per inch of thickness. Crushing strength, about 12 pounds per square inch. Water penetration into coated board is slow and inconsequential unless the board is exposed to a constant head of water, in which case this water may disintegrate the binder. Use a coated board or apply coal-tar pitch or asphalt to uncoated board. Coat all edges. Follow manufacturer's instructions for cutting. Placement of the insulation inside the vapor barrier will afford some protection.

3. *Foamed plastic* (polystyrene, polyurethane, and others) insulation in sheet form, usually available in thicknesses of ½, 1, 1½, and 2 inches. At normal temperatures the *R* factor varies from 3.7 for polystyrenes to over 6.0 for polyurethane for a 1-inch thickness. These materials generally have low water-vapor transmission rates. Some are low in crushing strength and perhaps are best used in a vertical position and not under the slab where crushing could occur.

4. *Insulating concrete.* Expanded mica aggregate, 1 part cement to 6 parts aggregate, thickness used as required. *R* factor, about 1.1 per inch of thickness. Crushing strength, adequate. It may take up moisture when subject to dampness, and consequently its use should be limited to locations where there will be no contact with moisture from any source.

5. *Concrete made with lightweight aggregate,* such as expanded slag, burned clay, or pumice, using 1 part cement to 4 parts aggregate; thickness used as required. *R* factor, about 0.40 per inch of thickness. Crushing strength, high. This lightweight aggregate may also be used for foundation walls in place of stone or gravel aggregate.

Under service conditions there are two sources of moisture that might affect insulating materials: 1) vapor from inside the house and 2) moisture from soil. Vapor barriers and coatings may retard but not entirely prevent the penetration of moisture into the insulation. Dampness may reduce the crushing strength of insulation, which in turn may permit the edge of the slab to settle. Compression of the insulation, moreover, reduces its efficiency. Insulating materials should perform satisfactorily in any position if they do not change dimensions and if they are kept dry.

Protection Against Termites

In areas where termites are a problem, certain precautions are necessary for concrete slab floors on the ground. Leave a countersink-type opening 1-inch wide and 1-inch deep around the plumbing pipes where they pass through the slab, and fill the opening with hot tar when pipe is in place. Where insulation is used between the slab and the foundation wall, the insulation should be kept 1 inch below the top of the slab and the space should also be filled with hot tar.

13.3 GROUND SLAB REINFORCING, GRADE BEAMS AND FOUNDATION WALLS

The factors for determining the type of underpinning for residential construction are local ground conditions, the climate, and the local building code. At Fig. 13.1 is shown a combined slab and foundation which is reinforced with wire rods and wire mesh. Note the caulking, the anchor bolt, and the vapor barrier. For a definition of wire mesh see Chapter 10.

The grade beam at Fig. 13.2 shows a method of providing relatively inexpensive underpinning in areas where it would be too costly to excavate completely. The piers go down to solid bearing, through the frost line, water table, filled ground, and so on. They can be used for building on the brink of steep hills, thereby using land to its utmost value for spectacular views.

The full foundation wall for cold climates shown at Fig. 13.3 gives an excellent example of a method of avoiding creeping cold perimeters by the introduction of heat into the perimeter duct.

At Fig. 13.4 is shown a floor-joists system supported on a ledge formed at the top of the concrete wall. Note the brick veneer facing wall with an air space to the framed wall. Such veneer walls are tied to the framing with metal ties.

13.4 JOIST ENDS EMBEDDED IN CONCRETE; BALLOON FRAMING SILL

In cold climates, many houses are built with a full eight feet of clearance for basements. This area affords excellent facilities for the installation of the heating system, laundry room, games room, cold storage room, workshop, and so on. During frigid cold spells such basements are a boon to parents with young children. Check with the local authority for any special building specifications for habitable basement rooms, and be aware that local taxes are greater for houses with such rooms than for those without.

In many areas it is the custom to embed (in wet concrete) the ends of treated joists at the top of the basement wall. It will be seen from Fig. 13.5 that the header and end joist (rim joists) will contain the wet concrete on the outside of the wall, but it will require formwork cut in between the joists to form the top of the concrete on the inside.

Note carefully, too, that *the concrete is never filled to the top of the joists*. If this were done, the joists would absorb water and then shrink, leaving the concrete above the surface of the joists. *This is important.* The space between the top of the concrete wall and the top of the joists is later filled with insulation. This also is important.

The balloon-frame sill construction shown at Fig. 13.6, should be closely studied. A great advantage of this method is in the reduction of settlement shrinkage (especially in construction of several floors). Note that the stud runs down to the sill plate, and as there is virtually no shrinkage in the wood lengthway of the grain, the shrinkage here is reduced to that of the sill plate.

In the floor assembly construction, the shrinkage would take place in the following members: sill plate; header joists; subfloor;

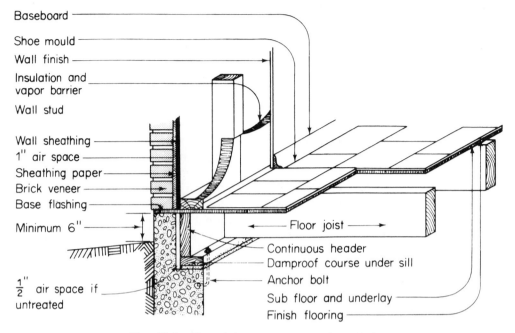

Baseboard
Shoe mould
Wall finish
Insulation and vapor barrier
Wall stud
Wall sheathing
1" air space
Sheathing paper
Brick veneer
Base flashing
Minimum 6"
$\frac{1}{2}$" air space if untreated

Floor joist
Continuous header
Damproof course under sill
Anchor bolt
Sub floor and underlay
Finish flooring

Fig. 13.4 Floor joists are supported on ledge formed in foundation wall. Joists are toe-nailed to header and sill plate. Masonry veneer supported on top of foundation wall. Wall framing supported on top of the subfloor. *(Courtesy of the Department of Forestry and Rural Development and the Canada Mortgage and Housing Corporation, Ottawa.)*

and the sole plate of the wall, in all, a possible shrinkage (in depth) of say 15", against a possible shrinkage of only 2" in the balloon framing method.

13.5 TYPES OF CENTRALLY LOCATED SUPPORTS FOR FLOOR ASSEMBLIES

There are many methods of supporting first floor joists above a basement or cellar floor.
Note: *An accepted definition of a basement is that it is more than half way out of the ground; a cellar is more than half way in the ground.*

The first floor joists may be supported on masonry walls and:

1. Brick or masonry columns supporting a wood or steel beam.

2. Monolithic columns supporting a steel beam.

3. Standard steel pipes supporting wood or steel beams.

4. Telescopic metal posts supporting wood or steel beams.

5. Lally posts, which are cylinders filled with concrete (named after their originator).

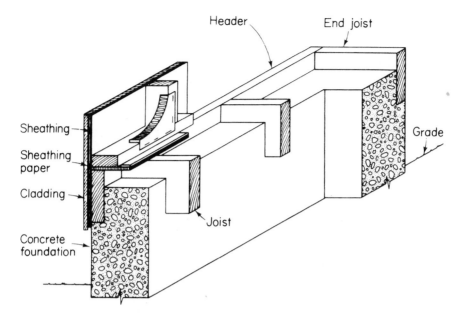

Fig. 13.5 Floor joists embedded in top of foundation wall. *(Courtesy of the Department of Forestry and Rural Development and the Canada Mortgage and Housing Corporation, Ottawa.)*

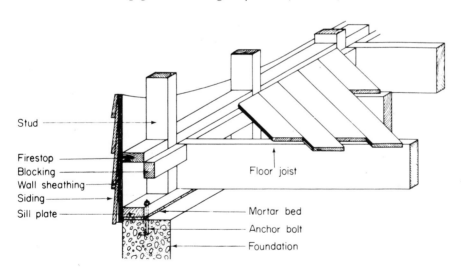

Fig. 13.6 Type of sill used in balloon-frame construction. *(Courtesy of the Department of Forestry and Rural Development and the Canada Mortgage and Housing Corporation, Ottawa.)*

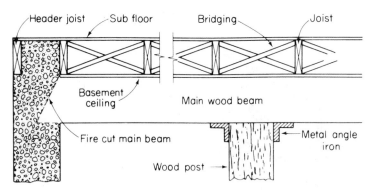

Fig. 13.7 Main wood beam supported on solid wood post.

6. A wood frame partition directly supporting wood joists without a beam.

7. Concrete block wall with a wall plate.

Main wood beams should be metal strapped or secured by angle irons to the solid wood posts supporting them. Wood posts may also be built up by spiking together 2 × 8's or 2 × 10's and then finishing them off with a decorative plywood veneer.

Note the fire cut in the main beam, (Fig. 13.7). Such cuts are made so that in case of fire the beam may fall free without fracturing the wall. This is especially true for wood beams at their intersections with masonry walls in upper floors. Instead of a fire cut, wood beams may be anchored in metal stirrups.

Note the arrangement of the floor joists with a header on the outside of the wall, and a joist placed immediately inside the concrete wall. This is done to provide nailing for ceiling on the underside of the joists in a basement.

Standard sized 4'-0" × 8'-0" plywood subfloors may be laid in the usual manner but with a filler starter strip of plywood from the header to the first floor joist, shown at the top of the fire cut.

The disadvantage of this floor assembly is that the beam projects below the underside of the joists, a feature avoided in Figures 13.8 through 13.10.

Ledgers spiked to the sides of wood beams as in Fig. 13.8 is a satisfactory method of constructing a floor assembly without a

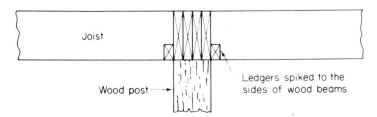

Fig. 13.8 Main wood beam with ledgers, supported on wood post.

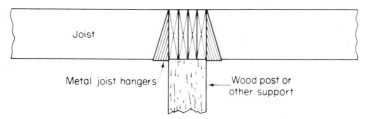

Fig. 13.9 Metal joist hangers attached to wood beam.

main beam. A further extension of this system is shown at Fig. 13.9 where the joists are secured to the built up beam with metal joist hangers (stirrups). This method prevents the ends of the joists from twisting while they are drying.

Another method of supporting wooden joists is shown in Fig. 13.10 where a metal column supports an "I"-beam; this method also gives clear headroom in the basement below, without a beam showing.

An acceptable method of supporting floor joists is shown in Fig. 13.11. With careful planning, a 2 × 6 wood framed wall may be erected to carry the joists (without a main beam) at any desirable place in the basement. Such a wall may be constructed with openings for doors, heating outlets, bathroom cabinets, electric outlets, and so on. Thought must be given to the kind of finish that will be applied to the wall; for decorative fiber boards, the spacing of the studs should be arranged to minimize waste.

Note the pier pad (upon which stands the wall) which is raised above the level of the floor to prevent damp penetration to the sole plate (bottom plate) of the wood framed wall.

Floors supported on telescopic legs as at Fig. 13.12 have the advantage of being adjustable, and may be raised or lowered according to the settlement of the building.

At Fig. 13.13 is shown a concrete block wall with a top wall plate and its anchor bolt. With careful planning, decorative colored concrete blocks (on one side or both) may be used in the construction of such walls to form a pleasing design in the basement rooms. Here also there is no obstruction by a beam of any kind.

13.6 BRIDGING FOR FLOOR JOISTS

Three types of cross bridging are shown in Fig. 13.14. Read your local building code for maximum allowable joist spans without

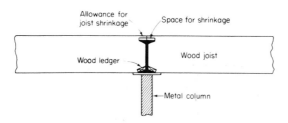

Fig. 13.10 Metal column supporting steel beam.

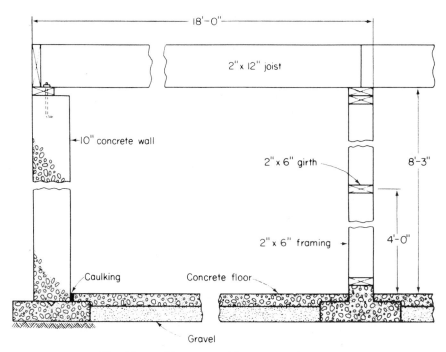

Fig. 13.11 Floor assembly supported on 2 × 6 framing.

bridging. See also Fig. 13.19 for in-place cross bridging.

Solid Bridging has the disadvantage of the possible shrinkage of the floor joists in thick-

ness. Assume that a row of solid bridging is placed between sixteen consecutive joists, the total thickness of joists subject to shrinkage is 17 × 2 = 34 inches nominal. This could total one inch or more of shrinkage and loosen the bridgings.

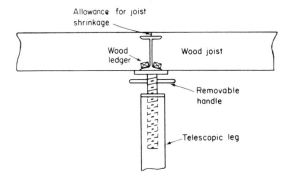

Fig. 13.12 Floor assembly supported on telescopic legs.

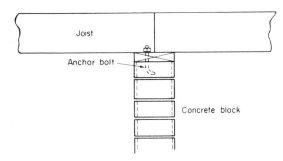

Fig. 13.13 Floor assembly supported on concrete block wall.

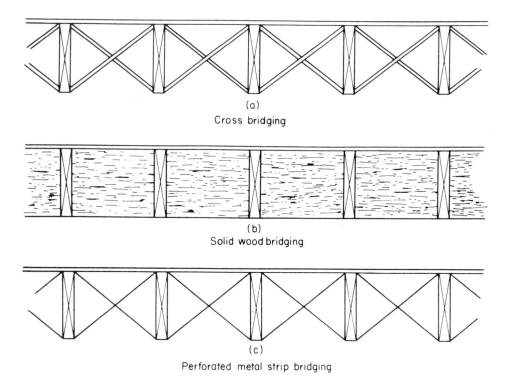

(a)
Cross bridging

(b)
Solid wood bridging

(c)
Perforated metal strip bridging

Fig. 13.14 Bridging for floor joists.

When Cross Bridging is Used, the bottoms may be left without nailing until the shrinkage has taken place; later the bridgings may be hammered and nailed into place.

When Metal Strip Bridging is Used, the shrinkage of the joists may cause the metal stripping to become progressively looser.

13.7 JOIST SUPPORTS OVER WOOD BEAMS

Three methods of supporting floor joists and securing their ends from twisting are shown in Figures 13.15, 13.16, and 13.17. It is important to remember that all joists should be placed to give the maximum rigidity to the floor and to allow for the minimum waste in subfloor material.

If tongue and groove plywood in sheets of four feet by eight feet sizes is used, it is imperative to know exactly what area these sheets will actually cover. If they are machine cut into exact sizes of four by eight pieces *and then tongued and grooved,* the actual floor coverage will be less and a narrower setting of the joists will be necessary. Manufacturers will produce plywood in sizes to order. *Check and be careful!*

13.8 IN-LINE JOIST SYSTEM AND FLOOR FRAMING

Figure 13.18 shows the joist arrangement for a simple span. The joists should be accurately set out on each wall plate, and nailed to the header. A mason's line should then be

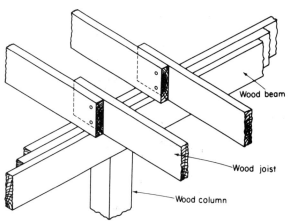

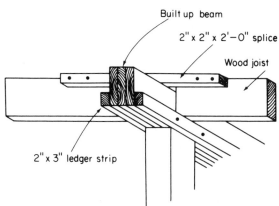

Fig. 13.15 Joists supported on top of wood beam and fastened to the beam by toe-nailing. Two 3¼ inch nails used for each joist. *(Courtesy of the Department of Forestry and Rural Development and the Canada Mortgage and Housing Corporation, Ottawa.)*

Fig. 13.16 Joists supported on ledger strip nailed to beam with two 3¼ inch nails per joist. Splice nailed to joist with two 3¼ inch nails at each end. *(Courtesy of the Department of Forestry and Rural Development and the Canada Mortgage and Housing Corporation, Ottawa.)*

stretched alongside each in-line joist and the joists nailed to the center beam true to line. *It cannot be emphasized enough that all floor and wall framing systems should be*

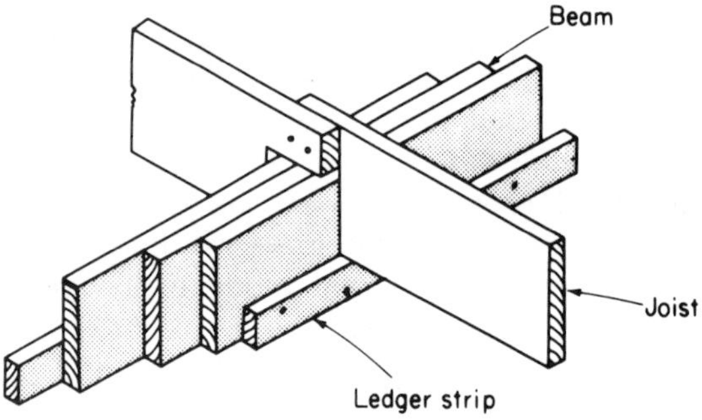

Fig. 13.17 Joists supported on ledger strip nailed to beam with two 3¼ inch nails per joist. Joists lapped and nailed together with two 3¼ inch nails. *(Courtesy of the Department of Forestry and Rural Development and the Canada Mortgage and Housing Corporation, Ottawa.)*

checked thoroughly for squareness before completing the nailing. Use the 30:40:50 system of triangulation.

Study the floor assembly as shown at Fig. 13.19, and note the two systems of subflooring, plywood or diagonally boarded. The diagonally placed floorboards stiffen the whole assembly and enable other coverings such as hardwood flooring to be nailed at any point on its surface. Floorboards placed diagonally also avoid the possibility of the edges of some longitudinally placed subfloor boards falling directly under the longitudinally placed hardwood flooring. *Remember that hardwood floors should be especially well nailed at doorways and near windows and wherever the line of traffic may be; this will prevent squeaky floors.*

Plywood subfloors are suitable for the direct application of an underfelt for wall-to-wall carpeting, or for the application of resilient or other floor coverings.

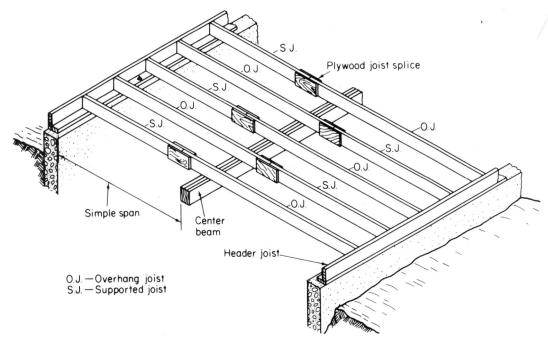

Fig. 13.18 "In-line" joist system. Alternate extension of joists over the center support with plywood gusset joint allows the use of a smaller joist size. *(Courtesy of the Forestry Products Laboratory, U.S. Department of Agriculture.)*

13.9 JOIST LAYOUT, 16" ON CENTERS

It is important to select floor joists for their respective positions in the floor assembly as follows:

1. Select the straightest joists for placing under door openings.

2. Select straight joists for making built-up (spiked together) wood beams.

3. Place the crown side (round side) of joists, headers, ceiling and roof members uppermost.

4. When looking for the crown side of lumber, be sure to hold the width horizontal. If it is held in the opposite direction, its own weight may cause it to appear to have the crown side down.

When making the layout for the floor joists, proceed as follows. See Fig. 13.20.

Step 1: Nail the long header to the short one.

Step 2: From the left hand end of the header, lay off 16" to the center line of No. 1 joist, as shown at Fig. 13.20.

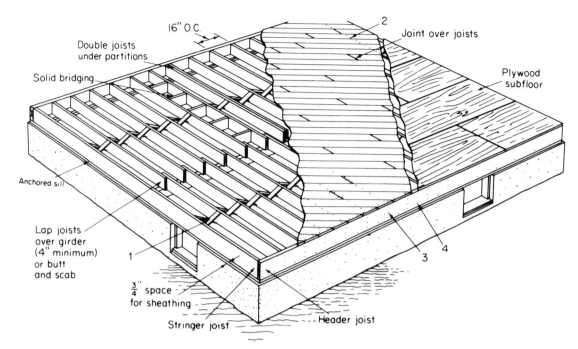

Fig. 13.19 Floor framing: (1) Nailing bridging to joists, (2) nailing board subfloor to joists, (3) nailing header to joists, and (4) toe-nailing header to sill. *(Courtesy of the Forestry Products Laboratory, U.S. Department of Agriculture.)*

Step 3: Lay off on either side of the ℄, half the thickness of the joist. **This is important!**

Step 4: Lay off 16″ from the right hand side of No. 1 joist to the right hand side of No. 2 joist. Mark this on the header with a square line and ticked to the left as shown on the drawing. Nail the right hand side of the joist to the square line.

Step 5: Lay off 16″ from the right hand side of No. 2 joist to the outside edge of No. 3 joist and mark it on the header similar to that for No. 2.

Step 6: It will be seen that from the outside edge of the header to the ℄ of joist No. 3,

it is exactly 4′-0″ which is the standard size of plywood subflooring.

Step 7: To avoid "creeping" by measuring in short 16″ steps it is better to run out a tape from the right hand mark of Joist No. 1 (not from the header), and mark 4′-0″, 8′-0″, and 16′-0″ spacings, and so on. These measures establish the certainty of the modular 4′-0″ spacings for receiving the plywood subfloor. From these spacings, lay off the 16″ ticked marks for the intermediate joists.

Note: Where metric system measurements are to be used, wood panel dimensions and OC spacings will be different from those given above. Joist spacings must accommo-

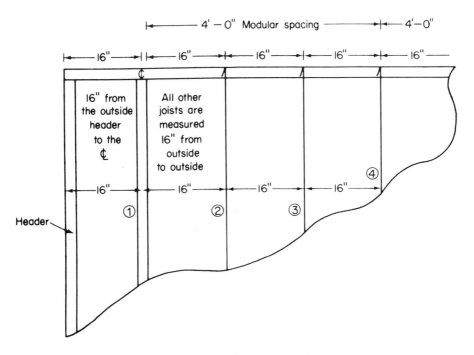

Fig. 13.20 Floor joist layout, 16 inch OCs.

date standard panel products. For example, as the 4'-0 by 8'-0 panel size becomes 1200 mm by 2400 mm, the joist spacings will probably be 400 mm (or 600 mm, where spacings had been 24" OC).

13.10 FRAMING FLOOR OPENINGS

Figure 13.21 illustrates the framing system for floor openings. Remember that openings in floors for stairwells and so on should in no way alter the basic layout of 16" OCs for the joists. The same thing applies for framed walls. You should imagine the floor (or wall) as being completely covered with sheathing, and then visualize how the openings would be cut into the framing with double members surrounding the openings. *Repeat: never alter the pattern of OC joists to suit a floor*

opening; make the opening as if it were to "guillotine" itself into the floor assembly.

It is important to remember to make framed openings large enough to receive the finished stair, window, or door.

Inside Chimney Openings must be large enough so that no combustible material shall be less than 2" from the masonry of the chimney. Floor openings for laundry chutes, and so on, must be large enough to accommodate any internal trim; they must not impede heating, plumbing, or air conditioning lines.

Stairwell Openings must be checked against the drawings, and, also, against the physical possibilities of installing the staircase as shown on the drawings. *Drawings are not*

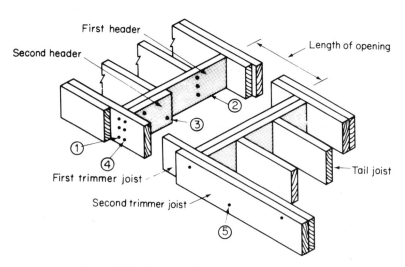

First header

Second header

Length of opening

Tail joist

First trimmer joist

Second trimmer joist

Fig. 13.21 Framing for floor openings where double headers and double trimmers are used. *(Courtesy of the Department of Forestry and Rural Development and the Canada Mortgage and Housing Corporation, Ottawa.)*

always correct! Assume that part of the specifications for a stairway are as follows:

The height of the stair from the finish of one floor to the finish of the one immediately above shall be 9'-0". The stair shall have fifteen equal risers and fourteen treads. The stair shall have a minimum perpendicular headroom from the angle of flight of 6'-4". Each riser shall be 7.2" (seven decimal two inches), and the treads shall be 9.8" *excluding the width of the tread nosings.* The upper floor assembly shall be 12" from finished ceiling to finished floor.

To check the stairwell opening, take a piece of plywood about two feet square and using a scale of 1½" to 1'-0", make a sectional drawing of the staircase.

Note carefully that the scale of 1½" to 1'-0", is ideal for on-the-job drawings using a carpenter's pencil, tape and framing square; where one eighth of an inch on scale rep-

resents one inch actual; and one and a half inches on scale represents one foot actual. Proceed as follows:

Step 1: Near the top of the plywood draw two faint parallel lines 12" apart and of indefinite length representing the floor assembly as at a-b and c-d in Fig. 13.22.

Step 2: From -a-, project a perpendicular line 9'-0" in length to -e- to intersect with the lower finished floor line e-f.

Step 3: Read the drawings and specifications and multiply the width of one tread by the total number of treads, thus 9.8 × 14 = 137" or 11'-5" nearly.

Step 4: On line e-f, from -e- measure 11'-5" to -g-, and project the perpendicular line to the first riser 7.2 to -h-.

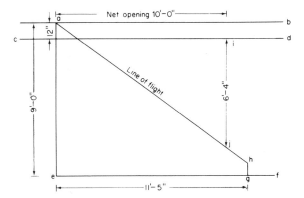

Fig. 13.22 Establishing a stairwell opening a-b, upper floor finish; c-d, total thickness of floor assembly; e-f, lower floor level; g-h, height of the first riser; h-a, line of flight of the stairs; and i-j, minimum headroom clearance.

Step 5: From -h-, project a line (angle of flight, or slope of the stair) to -a-. *It is important to remember that the line of flight starts at the top of the first riser or step to the*

upper floor and not from the lower floor level. **This is very important.**

Step 6: At right angles to the *underside* of the ceiling line, project a perpendicular line 6'-4" long to intersect with the line of flight as at i-j. This is the headroom allowance. Many jurisdictions state that the minimum headroom clearance for houses shall not be less than 6'-4", and for all others not less than 6'-9".

Step 7: The *net* length of the **stairwell opening** is the horizontal distance between the perpendiculars a-e and i-j, which is 10'-0". Additionally, an allowance must be made for fitting the stair at its intersection with the upper floor and also for the fascia board (trim) at the other end of the opening.

Step 8: To the net length of the opening add (say) 3" for the fitting at the upper floor level,

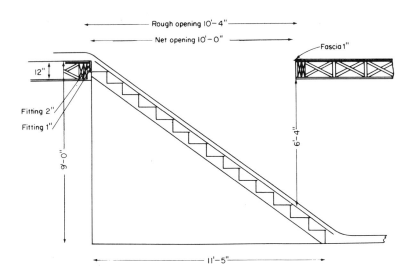

Fig. 13.23 Stair elevation.

plus 1″ for the fascia board at the other end, making a total of four inches. See Fig. 13.23.

Step 9: The total length of the opening will be 10′-0″ in all to allow for the thickness of wall finishes. To determine the width of the stairwell remember the thickness of the wall finish.

Review

1. List eight underpinning member terms.

2. Research and list all the different types of insulation recommended in your area.

3. Why should the tops of concrete basement walls be kept below the concrete embedded joists?

4. Make neat freehand sketches of floor joists supported on:

   a. wooden ledgers spiked to the sides of a wooden beam;

   b. metal hangers attaching joists to wood post supporting a wooden main beam;

   c. section of floor assembly supported on a telescopic steel leg.

14

Concrete Forms, Plywood, and Hardware

Much of the material in this chapter is excerpted from the booklet *Plywood Concrete Formwork,* a publication of the Council of Forest Industries of British Columbia, and is used with the permission of the copyright holder.

The statements are descriptive of how Douglas Fir plywood is used and explain why it is used in formwork. Data sheets for other formwork materials should be collected, filed, and compared.

14.1 THE ADVANTAGES OF PLYWOOD FOR CONCRETE FORMING

The selection of formwork materials should be based on maximum overall operating economy consistent with safety and the quality of finish required. Many contractors have found that, for the reasons noted below, Douglas Fir plywood satisfies the requirements of economy, safety and quality for the majority of concrete formwork applications.

Working with Plywood

Plywood can be easily worked with conventional hand or power rools. The following suggestions are offered to ensure best results:

Sawing. Sharp, fine-toothed saws with little set should be used. For radial arm, table or hand saws, place good face up; for portable power saws, place good face down.

Machining/Drilling. High-speed tools with sharp cutting edges should be used. Drill from good face whenever possible and do not drill closer than 7 mm to the panel edge.

Edge Sealing. Edges and cut-outs should be sealed with an edge sealer such as aluminum wood primer.

Storage. Panels should be stacked flat on a dry, level platform under shelter. If outside storage is unavoidable, panels must be protected against rain, but free air circulation must be provided.

Stripping. To minimize damage during form removal, stripping procedures should be studied during form planning with reference to surface contours and special conditions. While forms must be left in place a sufficient time to permit proper curing and protection of the fresh concrete, it is generally desirable to remove forms as soon as these requirements have been met.

Douglas Fir plywood is a rugged material, but like other types of panel forms, plywood can be damaged by prying with crowbars or by dropping panels on their edges from a height. If a good release agent has been properly applied to the plywood, stripping should present no difficulty. If it is necessary to use force, wooden wedges rather than metal pries should be employed.

Advantages of Using Plywood for Form Construction

Strength Cross-lamination of veneers tends to equalize strength of panel with and across face grain, permitting the panel to act as a plate when suitably supported.

Impact Resistance Cross-lamination results in high resistance to impact.

Split-Proof Nails can be driven close to panel edge without causing splitting.

Stability Construction of plywood creates a panel which is shrink resistant.

Less Handling Large panel size reduces number of pieces required. Reduces on-site labor.

Re-usability The number of re-uses is related to care in handling and stripping, and reduction of panel cutting by modular detailing. Five to twenty uses are common for quality finish industrial work. Between 50 and 100 uses can be expected for residential foundations.

Fewer Joints With fewer joints than boards and other materials, plywood forms are tighter. There is less leakage.

Insulation Plywood protects concrete from rapid temperature changes and assists in retention of concrete heat in freezing weather.

Salvage Value Even after many re-uses, plywood may be put to work in countless other applications, such as subflooring, ramps, protective barriers and temporary structures.

Easy to Bend Fir plywood can be bent dry to radii determined by thickness of plywood, direction of bend and the bending procedure itself. Soaking or steaming permits bending to smaller radii.

Smooth Face Large, flat plywood panels provide a concrete surface of uniform smoothness. Rubbing down and filling are kept to a minimum.

Simplicity of Repair Complex tools are not needed to patch and repair plywood.

Easy to Tally Stacked plywood panels can be readily checked by counting the panels or measuring the depth of the pile.

Less Storage Space Uniform size of large, flat Douglas Fir plywood panels makes them easy to store, on or off the job.

T&G Edges Available Tongue and groove Douglas Fir plywood panels may be used to construct forms on the site, eliminating the need for blocking at panel edges and providing a smooth, joint-free surface.

Ease of Fabrication Douglas Fir plywood is easily sawn, bored, routed, etc., with ordinary woodworking tools and therefore lends itself to special requirements of custom form jobs.

Cleaning

Proper supervision of forming operations on the job site should extend to the cleaning and repair of forms. Plywood forms, in common with all other types, should be cleaned immediately after stripping. Concrete particles may be removed by using a wide blunt blade, straw broom or burlap sacking. Many contractors use a power-driven nylon brush. There are also several proprietary solutions available for softening concrete adhering to the plywood.

Projecting nails should be withdrawn to prevent scarring of panels when stacking. Panels should be stacked flat, preferably out of the sun to reduce face checking.

Repairing

It is recommended that plywood forms be inspected after each use and repairs such as patching or renailing carried out as required.

Plywood forms should be clean and dry before repairs are carried out. Where the grade of plywood and the type of form are suitable, the plywood may be reversed. Small splits and depressions can be filled with a suitable patching compound sanded flush. Unwanted holes through the plywood may be patched by:

1. Driving a wooden plug in tightly and sanding flush.
2. Backing up the hole with scrap wood, filling with patching compound and sanding flush.
3. Driving a metal patching disc into the plywood face.

Experience has shown that even if a plywood form is damaged beyond economical repair, the plywood itself can be salvaged and usefully reemployed in numerous fields, for example as stiffening gussets on new formwork, as rough foundation formwork, and in those areas where formwork is difficult to remove and must be left in place.

Handling

It is generally acknowledged that the greatest damage to forms occurs during the various handling operations. Thorough planning of the whole forming operation will keep handling to a minimum. In the interests of speed and efficiency, mechanical handling devices should be used whenever possible.

14.2 RELEASE AGENTS FOR PLYWOOD CONCRETE FORMS

The application of a release agent to the form face facilitates stripping the formwork and prevents scaling of the concrete surface when the forms are removed.

Release agents have a far greater influence upon the surface finish of concrete than is generally supposed—the color, texture, and durability of the surface are determined as much by the formwork and its treatment with a release agent as by nearly all other factors combined.

Many different proprietary brands of release agents are available in North America. These brands vary in composition to suit various applications but may for general purposes be divided into three broad categories: lacquers and paints, oils and greases, and emulsions. It is recommended that contractors use only proprietary brands of release agents applied according to the manufacturer's instructions.

Lacquers and Paints

These release agents are applied as liquids and dry into waterproof, alkali-resistant films of varying degrees of hardness. The manufacturer's directions should be followed as proper application is of great importance. Grain rise and face checking will be reduced, form cleaning will be easier, and the plywood itself will be protected from moisture variations. A good lacquer coating should last three or four re-uses before recoating is required. If form oil is applied in addition to the lacquer coating, up to thirty re-uses can be expected. Generally, the release agents are colored so that untreated areas are easily noticed.

Oils and Greases

Form oils and greases generally have a paraffin wax or mineral oil base. Panels should be well cleaned before applying oil. Care should be taken not to put too much oil on the panel surface as this may result in staining of the concrete. Most oils eventually oxidize, causing them to dry up, or else they soak into the plywood. Therefore oil should not be applied too far in advance of the time the forms are needed. Oil may be applied with spray equipment or by brushes or rollers. If oil is to be used as the release agent, a paraffin base oil is preferable when it is intended to paint the concrete surface. The life of a panel can be extended by initially applying a liberal amount of form oil to the entire panel. This should be done just a few days before first use to allow deep penetration and some degree of drying. For re-use, only the face of the form is oiled in the normal manner, taking care not to apply an excessive amount which may stain the concrete. When staining does occur, it can nearly always be attributed to the excessive application of oil to the forms or traced to impurities contained within the oil itself.

Emulsions

Several emulsifiable oil or wax base concentrates are available. Generally, these are diluted with water or kerosene. To obtain proper results, the dilutions recommended by the manufacturer should not be exceeded. The emulsion is then applied for each re-use like a regular form oil. There are also several proprietary compounds available which react with chemicals in the concrete to form a film which permits easy stripping.

Coated Panels

Other types of plywood panels manufactured for use as concrete formwork include those with resin-fiber overlays or surface coatings of epoxy resin, modified polyurethanes, or other proprietary compositions developed in the research laboratories of the plywood industry. They simplify form stripping and cleaning, improve the quality of concrete finish, and extend the service life of the form. The overlays and coatings seal the plywood surface and make it impervious to oil and water. Many of the compositions are self-lubricating, making release agents unnecessary.

14.3 HARDWARE FOR PLYWOOD CONCRETE FORMS

Contractors should obtain their hardware only from recognized suppliers who can furnish proof of the strength of their accessories by laboratory or field tests. Although many different types of form hardware have been developed, all standard types are suitable for use with plywood. Of particular interest are various kinds of high tensile steel ties or bolts which have been specifically designed for plywood.

Snap-ties made from high tensile wire are popular as an inexpensive method of form support. These ties are designed to prevent the forms from separating under pressure. Stripping the forms should be done only after concrete has set. After the forms have been removed, a tie breaker is applied to the exposed end of the snap-tie and bent at right angles as close to the wall surface as possible. The unit is then turned with a clockwise circular motion until the snap-tie breaks at break-off point.

For most commercial concrete finishes a rod or bar tie with integral spreaders is customary. Such ties generally have a notch or similar reduction in section which allows the tie to be broken back a set distance from the wall surface.

Examples of typical form hardware are shown in Fig. 14.1. It is not intended to imply that those shown are better than others—nor is it intended to imply that hardware not shown is unsuitable or inferior. Limitations of space preclude showing the full range of concrete form hardware suitable for use with plywood.

14.4 FRAMED FORMS

Detailing for Plywood

Formwork costs can be substantially reduced if certain basic details of dimensioning are borne in mind by building planners. Beams and columns preferably should have the same outside dimensions from foundation to roof, allowing beam and column forms to be re-used without alteration.

A column should preferably be the same width as a beam framing into it. The column form then becomes a rectangular or square box with no cutouts, and the slab forms do not require cutting at the column corners.

Hardware for Plywood Concrete Forms

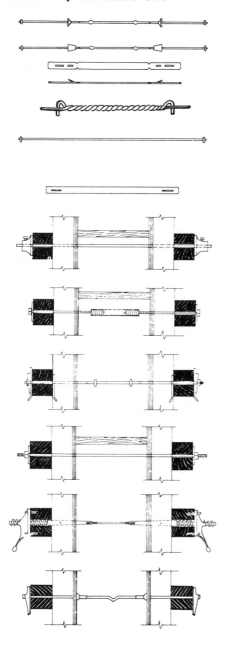

Rod ties are shaped to prevent rotation in the concrete when the rod is snapped off by twisting.

The bar tie shown here has a breakback notch and spurs which act as a spreader.

Twisted galvanized wire tie with integral spreader and backbreak features.

This type of tie, designed to be used where breakback is not required, consists of a straight unthreaded pencil rod with buttons. Clamps are slipped over the rod and bear against the walers.

A separate spreader must be used.

A bar tie may be used with wedges through the slots in the end of the tie.

Unthreaded pencil rod tie with end fittings to bear against the walers. Ties may be oiled to prevent concrete bonding to them.

A separate spreader must be used, and rods are entirely withdrawn from the wall when forms are stripped.

Tie consisting of two removable threaded rods and a part that remains in the wall into which the rods are threaded.

No metal must remain closer than 38 mm to wall surface with rods removed.

A separate spreader must be used.

A snap rod tie which breaks back at the required distance of 38 mm from the wall surface.

Spreader plates or separate spreaders may be used.

Threaded rod tie with nut and plate at each end.

A separate spreader is used and the rod entirely withdrawn from the wall.

Rod may be oiled or installed in sleeve which remains in the wall.

This tie permits removal of all metal by disconnecting one outside rod. The other outside rod, nut, washer and inside rod are withdrawn with a rod puller.

Ties of this type — more costly ties of larger diameter — have a disconnecting feature permitting re-use of the end portions.

The outer unit may be re-attached to secure knee-braces for scaffolding or cantilevered forms, eliminating offsets at construction joints.

Note: Drawings and text adapted from *Forms for Architectural Concrete*, Portland Cement Association.

Fig. 14-1. Hardware for Plywood Concrete Forms.

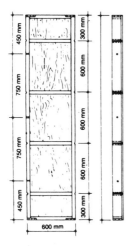

Fig. 14-2. A standard 600 mm by 2400 mm light modular framed panel of 17 mm Douglas Fir plywood and 38 mm by 89 mm lumber.

PANEL CLAMP

Fig. 14-3. A bolt and wedge device ensures a tight fit between framed panels.

It is highly desirable that columns, beams, stairwells and other items be so dimensioned that 1200 mm by 2400 mm panels of plywood can be cut with a minimum of waste.

If column centers are set so that the distance between faces of beams is a multiple of 1200 mm plus an allowance to facilitate panel removal, whole panels of plywood may be used without cutting for slab forms.

Wall Forms: Site Built. It is economical to fabricate as much of the formwork as possible on the ground, making sections as large as can be conveniently handled by the lifting equipment or manpower available. Where small pieces are required for such things as stepdowns and special shapes, plywood can be cut to the exact size required.

Horizontal joints between panels may be backed up by headers or nailing strips to eliminate leakage and produce a smoother joint. For special circumstances where a

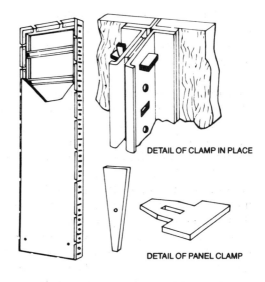

DETAIL OF CLAMP IN PLACE

DETAIL OF PANEL CLAMP

Fig. 14-4. A typical 600 mm by 2400 mm metal framed panel. One of the advantages of these patented panel systems is that the framing protects the plywood edges. The metal frames themselves have a long life and the plywood can easily be replaced or reversed.

smooth joint-free or fin-free surface is required, the use of tongue and groove plywood should be considered. It should be noted, however, that special care must be taken to prevent damage to panel edges. Some contractors overcome the joint problem in high-quality finish concrete surfaces by taping joints with thin, pressure-sensitive plastic tape.

Nails to fasten plywood to supports should be as small and as few as practical. For plywood up to 17 mm thick, nails should be 44 mm* (1¾") long. For 18.5 mm or thicker plywood, nails should be 51 mm* (2") long.

Wall Forms: Panel Systems. In the forming of large areas, standard sized prefabricated panels can be used for most structures. As the ties pass through pre-drilled holes it is essential that the forms be aligned correctly on a level footing. Panel form systems can be divided into two broad classes—unframed and framed.

Unframed Forms. Unframed forms are usually 19 mm plywood panels. The number of studs or walers is limited. Forms are aligned by means of a toe plate and top waler. Ties are inserted through holes cut in the panels. A slip-through bar or rod passed through the ends of ties holds panels together. Forms of this type are most commonly used for residential and other foundations below grade, and for concrete walls above grade where the highest architectural finish is not required. They are easy and light to handle, requiring little framing lumber. Fabrication by the contractor is simple. Another advan-

tage is that both faces of plywood can be used.

Framed Forms. These forms consist of a plywood face from 11 mm to 19 mm thick with a wood or metal frame. Plywood dimensions may be 1200 mm by 2400 mm or 600 mm by 2400 mm with miscellaneous filler pieces. A great variety of hardware is available. Ties pass between or through the panels depending on panel size. Framed forms are widely used for straight wall foundation work, both residential and commercial; above ground concrete work, including walls, columns, slabs, spandrel beams and joists; heavy industrial concrete work; and architectural concrete. Framed forms assist in the production of the highest quality wall obtainable and by the nature of their construction withstand rougher use than unframed forms. The framed form system lends itself to gang forming.

Column Forms. There are several methods of forming square and rectangular columns. Whenever possible, the size of the column should be selected to permit the use of standard 1200 mm by 2400 mm plywood panels.

Slab Forms. Plywood is easily adapted to accommodate a variety of support spacings and section changes in slab forming. Concrete may be poured on panels placed directly over supporting framework. In all cases, the formwork must safely support the vertical and horizontal loads placed upon it.

Miscellaneous Forms. There are so many shapes and types of structures for which individual consideration is insulating properties. In some cases plywood forms have been found sufficient protection at temperatures between −4°C and −1°C to avoid use

*Values represent approximations of the imperial sizes within a reasonable degree of accuracy and are not new metric sizes.

of extra insulation, except at corners and exposed concrete surfaces where heat losses are higher. At lower temperatures, insulated reusable plywood panels have been employed with good results, especially with heated concrete.

14.5 DESIGN OF PLYWOOD FORMWORK

Because of uncertainties such as swelling of form members, uneven tightening of form hardware, and variable construction loads, it is necessary to base form design on conservative material stresses and to select safety factors that are consistent with the hazards of the application.

Although authorities differ as to the pressures to be used in form design, the information given here follows the latest recommendations of the American Concrete Institute.

Definitions. A column form is defined as a form having a maximum horizontal dimension of 1.8 m.

All other vertical forms are classed as wall forms, except for those used in mass concreting, which are in a special classification.

Wall and Column Form Loads. Vertical formwork must be designed to resist both lateral concrete pressure and horizontal loads due to wind and impact.

Lateral Concrete Pressure. This is affected by many factors, the most important of which are:

Rate of placement,
Temperature of the concrete,
Effect of vibration,

Weight of concrete,
Type of cement,
Consistency of mix.

The calculation of lateral pressures is based on the following.

Weight of Concrete. Consult a handbook or data sheet for weights of locally mixed concrete. (Without such data one may assume a weight of 2403 kg per cubic meter.) Use selected data from a table to determine actual pressures of fluid mix.

Type of Cement. Average Type 1 Portland Cement is assumed. The cement manufacturer's instructions should always be followed closely. When slow-setting cements or retarding admixtures are used, the lateral pressures will be greater than those shown in the graph. In such cases, the lateral pressure should be assumed to be that exerted by a fluid weighing 2403 kg/m³, i.e. the lateral pressure in kilonewtons per square meter is equal to 23.5 times the height of the pour in meters.

Consistency of Mix. The assumption is made that the slump will be 100 mm or less. For more liquid mixes, use a lateral pressure closer to the full liquid head pressure, keeping in mind the pressure-reducing effects of setting concrete.

Vibration

For Walls. Normal internal mechanical vibration of the top 1.2 m is permitted within 15 minutes of placing. To permit complete vibration the height of each lift should not exceed 1.2 m. Such vibration must be for consolidation only, not for moving the concrete horizontally in the forms.

For Columns. Internal vibration is permitted throughout the entire height of one lift, up to a maximum of 5.5 m, in a short time. Forms must be specially designed for external vibration or revibration of the concrete.

Formulae

The following formulae for concrete pressures are recommended by the American Concrete Institute.

For Columns. The height of a single pour in column forms should be limited to 5.5 m. For greater column heights, an interval of at least 2 hours should elapse between each 5.5-meter lift and the next pour. The lateral concrete pressure, P, is given by:

$$P = 7.2 + \frac{785R}{T + 17.8}$$

(but not to exceed 144 kN/m² or 23.5H, whichever is smaller) where:

H = Height of fresh concrete (m)

R = Rate of placement (m/hr)

T = Concrete temperature in forms (°C)

For Walls. For a rate of placement of 2 m per hour or less:

$$P = 7.2 + \frac{785R}{T + 17.8}$$

(but not to exceed 95.8 kN/m² or 23.5H, whichever is smaller).

For a rate of placement of over 2 m per hour:

$$P = 7.2 + \frac{1156}{T + 17.8} + \frac{244R}{T + 17.8}$$

(but not to exceed 95.8 kN/m² or 23.5H, whichever is smaller).

Types of Plywood for Formwork

From your local or regional supplier obtain data for plywood sold in your area. Look for specifications with respect to waterproof glue, load-spans, nominal sizes, grade, and species. The manufacturing mill should also be noted. After reading the data sheets, actually find marked sheets of plywood identified according to the data given.

One example of specifications for formwork plywood is given in Section 14.6.

14.6 CERTIFICATION MARKS ON COFI PLYWOOD

The registered certification marks shown in Fig. 14.5 appear on all standard grades of COFI EXTERIOR Douglas Fir and COFI EXTERIOR Canadian Softwood plywood manufactured by members of the Council of Forest Industries of British Columbia and meeting the requirements of CSA 0121-M1978 and CSA 0151-M1978. The COFI mark which appears on sanded and unsanded grades, is an assurance to the buyer that the plywood meets the high standards established by the industry and that it will perform in a satisfactory and predictable manner.

CERTIFICATION MARKS ON COFI PLYWOOD

The registered certification marks shown below appear on all standard grades of COFI EXTERIOR Douglas Fir and COFI EXTERIOR Canadian Softwood plywood manufactured by members of the Council of Forest Industries of British Columbia and meeting the requirements of CSA O121-M1978 and CSA O151-M1978. The COFI mark which appears on sanded and unsanded grades, is an assurance to the buyer that the plywood meets the high standards established by the industry and that it will perform in a satisfactory and predictable manner.

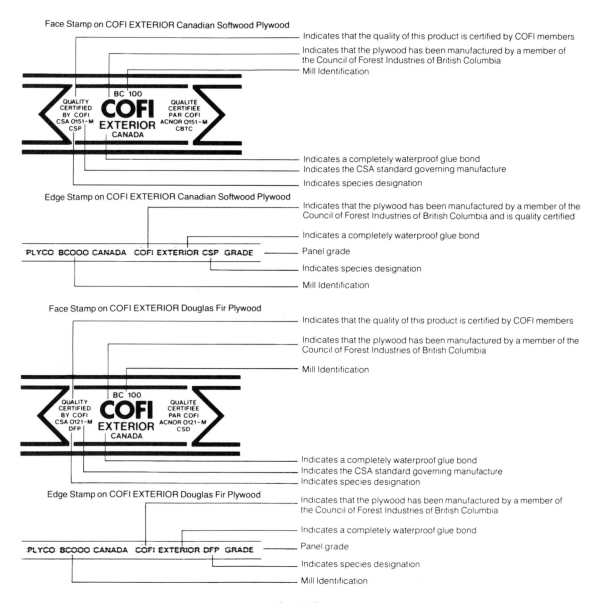

Face Stamp on COFI EXTERIOR Canadian Softwood Plywood
— Indicates that the quality of this product is certified by COFI members
— Indicates that the plywood has been manufactured by a member of the Council of Forest Industries of British Columbia
— Mill Identification
— Indicates a completely waterproof glue bond
— Indicates the CSA standard governing manufacture
— Indicates species designation

Edge Stamp on COFI EXTERIOR Canadian Softwood Plywood
— Indicates that the plywood has been manufactured by a member of the Council of Forest Industries of British Columbia and is quality certified
— Indicates a completely waterproof glue bond

PLYCO BCOOO CANADA COFI EXTERIOR CSP GRADE — Panel grade
— Indicates species designation
— Mill Identification

Face Stamp on COFI EXTERIOR Douglas Fir Plywood
— Indicates that the quality of this product is certified by COFI members
— Indicates that the plywood has been manufactured by a member of the Council of Forest Industries of British Columbia
— Mill Identification
— Indicates a completely waterproof glue bond
— Indicates the CSA standard governing manufacture
— Indicates species designation

Edge Stamp on COFI EXTERIOR Douglas Fir Plywood
— Indicates that the plywood has been manufactured by a member of the Council of Forest Industries of British Columbia
— Indicates a completely waterproof glue bond

PLYCO BCOOO CANADA COFI EXTERIOR DFP GRADE — Panel grade
— Indicates species designation
— Mill Identification

Fig. 14-5.

Review

1. What type of saw should be used for sawing plywood?

2. How would you protect panels of plywood stacked on site?

3. Research and list the release agents for plywood used in concrete forms in your area.

4. Research and obtain literature on all the types of form hardware that are marketed in your area.

15

Wall Framing, Anchors, and Fasteners

In this chapter we shall present wall anchors: conventional nailing methods, and metal wood fasteners in wood framing; steel studs; floor decks; and an actual case study of a housing development.

15.1 CONVENTIONAL WALL FRAMING

Before making any wall frame layout, the openings in the subfloor should be checked for the correctness of their locations and sizes. At this stage, it is relatively inexpensive to correct any fault before further construction begins. See article 13.10 for stairwell openings. When everything is satisfactory, the floor should be swept clean, and the following suggested steps taken to lay out the floor plates (sole plates).

Step 1: Study Figs. 15.1 and 15.2 and decide what type of stud assembly is to be used for corners and intersecting internal partitions. In this discussion, we will use the stud assembly in Fig. 15.1a.

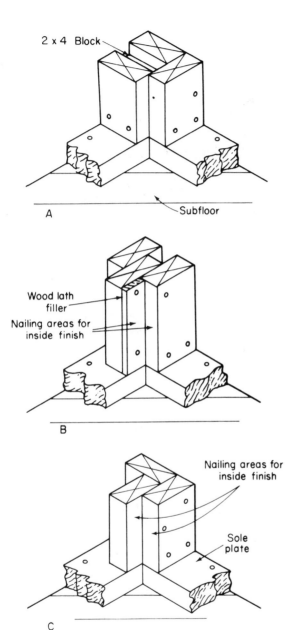

Fig. 15.1. Examples of corner stud assembly: (a) standard outside corner; (b) special corner with lath filler; (c) special corner without lath filler. *(Courtesy of Forest Products Laboratory, U.S. Department of Agriculture.)*

Step 2: Examine the drawings. (Some contractors glue them onto pieces of plywood, and clear-varnish them as a protection against the weather and to prevent persons defacing them with pencil sketches and calculations.) Check to see if partition and wall openings, such as doors and windows, are dimensioned to center lines; if so, make an allowance on either side for half their widths, and that of the sole plate of wall partitions.

Step 3: Strike chalk lines on the subfloor for partitions, and check the diagonals for square.

Step 4: From the lumber pile, select the straightest and best material for corner posts, window and door openings, and sole plates.

Step 5: Square-cut the ends of two pieces of sole plate, and loosely place them on the subfloor at right angles to each other as in Fig. 15.3. Using a square-ended piece of 2 × 4, about a foot long (called a short end), stand it square to the end of the plate; with a sharp pencil, draw the position of the corner stud and mark it as in Fig. 15.3(a). *You will never waste time by sharpening a pencil or any other tool.*

Step 6: From the corner post thus marked, again stand the short end and mark its width as in Fig. 15.3(b), which represents the thickness of the blocking for the built up corner post. See also Fig. 15.12.

Step 7: From the blocking mark, draw the inside starter stud as in Fig. 15.3(c).

Step 8: Place the other wall plate at right angles snug to the long one. Stand the short end as shown on the drawing and mark the inside starter stud of the short wall plate as in Fig. 15.3(d). It is recommended that the

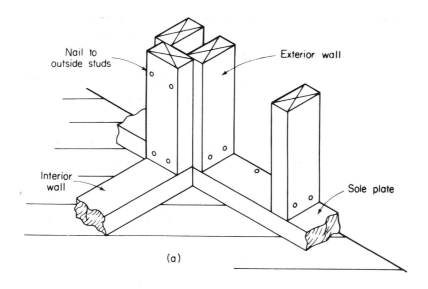

(a)

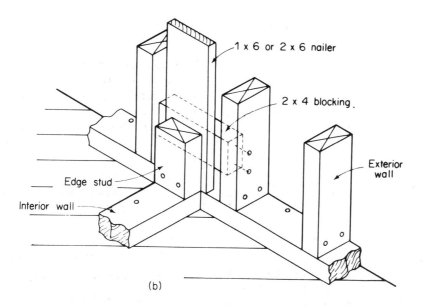

(b)

Fig. 15.2. Intersection of interior wall with exterior wall: (a) with doubled studs on outside wall, (b) partition between outside studs. (*Courtesy of Forest Products Laboratory, U.S. Department of Agriculture.*)

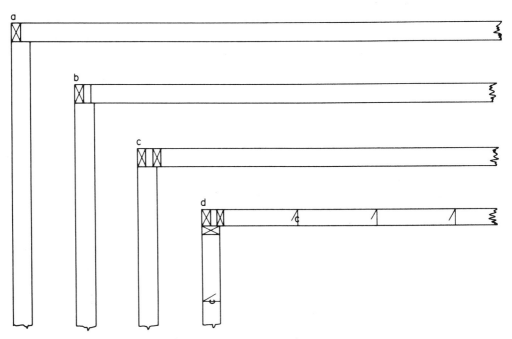

Fig. 15.3. Corner post layout.

actual material be used (instead of a ruler) for layout wherever practicable.

Step 9: From the inside intersection of the sole plates, measure 16″ each way as in Fig. 15.4. There are the center lines of the No. 2 studs, respectively. **This is important.** On either side of the center line, mark 3/4″ as shown. This is the location of the No. 2 stud for each wall plate.

Step 10: From the outside edge of each **No. 2 stud** (the edge furthest away from the intersection of the plates), run out a tape and mark 4′-0″ intervals (with ticked marks) as shown. The tick will be covered later by the nailed studs. Then lay off the intermediate studs with the 16″ tongue of a carpenter's framing square as shown. The reason for laying off the 4′-0″ intervals with a tape is to avoid the creeping which may occur if all

the studs are stepped off with the framing square. This way it is certain that all 4′-0″ wide fiber boards will fall exactly on the center line of a stud. See Fig. 15.5 for the named members of a rough frame opening.

Note: Where metric system measurements are to be used, sizes of dimension lumber and panels of wood, fiber, and gypsum must be accommodated.

1. 4′-0 × 8′-0 panel dimensions are replaced by 1200 mm by 2400 mm.

2. Panel thicknesses are given in mm.

3. Stud spacing becomes 600 mm (replacing 24″ OC) or 400 mm (replacing 16″ OC) or 300 mm (replacing 12″ OC).

4. Lumber dimensions will be actual dimensions measured in millimeters. Nominal dimensions will not be used. For exam-

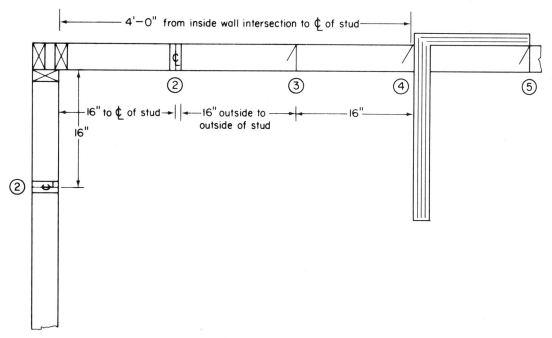

Fig. 15.4. Plate layout.

ple, the nominal sized 2 × 4, of actual size 1½" × 3½", becomes 38 mm × 89 mm.

15.2 THE CARPENTER'S TRADITIONAL FRAMING SQUARE

1. The body of the framing square is 2 inches wide and 24 inches long.

2. The tongue is 1½ inches wide and 16 inches long. In some countries, the tongue is 18 inches long.

3. The tool has two rectangular parts at right angles to each other. It usually has the rafter tables and the name of the manufacturer on the face side.

4. There are eight edges on the framing square. Each edge is divided into inches

and fractions of an inch. Readings of 1/16", 1/8", 1/4", 1/2", 1/10", 1/5", or 1/3", may be made on one or more edges. The use to which such graduations may be put in carpentry layout is indicated in the following example.

A one-twelfth scale drawing is to be made of a rectangular building measuring 12'-3" by 20'-6". By use of the framing square edge having 1/12" graduations, these measurements can be scaled down immediately to read 12 3/12" by 20 6/12". The drawing may be done quickly and may just as easily be read. See Fig. 15.6.

The Metric Framing Square(s)

1. Bodies of the squares are 600 mm long, and the tongues 400 mm.

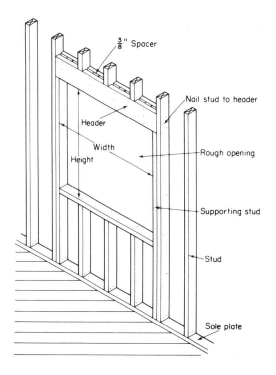

Fig. 15.5. Headers for windows and door openings. *(Courtesy of Forest Products Laboratory, U.S. Department of Agriculture.)*

2. Edges are graduated in either one or two millimeters.

3. Scale drawings one tenth full size, may be readily created.

Note: For additional information with respect to metric squares and their uses see Chapters 6, 7, and 8 of *Residential Roof Framing* (1980), by Wass and Sanders (Published by Reston Publishing Co. Inc., Reston, Virginia).

15.3 ROUGH OPENINGS FOR DOORS AND WINDOWS

Irrespective of the sizes or numbers of doors or window openings in a wood frame wall, the 16″ OCs of all studs must be constant; the framing for the openings is imposed on the main framing at the place desired.

It is important to read the manufacturer's catalog, which gives the actual sizes of door and window frame units and the **relative sizes for the rough openings.** Assuming that a newly framed wall has been sheathed, insulated, and finished with hardboard before it was discovered that the opening was too small for the unit, this would be a major (and expensive) mistake to correct. If units are delivered onto the job before the wall framing has begun, take the widths and heights on a piece of lath and allow sufficient clearance for fitting them into the rough openings. From my personal experience, I would never use a tape if I could manage without it. Similarly, it is better to take the height or width of an opening on a pair of slip sticks, transfer this length to the lumber to be fitted into the opening, and cut!

15.4 PREFABRICATION AND SEMI-PREFABRICATION

If an area is indiscriminately subdivided into building lots and uses a basic plan with variations of doors, windows, and roof treatments, a number of houses in any given district may complement each other. Such a development lends itself to intensive prefabrication methods such as prefabricated basement walls; floors; walls; pre-fitted windows and doors complete with hardware; meter boxes; ceilings; roofs; chimneys;

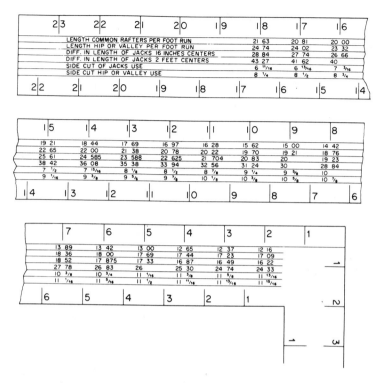

Fig. 15.6. The carpenter's traditional framing square.

hearths; firegrate surrounds; clothes closets; complete bathrooms with plumbing units, vanities, towel rails, and mirrors; kitchen cabinets; ranges, refrigerators.

In addition, the construction industry lends itself to an ever increasing number of specializing subtradesmen. This new age of house prefabrication requires administrators, with special organizing ability, who can co-ordinate the different assembly operations, so that a whole complex of houses may be given consecutive treatment by consecutive specializing crews of workmen with their own special tools, equipment, and techniques.

Semi-Prefabrication has been practiced, with continuing success in the saving of material and labor costs, for many years. As an example, it is particularly important when working in frigid or very hot temperatures to afford men some cover as soon as possible. When the underpinning has been completed, the following method (with your own variations) may be adopted:

Step 1: On the completed subfloor, pre-fabricate one long wall (complete with its sheathing, small glazed windows, and hard-ware fitted prehung doors secured in their respective positions) and complete with out-

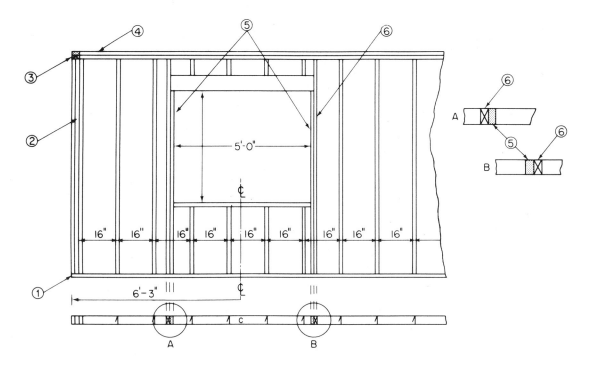

Fig. 15.7. Wall framing with rough opening for window. Note: all regular studs are spaced 16 inches OCs. (1) Bottom or sole plate, (2) built-up corner post, (3) top plate, (4) cap plate, (5) trimmer stud, and (6) window framing through stud.

side trim. Meanwhile, on the floor, the top plates should be marked off for the positions of the prefabricated roof trusses that will be spaced at 16″ or 24″ OCs. *Remember that, the less work that has to be done in space, the safer, faster, and more profitable will be the enterprise.*

Step 2: Raise the wall into position and brace it well, *especially if it has to be left overnight.* Nail the sole plate through the subfloor to the joist header, but leave four or five feet unnailed at each end of the wall ready for jockeying the end walls into posi-

tion. See a case study of housing development, pages 182–184.

Step 3: If the door and window units are not placed before the wall is raised, cover the rough opening with 4 mil polyethylene.

Step 4: Prefabricate the opposite long wall and raise it into its position as in Step 2.

Step 5: Prefabricate one short wall, raise it into position by jockeying it between the unnailed end plates of the long walls, position it carefully, nail it through to the floor joists. Then spike its end studs to the long wall corner studs.

Step 6: Prefabricate the other short wall and give it the same treatment as in Step 5.

Step 7: The roof trusses may be made on the subfloor, or bought from and delivered to the job by the manufacturer. Be sure to have them on hand when required. The delivery truck should place sufficient trusses for each house and as near to each as possible. If you are making your own trusses, you could use one subfloor upon which to lay out a jig and make a great number, on the job, with a steady work crew.

Step 8: Raise the roof trusses and spike them to their premarked positions on the top plate of the walls.

Step 9: Sheath the roof and apply shakes, shingles or other roofing material, and the place is virtually stormproof. Notice at this stage that no internal walls have been made or positioned. At this stage, the four walls with the roof is a free-standing building, which should be well braced against sudden gusts of wind.

Step 10: Neatly install the insulation around the inside perimeter walls. Note that this is another reason why all wall studs should be

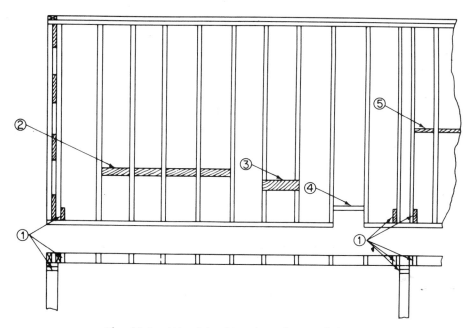

Fig. 15.8. Wood backing for other trades. (1) Short end of 2 × 4 nailed to all framing intersections for fixing baseboards, (2) backing for towel rails, (3) backing for plumbers unit, let in flush, (4) framing for sheet metal workers, hot air register, and (5) girts, or fire stops.

placed 16″ OCs irrespective of any wall openings.

Step 11: As soon as the internal walls are secured in position, the structure is ready for the electrician, plumber, and sheetmetal worker; for heating ducts, air conditioning, telephone, cable television, and the building inspectors.

With careful planning, an excellent field type of production line assembly can be achieved with excellent worker participation. Men like to see fast physical production, especially when their work is quickly shaded from extremes of climate. Remember, too, that subtrades will have prefabricated some of their plumbing lines, ducts, and so on, in their own shops.

Metric System of Measurement

The general use of the metric system will bring about changes in sizes and spacings of framing members. Existing framing methods will probably remain.

15.5 WOOD BACKING FOR SUBTRADES

Before the carpenters' rough wood framing is completed and handed over to other trades, inspect thoroughly each room to be sure that wood backing has been provided for affixing units. See Fig. 15.8. It will be seen from an inspection of the intersection of any wall frame with another, that without a short end of 2 × 4 nailed at the foot of all intersecting wall studs, the carpenter will not have sufficient bearing to readily nail the baseboard. The time taken in spiking these

nogs in place will be well repaid in the time saved by the finishing carpenter.

A list of other units, or items requiring backing is as follows:

Towel rail	Bathroom:
Plumbing units	toilet, wash basin,
Hot air registers	vanity towel bars, coat hangers,
Girts or fire stops	cabinets, soap and
Chimney hearths and fireplaces	toilet tissue holders, shower faucets and doors, curtain rods,
Undercarriage for stairs	facilities for repairing— plumbing services
Stair handrail brackets	behind all faucets (may be a loose door in the adjoining room).
Drywall backing at ceiling intersections with walls	
	Clothes chutes
Ceiling vents, fans, and chandeliers	Ceiling access door
Plaster grounds	Ironing board
Closet shelves and rails	Backing for telephone cable vision, electric and vacuum cleaning
Window valance	outlets.

This list is not exhaustive, and it should be added to with each new experience. It is expensive to have to call a carpenter from another job to provide backing, especially after the hardboard to all the walls has been completed. Check and be careful!
See Figs. 15.9, 15.10, and 15.11.

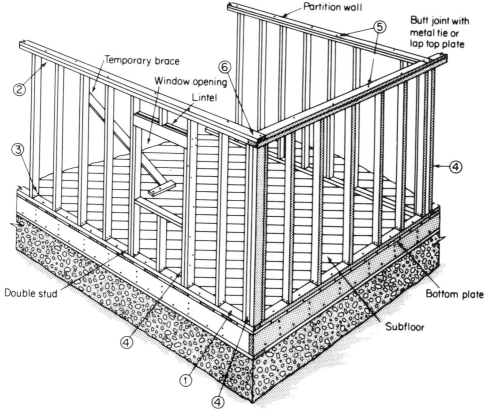

Fig. 15.9. Wall framing used with platform construction. *(Courtesy of the Department of Forestry and Rural Development and the Central Mortgage and Housing Corporation, Ottawa.)*

15.6 STRUCTURAL WOOD FASTENERS

Wood fasteners for wood framing are finding increasing favor among builders and contractors. They are comparatively inexpensive for original cost and especially for labor costs. The information shown on pages 173 to 181 has been excerpted from booklets published by the "Teco Engineering Company", and is here reproduced with the permission of the copyright holder.

Note carefully the types of anchors used in the walls. Check the local by-laws; the stronger the wind pressure the more stringent will be the requirements for anchorage of buildings to their foundations.

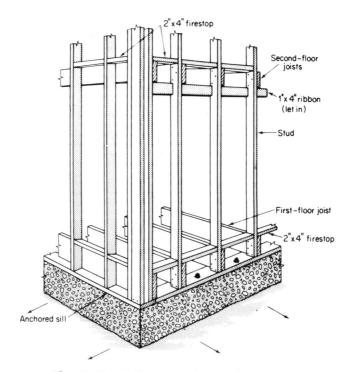

Fig. 15.10. Balloon framing. *(Courtesy of the Department of Forestry and Rural Development and the Canada Mortgage and Housing Corporation, Ottawa.)*

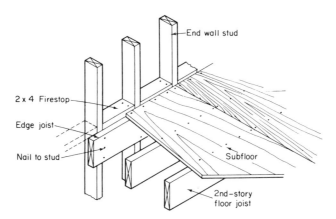

Fig. 15.11. End wall framing for balloon construction (junction of first-floor ceiling and upper-story floor framing. *(Courtesy of Forest Products Laboratory, U.S. Department of Agriculture.)*

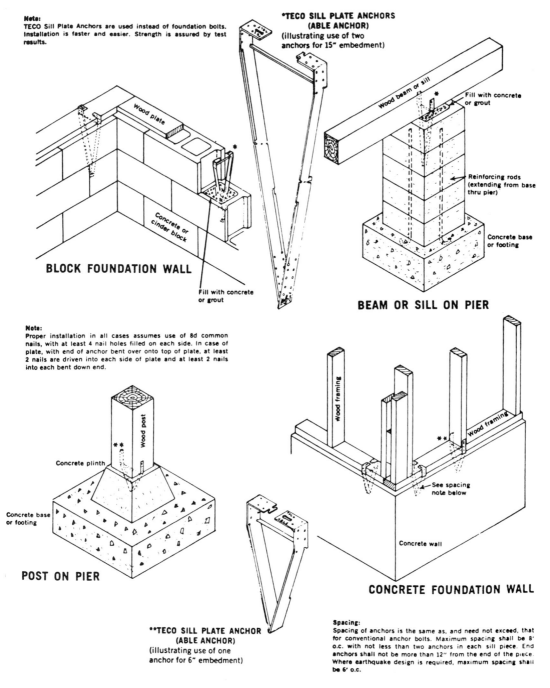

Note:
TECO Sill Plate Anchors are used instead of foundation bolts. Installation is faster and easier. Strength is assured by test results.

*TECO SILL PLATE ANCHORS
(ABLE ANCHOR)
(illustrating use of two anchors for 15" embedment)

Wood plate

Wood beam or sill

Fill with concrete or grout

BLOCK FOUNDATION WALL

Concrete or cinder block

Fill with concrete or grout

Reinforcing rods (extending from base thru pier)

Concrete base or footing

BEAM OR SILL ON PIER

Note:
Proper installation in all cases assumes use of 8d common nails, with at least 4 nail holes filled on each side. In case of plate, with end of anchor bent over onto top of plate, at least 2 nails are driven into each side of plate and at least 2 nails into each bent down end.

Wood post

Concrete plinth

Wood framing

Wood framing

See spacing note below

Concrete base or footing

Concrete wall

POST ON PIER

**TECO SILL PLATE ANCHOR
(ABLE ANCHOR)
(illustrating use of one anchor for 6" embedment)

CONCRETE FOUNDATION WALL

Spacing:
Spacing of anchors is the same as, and need not exceed, that for conventional anchor bolts. Maximum spacing shall be 8' o.c. with not less than two anchors in each sill piece. End anchors shall not be more than 12" from the end of the piece. Where earthquake design is required, maximum spacing shall be 6' o.c.

Fig. 15.12. Methods of Framing: Foundation Level

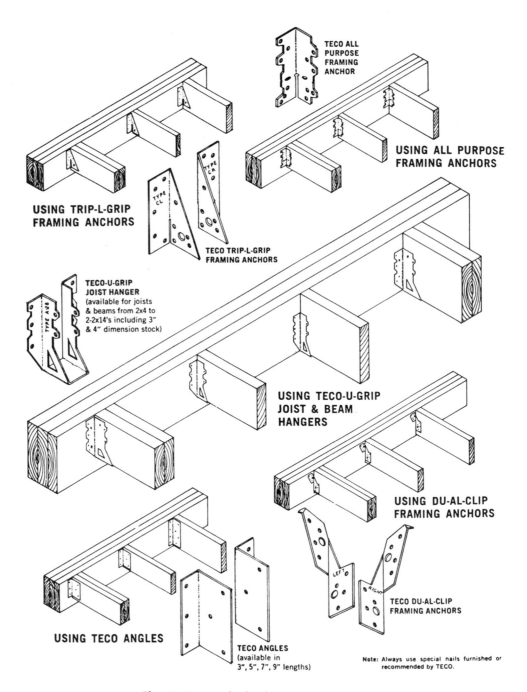

TECO ALL PURPOSE FRAMING ANCHOR

USING ALL PURPOSE FRAMING ANCHORS

USING TRIP-L-GRIP FRAMING ANCHORS

TYPE CL

TYPE CR

TECO TRIP-L-GRIP FRAMING ANCHORS

TECO-U-GRIP JOIST HANGER
(available for joists & beams from 2x4 to 2-2x14's including 3" & 4" dimension stock)

TYPE A28

USING TECO-U-GRIP JOIST & BEAM HANGERS

USING DU-AL-CLIP FRAMING ANCHORS

LEFT

RIGHT

TECO DU-AL-CLIP FRAMING ANCHORS

USING TECO ANGLES

TECO ANGLES
(available in 3", 5", 7", 9" lengths)

Note: Always use special nails furnished or recommended by TECO.

Fig. 15.13.   Methods of Framing: FLOOR LEVEL

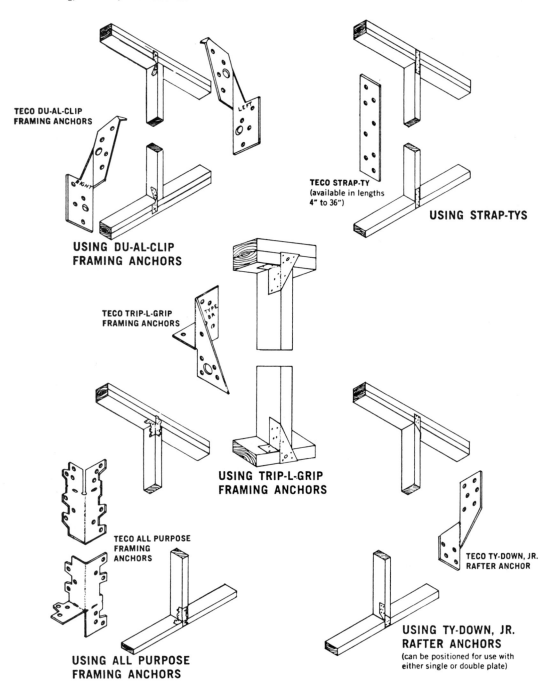

TECO DU-AL-CLIP FRAMING ANCHORS

LEFT

RIGHT

USING DU-AL-CLIP FRAMING ANCHORS

TECO STRAP-TY (available in lengths 4" to 36")

USING STRAP-TYS

TECO TRIP-L-GRIP FRAMING ANCHORS

TYPE BR

USING TRIP-L-GRIP FRAMING ANCHORS

TECO ALL PURPOSE FRAMING ANCHORS

USING ALL PURPOSE FRAMING ANCHORS

TECO TY-DOWN, JR. RAFTER ANCHOR

USING TY-DOWN, JR. RAFTER ANCHORS (can be positioned for use with either single or double plate)

Fig. 15.14. Methods of Framing: WALL CONNECTIONS

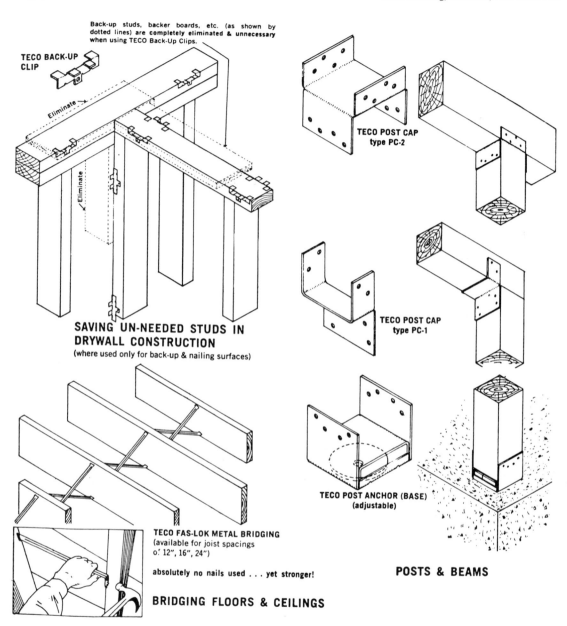

Back-up studs, backer boards, etc. (as shown by dotted lines) are **completely eliminated & unnecessary** when using TECO Back-Up Clips.

TECO BACK-UP CLIP

Eliminate →

Eliminate →

SAVING UN-NEEDED STUDS IN DRYWALL CONSTRUCTION
(where used only for back-up & nailing surfaces)

TECO POST CAP type PC-2

TECO POST CAP type PC-1

TECO POST ANCHOR (BASE) (adjustable)

TECO FAS-LOK METAL BRIDGING (available for joist spacings of 12", 16", 24")

absolutely no nails used . . . yet stronger!

BRIDGING FLOORS & CEILINGS

POSTS & BEAMS

Fig. 15.15. Methods of Framing: MISCELLANEOUS APPLICATIONS

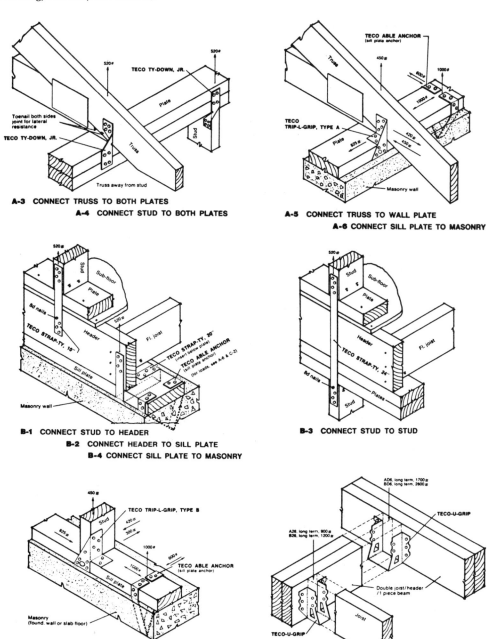

Fig. 15.16. Methods of Framing: WALL FRAM-ING ANCHORS

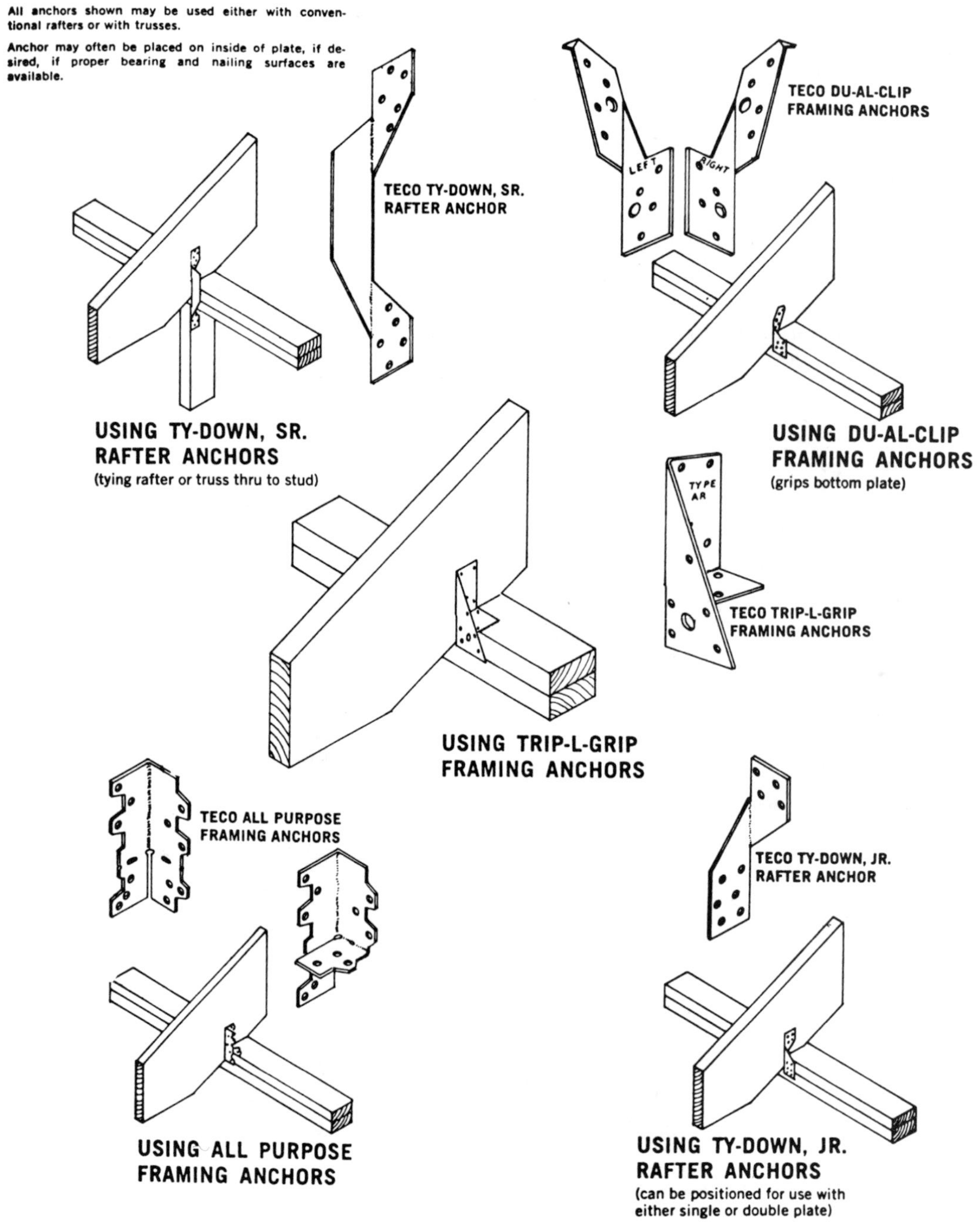

All anchors shown may be used either with conventional rafters or with trusses.

Anchor may often be placed on inside of plate, if desired, if proper bearing and nailing surfaces are available.

TECO TY-DOWN, SR.
RAFTER ANCHOR

TECO DU-AL-CLIP
FRAMING ANCHORS

LEFT   RIGHT

**USING TY-DOWN, SR.
RAFTER ANCHORS**
(tying rafter or truss thru to stud)

**USING DU-AL-CLIP
FRAMING ANCHORS**
(grips bottom plate)

TYPE
AR

TECO TRIP-L-GRIP
FRAMING ANCHORS

**USING TRIP-L-GRIP
FRAMING ANCHORS**

TECO ALL PURPOSE
FRAMING ANCHORS

TECO TY-DOWN, JR.
RAFTER ANCHOR

**USING ALL PURPOSE
FRAMING ANCHORS**

**USING TY-DOWN, JR.
RAFTER ANCHORS**
(can be positioned for use with
either single or double plate)

Fig. 15.17. Methods of Framing: ROOF AN-
CHORAGE

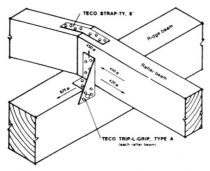

E-1 CONNECT RAFTER BEAMS TO RIDGE BEAM

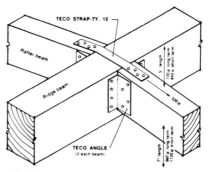

E-2 CONNECT RAFTER BEAM TO RIDGE BEAM

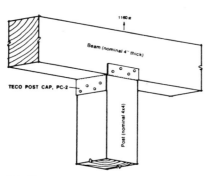

F-1 CONNECT BEAM TO POST

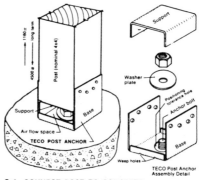

G-1 CONNECT POST TO CONCRETE

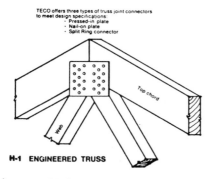

H-1 ENGINEERED TRUSS

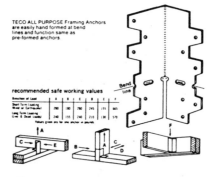

In geographical areas where storm severity is not as great as in hurricane, tornado, and earthquake zones, it may not be essential to use anchorage devices on **all** joints along the length of the building. However, in locations where anchorage devices are used, they should be in-line from top to bottom of the building to provide a continuous tie between roof and foundation.

Fig. 15.18.   Continuous Ties: ROOF TO FOUNDATION

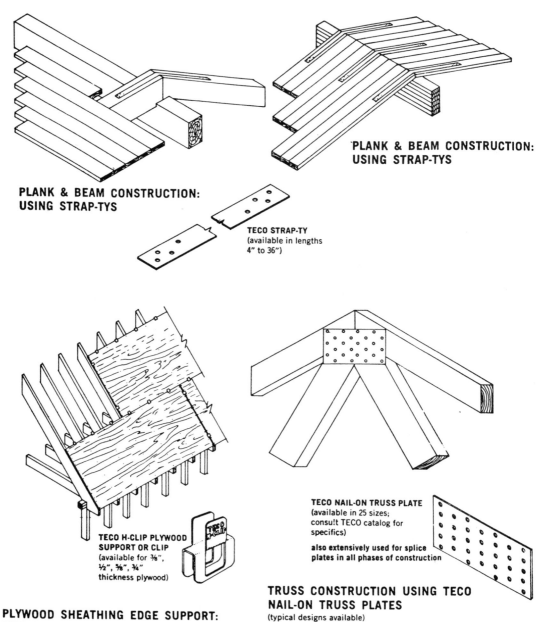

PLANK & BEAM CONSTRUCTION: USING STRAP-TYS

PLANK & BEAM CONSTRUCTION: USING STRAP-TYS

TECO STRAP-TY
(available in lengths
4" to 36")

TECO H-CLIP PLYWOOD SUPPORT OR CLIP
(available for ⅜",
½", ⅝", ¾"
thickness plywood)

PLYWOOD SHEATHING EDGE SUPPORT: USING TECO H-CLIPS TO SAVE WOOD BLOCKING
(also provides automatic end spacing for expansion &
contraction of plywood)

TECO NAIL-ON TRUSS PLATE
(available in 25 sizes;
consult TECO catalog for
specifics)

also extensively used for splice plates in all phases of construction

TRUSS CONSTRUCTION USING TECO NAIL-ON TRUSS PLATES
(typical designs available)

Fig. 15.19. Methods of Framing: ROOF CON-
STRUCTION

TRUSS PLATES (nailed type)

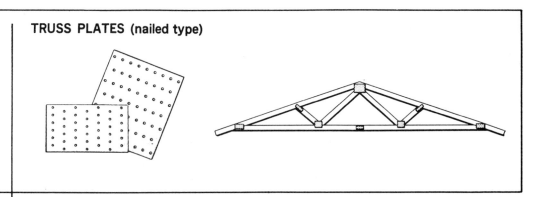

where used

Where single plane assembly of residential and other types of light roof trusses is desired, TECO Truss Plates provide economical clear span construction without the requirement for costly fabricating equipment. No special presses or rollers are needed for the proper assembly of members. In most situations an efficient fabricating line can be set up for less than $300.00.

description

Manufactured from 20 gauge zinc coated sheet steel, TECO Truss Plates are pre-punched to receive 8d 1½″ length nails. The TECO plate system accommodates spans ranging from 16′ to 32′ and slopes of from 3:12 to 7:12. Designed in accordance with HUD

(FHA) Construction Standards, the system is covered by HUD (FHA) Bulletin SE 297.
Complete details on design and fabrication with TECO Truss Plates are available free upon request.

suggested specification

Trusses shall be built using TECO Truss Plates (nailed type), as manufactured by Timber Engineering Company, Washington, D.C. Nails shall be either 1½″ x 0.133″ diameter (square barbed) or 1½″ x 0.131″ diameter (round barbed) and shall be placed in requisite number of nail holes as shown on TECO designs.

shipping information

Packed: in varying quantities, dependent on sizes. Contact nearest TECO distributor (or TECO) for standard packing. Nails are packed in 50# cartons.

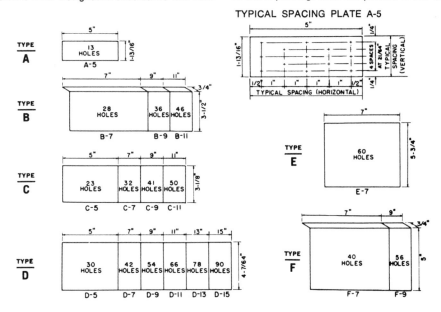

Fig. 15.20. Truss Plates

15.7 CASE STUDY OF A HOUSING DEVELOPMENT

The following case study of Acadia Park Housing Development project is here reproduced through the courtesy of the Forest Industries of B.C.

Acadia Park Housing Development

Over 180,000 sq. ft of 5/8 inch tongue-and-groove fir plywood was used for combined subfloor and underlayment at Acadia Park, a 175-unit row-housing development for married students at the University of British Columbia. The project's architect, Vladimir Plavsic, specified T&G fir plywood flooring throughout Acadia Park for two reasons. "It goes down faster," he said, and "it gives a better surface for the application of the finished flooring."

Speed was important in the construction of Acadia Park for the 25-acre site had to go from wilderness to finished housing in just ten months. The project is the university's first venture into housing specifically designed for married students, which each year make up an increasingly large percentage of UBC's student body.

The two story houses are grouped in a series of nine U-shaped clusters, each enclosing a parking and play area. Kitchen windows face this area so mothers can keep an eye on children playing outside. The living rooms and bedrooms are located at the rear, to provide more peace and privacy.

The development consists of 1- and 2-bedroom suites, with a small number of 3-bedroom units. In addition to the 175-unit housing development, there is a 100-suite highrise apartment building, the first on the university campus.

Fig. 15.21. Tongue-and-groove fir plywood was used for combined subflooring and underlayment throughout Acadia Park. Wall sections were preassembled at the site, then lifted into place.

Fig. 15.22. Roof trusses and gable ends were prefabricated by Fiscus Components of North Vancouver, B.C.

Families with several small children rent the houses, while the apartments are for couples with no children or with babies. The 15-story apartment building has study rooms on the top floor and students who use them are issued special keys. Other specialized features of Acadia Park include an enclosed play area, communal laundry facilities, and a social area as part of the study facilities on the top floor of the highrise.

Timber frame construction was used throughout the housing project, which was built by Laing Construction and Equipment Ltd. Prefabrication was called for wherever possible, in an effort to speed construction.

Fig. 15.23. Use of tilt-up plywood-sheathed wall sections helped speed construction of Acadia Park.

A total of 1600 pre-assembled roof components, including more than 1400 roof trusses, were prefabricated by Fiscus Building Components of North Vancouver. The trusses, each spanning 27 ft, have machine-nailed plywood gussets and 2 × 4 hemlock framing members.

Fig. 15.24. Erected wall unit is held in place with lumber while crew completes nailing.

Fig. 15.25. Two-story townhouse development was University's first venture into housing for married students.

Architect Plavsic called for plywood wall sheathing to speed construction and provide a good base for finish materials. The lower storys were faced with brick, and white stucco was applied on the upper storys.

The living rooms have hardwood flooring; kitchens and bathrooms have vinyl sheet flooring; and other areas have vinyl tiles. All flooring materials were applied directly over the plywood tongue-and-groove subflooring.

Many of the trees were left standing during construction so the development still retains a pleasant wooded atmosphere. Although design and finish materials of the 175 units are identical, the alternating roof slopes and cluster groupings give an impression of design variety.

The $4.5 million project was financed

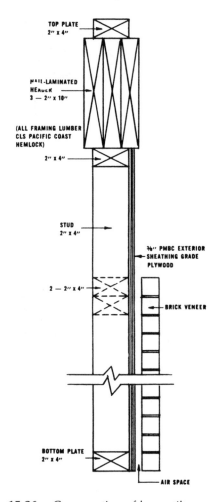

Fig. 15.26. Cross section of lower tilt-up wall.

through Canada Mortgage and Housing Corporation, which provided 50-year mortgages at 6 1/8 percent for student residences on university campuses. The development was planned to be a self-sustaining, self-liquidating operation with rents covering operating costs, principal and interest.

15.8 STEEL FLOOR JOISTS AND STUDS

As an alternative to wood members, steel members may be used. Data sheets for IN-RYCO/MILCOR steel framing are included here as examples of typical members. Sheets on steel floor joists, structural steel studs, standard steel studs, cold rolled channels, drywall steel studs, track and furring channels, accessories, and fasteners are provided. For your file development, obtain sets of technical data sheets with respect to locally supplied steel products for residential construction.

Review

1. Make a neat freehand sketch of what you believe to be the best corner stud framing assembly. Support your view in 200 words or less.

2. List eight advantages of semi-prefabrication of framing walls for housing units.

3. Define wood backing in wood framed walls as provided for subtrades.

4. Which should be used for the best job, traditional nail spiking wood framing or metal structural wood fasteners? Support your view by listing points in order of importance.

Steel floor joists

description

These unpunched "C" sections serve as an alternative to the use of wood joists in single and multi-unit residential construction and light commercial applications. Available in seven sizes. The 7¼" and 9¼" sizes match the depth dimensions of 2x8 and 2x10 wood joists, enabling them to be used in conjunction with wood members when required. Wood subflooring or permanent metal form material for concrete slabs are quickly and firmly attached to Inryco Joists with Milcor Titelock Screws or with air-driven nails.

product data

MATERIAL: 12 ga., 14 ga., 16 ga., 18 ga. — Steel, prime painted with red oxide paint; or Galvanized Steel.

SIZES: 6", 7¼", 8", 8¼", 9¼", 10" and 12".

FLANGES: 1⅝", 2" or 2½" as indicated in table below.

LENGTHS: 7-ft. to 37-ft. in increments of one inch.

TRACK: See page 5 for track sections suitable for end closures.

BRIDGING: See page 25.

physical and structural properties (See pages 22, 23 and 24 for load tables.)

Member (Code*-Size x Ga.)	Dimensions (Inches)			Weight (Lbs. per Ft.)	Cross Sectional Area (Sq. In.)	Allowable Compression Stress (Lbs. per Sq. In.)	About Major Axis (x-x)			About Minor Axis (y-y)			Resistance Moment (In.-Lbs.)
	A	B	E				I (In.⁴)	S (In.³)	r (In.)	I (In.⁴)	r (In.)	D (In.)	
JWE-12 x 12	12	2½	13/16	6.528	1.611	30,000	36.074	6.012	4.400	1.225	0.834	0.556	180,360
JWE-12 x 14	12	2½	¾	4.682	1.156	30,000	26.099	4.350	4.417	0.890	0.839	0.542	130,500
JWE-10 x 12	10	2½	13/16	5.798	1.402	30,000	23.120	4.624	3.739	1.143	0.864	0.619	138,720
JWE-10 x 14	10	2½	¾	4.160	1.007	30,000	16.763	3.353	3.759	0.831	0.869	0.605	100,590
JW-10 x 12	10	2	11/16	5.340	1.277	30,000	20.228	4.046	3.638	0.619	0.659	0.444	121,380
JW-10 x 14	10	2	⅝	3.819	0.913	30,000	14.576	2.915	3.652	0.447	0.661	0.428	87,450
JWE-9¼ x 12	9¼	2½	13/16	5.524	1.323	30,000	19.143	4.139	3.488	1.105	0.876	0.647	124,170
JWE-9¼ x 14	9¼	2½	¾	3.965	0.951	30,000	13.894	3.004	3.507	0.803	0.881	0.633	90,120
JW-9¼ x 12	9¼	2	11/16	5.069	1.198	30,000	16.683	3.607	3.394	0.601	0.670	0.465	108,210
JW-9¼ x 14	9¼	2	⅝	3.625	0.857	30,000	12.033	2.602	3.409	0.434	0.672	0.449	78,060
JWE-8¼ x 12	8 3/16	2½	13/16	5.137	1.212	30,000	14.267	3.485	3.126	1.044	0.893	0.692	104,550
JWE-8¼ x 14	8 3/16	2½	¾	3.688	0.871	30,000	10.374	2.534	3.146	0.760	0.898	0.677	76,020
JWE-8¼ x 16	8 3/16	2½	9/16	2.888	0.679	30,000	8.128	1.922	3.146	0.558	0.867	0.628	57,660
JW-8 x 14	8	2	⅝	3.302	0.764	30,000	8.438	2.109	2.996	0.407	0.692	0.489	63,270
JW-8 x 16	8	2	9/16	2.632	0.608	30,000	6.749	1.687	3.001	0.321	0.687	0.474	50,610
J-8 x 14	8	1⅝	9/16	3.073	0.699	30,000	7.450	1.862	2.920	0.235	0.541	0.362	55,860
J-8 x 16	8	1⅝	9/16	2.476	0.564	30,000	6.042	1.511	2.930	0.194	0.549	0.361	45,330
J-8 x 18	8	1⅝	9/16	1.990	0.453	19,800	4.881	1.220	2.938	0.159	0.555	0.360	24,156
JW-7¼ x 14	7¼	2	⅝	3.108	0.708	30,000	6.642	1.832	2.745	0.388	0.703	0.517	54,960
JW-7¼ x 16	7¼	2	9/16	2.476	0.564	30,000	5.316	1.467	2.751	0.306	0.698	0.502	44,010
JW-7¼ x 18	7¼	2	9/16	1.990	0.453	19,800	4.293	1.184	2.758	0.250	0.704	0.501	23,443
J-7¼ x 14	7¼	1⅝	9/16	2.878	0.643	30,000	5.835	1.610	2.675	0.224	0.553	0.384	48,300
J-7¼ x 16	7¼	1⅝	9/16	2.319	0.519	30,000	4.737	1.307	2.684	0.185	0.560	0.384	39,210
J-7¼ x 18	7¼	1⅝	9/16	1.865	0.417	19,800	3.829	1.056	2.692	0.152	0.566	0.383	20,908
JW-6 x 14	6	2	⅝	2.781	0.614	30,000	4.201	1.400	2.316	0.348	0.723	0.573	42,000
JW-6 x 16	6	2	9/16	2.215	0.489	30,000	3.368	1.123	2.324	0.275	0.718	0.557	33,690
JW-6 x 18	6	2	9/16	1.781	0.393	19,800	2.723	0.908	2.330	0.225	0.724	0.557	17,978
J-6 x 14	6	1⅝	9/16	2.555	0.549	30,000	3.656	1.219	2.258	0.202	0.572	0.429	36,570
J-6 x 16	6	1⅝	9/16	2.059	0.444	30,000	2.972	0.991	2.267	0.167	0.579	0.428	29,730
J-6 x 18	6	1⅝	9/16	1.656	0.358	19,800	2.406	0.802	2.274	0.137	0.585	0.427	15,879

**Unit Code Letters – "JWE" = Joist with 2½" flanges; "JW" = Joist with 2" flanges; "J" = Joist with 1⅝" flanges.*

Structural steel studs

Inryco/Milcor® steel framing

description

Efficient and economical members for use in interior load bearing walls and exterior load bearing or curtain walls with metal lath and plaster or cementitious facings. They also offer savings in interior partition construction — one structural stud, for instance, will serve in place of the two standard or drywall studs normally required on each side of door openings.

product data

MATERIAL: 16 ga. — Steel, prime painted with red oxide paint; or Galvanized Steel. 18 ga. furnished on special order.

SIZES: 2½", 3⅝", 4" and 6".

LENGTHS: 7-ft. to 32-ft. in 1" increments.

TRACK: See page 5.

BRIDGING: See bridging recommendations — pg. 25; cold rolled channels — below.

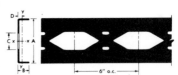

physical and structural properties

Member (Code*-Size x Ga.)	Dimensions (Inches) A	B	C	Weight (Lbs. per Ft.)	Cross Sectional Area (Sq. In.)	Allowable Compression Stress (Lbs. per Sq. In.)	Column Factor (Q)	About Major Axis (x-x) I (In.⁴)	S (In.³)	r (In.)	About Minor Axis (y-y) I (In.⁴)	r (In.)	D (In.)	Resistance Moment (In.-Lbs.)
S-6 x 16	6	1	2½	1.326	0.316	22,670	0.761	1.937	0.646	2.476	0.026	0.289	0.209	14,645
S-6 x 18	6	1	2½	1.061	0.255	15,990	0.715	1.568	0.523	2.482	0.022	0.291	0.204	8,363
S-4 x 16	4	1	1½	1.016	0.256	22,670	0.840	0.715	0.357	1.671	0.024	0.306	0.251	8,093
S-4 x 18	4	1	1½	0.813	0.207	15,990	0.800	0.581	0.290	1.676	0.020	0.308	0.245	4,637
S-3⅝ x 16	3⅝	1	1½	0.989	0.249	22,670	0.840	0.565	0.312	1.508	0.024	0.309	0.257	7,073
S-3⅝ x 18	3⅝	1	1½	0.791	0.201	15,990	0.800	0.460	0.254	1.514	0.019	0.310	0.252	4,061
S-2½ x 16	2½	1	1¼	0.755	0.181	22,670	0.840	0.226	0.181	1.118	0.019	0.323	0.342	4,103
S-2½ x 18	2½	1	1¼	0.604	0.147	15,990	0.800	0.185	0.148	1.123	0.016	0.325	0.336	2,366

*Code Letter "S" = Structural Steel Stud.   Weights listed are for prime painted steel. Galvanized steel weights furnished on request.

NOTES: 1. Studs are formed from steel meeting the following criteria: *Painted Steel* — 16 ga. conforms to ASTM A570-75, except that the steel shall be 50,000 psi — 18 ga. conforms to ASTM A611-72, Grade C; *Galvanized Steel* — 16 ga. conforms to ASTM A446-72, Grade D — 18 ga. conforms to ASTM A446-72, Grade A.
2. Q values listed are to be used when computing axial loads, and are based on the net areas of the sections.
3. All structural properties are computed in accordance with A.I.S.I. "Specification for the Design of Cold Formed Steel Structural Members."

Standard steel studs

description

Used to supplement the structural stud framing system — dimensioned to fit into structural stud track for use in spandrel walls, as jack studs, etc. Can be used in relatively low walls subject to wind load only. Also serve to frame interior partitions with plaster facings.

product data

MATERIAL: 18 ga. — Steel, painted black; or Galvanized Steel. 16 ga. on special order.

SIZES: As listed in table. 1⅝" and 2" also available — see Inryco Metal Lath Products catalog 37-9 for properties.

LENGTHS: 7-ft. to 32-ft. in 1" increments.

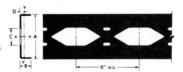

physical and structural properties

Member (Code*-Size x Ga.)	Dimensions (Inches) A	B	C	Weight (Lbs. per Ft.)	Cross Sectional Area (Sq. In.)	About Major Axis (x-x) I (In.⁴)	S (In.³)	r (In.)	About Minor Axis (y-y) I (In.⁴)	r (In.)	D (In.)
N-6 x 18	6	½	4½	0.707	0.111	0.841	0.280	2.758	0.002	0.146	0.122
N-4 x 18	4	½	2½	0.566	0.111	0.344	0.172	1.764	0.002	0.146	0.122
N-3⅝ x 18	3⅝	½	1½	0.589	0.129	0.292	0.161	1.508	0.003	0.140	0.109
N-3¼ x 18	3¼	½	1½	0.527	0.123	0.215	0.132	1.393	0.002	0.146	0.122
N-2½ x 18	2½	½	1¼	0.442	0.099	0.113	0.090	1.069	0.002	0.146	0.134

*Code Letter "N" = Standard Steel Stud.   Weights listed are for painted steel. Galvanized steel weights furnished on request.

NOTES: 1. All 18 ga. members are formed from steel meeting the following criteria: *Painted Steel* — conforms to ASTM A611-72, Grade C; *Galvanized Steel* — conforms to ASTM A446-72, Grade A.
2. All structural properties are computed in accordance with A.I.S.I. "Specification for the Design of Cold-formed Steel Structural Members."

Deflections of 18 ga. Inryco Standard Steel Studs with 100 lb. concentrated load in a 5 ft. span are below the maximum allowable deflections of .20" for 2½" studs, .15" for 3¼" studs and .10" for 4" and wider studs specified in the requirements of the United States Corps of Engineers, General Services Administration and Veterans Administration.

Cold rolled channels

description

These sections serve many uses, including: bridging (lateral support) in walls carrying axial and/or wind loads; stiffeners in standard steel stud partitions; framing around utility boxes; bracing studs at door bucks; and furring for ceilings. They are also used with metal lath and plaster in partitions, ceilings, column and beam fireproofing, etc.

product data

MATERIAL: 16 ga. — Steel, painted black; or Galvanized Steel.

LENGTHS: 16-ft. and 20-ft.

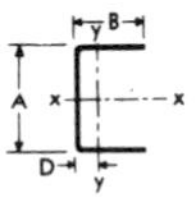

physical and structural properties

Member (Code*-Size x Ga.)	Dimensions (Inches) A	B	Lbs. per M ft.	Cross Sect. Area (Sq. In.)	About Major Axis (x-x) I (In.⁴)	S (In.³)	r (In.)	About Minor Axis (y-y) I (In.⁴)	S (In.³)	r (In.)	D (In.)
CRC-2 x 16	2	¹⁹⁄₃₂	590	0.167	0.095	0.095	0.736	0.005	0.010	0.170	0.140
CRC-1½ x 16	1½	⁹⁄₁₆	475	0.138	0.043	0.057	0.558	0.004	0.010	0.170	0.147
CRC-1¼ x 16	1¼	⁹⁄₁₆	458	0.124	0.028	0.045	0.475	0.004	0.010	0.180	0.160
CRC-¾ x 16	¾	½	300	0.085	0.008	0.021	0.291	0.002	0.006	0.153	0.163

*Code Letters "CRC" = Cold Rolled Channels.   Weights listed are for painted steel. Galvanized steel weights furnished on request.

Drywall steel studs, track and furring channel

description
Roll formed, channel type, non-bearing steel members, with outer flanges knurled to prevent screw "ride" and expedite attachment of gypsum wallboard. Used for hollow partitions, column fireproofing and framing-in drywall ceilings. Flanges are of slightly different depths so that the studs may be turned and nested together to form a close-fitting interlocked splice. Service punchouts facilitate installation of any required bridging, pipe and conduit. Drywall track is dimensioned to receive the stud. Flanges angle inward slightly for a spring hold on the

studs to expedite positioning.

The drywall furring channel is a convenient accessory for use in furred ceilings or for furring out from masonry walls. Its knurled face facilitates screw attachment of wallboard.

product data
MATERIAL: Standard gage or 20 gage Steel.
SIZES: Standard sizes are listed in tables. 2", 3" and 3½" Studs and Track furnished on special order.
LENGTHS: Standard lengths are listed in tables. Special lengths available on request.

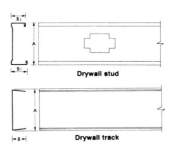

Drywall stud

Drywall track

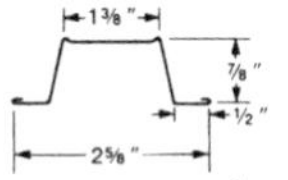

Drywall furring channel

Drywall studs

sizes, weights, lengths and packing

Member (Code*-Size x Gage)	Dimensions (Inches)			Net Weight (Lbs. per Ft.)	Standard Lengths (Feet)	Packing (Pcs. per Bundle)
	A	B_1	B_2			
DW-1⅝ x Std.	1⅝	1²⁵⁄₆₄ nom.	1¹⁹⁄₆₄ nom.	0.350	8, 9 and 10	10
DW-2½ x Std.	2½	1²⁵⁄₆₄ nom.	1¹⁹⁄₆₄ nom.	0.420	8, 9, 10, 12 and 14	10
DW-3⅝ x Std.	3⅝	1²⁵⁄₆₄ nom.	1¹⁹⁄₆₄ nom.	0.504	8, 9, 10, 12, 14 and 16	10
DW-4 x Std.	4	1²⁵⁄₆₄ nom.	1¹⁹⁄₆₄ nom.	0.533	10, 12 and 14	10
DW-6 x Std.	6	1²⁵⁄₆₄ nom.	1¹⁹⁄₆₄ nom.	0.684	10, 12 and 14	10
DW-2½ x 20	2½	1²⁵⁄₆₄ nom.	1¹⁹⁄₆₄ nom.	0.636	10, 12, 14 and 20	10
DW-3⅝ x 20	3⅝	1²⁵⁄₆₄ nom.	1¹⁹⁄₆₄ nom.	0.771	10, 12, 14 and 20	10
DW-4 x 20	4	1²⁵⁄₆₄ nom.	1¹⁹⁄₆₄ nom.	0.816	10, 12, 14 and 20	10
DW-6 x 20	6	1²⁵⁄₆₄ nom.	1¹⁹⁄₆₄ nom.	1.055	10, 12, 14 and 20	10

Drywall stud track

Member (Code*-Size x Gage)	Dimensions (Inches)		Net Weight (Lbs. per Ft.)	Standard Lengths (Feet)	Packing (Pcs. per Bundle)
	A	B			
TDW-1⅝ x Std.	1¹³⁄₁₆	1⅛ nom.	0.255	10	10
TDW-2½ x Std.	2¹¹⁄₁₆	1⅛ nom.	0.316	10	10
TDW-3⅝ x Std.	3¹³⁄₁₆	1⅛ nom.	0.396	10	10
TDW-4 x Std.	4³⁄₁₆	1⅛ nom.	0.422	10	10
TDW-6 x Std.	6³⁄₁₆	1⅛ nom.	0.563	10	10
TDW-2½ x 20	2¹¹⁄₁₆	1⅛ nom.	0.563	10	10
TDW-3⅝ x 20	3¹³⁄₁₆	1⅛ nom.	0.698	10	10
TDW-4 x 20	4³⁄₁₆	1⅛ nom.	0.742	10	10
TDW-6 x 20	6³⁄₁₆	1⅛ nom.	0.982	10	10

Drywall furring channel

Size (Depth)	Net Weight (Lbs. per Ft.)	Standard Length (Feet)	Packing	
			Pieces per Bundle	Feet per Bundle
⅞"	0.297	12	10	120

8 *Unit Code Letters – "DW" = Drywall Stud; "TDW" = Drywall Stud Track.*

Accessories

Inryco Snap-in bridging
Patent Pending

Used for lateral support of studs, affording resistance to both rotation and minor axis bending. Notches at ends engage stud web — no weld or screw attachments required. Can be used with both 3⅝" and 4" studs. (See page 25.) MATERIAL: 18 gage galvanized steel. SIZES: To fit 16" or 24" o.c. stud spacing.

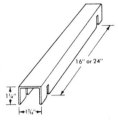

Vertical slide clip (VSC)
Patent Pending

For attachment of curtain wall to the building structure. Permits vertical movement of the structure without transferring vertical loading to the exterior wall. (See installation details on page 33.) MATERIAL: 12 gage galvanized steel.

Channel bearing clip (CBC)

For joist web reinforcement and transfer of axial loads through joists — normally at a center support. MATERIAL: 16 gage red oxide prime painted steel or galvanized steel. WIDTHS: 3⅝", 4", 6" or 8". HEIGHTS: 6", 7¼", 8", 8⅜", 9¼", 10" or 12". Contact Inryco for axial capacity.

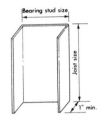

Angle bearing clip (ABC)

For joist web reinforcement and transfer of axial loads through joists — normally at end support. Permits shear connection and load transfer at perpendicular joist intersection. MATERIAL: 14 gage galvanized steel. HEIGHTS: 6", 7¼", 8", 8⅜", 9¼", 10" or 12". Contact Inryco for axial capacity.

Diagonal tension strapping (DTS)

Positioned diagonally for resisting wind and seismic racking loads. May be used for miscellaneous tension loads. Normally, 16 gage is used for joist lateral bridging. MATERIAL: Red oxide prime painted steel or galvanized steel. SIZES and GAGES: 2" — 16 gage; 2", 3" or 4" — 14 gage; 3", 4" or 5" — 12 gage. STANDARD LENGTHS: 12-ft. and 20-ft.

Anchor angle

Provides for anchorage of diagonal tension straps at the building foundation and at intermediate floors. (See installation details on page 31.) Anchor bolt or rod secures the horizontal leg, resisting uplift and horizontal shear forces. MATERIAL: Hot rolled steel, red oxide prime painted.

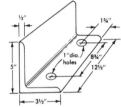

Hat channel sub-girt (HCG)

For attachment of vertical sidings such as metal wall panels. Also used for furring over masonry walls. MATERIAL: 16 gage and 18 gage galvanized steel. STANDARD LENGTH: 10-ft.

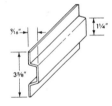

Cold rolled angle (CRA)

For miscellaneous connections and secondary bracing. MATERIAL: 16 gage galvanized steel. STANDARD LENGTH: 20-ft. SIZES: 1¼" x 1¼" is standard size. Other sizes and lengths available on request.

Permapanel® floor and roof form deck
LENGTHS: 6-ft. through 32-ft.

Section properties Per foot of width						Allowable uniform load (PSF) 3 or more equal spans		
Gage	I$_x$ (In.⁴)	S$_x$ (In.³)	F$_y$ (KSI)	F$_b$ (KSI)	Weight (PSF)	Span — c-c of supports (In.)		
						16	24	32
Std.	.0041	.0165	80	48	.75	422	175	78

9

Fasteners

Milcor Titelock screws

Self-drilling, self-tapping. Used for fastening various facing materials to steel framing components — maximum 12 gage.

No. 8-CR Comp-Rated

Attaches metal lath to studs. Projecting head engages cementitious facing to create a composite struct .ral section, increasing bending capacity of assembly. Has #8 shank. Length 1".

No. 6-DG

For drywall or gypsum lath attachment. The 5⁄16" flared head seats firmly without rupturing paper skin. Has #6 shank. Lengths: 1" and 1⅝".

No. 8-ML

Attaches metal lath and accessories, metal panels, etc. The 7⁄16" dia. pan washer head spans lath openings. Has #8 shank. Length ½".

No. 6-PL

For plywood sub-flooring up to ¾" thick. Has 5⁄16" flared head and #6 shank. Length 1⅞".

No. 8-WH

For self-furring metal lath attachment through sheathing. Has ½" dia. flat wafer head and #8 shank. Lengths: ½" and 1¼".

No. 6-FH

For installing interior wood trim. Has 5⁄32" dia. flared head and #6 shank. Length 2¼".

No. 8-FS

Attaches fiber sheathing, rigid insulation, etc. Has 7⁄16" dia. flared head and #8 shank. Length 1¼".

No. 10-HH

Used for steel to steel connections. Has ⅜" dia.' indented hex washer head and #10 shank. Length ¾".

Suggested design loads for screw connections (pounds)

Steel Thickness (Gage)	Screw Size							
	No. 12-14 (D = .177")		No. 10-16 (D = .153")		No. 8-18 (D = .125")		No. 6, S-12 (D = .106")	
	Type of Loading							
	Shear or Bearing	Pullout	Shear or Bearing	Pullout	Shear or Bearing	Pullout	Shear or Bearing	Pullout
12	861	610	N.A.	656	N.A.	536	N.A.	548
14	788	444	636	394	N.A.	388	N.A.	313
16	733	320	621	296	498	277	381	241
18	505	230	474	206	401	196	351	172
20	344	144	334	146	310	118	263	112
22	N.P.	N.P.	N.P.	N.P.	243	79	191	76
25	N.P.	N.P.	N.P.	N.P.	N.P.	42	153	56

N.A. = Not applicable: two steel thicknesses of this gage cannot be connected by this size screw.
N.P. = Not practical: a smaller size screw should be used to connect two thicknesses of this gage.

NOTES: 1. Shear and pullout strengths are based on average test results divided by a safety factor of 2.5.
2. Minimum screw spacing and distance from edge shall not be less than 1½D nor less than $P/.6F_yt$.
3. When connecting materials of different gage, use loads shown for the lighter gage.

Suggested design loads for fillet and flare-bevel groove welds

Steel Gage	Design Thickness (Inches)	Weld Size (Inches)	Allowable Load (Lb./In.) Fillet	Allowable Load (Lb./In.) Flare-bevel Groove
12	.1046	5⁄32	1035	828
14	.0747	⅛	740	592
16	.0598	⅛	592	473
18	.0478	⅛	473	379
20	.0359	⅛	355	284

NOTES: 1. Values listed may be increased by ⅓ for wind or seismic loading.
2. Welds may be positioned so they are subject to either shear or tensile stress.
3. When joining materials of different gage, use loads shown for the lighter gage.
4. Values are based on an allowable stress of 0.3 x yield stress of the material.
5. Flare-bevel groove welds are welds that occur between the outside radius of one member and the flat of an adjacent member.

16

Scaffolding

In this chapter several types of wooden scaffolding and an example of a metal scaffolding are presented. It is important to remember that all wood used in scaffold building shall be new, straight grained, and free from dead knots and that the completed scaffold shall be capable of withstanding four times the weight that may be imposed on it.

Specifications given in the text are typical. Local regulations and design restrictions should be thoroughly researched and adhered to for safety reasons.

Figures 16.1, 16.2, and 16.3 describe half-horse, double-pole, and single-pole wooden scaffolds respectively. All are useful for constructing one-story buildings. Double-pole scaffolds are safer for increased heights. Each has advantages and disadvantages for specific applications.

16.1 HALF-HORSE SCAFFOLD

Persons who can build a splayed and spread sawhorse can build a half-horse scaffold. It is easily constructed, less costly than a dou-

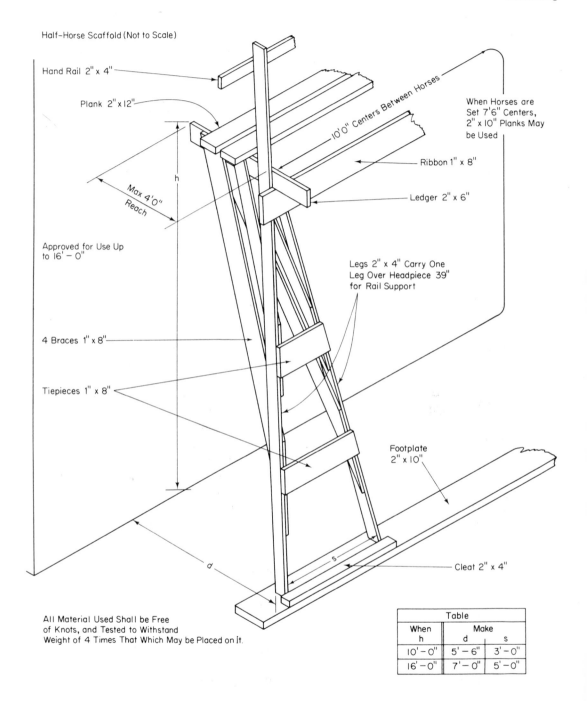

Half-Horse Scaffold (Not to Scale)

Hand Rail 2" x 4"

Plank 2" x 12"

10'0" Centers Between Horses

When Horses are
Set 7'6" Centers,
2" x 10" Planks May
be Used

Ribbon 1" x 8"

h

Max 4'0"
Reach

Ledger 2" x 6"

Approved for Use Up
to 16' – 0"

Legs 2" x 4" Carry One
Leg Over Headpiece 39"
for Rail Support

4 Braces 1" x 8"

Tiepieces 1" x 8"

Footplate
2" x 10"

s

d

Cleat 2" x 4"

All Material Used Shall be Free
of Knots, and Tested to Withstand
Weight of 4 Times That Which May be Placed on İt.

Table		
When h	Make	
	d	s
10' – 0"	5' – 6"	3' – 0"
16' – 0"	7' – 0"	5' – 0"

Fig. 16.1   Half horse scaffold (not to scale).

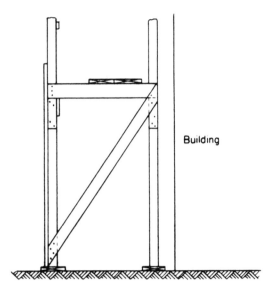

Fig. 16.2 Double pole scaffold.

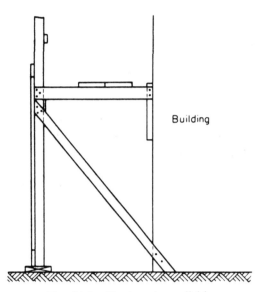

Fig. 16.3 Single pole scaffold.

ble-pole type, easily moved, and easily stored. If it is standing on a footplate, it is relatively safe if built within design limits. (See Fig. 16.1).

Height limits, narrow platform, and weight carrying limits suggest better use by carpenters than by bricklayers.

16.2 DOUBLE-POLE SCAFFOLD

This scaffold, while more costly in terms of labor and materials, can be strong and relatively safe with a wide working platform. It is more difficult to move than the half-horse scaffold but allows better passage of cladding materials along the wall. (See Fig. 16.2.)

16.3 SINGLE-POLE SCAFFOLD

With only one pole to ground, this scaffold may be less safe. One end of the platform beam is carried by a nailed-on strap or scab. Less material is used than for the double-

pole scaffold, so it is therefore cheaper and more easily moved. A wide platform is provided, but load limits must be recognized. Bracing to the building will increase stability. (See Fig. 16.3.)

Local regulations with respect to scaffolding must be known. With such information, the builder can decide which types of wooden scaffolding to use or whether approved metal scaffolding would be better.

16.4 METAL SCAFFOLDING

Metal scaffolding and towers are shown in Figs. 16.4 and 16.5. These examples are reproduced from publications of the Morgen Manufacturing Company and are reproduced with the permission of the copyright holder.

An excellent source of information regarding all types of scaffolding is your local Workers' Compensation Board. As with all other aspects of building construction, better and safer general working conditions are being developed. It must be kept in mind that scaffolding may have to withstand the rigors of frigid temperatures, occasional unexpected gusts of wind, extremes of heat, hail, snow, or torrential rain. The material on pages 195 through 196 has been excerpted from literature supplied by the Morgen Manufacturing Company and is here reproduced with the permission of the copyright holder.

16.5 SCAFFOLD MAINTENANCE

All scaffolds should be regularly and thoroughly checked for signs of deterioration, for broken parts, and for possible unsafe surfaces. Wooden scaffolds, and ladders particularly, need careful inspections. Pigmented finishes, sometimes applied to extend the life of such equipment, make such inspections most difficult.

Review

1. List four standards of quality that all pieces of wood should have for building wooden scaffolds.

2. Describe:

   a. a half horse scaffold

   b. a double pole scaffold

   c. a single pole scaffold.

3. Make a neat freehand sketch of all the different wooden scaffolds and state where they should be used.

4. On what types of residential construction would it be profitable to use metal scaffolding?

5. Assume that you are checking wooden scaffolding members. What five points should you be looking for in signs of deterioration?

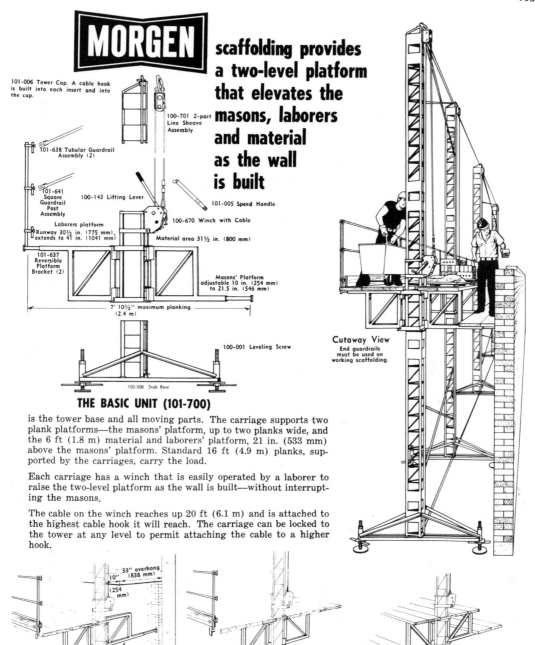

MORGEN scaffolding provides a two-level platform that elevates the masons, laborers and material as the wall is built

101-006 Tower Cap. A cable hook is built into each insert and into the cap.

100-701 2-part Line Sheave Assembly

101-638 Tubular Guardrail Assembly (2)

101-641 Square Guardrail Post Assembly

100-143 Lifting Lever

101-005 Speed Handle

100-670 Winch with Cable

Laborers platform Runway 30½ in. (775 mm), extends to 41 in. (1041 mm)

Material area 31½ in. (800 mm)

101-637 Reversible Platform Bracket (2)

Masons' Platform adjustable 10 in. (254 mm) to 21.5 in. (546 mm)

7' 10½" maximum planking (2.4 m)

100-001 Leveling Screw

100-006 Stub Base

Cutaway View
End guardrails must be used on working scaffolding.

THE BASIC UNIT (101-700)

is the tower base and all moving parts. The carriage supports two plank platforms—the masons' platform, up to two planks wide, and the 6 ft (1.8 m) material and laborers' platform, 21 in. (533 mm) above the masons' platform. Standard 16 ft (4.9 m) planks, supported by the carriages, carry the load.

Each carriage has a winch that is easily operated by a laborer to raise the two-level platform as the wall is built—without interrupting the masons.

The cable on the winch reaches up 20 ft (6.1 m) and is attached to the highest cable hook it will reach. The carriage can be locked to the tower at any level to permit attaching the cable to a higher hook.

33" overhang (838 mm)

10" (254 mm)

CAN BE REMOVED TO CLEAR OVERHANG

Normal Two-Level Planking

Planked Flat for Inside Work or Overhead Obstructions

Three-Level Planking for Stairwells, Elevator Shafts or Special Applica

Fig. 16.4   Metal scaffolding

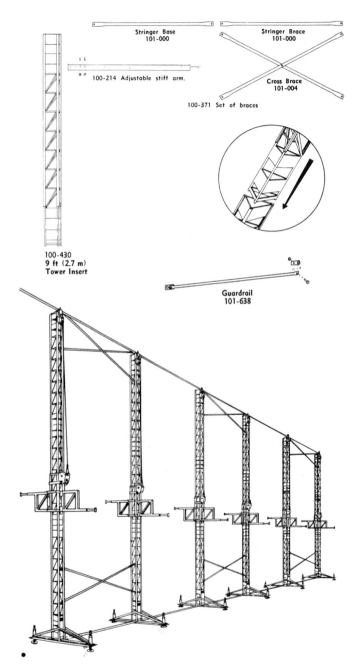

TOWERS

of any desired height are erected using nine-foot sections called inserts. The male end of the insert fits into a female sleeve. You can plug any insert into any base or any other insert. Basic towers, up to 38½ ft (11.7 m), are erected by a fork lift truck. If necessary, additional inserts are added to reach full wall height by one of several methods—a fork lift, a crane, or men with a gin pole.

GUARDRAILS

consist of a 101-000 stringer brace having a 101-682 end connector kit installed at each end. Two tubular guardrails are required between each tower to connect to a 101-641 square guardrail post. Toe board end brackets are available to make toe boards from contractor-supplied lumber.

A PAIR OF TOWERS

makes a free-standing unit. Making a pair requires a stringer brace at the bottom and a stringer and cross brace for every nine feet (2.7 m) of height. These braces automatically space the tower 7½ ft (2.3 m) apart. Pairs of towers are connected by stringer braces to make continuous scaffolding for any desired length of wall.

SAFETY APPROVED
UNITED STATES AND CANADA

Morgen Scaffolding meets the safety requirements for scaffolding as prescribed by the Occupational Safety and Health Administration, Department of Labor, under Section 1910. 28 of Subpart D of the Occupational Safety and Health Standards. Morgen Scaffolding has also been approved by all states and provinces which grant safety approvals.

Fig. 16.5   Towers

17

Post and Beam Construction

In this chapter are presented some typical wood post and beam construction methods which are well adapted for modular residential construction where curtain wall (and roof planking) may be erected between the supporting posts and/or beams. There is nothing new about post and beam construction as may be attested to by much of the existing architecture erected by the Greeks and the Romans.

17.1 POSTS AND BEAMS

Both posts and beams are designed to carry the superimposed loads, and although posts are usually of solid wood, the beams may be fabricated in several different ways to meet either cost, or appearance, or both. The types of beams most used in residential construction are as follows:

1. Solid single pieces of lumber which may be dressed, or faced with finished plywood, or cedar boards, and so on, see Fig. 17.1.

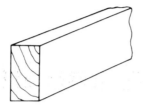

Fig. 17.1. Solid wood beam.

2. Laminated wood beams built up (on the job) with several pieces of lumber that are dry nailed together; such beams are often used as a main beam for underpinning the first floor joists, see Fig. 17.2.

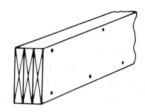

Fig. 17.2. Wood laminated beam.

3. Glue-laminated beams, built up from precision dressed pieces of lumber which are glued together under controlled conditions, and with the exposed faces sanded and stained to meet the aesthetic taste of the owner, see Figs. 17.3 and 17.4.

4. Built up solid plywood beams, see Fig. 17.5.

5. Box beams which are fabricated with select frame members separating the plywood skin finish which may be nailed and/or glued together, see Fig. 17.6.

17.2 CURTAIN WALLS IN POST AND BEAM CONSTRUCTION

Where post and beam modular methods are used in residential construction, the posts are usually placed at 4'-0" OCs between which curtain walls are erected. Such curtain walls may be built from:

1. Standard wood wall framing.

2. Brick or brick veneer.

3. Fiber, metallic, ceramic, or plastic standard 4'-0" × 8'-0" panels.

4. Stucco over other materials.

5. Stone or concrete block.

6. One modular section that may lend itself for the accommodation of the chimney for a solid fuel fire grate.

7. Glass blocks.

8. Glass windows which are designed to complement the total modular design.

Brick and concrete block will lay-up into the exact width of the curtain walls. Modular brick will lay-up to 8" in length requiring six bricks between 4'-0" OC posts, and concrete block will lay-up three blocks of 16" units in the same length.

The construction of the perimeter walls and the roof and roofing will afford more tolerable working conditions for the workmen to erect free-standing interior walls and partitions; additionally, this type of construction permits the future changing of the positions of interior walls and partitions to meet new needs, and without any temporary support for the beams during alteration work.

Article 17.3 and Figs. 17.7 and 17.8 are here reproduced through the courtesy of the Canadian Wood Council. The typical

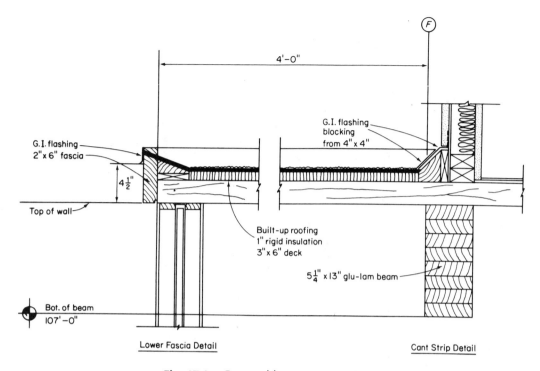

Fig. 17.3. Post and beam construction.

Fig. 17.5. Solid plywood beam.

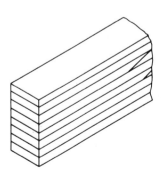

Fig. 17.4. Laminated on flat.

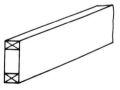

Fig. 17.6. Plywood box beam with wood frame members.

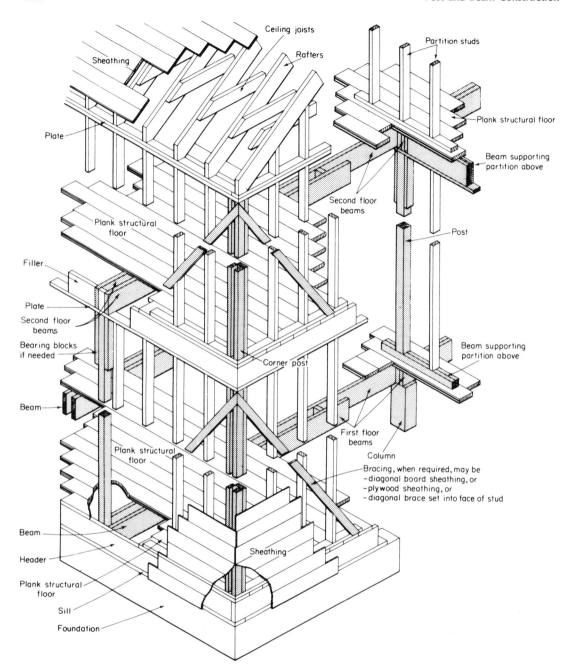

Ceiling joists

Rafters

Sheathing

Plate

Partition studs

Plank structural floor

Beam supporting partition above

Second floor beams

Post

Plank structural floor

Filler

Plate

Second floor beams

Bearing blocks if needed

Corner post

Beam supporting partition above

Beam

First floor beams

Column

Plank structural floor

Bracing, when required, may be
-diagonal board sheathing, or
-plywood sheathing, or
-diagonal brace set into face of stud

Beam

Header

Plank structural floor

Sheathing

Sill

Foundation

Fig. 17.7. Post and beam framing combined with conventional framing in two-story house. (*Courtesy of Canadian Wood Council, Ottawa.*)

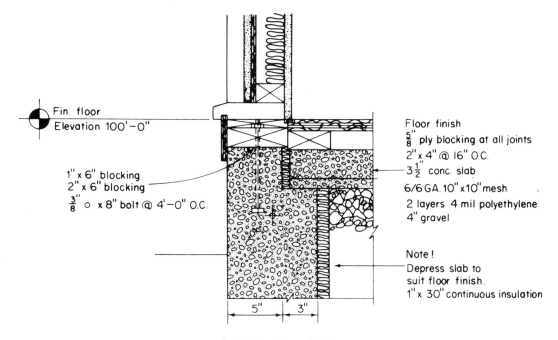

Fin. floor
Elevation 100'-0"

1" x 6" blocking
2" x 6" blocking
$\frac{3}{8}$" ⌀ x 8" bolt @ 4'-0" O.C.

Floor finish
$\frac{5}{8}$" ply blocking at all joints
2" x 4" @ 16" O.C.
$3\frac{1}{2}$" conc. slab
6/6 GA. 10" x10" mesh
2 layers 4 mil polyethylene
4" gravel

Note !
Depress slab to
suit floor finish.
1" x 30" continuous insulation

5"   3"

Fig. 17.8. Base detail.

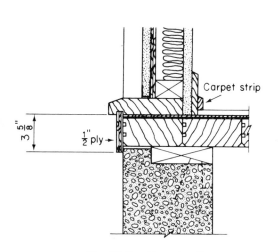

Carpet strip

3 $\frac{5}{8}$"

$\frac{1}{2}$" ply

Fig. 17.9. Base detail.

post and beam details, Fig. 17.3 and Figs. 17.9 through 17.11 (which are used in the construction of a residence) are here reproduced through the courtesy of Mr. Alton M. Bowers, architect, Calgary, Alberta.

Metrification of the construction industry introduces a different set of materials sizes. Standard panels for curtain walls are 1200 mm × 2400 mm rather than 4'-0" × 8'-0". Posts, set to accommodate panels, are at 1200 mm OC, not 4'-0", a difference of more than 19 mm.

So that safety standards and quality levels may be maintained or improved, builders must adjust to metric specifications for materials. Changes in sizes and unit strengths mean different load and span limits for post and beam construction. (See approved metric span tables for wood joists, rafters, and beams.)

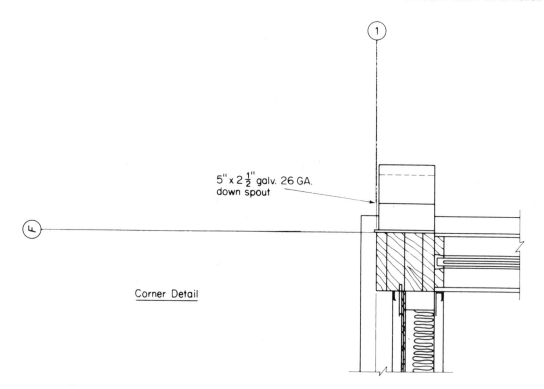

5" x 2½" galv. 26 GA.
down spout

Corner Detail

Fig. 17.10.   Corner detail

17.3 POST AND BEAM: DESCRIPTION AND DESIGN FACTORS

General Description

The post and beam system is essentially a framework made up of decking, beams, and posts supported on a foundation. The floor and roof decks transfer loads to the beams which, in turn, carry them to posts and on down to the foundation.

Post and beam construction dates back to some of the earliest buildings of Greece and shows up in traditional Japanese homes, half-timbered Tudor houses, and early American and English Colonial homes. This construction was followed, in the middle of the 19th century in North America, by the development of conventional frame construction which used more and lighter construction members than post and beam construction; the construction members were concealed in the frame.

Posts and beams are larger and spaced farther apart than studs, joists, and rafters of conventional framing (Figures 17.7 and 17.8). Horizontal spaces between beams are normally spanned by plank decking, but conventional joist construction is sometimes used. Spaces between posts can be filled with wall panels, glass, or supplementary framing and sheathing.

In recent years, trends in architecture have separated the posts and beams from the conventional frame and made them visible as a prominent part of the construction sys-

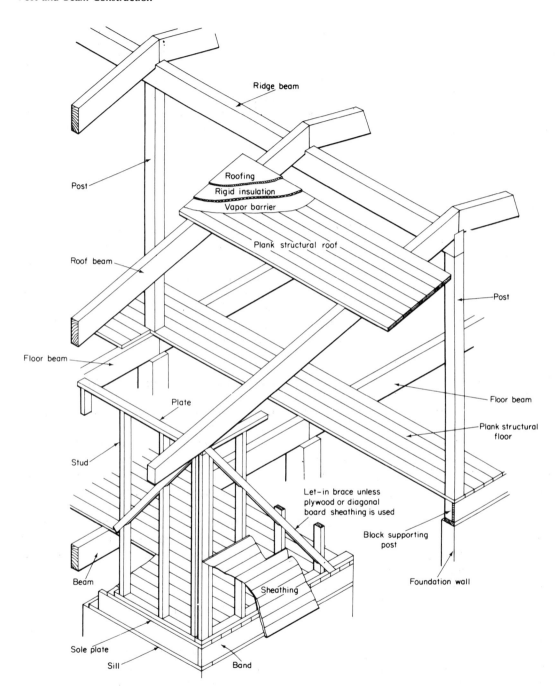

Fig. 17.11. Typical post and beam framing.
(*Courtesy of Canadian Wood Council, Ottawa.*)

tem. This concept is used in many types of buildings. Residential, commercial, industrial, and recreational buildings are some examples where post and beam framing is used, either by itself or in combination with conventional framing. The architectural style of post and beam is both charming and impressive but, like other systems, should be used with discrimination.

Post and beam, though similar in style, should not be confused with heavy timber construction; in building codes, "heavy timber" is classed by itself and calls for specific minimum sizes of beams, columns, and other components.

17.4 ADVANTAGES OF POST AND BEAM

Surface Finishes

Exposed posts, beams, and planks can be stained to preserve natural color, texture, and grain characteristics of the wood. Stain is long lasting and, unlike paint films, does not form a semi-permeable membrane.

Paint retards fluctuations of moisture content in the wood, thus minimizing checking. Colors can be chosen that blend with furniture and the surroundings. Unpigmented varnishes should not be used if exposed to the sunlight. Lack of pigments in the varnish allows ultra-violet rays to penetrate through the varnish to the wood surface. This causes the surface of the wood to deteriorate, leaving unsightly finishes.

Freedom in Planning

Partitions in post and beam construction do not normally carry vertical loads; therefore, their location is not controlled by structural considerations. This allows the designer freedom in layout of interior floor plans. Because posts and beams can be spaced far apart, the building interior is more spacious, allowing furniture and interior decorations to be arranged in many different ways. Posts, beams, and planks may be exposed or closed in. Spaces between posts may be filled with glass, decorative panels, or conventional framing.

Speed of Erection

Well-planned post and beam framing has fewer but larger-sized pieces than conventional framing. This results in simple details, fewer joints and therefore faster erection. The roof soon covers the floor, giving protection for all further work. The remainder of the house can be fabricated in the shop and inserted into the structure.

Reduction in Building Height

In post and beam framing, room height is measured from the floor to the underside of the plank, whereas in conventional construction, it is measured from the floor to the underside of the joist. The difference between thickness of the plank and depth of the joist provides a reduction in total height of the building. This makes possible a saving in sheathing, siding and length of studs, as well as down-spouting, stairs and other services.

Thermal Performance

Because wood is a good insulator, the amount of additional insulation required in walls and roofs is less than for other construction materials; if the climate is not too severe, wood may provide all the insulation necessary.

Review

1. What is the difference between glued laminated and solid wood beams?

2. Describe in 150 words or less:
   a. Traditional modular construction centers.
   b. Metric modular construction centers.
   Include information with respect to tools for measurement.

3. Make neat freehand sketches of:
   a. Solid plywood beam.
   b. Plywood box beam with wood frame members.

18

Ceilings and Flat Roofs

In this chapter we shall discuss various types of ceiling framing, both for flat roofs which support a roof deck and ceiling and for pitch roofs; and methods and materials used in the building of roof decks. This is followed with information about softwood and heavy timber roof decks.

18.1 CEILING FRAMING

In most residential construction a ceiling of gypsum boards or plaster—but not a flat roof deck—can be attached to standard wood ceiling joists placed at 16" OCs. *It is imperative that these OCs be placed accurately to receive a modular sized plaster lath.* Be familiar with your local building code!

Figure 18.1(a) shows two methods of securing the ends of ceiling joists over a load-bearing partition. As an additional precaution, to prevent the ends of the joists from twisting and warping, a 1 × 4 may be nailed on top of the ends of the joists. Remember to place the crown sides of all ceiling rafters uppermost. Figure 18.1(b) shows the outer ends of ceiling joists which

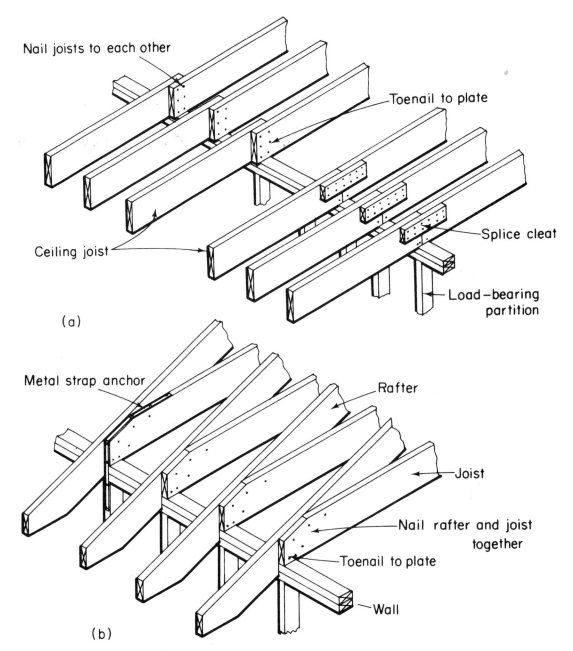

Fig. 18.1. Ceiling joist connections: (a) at center partition with joists lapped or butted, and (b) at outside wall. *(Courtesy of Forest Products Laboratory, U.S. Department of Agriculture.)*

may be secured to the rafters over the wall-plates. This is excellent practice where the rafters and joists are placed with similar OC spacings. It lends stability to the ceiling joists, and gives a truss effect to the roof rafters.

Figures 18.2 and 18.3 show methods of framing ceiling joists to a flush beam, and Fig. 18.4 shows ceiling framing with the joists running in two directions.

Figures 18.5 and 18.6 show three methods of providing good nailing for gypsum and other boards at internal partitions.

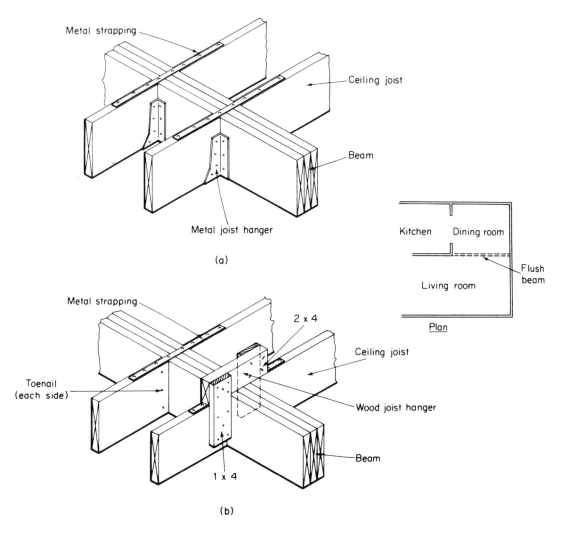

Fig. 18.2. Flush ceiling framing: (a) metal joist hanger, and (b) wood hanger. *(Courtesy of Forest Products Laboratory, U.S. Department of Agriculture.)*

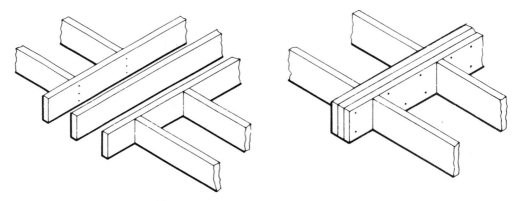

Fig. 18.3. Joists nailed to flush beam.

Note: For metric nomenclature for surfaced softwood lumber products, refer to tables 18.1 to 18.4 at the end of this chapter.

Hanging Beam. Check your local building code for allowable spans (in different species of wood) for the various sizes of lumber, and

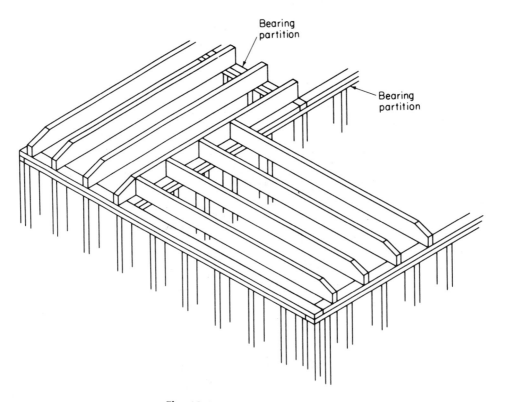

Fig. 18.4. Joists running two ways.

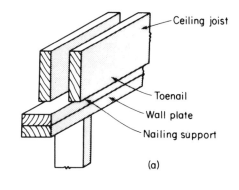

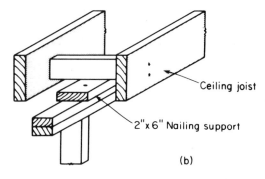

Fig. 18.5. Horizontal nailing support for interior finish.*(Courtesy of the Department of Forestry and Rural Development, Ottawa.)*

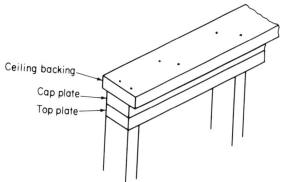

Fig. 18.6. Ceiling backing.

permitted OC spacings for ceiling joists supporting a ceiling; also for joists supporting a roof deck, snow load, and ceiling. For some ceiling framing, stiffeners are mandatory. Bridging or hanging beams may be used.

Step 1: Read Fig. 18.7 with these steps.

Step 2: String a taut mason's line alongside the central ceiling joist (crown side up) and set it true to line.

Step 3: Place a 1 × 4 at right angles to the central joist and temporarily nail it.

Step 4: Starting from the central ceiling joist and working both ways, place and tempo-

rarily nail all the remaining joists *at their exact specified OCs.*

Step 5: If a hanging beam is specified, select a sound piece of lumber of the correct dimensions, and with its crown side up, set it centrally at right angles over the ceiling joists as in Fig. 18.7. Toenail the ceiling joist to the hanging beam and secure it further by nailing 2 × 2 wooden hangers on alternate sides as shown on the drawing. Metal hangers may also be used for this purpose. This method will give rigidity to the whole assembly. The ends of the hanging beam are secured to opposite wall plates.

Step 6: Nail two or three boards closely to the top of the ceiling joists so that workmen may later walk or crawl to make periodic inspections.

Access Hatchway. All ceilings that have a space of 2'-0" or more between the top of the ceiling joists and the bottom of the roof rafters should be provided with an access hatchway. This is usually placed in an inconspicuous part of the residence, sometimes in the ceiling of a large clothes closet, or in a utility room. This is provided so that

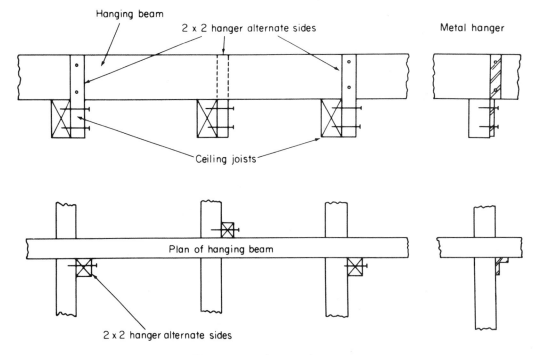

Fig. 18.7. A hanging beam.

an inspection of the chimney, the insulation, ventilation, electric lines, and so on may be made for maintenance purposes. Read your local building code for the minimum size of an access hatchway to be provided; for apartment blocks it would be larger than for single residences. Such a hatchway must be provided with a trap door, and the door must be insulated. There is also a mandatory minimum area to be made for ventilation in all roofs.

Figure 18.8 shows two flat-roof designs where the roof rafters may serve also as ceiling joists, and Fig. 18.9 shows a framing method for a flat roof overhang. Note carefully the centrally drilled ventilation holes for ceiling ventilation. Any holes drilled in any wooden construction member for the accommodation of service lines or ventila-

tion must be drilled centrally in order to cause a minimum of weakening in the member.

18.2 TILED CEILINGS

Furring strips of wood, usually 1 × 2, may be nailed to the underside of wooden ceiling joists to support ceiling tiles. Assuming that the tiles are 12″ × 12″, to line up the furring strips, proceed as follows:

Step 1: Measure the length of each ceiling joist **which is nearest to the opposite walls of the room,** and mark the center.

Step 2: Assume that the width of the furring strip is exactly 2″; on each wall ceiling joist

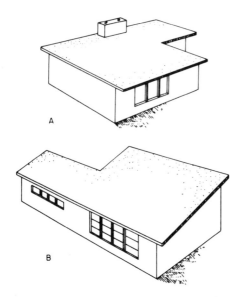

A

B

Fig. 18.8. Two flat-roof designs. Rafters may also serve as ceiling joists. *(Courtesy of the Department of Forestry and Rural Development and the Canada Mortgage and Housing Corporation, Ottawa.)*

center line, lay off 1" and set a nail; but be sure that these are both spotted on the same (say north) side.

Step 3: From nail to nail, strike a chalk line with the mason's line; to this, align and nail the first full length furring strip.

Step 4: Using a 6'-0" straightedge, shim down with a shingle (between the top of the furring strip and the bottom of the ceiling joist) the high spots until the first furring strip is true to line and level on its underside plane.

Step 5: Nail all the other 1 × 2 strips to their exact 12" OCs, and set them true to line and shimmed down to bring the total area into one even plane.

Step 6: Find the exact center of the room, and from this center lay up all the tiles. Note carefully that, by working from the exact center of the room, the perimeter or marginal tiles will be of the same width at opposing walls. Supposing that the room measures 16'-9" × 10'-8", then the tiles on the 16'-9" wall sides would be 4" in width and the 10'-8" wall sides would have 4½" wide tiles, and the ceiling would appear to be symmetrical. *This is important!*

Ceiling Suspension Systems. There is a wide choice of suspended ceiling systems with lighting systems installed above, below, or as inserts in the panels forming the ceiling. This type of installation is used extensively in the vestibules and hallways of apartment buildings.

The suspended "T's" may be finished with baked enamel in a variety of colors, and the panel textures and colors may be selected to match any intended decor. The removable panels lend themselves for easy access to many service lines such as telephone, cable TV, electric, and plumbing. The installation of suspended ceiling systems is a subtrade.

18.3 TONGUE AND GROOVE SOFTWOOD PLYWOOD ROOF DECKS

The material for this section and sections 18.4 and 18.5 has been excerpted from one of the publications of the Plywood Manufacturers of British Columbia and is reproduced with permission. Similar construction for roof decks is used in all states of America, and in all provinces of Canada.

Tongue and Groove Western Softwood Plywood for Roof Decks and Subfloors

Tongue and Groove (T&G) western softwood plywood is a Sheathing or Select Sheathing grade plywood panel with a factory-machined tongue along one of the long edges and a groove along the other. T&G plywood is usually manufactured from a standard 48″×96″ panel blank in thicknesses of 1/2″, 5/8″, and 3/4″, although net 48″ wide panels and other grades, sizes, and thicknesses are available on special order.

Lightweight T&G plywood panels can be easily handled and quickly applied over joists or rafters. In addition to eliminating costly blocking at panel edges, T&G plywood panels save on nails and nailing time. Time studies have shown that a typical floor or roof area can be sheathed with T&G panels in approximately two-thirds the time usually required for square-edge panels and edge blocking—and fewer nails are required.

T&G plywood panels interlock to ensure the effective transmission of loads across panel joints, eliminating differential deflection between panel edges and providing a strong, uniform deck suitable for any finish flooring or roofing material.

For complete installation instructions for T&G plywood see the PMBC publication "Tongue and Groove Plywood."

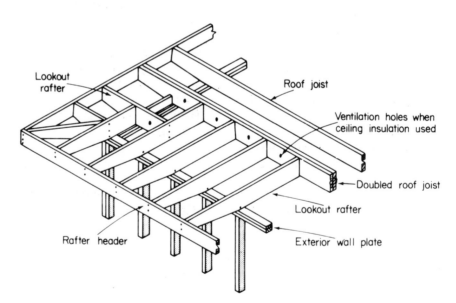

Fig. 18.9. Typical construction of flat roof with overhang. Ventilation holes are drilled in framing members to provide continuous ventilation over ceiling insulation. *(Courtesy of the Department of Forestry and Rural Development and Canada Mortgage and Housing Corporation, Ottawa.)*

18.4 FLOORS

Floors may be constructed of glued laminated or solid sawn plank. When laid flat, the floor planks should be tongue and groove, or splined. When laid on edge, they should be spiked together. Planks are splined together by inserting strips of thinner wood (called splines) into grooves cut into opposing edges of abutting planks to form a continuous joint.

Planks should be laid so that mid-span end joints are staggered; a continuous line of end joints is permissible only over points of support. Floor planks should be covered by one-inch nominal tongue and groove flooring laid crosswise or diagonally, or by half-inch tongue and grooved phenolic-bonded plywood. A half-inch clearance to end walls should be allowed for expansion,

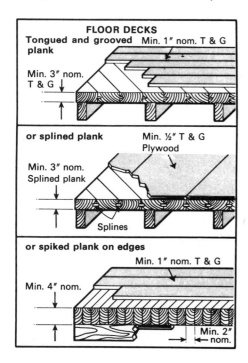

Fig. 18.10. Floor decks

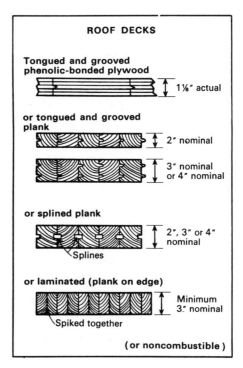

Fig. 18.11. Roof decks

and the gap between flooring and end wall should be fire stopped at top or bottom.

18.5 ROOFS

Heavy timber roof decks may be built of solid sawn or glued laminated material, or tongue and groove phenolic-bonded plywood. Use of plywood as a heavy timber roof deck material is new to the 1970 National Building Code, providing greater flexibility for the designer and builder. Recent fire tests in the United States indicate that 1⅛ inch plywood performs as well under fire exposure as traditional heavy timber roof deck materials. Noncombustible decking may also be substituted for wood material, as provided for in previous editions of the code.

Tongue and groove or splined plank roofs must be at least two inches thick. Laminated decks of planks set on edge, with joints staggered as required for floors, must be at least three inches thick; and if tongue and groove plywood is used for roof decking, it must be at least 1⅛ inches thick.

18.6 METRIC NOMENCLATURE FOR SURFACED SOFTWOOD LUMBER PRODUCTS

See the tables on pages 217–219.

Review

1. Figure 18.1(a) shows two methods of connecting ceiling joists over a load-bearing partition. State which method you prefer and support your view in 100 words or less.

2. Sketch the type of metal fasteners you would select in order to secure the ends of the ceiling joists in question 1 above.

3. Under what circumstances is it advantageous to connect a supporting ceiling beam with flush ceiling joists?

4. What trades will be advantaged by flushing ceiling joists to a supporting ceiling beam? What trades may be disadvantaged by this method?

5. Examine Fig. 18.4, page 210 and give the reason why ceiling joists are sometimes placed to run both ways.

6. Write ceiling backing specifications. See Fig. 18.6, page 211.

7. Make a freehand sketch of a plan, front and side elevation of a hanging beam and define it.

8. Make a freehand sketch of a section of a splined plank as used in roofing.

9. What is the minimum sized access hatchway to ceilings in houses and also in apartment blocks in your area?

10. Sketch the plan of the wood framing for a ceiling access hatchway, and name and draw arrows to the parts.

Metric Nomenclature for Surfaced Softwood Lumber Products

TABLE 18.1.[*]

Rough Lumber

Item	Thickness			Width		
	Nominal inches	Actual Size inches	Metric Nomenclature mm	Nominal inches	Actual Size inches	Metric Nomenclature mm
	1	1	25	2	2	51
	$1\frac{1}{4}$	$1\frac{1}{4}$	32			
	$1\frac{1}{2}$	$1\frac{1}{2}$	38	3	3	76
	$1\frac{5}{8}$	$1\frac{5}{8}$	41	4	4	102
	$1\frac{3}{4}$	$1\frac{3}{4}$	44	5	5	127
	$1\frac{7}{8}$	$1\frac{7}{8}$	48	6	6	152
Rough	2	2	51	7	7	178
Lumber	$2\frac{1}{2}$	$2\frac{1}{2}$	64	8	8	203
	3	3	76	9	9	229
	$3\frac{1}{2}$	$3\frac{1}{2}$	89	10	10	254
	4	4	102	11	11	279
	$4\frac{1}{2}$	$4\frac{1}{2}$	114	12	12	305
	5	5	127	14	14	356
	6	6	152	16	16	406
	7	7	178	18	18	457
	8	8	203	20	20	508
	9	9	229			
	10	10	254			
	11	11	279			
	12	12	305			
	14	14	356			
	16	16	406			
	18	18	457			
	20	20	508			

*Metric Manual for Wood Products (10M78.09, 10M79.03), p. 12.

Metric Nomenclature for Surfaced Softwood Lumber Products

TABLE 18.2.

Studs, Light Framing, Joist and Plank

Item	Thickness				Width			
		Actual				Actual		
	Nominal inches	Dry inches	Green inches	Metric Nomenclature mm	Nominal inches	Dry inches	Green inches	Metric Nomenclature mm
Studs,	2	$1\frac{1}{2}$	$1\frac{9}{16}$	38	2	$1\frac{1}{2}$	$1\frac{9}{16}$	38
Light	$2\frac{1}{2}$	2	$2\frac{1}{16}$	51	3	$2\frac{1}{2}$	$2\frac{9}{16}$	64
Framing,	3	$2\frac{1}{2}$	$2\frac{9}{16}$	64	4	$3\frac{1}{2}$	$3\frac{9}{16}$	89
Joist	$3\frac{1}{2}$	3	$3\frac{1}{16}$	76	5	$4\frac{1}{2}$	$4\frac{5}{8}$	114
and	4	$3\frac{1}{2}$	$3\frac{9}{16}$	89	6	$5\frac{1}{2}$	$5\frac{5}{8}$	140
Plank	$4\frac{1}{2}$	4	$4\frac{1}{16}$	102	7	$6\frac{1}{2}$	$6\frac{5}{8}$	165
					8	$7\frac{1}{4}$	$7\frac{1}{2}$	184
					10	$9\frac{1}{4}$	$9\frac{1}{2}$	235
					12	$11\frac{1}{4}$	$11\frac{1}{2}$	286
					14	$13\frac{1}{4}$	$13\frac{1}{2}$	337
					16	$15\frac{1}{4}$	$15\frac{1}{2}$	387

Note: Shiplap and center match will use the same nomenclature as the S4S boards above, regardless of the length of the lap or tongue.

Metric Handbook for Canadian Softwood Lumber (First Edition, November, 1977) p. 7. Compiled by Metric Sub-Sector Committee 8.21—Softwood Lumber for Metric Commission of Canada.

TABLE 18.3

Boards, Shiplap and Center Match

Item	Thickness				Width			
		Actual				Actual		
	Nominal inches	Dry inches	Green inches	Metric Nomenclature mm	Nominal inches	Dry inches	Green inches	Metric Nomenclature mm
Boards,	1	$\frac{11}{16}$	$\frac{3}{4}$	17	2	$1\frac{1}{2}$	$1\frac{9}{16}$	38
Shiplap	1	$\frac{3}{4}$	$\frac{25}{32}$	19	3	$2\frac{1}{2}$	$2\frac{9}{16}$	64
and	$1\frac{1}{4}$	1	$1\frac{1}{32}$	25	4	$3\frac{1}{2}$	$3\frac{9}{16}$	89
Center	$1\frac{1}{2}$	$1\frac{1}{4}$	$1\frac{9}{32}$	32	5	$4\frac{1}{2}$	$4\frac{5}{8}$	114
Match					6	$5\frac{1}{2}$	$5\frac{5}{8}$	140
					7	$6\frac{1}{2}$	$6\frac{5}{8}$	165
					8	$7\frac{1}{4}$	$7\frac{1}{2}$	184
					9	$8\frac{1}{4}$	$8\frac{1}{2}$	210
					10	$9\frac{1}{4}$	$9\frac{1}{2}$	235
					11	$10\frac{1}{4}$	$10\frac{1}{2}$	260
					12	$11\frac{1}{4}$	$11\frac{1}{2}$	286
					14	$13\frac{1}{4}$	$13\frac{1}{2}$	337
					16	$15\frac{1}{4}$	$15\frac{1}{2}$	387

Note: Shiplap and center match will use the same nomenclature as the S4S boards above, regardless of the length of the lap or tongue.

Metric Handbook for Canadian Softwood Lumber (First Edition, November, 1977) p. 7. Compiled by Metric Sub-Sector Committee 8.21—Softwood Lumber for Metric Commission of Canada.

Metric Nomenclature for Surfaced Softwood Lumber Products

TABLE 18.4.

Lengths

Nominal Length feet	Metric Length meters
3	0.91
4	1.22
5	1.52
6	1.83
7	2.13
8	2.44
9	2.74
10	3.05
11	3.35
12	3.66
13	3.96
14	4.27
15	4.57
16	4.88
17	5.18
18	5.49
19	5.79
20	6.10
21	6.40
22	6.71
23	7.01
24	7.32
26	7.92
28	8.53
30	9.14
32	9.75
34	10.36
36	10.97
38	11.58
40	12.19
42	12.80
44	13.41
46	14.02
48	14.63
50	15.24

Metric Handbook for Canadian Softwood Lumber (First Edition, November, 1977) p.12.

19

Pitch Roofs

In this chapter we shall discuss in depth how to cut (on the ground) wood framing members for a regular hip roof: common rafters, hip rafters, and jack rafters. That information is then related to construction truss shapes and truss systems, without examination of technical design aspects. The chapter concludes with an introduction to metric framing square settings.

19.1 TYPES OF ROOFS

Flat Roof

This is a roof in which heavy ceiling joists are used as rafters. It has a minimum slope for drainage. It must be well supported at the walls. It must be heavily waterproofed.

Shed or Lean-to Roof

This is a roof which has one sloped surface only. The slope is across the width of the

221

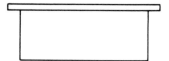

Fig. 19.1. Flat roof.

building. The horizontal distance over which the slope passes is the RUN. The lean-to roof is so named because it leans against another building or wall. It saves the expense of building one wall. It is the simplest roof that a carpenter may have to build.

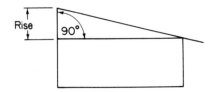

Fig. 19.2. Lean-to or shed roof.

Gable Roof

This is a roof which has two sloped surfaces meeting at the RIDGE. For a regular roof, the horizontal distance from the foot of one rafter to the foot of the opposite rafter is called the SPAN. Half the span over which each rafter passes is the RUN. This roof is like two lean-to roofs placed together.

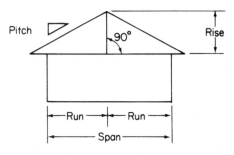

Fig. 19.3. Gable roof.

Hip Roof

This is a roof which has a sloped surface from each wall towards the RIDGE. The rafters that fit against the ridge are called COMMON RAFTERS (afterwards in the text they are named CRs). The main part of the roof whose members are CRs is like two lean-to roofs placed together.

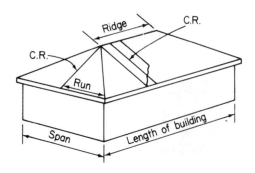

Fig. 19.4. Hip roof.

Gambrel or Barn Roof

This is a gable-type roof which has more than one slope on one face. It is used extensively by farmers. The upper portion is like two lean-to roofs placed together. The lower slopes are like lean-to roofs.

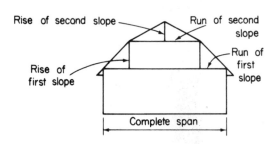

Fig. 19.5. Gambrel or barn roof.

Saw-tooth Roof

This is a series of roofs which, when viewed from the ends, resembles the angles of saw teeth. It is a factory type of roof. It allows for the placing of glass on one slope to light the floor area below. Each pair of slopes resembles two lean-to roofs of different runs and slopes but of the same height.

A plumb line is a vertical line. A run line is a horizontal line. The angle between a plumb line and a run line is 90°.

Roof framing principles are based on right-angle triangulation.

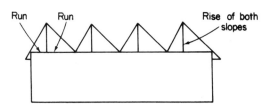

Fig. 19.6. Saw-tooth roof.

19.2 DEFINITIONS OF ROOF TERMS

Starting at the top of Fig. 19.7, the definitions are as follows:

Ridge board: The uppermost member of a roof against which the CRs (common rafters) fit. The rafters are shortened half the thickness to allow for it.

Back of the rafter: The top side of a rafter to which the roof sheathing is nailed. *The crown side of all placed uppermost.*

Center line ℄: The hypotenuse of a right triangle having the run of a rafter for its base; and the rise of the roof for its height.

Rise: The perpendicular distance from the top of the wall plate to its intersection with the center line.

Seat of birdsmouth: The horizontal and plumb cuts of a rafter at its nailing point to the cap plate.

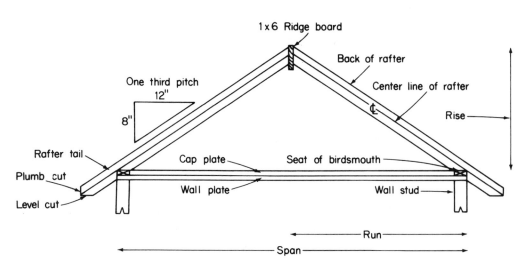

Fig. 19.7. The elevation of a one-third pitch roof using 2 × 4's for rafters.

Wall stud   The perpendicular framing stud supporting the plates and rafters.

Run (for a regular roof):   The run is half the span.

Span (for a regular roof):   The shortest horizontal distance between opposite outside walls.

Wall plate: The first plate of the wall framing over which is nailed the cap plate.

Cap plate: The top plate which is nailed to the framing plate.

Rafter tail: That part of the rafter that extends beyond the wall plates.

Plumb and level cuts: The design of the rafter tail to receive a fascia board and a soffit.

Pitch: The slope of a roof. For a regular roof, it is the relationship of the rise of a roof to the span. A quarter pitch roof has a rise equal to one-quarter of its span, and a one-third pitch roof has a rise equal to one-third of its span, and so on. It is usually shown on the drawing of a roof by a right-angle triangle (◥) with the rise shown in inches and the run of the rafter shown in inches. These figures are used by the carpenter to lay out rafters with a framing square. See Fig. 19.7.

The line length of a common rafter is measured on the center line, and extends from No. 1 plumb cut line to its intersection with lines 2 and 3 at the birdsmouth as shown at Fig. 19.13, page 227.

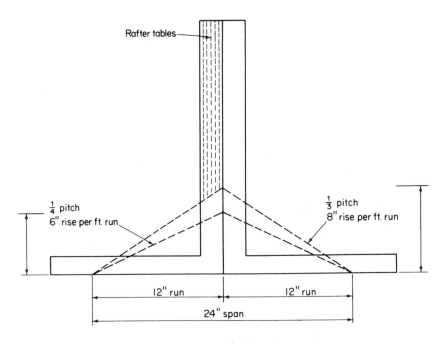

Fig. 19.8.   Two framing squares back to back.

23	22	21	20	19	18	17	16	15	14	13	12
LENGTH COMMON RAFTERS PER FOOT RUN					21 63	20 81	20 00	19 21	18 44	17 69	16 97
LENGTH HIP OR VALLEY PER FOOT RUN					24 74	24 02	23 32	22 65	22 00	21 38	20 78
DIFF. IN LENGTH OF JACKS 16 INCHES CENTERS					28 84	27 74	26 66	25 61	24 585	23 588	22 625
DIFF. IN LENGTH OF JACKS 2 FEET CENTERS					43 27	41 62	40	38 42	36 08	35 38	33 94
SIDE CUT OF JACKS USE					6 $\frac{11}{16}$	6 $\frac{15}{16}$	7 $\frac{3}{16}$	7 $\frac{1}{2}$	7 $\frac{13}{16}$	8 $\frac{1}{8}$	8 $\frac{1}{2}$
SIDE CUT HIP OR VALLEY USE					8 $\frac{1}{4}$	8 $\frac{1}{2}$	8 $\frac{3}{4}$	9 $\frac{1}{16}$	9 $\frac{3}{8}$	9 $\frac{5}{8}$	9 $\frac{7}{8}$
22	21	20	19	18	17	16	15	14	13	12	11	10

11	10	9	8	7	6	5	4	3	2	1
16 28	15 62	15 00	14 42	13 89	13 42	13 00	12 65	12 37	12 16	
20 22	19 70	19 21	18 76	18 36	18 00	17 69	17 44	17 23	17 09	
21 704	20 83	20	19 23	18 52	17 875	17 33	16 87	16 49	16 22	
32 56	31 24	30	28 84	27 78	26 83	26	25 30	24 74	24 33	
8 $\frac{7}{8}$	9 $\frac{1}{4}$	9 $\frac{5}{8}$	10	10 $\frac{3}{8}$	10 $\frac{3}{4}$	11 $\frac{1}{16}$	11 $\frac{3}{8}$	11 $\frac{5}{8}$	11 $\frac{13}{16}$	
10 $\frac{1}{8}$	10 $\frac{3}{8}$	10 $\frac{5}{8}$	10 $\frac{7}{8}$	11 $\frac{1}{16}$	11 $\frac{5}{16}$	11 $\frac{1}{2}$	11 $\frac{11}{16}$	11 $\frac{13}{16}$	11 $\frac{15}{16}$	
10	9	8	7	6	5	4	3	2	1	

Fig. 19.9.

19.3 THE CARPENTER'S TRADITIONAL FRAMING SQUARE

1. The body of the square is two inches wide and twenty-four inches long.

2. The tongue is one and a half inches wide and sixteen inches long.

3. The tool has two rectangular sides that meet at a right angle. It usually has the name of the manufacturer and the rafter tables on the face side.

4. The square has eight edges with different fractions of inches shown on each.

Figure 19.8 shows two traditional squares back to back with a quarter and one-third pitch outlined. To find the slope length of a CR per foot run, of a one-third pitch roof (8″ rise to 12″ run) as shown in Fig. 19.8, measure diagonally across the square from the 12″ mark to the 8″ mark. It measures, say, 14⅜″, or 14.42″. Don't accept this. Try it! Now try it for a one-quarter pitch roof.

Rafter Tables

Figure 19.9 shows in broken form a traditional square for the easy reading of the rafter tables during the study of the text.

First line Length of a common rafter per foot run.

Second line Length of hip or valley per foot run.

Third line   Difference in length of jack rafter 16″ centers.

Fourth line   Differences in length of jacks at 24″ centers.

Fifth line   Side cut of jacks use.

Sixth line   Side cut of hip or valley use.

Under the 8″ mark of the rafter tables at Fig. 19.9 read 14.42; this is the ready reckoned hypotenuse (the length of the slope of the rafter per foot run) of a right angle with a base of 12″, a rise of 8″, and a hypotenuse of 14.42. See Fig. 19.7 where a right angle with a one-third pitch is shown above the left hand CR.

Now measure from the 12″ mark to the 6″ mark on the framing square and compare your reading of the tape with the reading under the 6″ mark of the square.

Once the rise of a roof per foot run has been established (e.g., 8″), all the framing square information for that particular roof will be found under that same figure, in this case 8″. Under 8″ read length of common rafter per foot run 14.42; also under 8″ read length of hip rafter per foot run 18.76 and so on.

19.4 LAYOUT OF A COMMON RAFTER FOR A ONE-THIRD PITCH ROOF

Fig. 19.10 shows a framing square with the stair gauges set for the layout of the CR for a ⅓ pitch roof. The square is shown in position for the marking of the plumb cut. Stair gauges may be purchased in the tool section of most hardware stores, and they are almost indispensable in rafter framing with the square.

It is important to see that all the (numbered) layout lines of the small figures in this section correspond with those shown on the complete rafter layout in Fig. 19.13.

Specifications

1. Assume that a ⅓ pitch regular gable roof with a 1 × 6 ridge is to be erected on a building with a span of 36′-0″. The overhang is 16 inches.

2. Select a straight clean piece of 2 × 4 of suitable length. Examine the stock for the crown side by holding it with the wide face flat in the palm of the hand and sighting along the narrow face.

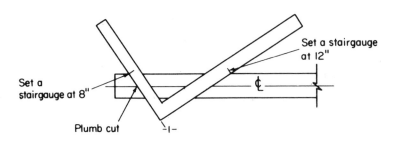

Fig. 19.10.   Stair gauges set for one-third pitch.

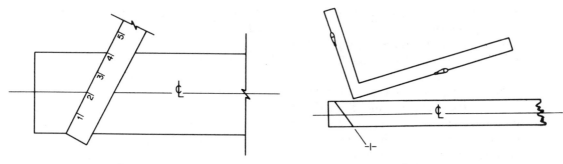

Fig. 19.11.   **Fig. 19.12.**

Place the stock on the sawhorses with the crown side away from you.

3. Draw a ₵ on the wide face of the 2 × 4.

    To find the center of a piece of 2 × 4, place a tape square across the 3½" face of the stock. Traverse the tape until the

4" mark may be read on the top edge of the stock. Spot the center. Set an adjustable square to the center spot and draw in a center line the full length of the 2 × 4. See Fig. 19.11. When the CR is raised into place, the ₵ is the LL (line length) of the CR.

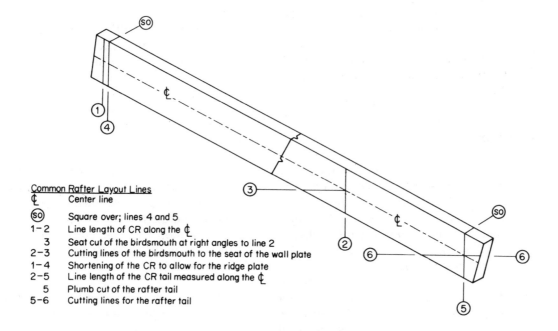

Common Rafter Layout Lines
₵   Center line

(SO)   Square over; lines 4 and 5
1-2   Line length of CR along the ₵
  3   Seat cut of the birdsmouth at right angles to line 2
2-3   Cutting lines of the birdsmouth to the seat of the wall plate
1-4   Shortening of the CR to allow for the ridge plate
2-5   Line length of the CR tail measured along the ₵
  5   Plumb cut of the rafter tail
5-6   Cutting lines for the rafter tail

Fig. 19.13.   Layout for a common rafter.

The horizontal distance over which it passes is the run.

The height that it is raised over the plate is the rise. See Fig. 19.7, page 223.

4. Set the stair gauges for a ⅓ pitch roof by attaching one gauge to the 8″ mark on the tongue of the square and the other to the 12″ mark on the body of the square. Be sure that both gauges are placed on the outside edges of the square.

5. The imaginary hypotenuse of the right-angle triangle is between the stair gauges.

Plumb Cut

1. Place the square with the plumb cut to the left and the stair gauges snug to the back of the rafter stock as in Fig. 19.10.

2. Draw in the plumb cut as in Fig. 19.12. Study the complete CR layout in Fig. 19.13.

Line Length

1. A little to the right of the plumb cut and actually on the CR, work out mathematically the LL of the CR. Multiply 14.42 (as read on the rafter tables) by the actual number of feet of run in the CR; that is 14.42 × 18 = 21′-7⅝″. The run is 18′-0″ and the total span is 36′-0″.

2. With a steel tape, measure on the center line of the rafter stock 21′-7⅝″ and draw the plumb cut line No. 2 as shown at Fig. 19.13.

Checking the LL of the CR by the Step Off Method

1. An excellent additional checking method, and one that should always be used by carpenters is the step off method. Place the stair gauges for the pitch of the roof. Set the framing square at Line 1 as in Fig. 19.10.

   Mark a short line on the run of the square to intersect with the top edge of the rafter stock.

   Slip the square along the rafter stock until the 8″ plumb marking line intersects with the run line already drawn.

   Repeat this operation until the number of steps taken is the number of feet of run in the CR.

   The last application at the run end of the framing square should reach to within ⅜″ of the LL as determined from the rafter tables.

   When the step off method checks to such a tolerance, accept the LL as reckoned from the rafter tables on the framing square and as measured by the tape.

   The carpenter should use the step off method for checking only—not for the original layout.

2. When using the traditional framing square, the run is always 12″. The number of steps to be taken would therefore always be the number of times that 12″ (or one foot) is contained in the run of the CR—in this case 18 times for a run of 18 feet.

3. With the plumb cut of the framing square to the left, draw in another plumb cut at the 21′-7⅝″ mark as in Fig. 19.14. Also see Fig. 19.13, line 2.

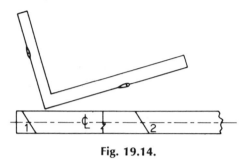

Fig. 19.14.

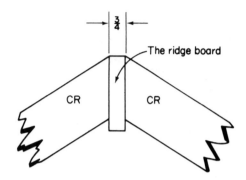

Fig. 19.16.   Shortening of CR at ridge board.

The Birdsmouth

1. Slip the framing square to the left until the level cut may be drawn to intersect with No. 2 plumb line at the ℄ as in Fig. 19.15.

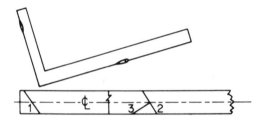

Fig. 19.15.

2. The meeting of Lines 2 and 3 at the ℄ lays out the birdsmouth. Lines 2 and 3 should be squared under the bottom edge of the rafter. After the birdsmouth has been removed, the level and plumb cuts fit to the wall plate.

Shortening of the CR

1. Referring to the specifications, you will see that the ridge board sawn size is 1 × 6. The actual size of this member would be ¾ × 5½". See Fig. 19.16.

2. It is possible to erect the roof without using a ridge board, but a ridge board simplifies the actual erection of a roof. An economy in labor time is effected, apart from any other reason.

3. It will be seen at Fig. 19.16 that the introduction of a ridge board necessitates the shortening of the CRs. The amount of shortening necessary on each CR is half the thickness of the ridge board, *measured at right angles to the plumb cut.*

4. The shortening is measured at right angles (that is on the run) to the plumb Line 1.

5. Place the framing square with the plumb marking line to the left on Line 1. Slip the square so that it is ⅜" back at right angles to Line 1 as in Fig. 19.17. The tape may be seen placed in the position of checking the shortening. Draw in Line 4 as in Fig. 19.17. See also Fig. 19.13, Line 4.

6. Square over Line 4 to the back of the rafter. This is the cutting line.

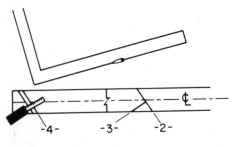

Fig. 19.17.

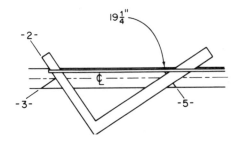

Fig. 19.18.

Tail LL of a CR

The tail length is reckoned in a manner similar to the LL of the CR.

1. Referring to the specifications on page 226 you will recall that the overhang is 16″ and that the pitch is ⅓.

2. On the CR, just to the right of Line 2, make the calculations for the line length of the tail for the overhang.

3. Reading on the framing square for a ⅓ pitch roof, we see that the rise per foot of run is 8″. On the first line of the rafter tables read 14.42 under 8″.

4. To find the LL of the tail of the CR, multiply the length of the rafter per foot run, 14.42, by the actual number of feet of run in the tail of the CR, which is 16″, or one and one-third feet of run.

5. 14.42″ × 1⅓″ = 19¼″, the LL of the tail. The tape may be seen in the position for checking the LL of the tail as in Fig. 19.18. Draw in Line 5.

Checking the LL of the Tail by the Step Off Method

With the plumb marking side of the framing square to the left and placed on Line 2, measure 1′-0″ on the run. Slip the square to

the right and measure a further 4″ as in Fig. 19.19. The 12″ and the 4″ together equal 16″, the given overhang *measured on the run*.

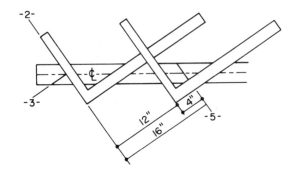

Fig. 19.19.

It will be seen that the procedure for the layout of the LL of the tail of a CR from Line 2 is exactly the same as for the layout of the LL for the CR.

Plumb Cut of the Tail of CR

1. When the rafter stock is of just sufficient length for the CR, it is necessary to turn the square over to draw Line 5. The square should be turned over so that the heel is away from the carpenter. The

plumb side of the square should be to the right, and the stair gauges should fit snug against the bottom of the rafter stock.

2. Figure 19.20 shows the measured LL of the tail of the rafter as calculated from the rafter tables, and as checked by stepping off with the framing square from Line 2 to Line 5.

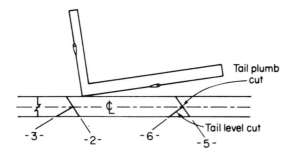

Fig. 19.20.

Level Cut of the Tail of the CR

1. Where a plumb and level cut is to be made at the end of a CR, place the square with the plumb side to the left. Adjust the position of the square until it will intersect with Line 5 at the ₵ .

2. The complete CR rafter layout with the Line numbering as in this chapter is shown in Fig. 19.13, page 227.

Actual Sawing Lines of the CR

The actual cutting lines are on:

Line 4 for the shortened plumb cut.
Line 3 and lower part of Line 2 for the birdsmouth.
Lines 5 and 6 for the plumb and level tailcut.

19.5 A REGULAR HIP ROOF

Assume that a regular hip roof with a 1 × 8 ridgeboard has a 24'-0" span, a length of 36'-0", and an overhang of 16" at the eaves, and a one-third pitch. Some simple facts can be deduced:

1. All slopes of the roof have the same pitch.

2. The rise of the CRs is the same as the rise of the HRs (hip rafters).

3. The runs of the six CRs shown in Fig. 19.21 are all equal. Two CRs are shown on each long wall, and one CR is shown on each short wall.

4. The run of the HR is equal to the diagonal of a square whose sides are equal to the run of a CR. Reread this!

5. Assume that a skeleton plan for a doll house is drawn with a span of 2'-0". The run of any CR would be equal in length to the side of a 12" square, and the run of the HR would be the *diagonal* of a square with 12" sides. Measure across one side of a framing square from the 12" marks on the outside edges (or you could lay it out across the desk at which you are sitting). It measures 17". Try it!.

6. For the layout of a CR with a one-third pitch, we set the stair gauges at 8" and 12"; see Fig. 19.10, page 226. For a HR for the same roof pitch, we set the gauges at 8" and 17". See Fig. 19.22.

7. To find the length of a CR per foot run for this roof, we read on the first line of the rafter tables under the 8" mark, 14.42 as at Fig. 19.9, page 225.

8. To find the length of the hip or valley per foot run of the CR, we also read

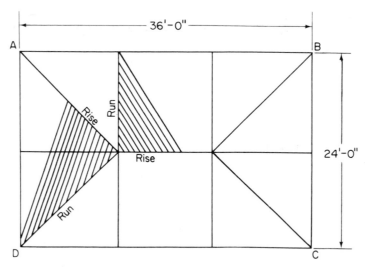

Fig. 19.21. Shows the runs of six CRs, four HRs, and the slopes of the CR and HR projected to a plane surface.

under the 8″ mark **on the second line of the rafter tables, 18.76.** Thus, for this roof, the right angle for the CR has a rise of 8″, a run of 12″, and a framing square rafter table reading of 14.42. In a similar manner the HR has a rise of 8″, and a run of 17″, and a framing square rafter table reading of 18.76.

9. Figure 19.21 shows the slope of a CR and HR projected to a flat plane. The rise in each case is equal to one-third of the span of the roof (one-third pitch). For

a bit of fun, make a tracing of this drawing, cut on the slopes and rise lines of the shaded portion, and fold the triangles up on their base lines (runs). Examine your work!

19.6 LAYOUT OF THE HIP RAFTER

1. Figure 19.22 shows a framing square on a piece of HR stock with its gauges set at 8″ rise and 17″ run.

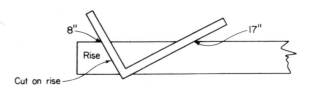

Fig. 19.22. Shows the square set for the layout of a HR having a one-third pitch.

2. Since the pitch of the roof is one-third and the run of the roof is 12'-0", read on the framing square rafter tables under the 8" mark and find 18.76. Multiply this figure by the number of feet of run of the CR which is twelve. Thus 18.76 × 12 = 18'-9⅛", which is the line length of the HR. Measure 18'-9⅛" on the back of the rafter and draw in the plumb lines shown at Fig. 19.23.

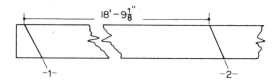

Fig. 19.23. Shows the line length of the CR.

It should be noted that, throughout this section, all positions of the framing square are in exactly the same relative positions as those for the larger drawings of the hip rafter layout shown on page 240, Fig. 19.43.

19.7 HIP RAFTER ORIGINAL LEVEL LINE AT THE BIRDSMOUTH

1. Figure 19.24 shows the pattern common rafter. On Line 2 at *a-ai* is shown the perpendicular height of the CR from the seat cut, Line 3, to the back of the rafter.

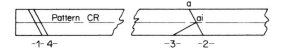

Fig. 19.24.

2. Figure 19.25 shows the pattern hip rafter. On Line 2 at *a-ai* is shown the

amount of rafter above the plate as measured from the common rafter and reproduced on the hip rafter. It will be seen that, since a 2 × 6 is used for the hip rafter, the latter will require a larger birdsmouth to be removed.

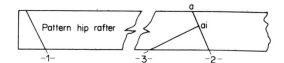

Fig. 19.25.

3. Figure 19.26 shows the framing square in position for drawing the level line. Draw the level Line 3.

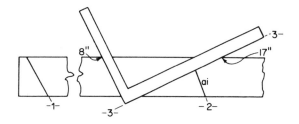

Fig. 19.26.

19.8 SHORTENING OF THE HIP RAFTER

1. From an inspection of Fig. 19.27, it will be seen that the run of the shortening of the hip rafter is equal to half the diagonal thickness of the common rafter as at Lines 1–4.

2. It should be constantly kept in mind that the hip rafter is shortened against the roof member against which it fits. It fits against the common rafters.

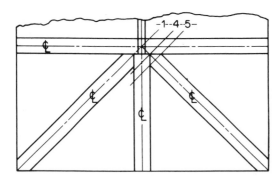

Fig. 19.27. Shortening of the hip rafter.

3. Measure back at right angles to Line 1, half the diagonal thickness of the CR. See Fig. 19.28. In this case, as a 2 × 4 is specified for the CR, half the diagonal of this member is 1⅛″. Draw in Line 4 measured at right angles to Line 1.

Fig. 19.28.

19.9 SIDE CUTS (CHEEK CUTS) OF THE HIP RAFTER

1. Upon close inspection of related plates and figures, it will be seen that the run of the side cuts of the hip rafter is equal to half the thickness of the hip rafter stock. The run of the side cut is measured on plan between Lines 4 and 5 as in Fig. 19.27.

2. Measure back at right angles from Line 4 half the thickness of the hip rafter stock. In this case, since a 2 × 6 is specified for the hip, half the thickness

Fig. 19.29.

of the hip is 13/16″. Draw in Line 5 as in Fig. 19.29. Lines 6 and 7, Fig. 19.30 are the hip rafter cheekcutting lines.

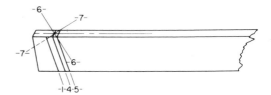

Fig. 19.30.

19.10 BACKING (BEVELING) OF THE HIP RAFTER

1. The sheathing of a roof is the material which is secured to the backs of the rafters. Usually, roofs are sheathed with common boards, shiplap, or plywood.

2. The sheathing of adjacent sides of the roof meets at a point above the center of the back of the hip rafter. *The steeper the pitch of the roof, the more acute will be the angle at the meeting place of the adjacent pieces of sheathing.*

3. Theoretically, and sometimes in actual practice for special projects, the back of the hip rafter must have the edges beveled to receive the sheathing. Unless some provision is made, the roof sheathing will not lie flat where it comes in contact with the edges of the hip rafter.

4. Closely examine Fig. 19.33 at Line 2. A perpendicular line through the center of the back of the hip on Line 2 at *a* would intersect with the inside intersection of the wall plates.

5. This perpendicular height corresponds to the perpendicular height of the common rafter from the seat cut Line 2 of the CR. See Figures 19.24 and 19.25.

6. The length of the run between Lines 2 and 8 on the plan is equal to half the thickness of the hip rafter stock. The length of the run is also equal to the run between Lines 4 and 5. The length of the run is shown between Lines 2 and 8, Fig. 19.31.

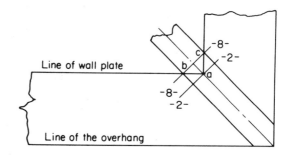

Fig. 19.33.

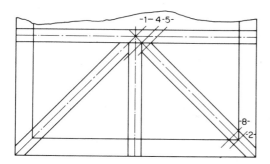

Fig. 19.31. Backing of the hip rafter.

7. On the pattern hip rafter draw Line 8 forward from Line 2, a distance of 13/16″ as in Line 8 Fig. 19.32. *This is very important.*

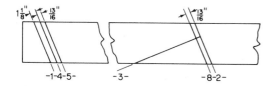

Fig. 19.32.

8. On the plan at Fig. 19.33, the top of the outside edges of the HR are vertical over the plates as at b and c on Line 8; but since the HR on plan is at an angle of 90° to the CR, when it is raised into position, its outside edges become higher than the plane of the CRs. *The steeper the pitch, the greater the difference.* See Fig. 19.34 where a HR with a steep pitch has been presented to emphasize this point.

9. The height of the (center) of the hip rafter above the wall plate was located as at *a-ai* on Line 2 of the pattern hip rafter layout. This is the same height as is measured from the back of the CR on Line 2 of the common rafter layout. See Figs. 19.24, 19.25 and 19.43.

10. The measurement from the wall plates to the outside edges of the HR where the HR passes directly over the wall plate is *a-ai* and must be measured from the back of the rafter on Line 8.

11. Measure down from the back of the hip rafter on Line 8 the same distance as on Line 2 at *a-ai*. Spot *bi* on Line 8 as in Fig. 19.34 and 19.43.

12. Place the framing square with the run to intersect Line 8 at *bi*. Draw a level line as at Line 9, Fig. 19.35.

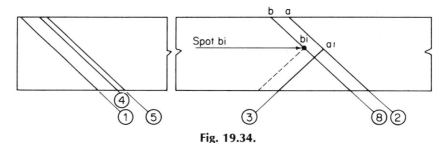

Fig. 19.34.

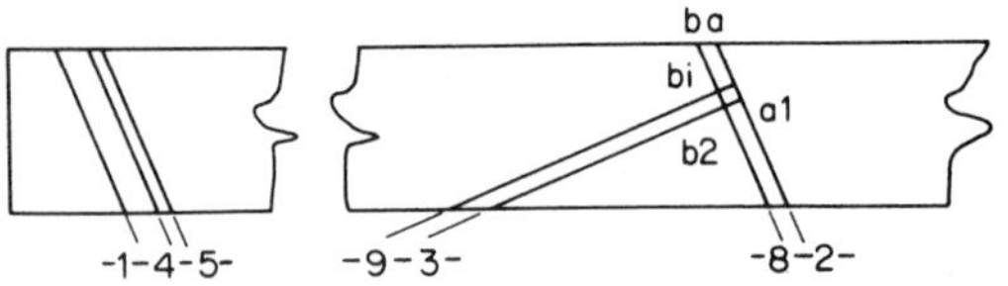

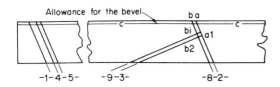

Fig. 19.35.

19.11 DROPPING THE HIP RAFTER

1. In general building practice, unless the hip rafter is of very large dimensions, it is the usual practice to drop the rafter, instead of backing it.

2. *Rule: A hip rafter must be either backed or dropped.* The amount that a hip rafter is dropped is the amount that otherwise it would be backed.

3. Since the amount to be dropped is equal to the amount that otherwise it would be backed, it follows that, if the rafter were to be dropped, the seat cut would be on Line 9. See Fig. 19.35.

4. If the rafter is to be backed, the seat cut should be on Line 3.

5. A hip rafter is either backed or dropped so that its edges will line up with the main plane of the roof.

13. The measurement between *bi* and *b2* (measured vertically) on Line 8 is the amount of bevel required on the hip rafter. From the back of the rafter on Line 8, gauge the amount of backing (beveling) required. See Fig. 19.36.

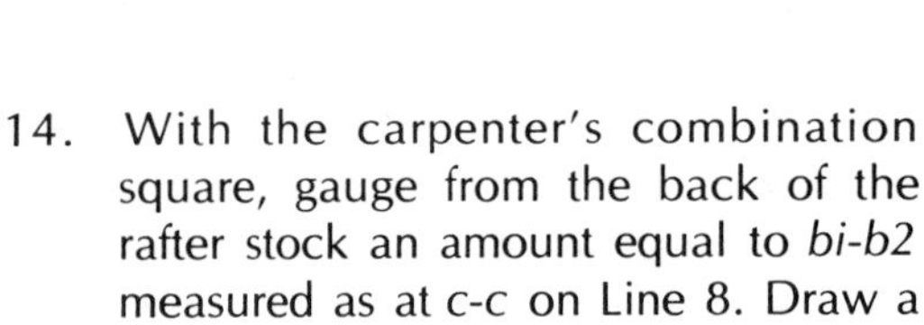

Fig. 19.36.

14. With the carpenter's combination square, gauge from the back of the rafter stock an amount equal to *bi-b2* measured as at *c-c* on Line 8. Draw a ₵ down the back of the rafter. The amount to be backed is shown in Fig. 19.37. Note *bi-b2* equals *b-c*.

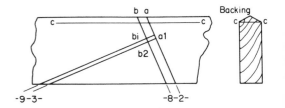

Fig. 19.37.

19.12 REVIEW OF THE LL OF THE TAIL OF THE COMMON RAFTER

1. Upon reviewing the operation for finding the LL of the tail of the common rafter, it will be recalled that reading under 8" on the first line of the rafter tables we find 14.42. To find the LL of the CR tail, multiply 14.42 by the number of feet and portions of feet of run in the CR overhang.

2. The number of feet and portions of feet of run in the CR overhang is 1'-4", or 1⅓ feet, or 1.33 feet. 14.42" × 1⅓ is 9¼" which is the LL of the tail of the common rafter to the nearest ⅛".

19.13 THE LL OF THE TAIL OF THE HIP RAFTER

1. The LL of the tail of the hip rafter is laid off from the plumb Line 2 of the original birdsmouth.

2. Make the calculations on the face of the rafter a little to the right of Line 2.

3. Read on the rafter tables of the framing square under 8" on the second line: LENGTH OF HIP OR VALLEY PER FOOT RUN . . . 18.76
(It will be recalled that this regular roof is specified to have a span of 24'-0", the pitch ⅓ and the overhang 16".)

4. Multiply 18.76" by the number of feet of run in the *common rafter tail*. The LL of the tail is therefore 18.76" × 1⅓' which equals 25" to the nearest ⅛".

5. Measure 25" along the back of the hip rafter from Line 2, and draw the plumb Line 10. This is the LL of the tail from Line 2. See Fig. 19.38.

19.14 CHECK THE LL OF THE HIP RAFTER BY THE STEP OFF METHOD

1. The run of the overhang of the tail of the hip rafter is the **diagonal** of the run of the overhang of the common rafter.

2. For every 1'-0" of run of the common rafter tail, the run of the hip rafter tail will be 17". (17" is the diagonal of 12" and 12".) Set the stair gauges to 8" and 17" for a ⅓ pitch hip rafter layout.

3. For every portion of 1'-0" of run of the common rafter tail, the hip rafter tail will require the diagonal of that portion of the common rafter tail. See Fig. 19.39.

4. Apply the framing square to the rafter stock with the plumb marking side of the square to the left, and placed on

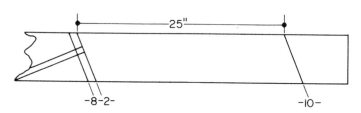

Fig. 19.38.

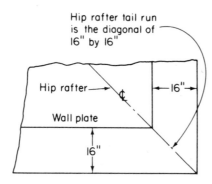

Hip rafter tail run is the diagonal of 16" by 16"

Hip rafter →

Wall plate

16"

16"

Fig. 19.39.

Line 2. Measure 17" on the run. This is the first step. Slip the square to the right so that the 8" setting of the tongue is at the 17" mark on the rafter. Draw a fine plumb line. See Figs. 19.40 and 19.41.

5. Slip the framing square further to the right from the marked plumb line and measure 5⅝" on the run as in Fig. 19.41. The measuring edge of the framing square should now be within ⅛" of Line 10. See Figs. 19.38 and 19.42.

6. The LL of the tail of the hip rafter (25") is measured on the back of the HR stock from Line 2 to Line 10. The run of the overhang is measured on the blade of the square and is 22⅝".

19.15 THE TAIL END SIDE CUTS OF THE HIP RAFTER

1. Where the eaves are to be boxed in, the tail end side cuts of the hip rafter will be the reverse of the side cuts at the ridge end of the hip rafter.

2. From Line 10 on the plan, lay off half the thickness of the rafter stock as at Line 11, Fig. 19.42.

3. On the hip rafter, measure back, at right angles from Line 10 towards the birds-mouth, half the thickness of the rafter stock. See Fig. 19.43. In this case, as a 2 × 6 is specified for the hip rafter, half the thickness of this member is 13/16". Draw Line 11.

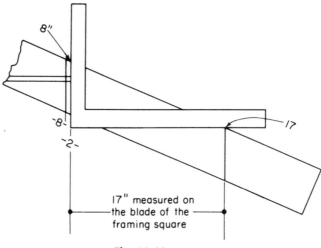

8"

8

2

17

17" measured on the blade of the framing square

Fig. 19.40.

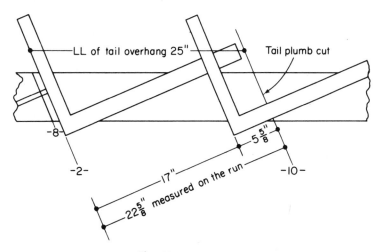

Fig. 19.41.

4. Draw a ℄ on the back of the rafter as at x-x. From Line 11 draw Lines 14 and 15 to intersect at the ℄ on Line 10. See Fig. 19.43, page 240.

5. Draw from Line 10 two level lines in the same relative positions as are Lines 3 and 9 from the back of the rafter at the birdsmouth. The final cutting level line at the end of the rafter will correspond to the cutting line at the birdsmouth. If the rafter is to be dropped, cut on Line 9 at the birdsmouth and on Line 13 at the tail end. If the rafter is to be backed, cut on Line 3 and on Line 12.

6. Study Fig. 19.43(b).

7. It is common practice in building operations to allow the hip rafter tail end to run out past the tail ends of the CRs and then to mark the actual length with a

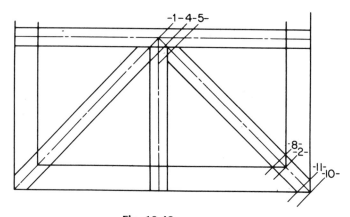

Fig. 19.42.

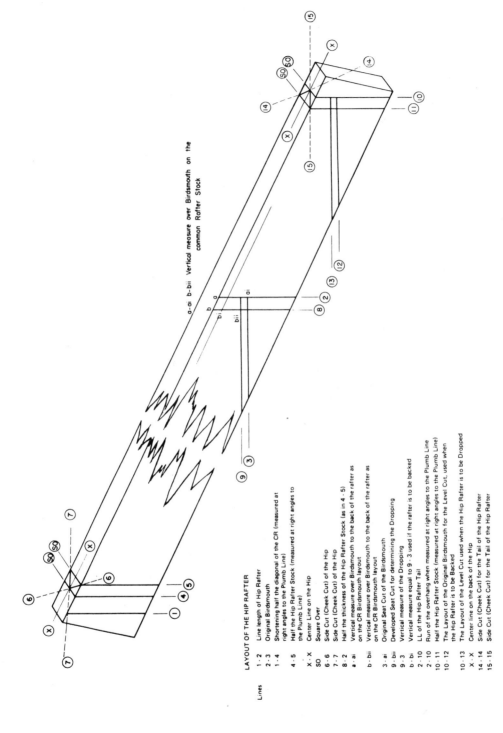

a-ai b-bii Vertical measure over Birdsmouth on the
common Rafter Stock

LAYOUT OF THE HIP RAFTER

Lines		
	1 - 2	Line length of Hip Rafter
	2 - 3	Original Birdsmouth
	1 - 4	Shortening half the diagonal of the CR (measured at right angles to the Plumb Line)
	4 - 5	Half the Hip Rafter Stock (measured at right angles to the Plumb Line)
	X - X	Center Line on the Hip
	SO	Square Over
	6 - 6	Side Cut (Cheek Cut) of the Hip
	7 - 7	Side Cut (Cheek Cut) of the Hip
	8 - 2	Half the thickness of the Hip Rafter Stock (as in 4 - 5)
	a - ai	Vertical measure over Birdsmouth to the back of the rafter as on the CR Birdsmouth layout
	b - bii	Vertical measure over Birdsmouth to the back of the rafter as on the CR Birdsmouth layout
	3 - ai	Original Seat Cut of the Birdsmouth
	9 - bii	Developed Seat Cut for determining the Dropping
	9 - 3	Vertical measure of the Dropping
	b - bi	Vertical measure equal to 9 - 3 used if the rafter is to be backed
	2 - 10	LL of the Hip Rafter Tail
	2 - 10	Run of the overhang when measured at right angles to the Plumb Line
	10 - 11	Half the Hip Rafter Stock (measured at right angles to the Plumb Line)
	10 - 12	The Layout of the Original Birdsmouth for the Level Cut, used when the Hip Rafter is to be Backed
	10 - 13	The Layout of the Level Cut used when the Hip Rafter is to be Dropped
	X - X	Center line on the back of the Hip
	14 - 14	Side Cut (Cheek Cut) for the Tail of the Hip Rafter
	15 - 15	Side Cut (Cheek Cut) for the Tail of the Hip Rafter

Fig. 19.43.

straight edge lined up with the tail ends of the CRs, from both sides of the roof.

19.16 JACK RAFTERS FOR A REGULAR HIP ROOF

Assume that a regular hip roof has a one-third pitch and a 24'-0" span. Some simple facts are as follows:

1. The run of any JR (jack rafter) is equal to its length from the outside edge of the wall plate to its intersection at the center line of the HR. See Fig. 19.44.

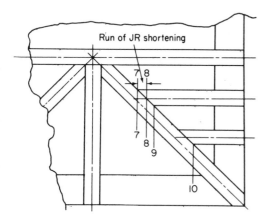

Fig. 19.44. Run of any JR equals its distance from outside corner of wall plates.

2. *With the exception of the cheek cuts for a JR, all other cuts are identical with those for the CR of the same roof.*

3. The common differences in the length of the JRs with 16" and 24" OCs (on centers) are given on the rafter tables of the framing square.

4. The example given in this section is based on JRs with 16" OCs. The common differences in lengths of adjoining JRs placed at 16" OCs is 19.23 as shown on the rafter tables, say, 19¼". Look under the 8" mark for this roof at Fig. 19.9, page 225.

5. The layout of the JRs is made on the pattern CR. See Figs. 19.45 and 19.47.

6. All JRs are shortened half the diagonal thickness of the HR against which they fit; if the HR stock is 1⅝", the diagonal thickness (*on plan*) is 1⅛".

19.17 LAYOUT OF JACK RAFTERS

1. For a one-third pitch the *longest* JR is 19¼" shorter than the CR, and each succeeding JR is 19¼" shorter still.

2. Since the JR fits against the HR at 45° *on plan*, it must be shortened half the diagonal thickness of the HR stock **on plan**. For an HR that is 1⅝" thick, half its diagonal **on plan** is 1⅛". See Fig. 19.44 for the run (plan) of the shortening (1⅛") of the JR between Lines 7 and 8; then see how it is measured *at right angles* from Line 7 to 8 at Figs. 19.45 and 19.47.

3. To lay out the side (cheek) cut of the JR, measure at right angles from Line 8 half the thickness of the JR stock (say ¾" for a 2 × 4). Draw Line 9 and square it over (SO). This is shown in Figs. 19.45 through 19.47.

4. Draw a center line on the back of the JR which will intersect with the square over (SO) Line 8, as shown at X—X at Fig. 19.47.

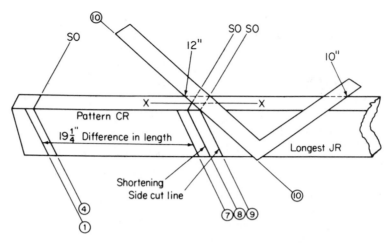

Fig. 19.45.

5. Across the back of the JR draw Line 10, which extends from Line 9 and intersects Line 8 at its intersection with the center line X—X as shown at Fig. 19.47.

6. To obtain the same line with the framing square, see Fig. 19.9, read on the fifth line of the rafter tables under the 8" mark for, "Side cut of jacks use . . . '', 10. Set the stair gauges at 12"

on the blade of the square and 10" on the tongue; with the 12" gauge on the left, apply the square across the back of the JR as shown at Fig. 19.45. It is the same line as in 5. above. Use either method. In effect, the cheek cut is a line which is pivoted on the back of the JR at the central spot on Line 8 to Line 9, producing the cutting line 10.

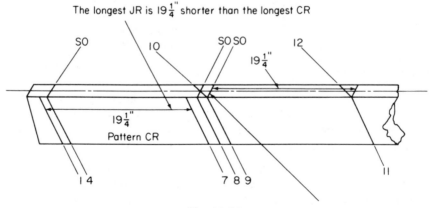

Fig. 19.46.

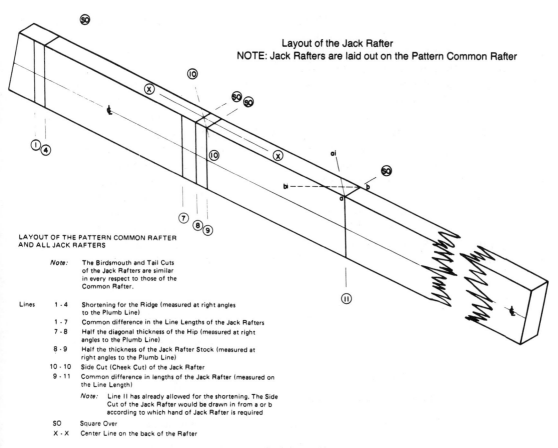

Layout of the Jack Rafter
NOTE: Jack Rafters are laid out on the Pattern Common Rafter

**LAYOUT OF THE PATTERN COMMON RAFTER
AND ALL JACK RAFTERS**

Note: The Birdsmouth and Tail Cuts
             of the Jack Rafters are similar
             in every respect to those of the
             Common Rafter.

Lines   1 - 4   Shortening for the Ridge (measured at right angles
                   to the Plumb Line)

         1 - 7   Common difference in the Line Lengths of the Jack Rafters

         7 - 8   Half the diagonal thickness of the Hip (measured at right
                   angles to the Plumb Line)

         8 - 9   Half the thickness of the Jack Rafter Stock (measured at
                   right angles to the Plumb Line)

         10 - 10 Side Cut (Cheek Cut) of the Jack Rafter

         9 - 11   Common difference in lengths of the Jack Rafter (measured on
                   the Line Length)

                  Note: Line II has already allowed for the shortening. The Side
                            Cut of the Jack Rafter would be drawn in from a or b
                            according to which hand of Jack Rafter is required

         SO   Square Over

         X - X   Center Line on the back of the Rafter

Fig. 19.47.

With an understanding of hip roof lay-out, a builder is able to apply his knowledge in hundreds of other ways to develop the length and fittings of other construction framing members.

For roofs that include valley rafters, cripple jack rafters, and rafters for unequal pitch roofs see RESIDENTIAL ROOF FRAMING (1980) Wass and Sanders, (Reston Publishing Co., Inc.)

19.18 WOOD ROOF TRUSSES

Strong, durable, and inexpensive wood roofs may be rapidly constructed with the use of (off-site) shop prefabricated quality controlled roof trusses. As a further advantage, where extremes of climate are encountered, the perimeter walls of housing units may be erected free standing; the roof trusses placed, and the roof covered, giving early tolerable working conditions for workmen to complete the erection of internal walls and all services.

Technical data in Figs. 19.48 and 19.49 was supplied by the Canadian Wood Council and is reproduced here with permission. As an introduction to truss construction, TECO Nail-on Truss Plates is included, with permission. (See Fig. 19.50.)

Truss shapes must be selected with care to make useful roof systems. Although general uses of valley rafters have not been given in this book, the application of roofing systems of girder and valley trusses should be noted (Fig. 19.49).

Rafter layouts for a regular hip roof should be thoroughly understood before attempting truss system construction such as "step down" or "hip louvre".

19.19 METRIC ROOF FRAMING

Metrification of the construction industry has led to the introduction of metric framing squares, two of which are on the market with different markings and sets of tables: one based on a unit run of 250 mm; and the other based on a unit run of 1000 mm (1 m).

Table 19.1 contains sets of roof framing data related to the two squares. Slope triangle information for each is equated in terms of "pitch". For example: 0.5 or ½ pitch is equivalent to slopes of 250 mm in 250 mm, or 1000 mm in 1000 mm.

Review

1. Make freehand line drawings of six different types of roofs.

2. Name and define eight different roof member terms.

3. What is meant by the term *traditional framing square?*

4. Make a sectional line drawing of a pitch roof and name all the parts drawn.

5. Make a freehand sketch showing how you would draw the center line on a rafter of indefinite width.

6. By how much is each common rafter shortened to allow for a ridge board?

7. Describe a regular hip roof.

8. Describe a jack rafter.

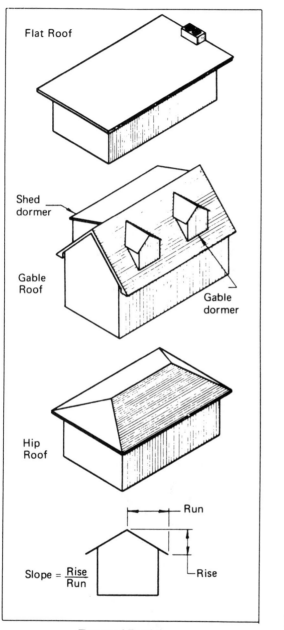

Types of Roofs[1]

[1]*Framing Techniques,* CWC Datafile WB-1, p. 18.

[2]*Light Frame Trusses,* CWC Datafile WC-3, p. 3.

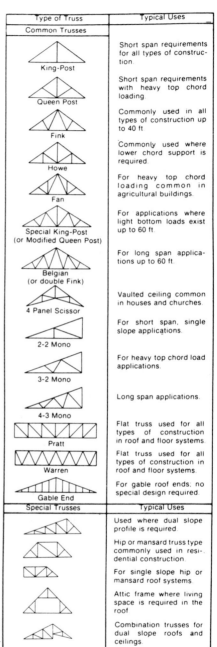

Truss Shapes[2]

Fig. 19.48. Truss Shapes

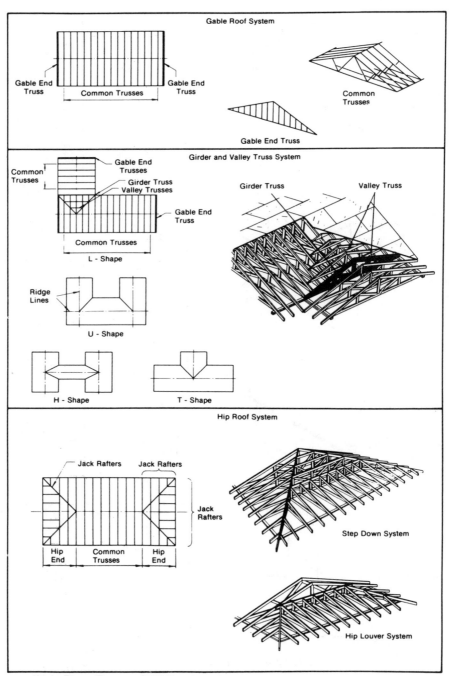

*Light Frame Trusses, CWC Datafile WC-3, p. 3.

Fig. 19.49. Trussed Rafter Systems

WHERE USED:

Where single plane assembly of residential, commercial, and farm trusses is desired, TECO truss plates provide economical clear span construction without the requirement for costly fabricating equipment. For residential construction, the TECO plate system is covered by HUD (FHA) Bulletin SE-297. This bulletin covers designs in accordance with HUD (FHA) construction standards for spans 16' to 32' and roof slopes 3:12 to 7:12. Design information is also available for other uses.

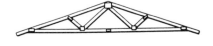

DESCRIPTION:

TECO Nail-On truss plates are manufactured from 20 gauge zinc coated sheet steel having the same physical properties as grade "A" structural steel (ASTM A-446). They are manufactured in flat and flanged styles. The plates have pre-punched 0.128" diameter holes.

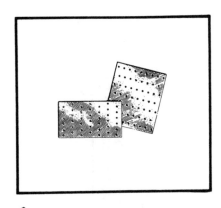

SUGGESTED SPECIFICATION:

Trusses shall be fabricated using TECO prepunched Nail-On truss plates as manufactured by Timber Engineering Company, Washington, D.C. Plate sizes, plate locations, and nail quantities shall be as shown on truss fabrication drawings. The nails are to be of uncoated steel wire 8d diameter (0.131") by 1½" long. Truss members shall be tight fitting at all joints.

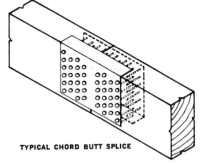

TYPICAL CHORD BUTT SPLICE

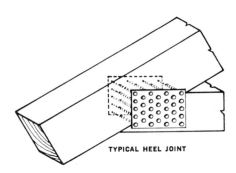

TYPICAL HEEL JOINT

Copyright Timber Engineering Company 1970

Fig. 19.50.   TECO Nail-On Truss Plates

TABLE 19.1

Roof framing data[1] related to two metric framing squares: one based on a unit run of 250 mm; and one based on a unit run of 1000 mm (1m)

	Unit Run of 250 mm					Unit Run of 1000 mm (1m)				
Angle to Plate (°) of CR	Slope Triangle (Run/Rise)	Unit Run	Span	Rise	Pitch	Rise	Span	Unit Run	Slope Triangle (Run/Rise)	Angle to Plate (°) of CR[2]
63.44	500 in 250	250	500	500	1.0	2000	2000	1000	2000 in 1000	[3]
60.95	450 in 250	250	500	450	0.9	1800	2000	1000	1800 in 1000	
58.00	400 in 250	250	500	400	0.8	1600	2000	1000	1600 in 1000	
54.46	350 in 250	250	500	350	0.7	1400	2000	1000	1400 in 1000	54.5
50.20	300 in 250	250	500	300	0.6	1200	2000	1000	1200 in 1000	50.2
45.00	250 in 250	250	500	250	0.5	1000	2000	1000	1000 in 1000	45.0
38.66	200 in 250	250	500	200	0.4	800	2000	1000	800 in 1000	38.7
30.96	150 in 250	250	500	150	0.3	600	2000	1000	600 in 1000	31.0
21.80	100 in 250	250	500	100	0.2	400	2000	1000	400 in 1000	21.8
11.31	50 in 250	250	500	50	0.1	200	2000	1000	200 in 1000	

[1]Most of the data is based on the definition that pitch is rise divided by span.
[2]Angle to plate may not be the same as angle of rafter cut shown on a framing square.
[3]Some angular measurements may not be shown on the square.

20

Wall Cladding, Fiber Boards, Insulation, and Vapor Barriers

In this chapter we shall discuss wall cladding and some of the materials and methods used in wood frame wall construction to control the passage of heat, cold, and sound, and also used in the decorative finish of both inside and outside surfaces. Builders should keep abreast of all new developments in these fields and be alert to the cost of materials, their applications, and the efficacy of the end results.

If just the correct amount of materials required by the workmen is placed in each residence, it will be easy to identify careless and wasteful workmen and dispense with their services. Remember to have the surroundings for workmen clear of all debris at all times so that nothing extraneous will impede their progress with the work on hand.

20.1 WALL CLADDING AND FIBER BOARDS

All materials attached to and forming an integral part of a wood frame wall are known as cladding. These include:

1. Fiber boards for both internal and external finish, which are usually manufactured in 4'-0" × 8'-0" sheets, (the height of most residential rooms) which may be of wood or simulated wood. For finished good class work, finishing panels are secured to the studs with glue or with nails of similar color to the panel; or the nail heads may be countersunk and stopped with matching color filling.

2. Plaster which is trowelled onto the wall and having expansive metal backing to reinforce over wall openings for doors and windows; external corners are reinforced with metal beads. Outside wall may be treated with stucco applied to a base of stucco wire with the knurls of the wire placed toward the wall surface. *This is important.*

3. Drywall which is manufactured in 4'-0" × 8'-0" standard sized sheets (or longer to order) and secured with manufacturers' specified nails at stated spacings. It is important that there be no joints over doorways; see Fig. 20.13.

4. Hard-pressed fiber board which may be purchased with a plain or decorative finish that will take all kinds of paint or wallpaper. Care should be taken to drill all holes for nailing to avoid bent nails and hammer face marks on the finished surface.

5. Plastic sheets in tile patterns used especially in bathrooms.

6. Asbestos sheets which are mandatory in some areas behind solid fuel stoves and heaters. They are also used as outside wall finish.

7. T & G (tongue and groove) boards which may be finished for interior use or used as an outside finish in varying patterns.

8. Aspenite sheets which are made from thin wafers of aspen wood bonded under heat and pressure with waterproof glue; unsanded or sanded. These panels, ¼" thick, may be used for a pleasing natural finish or for applying coloring stains and varnish. They are also used for outside finished walls. Panels are made in all thicknesses up to ¾" as used in floor sheathing.

9. Weldwood sheets which lend themselves to rich internal finishes.

10. Metallic sheets for outside siding.

11. Rough plywood sheathing that is available in standard sized sheets and in varying thicknesses to meet any specifications. The minimum thickness of plywood applied to outside wall sheathing such as shiplap is ¼". Unsheathed wall framing should have ⅜" plywood sheets for studs 16" OC, and ½" for studs placed 24" OC. The edges of plywood panels should be secured with corrosive resistant nails spaced 6" apart along the edges.

12. Shiplap or square-edged boards that may be used as sheathing both for walls and subfloors.

13. All wall sheathing which should be covered with building paper before applying the outside finish.

14. Outside finish that may be wood siding or other man-made fabrics simulating wood, rock, brick and so on. Rough-sawn cedar siding may be horizontally applied with the unmachined barked edge of the board exposed to give the lower edge a rustic appearance.

15. Masonry walls of brick or brick veneer, and concrete blocks in all colors (tex-

tured specially for their insulating qualities and having their cores filled with granulated inert insulation).

It is imperative that the starting panel of all the foregoing materials be placed correctly (for plumb and horizontals) since all other panels will be aligned against the first one placed. See the following pages and Fig. 20.8. Information in sections 20.2 through 20.7 has been provided by the Council of the Forest Industries of British Columbia and is reproduced here with permission.

20.2 BASIC PATTERNS

Manufacturers have developed a number of panelling profiles by varying the surface design. As a result, Western red cedar panelling is available with smooth or saw-textured surfaces; in clear or with knots; with vertical or flat grain; in different widths and thicknesses; in flush-joint; v-joint or channel patterns; with bevelled or bullnosed edges; with moulded or flat surfaces; and many other combinations of these variables. Three typi-

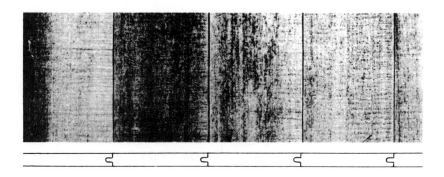

Fig. 20.1. Flush Surface Tongue and Groove Joint (saw-textured finish)

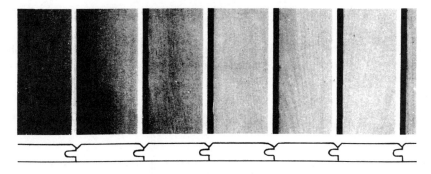

Fig. 20.2. V-Joint Surface Tongue and Groove Joint (milled finish)

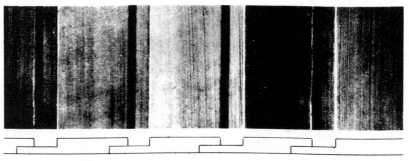

Fig. 20.3. Channel Surface Lapped Joint (milled finish)

cal types of panelling are shown here. For further information on available patterns and panelling manufacturers, contact Council of the Forest Industries of British Columbia.

20.3 NAILING TECHNIQUES

Western red cedar panelling should be applied with standard finishing nails long enough to penetrate at least an inch into the framing members. For all panelling up to ¾-inch thick (1-inch nominal), 2-inch nails are recommended for both face nailing and blind nailing.

Tongue and Groove

Tongue and groove panelling up to six inches in width should be blind nailed through the base of the tongue into the cross-blocking or nailing strips of the supporting wall. The nails should be countersunk to allow for flush application of the next panel.

Tongue and groove panelling more than six inches in width requires surface nailing as illustrated below. Countersink all surface nails. Since wood tones vary with the type of finish selected, nail holes are best concealed with a matching putty *after the final surface finish has been applied.*

Lapped

Lapped panelling less than six inches wide should be surface nailed using the standard countersink-and-fill method.

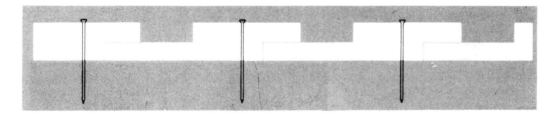

For lapped panelling more than six inches wide, use an additional surface nail taking care to avoid nailing through the underlying lap. Both nails should be countersunk below the surface of the panelling.

Since wood tones vary with the type of finish selected, nail holes are best concealed with a matching putty *after the final surface finish has been applied.*

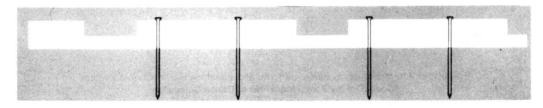

20.4 BASIC WALL CONSTRUCTION

Like all siding materials, the performance and permanence of Western red cedar will depend to a large extent on the quality and suitability of the frame to which it is applied. Correct installation will ensure excellent service and handsome appearance.

Figures 20.4 and 20.5 illustrate the recommended construction of walls for the application of cedar siding.

Structurally, the wall must have the ability to hold fastenings firmly in place, with standard studding and wood sheathing of

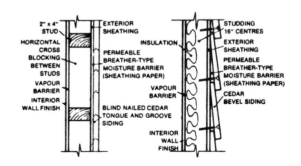

Fig. 20.4.

Vertical Application

(top section)

Fig. 20.5.

Horizontal Application

(cross section)

either shiplap boards or plywood. The interior side of the wall studs should be overlaid with a non-permeable *vapor barrier,* while the exterior sheathing should be covered with a permeable breather-type *moisture barrier* sheathing paper before applying the siding.

Vertical application of siding (Fig. 20.4) calls for the installation of 2" × 4" horizontal cross blocking between studs to provide a continuous base for nailing.

For siding up to ½-inch in thickness, cross blocking should be installed on 24-inch centers, floor to ceiling.

For ¾-inch material or thicker, blocking may be on 48-inch centers.

Horizontal application of siding (Fig. 20.5) does not require cross blocking. Nails are driven through the sheathing and directly into the studs.

20.5 TYPES OF NAILS

The type of nail selected for the application of siding will have a substantial bearing on the appearance and performance of the finished work.

The following recommendations are the result of a long-term research program conducted by the Western Red Cedar Lumber Association in laboratory tests and under conditions of actual use.

Qualities

Ideally, siding nails

will not rust or cause discoloring;
will have good holding power with no
tendency to pop out or pull through;

will minimize splitting;
will be easy to install yet strong enough
to resist bending;
will be relatively unobtrusive in the
finished wall.

Designs

The four designs recommended for the installation of siding are illustrated in Fig. 20.6.

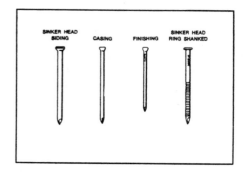

Fig. 20.6.

The two sinker head varieties and the casing nail are commonly used for face nailing. Of these, the ring shanked nail has superior holding properties. Sinker head nails are normally tapped flush with the surface of the siding; casing nails may be countersunk and puttied.

Finishes

The three corrosion-resistant nails recommended for siding are:

high tensile strength aluminum
stainless steel
galvanized—hot-dipped

Other finishes may cause discoloration or staining.

Nail Points

Nails are available with a variety of points for a variety of purposes. For good holding power in the application of siding, with little tendency to cause splitting, the blunt or medium diamond point and the blunt or medium needle point with a ring-threaded shank can be recommended.

Sizes

The correct size for siding nails will depend upon the type and thickness of the material being applied.

As a general rule, siding nails should be long enough to penetrate at least 1½ inches into studs and wood sheathing combined.

The following tables will be useful for estimating sizes and quantities.

SIZES			QUANTITIES				
Nail Length (in.)		U.S. Size	Siding Nails (no. per lb)		Pounds Required per 1,000 bd ft of Siding		
Aluminum	Hot-Dipped Galvanized		Aluminum	Hot-Dipped Galvanized	Aluminum	Hot-Dipped Galvanized	
1⅞	2	6d	566	194	2	6	
2⅛	2¼	7d	468	172	2½	6½	
2¾	2½	8d	319	123	4	9	
2⅞	3	10d	215	103	5½	11	

NUMBER OF NAILS REQUIRED PER THOUSAND SQUARE FEET OF SIDING	
6" Siding	1560
8" Siding	1180
10" Siding	960

20.6 BASIC PATTERNS AND APPLICATION

The four basic patterns of Western red cedar siding are: bevel, tongue and grove, channel, and board and batten.

Based on these patterns, siding manufacturers have developed a wide range of variations to meet personal preferences and the dictates of design: smooth surfaced or saw textured; clear or with knots; vertical or flat grain; different widths and thicknesses of material; v-joint or flush joint; rabbetted or plain bevel; straight-edged, wavy-edged, simulated log cabin style, and many others.

The application methods described here may be adapted to all variations of the four basic siding patterns.

For further information on available patterns and siding manufacturers, contact Council of the Forest Industries of B.C.

Bevel Siding (Horizontal Application)

For 4", 6", or 8" widths, ½" or ⅝" thick, use 2" nails; and 10" and 12" widths ¾" thick, use 2½" nails.

Use one nail per stud (Fig. 20.7[a])

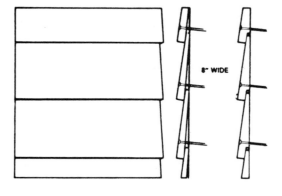

8" WIDE

Fig. 20.7.

taking care not to nail through both courses of the siding. The nail should miss the feather edge of the underlying piece by ⅛". This allows for expansion and contraction. For rabbetted bevel siding (20.7[b]), the nail should be driven 1" above the thick edge of the piece.

Nailing should be snug but not tight, with nail heads either tapped flush with the surface of the siding or countersunk and filled.

Tongue and Groove Siding (Vertical Application)

Narrower widths (4", 5", and 6") of tongue and groove cedar siding are normally blind nailed as shown (Fig. 20.8(a)). Use one 2" finishing nail per bearing, toenailing into the base of the tongue.

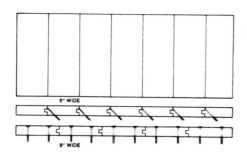

Fig. 20.8.

For widths over 6" (Fig. 20.8(b)) face nail the siding using two 2½" siding nails per bearing. If a smooth finish is desired, countersink all nails slightly and fill with wood putty or other filler.

20.7 APPLICATION AND ESTIMATING

In addition to proper nails and nailing techniques, a sound nailing surface is important for both new construction and remodelling.

Panelling Applied to Wall Frame

When applying panelling to an unfinished frame wall, 2" × 4" cross blocking between the wall studs provides a solid nailing surface. It is a good technique to turn the cross blocking so that the 4-inch surface is face-outwards. This provides a larger nailing surface and easy passage for electrical wiring. Spacing of cross blocking varies with the thickness of the panelling. For 1-inch panelling, 48-inch intervals are recommended. For ½-inch panelling, blocking should be set

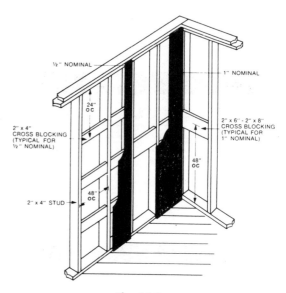

Fig. 20.9.

at 24-inch intervals. Extra care should be taken in aligning the first panel: do not rely on the adjacent wall to be plumb at the corner. Once the first panel has been nailed accurately in place, the other panels will align themselves.

Panelling Applied Over Plaster

When applying panelling over an existing plaster wall, the area to be panelled should be strapped with a series of 1″ × 3″ furring strips set horizontally at 24-inch centers. As illustrated in Fig. 20.10, a 1″ × 6″ strip at the floor level creates a recessed baseboard. In applying the strapping, use nails of sufficient length to penetrate the wall plaster and anchor firmly in the wall studs. The top length of strapping should be set at ceiling height. Accurate alignment of the first piece of panelling will ensure correct alignment of the panels to follow.

Plaster ceilings can be panelled using a similar technique. When applying ½-inch thick panelling, use furring strips set at 16-inch centers; for 1-inch panelling, set furring strips at 24-inch centers.

Estimating

The table below will assist in estimating the quantity of panelling required to cover a given wall area using either the lapped or the v-joint tongue and groove pattern.

Nominal Size (in.)		Quantity Required to Cover 1,000 sq ft of Wall Area (bd ft)*	
V-Joint	Channel	V-Joint	Channel
1 x 4	—	1,333	—
1 x 6	1 x 6	1,200	1,263
1 x 8	1 x 8	1,185	1,231
1 x 10	1 x 10	1,143	1,176
—	1 x 12	—	1,143

* Allow small additional footage for cutting and fitting.

20.8 REQUIREMENTS FOR SOUND CONTROL

Sound insulation or acoustic separation is a material's ability to reduce or resist the transmission of sound; the ASTM *Sound Transmission Class (STC)* rating system, based on the decibel, measures the sound insulating performance of construction assemblies in buildings. The National Building Code of Canada (NBCC) uses this *STC* rating system for measuring sound transmission loss. (ASTM *E-90-66T, Laboratory Measurement of Airborne Sound Transmission Loss of Building Partitions.*)

The NBCC sets a minimum *STC* rating of not less than 45 for construction in some areas of multiple dwelling structures as follows:

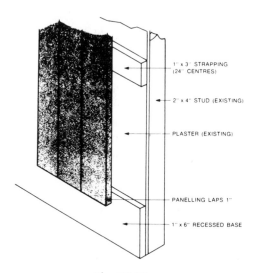

1″ x 3″ STRAPPING (24″ CENTRES)

2″ x 4″ STUD (EXISTING)

PLASTER (EXISTING)

PANELLING LAPS 1″

1″ x 6″ RECESSED BASE

Fig. 20.10.

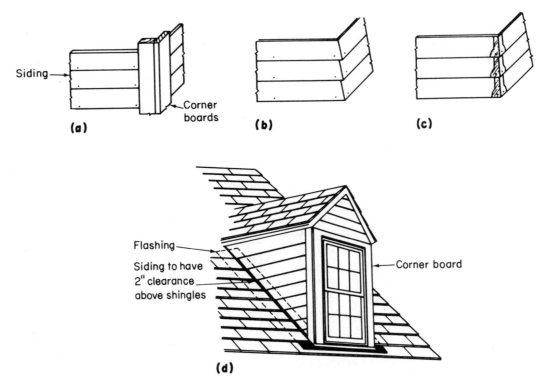

Fig. 20.11. Corner treatment of siding. *(Courtesy of the Forestry Products Laboratory, U.S. Department of Agriculture.)*

Between dwelling units in the same building.

Between a dwelling unit and any space common to two or more dwelling units.

Between dwelling units and service rooms or space serving more than one dwelling unit (e.g., storage room, laundry, workshop, building maintenance room or garage).

The NBCC does not cover situations other than those listed above, so the responsibility of selecting constructions with suitable *STC* ratings rests with the designer. He should use common sense and ensure that sound is properly controlled for the purpose for which the building will be used. It is difficult to satisfy all tenants all the time; a successful building is one that can accommodate the wide variety of tenants and tenant activities amicably.

Some things that should be considered are:

1. In *apartment buildings* and other multiple dwelling structures, consider transmission of noise from one dwelling unit to another, as well as local individual noise.

2. In *office buildings,* noise insulation requirements are less stringent than for apartment buildings because they are usually occupied for only about 8 out of 24 hours. A moderate amount of business noise is acceptable, and interference with sleep is rarely a concern; the main requirement is speech privacy. In cases where absolute privacy is needed, the insulation requirement might be about *STC* 35.

3. In *classrooms,* concert halls, and auditoriums, the primary consideration is the communication process. The occupants must be able to hear and understand the message being delivered. Room surfaces should be shaped to control and reflect sound and absorptive surfaces should be used to dampen excessive reverberation.

Sound Control

Acoustical problems can, in most cases, be solved in advance by good design. The importance of acoustics varies greatly, depending on the purpose for which a building is designed, but the problems should be considered early in the design stage.

Site Selection

Building sites should be located as far as possible from potential sources of noise such as airfields, industrial plants, railroads, and traffic arteries. Buildings should be placed to take advantage of rolling terrain, stands of trees, and other buildings which are natural noise barriers. Final site selection may be governed by the intended use of a building and degree of noise control required.

Building Layouts

One of the most important things in sound control is segregating noisy areas from quiet areas; this simplifies the problem of achieving adequate noise insulation. A few rules are:

1. In *manufacturing plants,* locate the offices as far as possible from sources of intense noise.

2. In *multiple dwelling structures,* arrange layouts so that the most critical rooms (bedrooms, living rooms) are protected from adjoining apartments by a buffer zone of non-critical sound areas such as bathrooms, kitchens, closets and hallways. The next best arrangement is to place quiet rooms such as bedrooms on the two sides of a party wall.

3. Keep windows and doors away from the noisy side of a building if possible.

Selecting Equipment and Services

In industry, vibration in the factory area is most important. Vibrations can be minimized by providing special foundations or vibration-isolating mountings such as rubber coil spring shock mountings.

Office equipment such as card-punching, sorting machines and reproduction equipment should be placed in a separate room. Air conditioners, furnace equipment and pumps for any building should be located in the basement, on roofs or on specially designed equipment floors.

Choosing Construction Assemblies

In sound conditioning a room, both sound absorption and sound insulation of floor, wall and ceiling materials should be considered. For sound emitted within a room, the objective is for the walls, floor and ceiling to absorb some of the sound energy. Absorptive requirements may be met in most residential rooms by ordinary furnishings such as drapes and carpets. For control of sounds emitted from a source outside a room, the sound insulation properties of the walls, floor and ceiling are important. The *STC* ratings for some typical window, door, wall and floor constructions are given in the text.

Windows are the weakest part of exterior walls for sound control; their effectiveness depends on the airtightness of the installation. Fixed windows provide more sound insulation than windows that can be opened, and double-glazed windows give more sound insulation than single-glazed windows.

Doors are the weakest part of interior walls for sound control; they determine the amount of sound control that can be provided. Solid-core doors provide better sound insulation than hollow-core doors. Gaskets can be installed between the door and jamb to improve sound insulation; this also softens the impact when the door is slammed.

Insulation of *walls* against air-borne sound depends on weight, stiffness, breaks in sound travel paths and sound absorption within the wall space.

Air-borne sound may be controlled with a heavy wall or one composed of several independent layers. To obtain high sound insulation without excessive weight, component members must be structurally isolated from each other. Generally speaking, a wall should be flexible to minimize effects of panel vibrations. Dividing a wall into two independent barriers will accomplish this, because the two relatively flexible layers replace a rigid structure. One highly efficient wall construction uses two sets of

wood studs, staggered or slightly offset from each other, so that the two surfaces are not linked. Thus there can be no direct sound transmission except through the top and bottom plates.

Doubling the weight of the surfaces improves performance by about 3 db; adding insulation or a porous material between wall surfaces also helps considerably. Another structure equally efficient utilizes resilient clips or channels to fasten facing materials to wood framing. Again, absorbing material in the wall space is of great value. The walls should extend from floor to ceiling and doors, windows and service outlets should be well sealed.

For air-borne sound, the principles for *floors* are the same as for walls. In addition, a problem of special importance in floors is impact sound (e.g., footsteps) originating as a vibration in the separating structure itself. Impact sound, in many cases, can lead to more complaints than air-borne sound.

Impact noise transmission can be reduced by soft floor coverings, by suspended ceilings, by sound absorbing materials between ceiling and floor and by separating floor surfaces from structural parts of the floor with strips of wood furring or other material.

Controlling Sound Efficiently

The key to efficient sound control is good layout of building interiors; sound problems in many cases can be eliminated, or at the very least, minimized. After the building layout is fixed, the designer then can select types of construction and materials that will satisfactorily control the sounds liable to occur. Designers should remember that no material will solve all problems and that sound control systems are no more efficient than their weakest link. Windows, doors, service outlets and the perimeter of partitions, floors and ceilings should be well sealed to minimize sound leakage. Failure to observe these basic principles will result in annoying problems for tenants, workers and users. If alterations are necessary after a structure is complete, they will be expensive and probably ineffective.

Wood panel products and framing members provide effective, economical sound insulation and absorption when properly utilized. Careful attention to the details of design will result in performance as intended.

Decibels

Good insulation reduces the transmission of heat, cold, and sound through floors, walls and ceilings. Sound is measured in decibels using the symbol db. The range of sound runs from that of a whisper, say 0–10 db, to the average radio, say 70 db, and to the noise of a jack-hammer which ranges between 110–120 db and is literally deafening.

20.9 INSULATION AND VAPOR BARRIERS

Of the many different types of insulation and sound proofing materials used in building construction, the following is a partial list; others described in this book may be seen by consulting the index:

1. Batt-types mineral, also obtainable in rolls, see Figs. 20.12 and 20.13.

2. Batt-type fiber, also obtainable in rolls.

3. Lightweight cellular concrete blocks.

4. Lightweight chemically treated wood shavings and cement.

5. Loose fill—inert or fiber.

6. Lightweight cellular plastic types.

7. Straw (chemically treated) boards.

8. Foam glass boards in 2'-0" × 4'-0" sheets of varying thicknesses.

9. Foamed-in-place insulation.

10. Vermiculite, polystyrene, urethane, and perlite.

11. Gypsum boards, mineral fiber boards, wood fiber boards.

12. Rigid urethane laminated roof insulation.

13. Reflective insulation in sheets of aluminum, copper foil, or sheet metal.

14. Polyethylene vapor barriers from .002 to .010.

Further information may be obtained from: Superintendent of Documents, U.S. Government Printing Office, Washington, D.C. 20402; also from Publication Section, Division of Building Research, National Research Council, Ottawa, Ontario; and from Sweet's "Construction Catalog File," which may be seen at your library.

Make a close study of the drawings shown in Figs. 20.12 through 20.16.

The material on pages 265 – 268 on Fiberglas building insulation has been excerpted from one of the publications of Owens-Corning Fiberglas Corporation, and is reproduced here with permission.

20.10 CONDUCTION (METRIC MEASUREMENTS OF HEAT TRANSFER)

Conduction through roofs, ceilings, walls and basements is the primary factor in heat loss calculations. The unit of heat flow is the

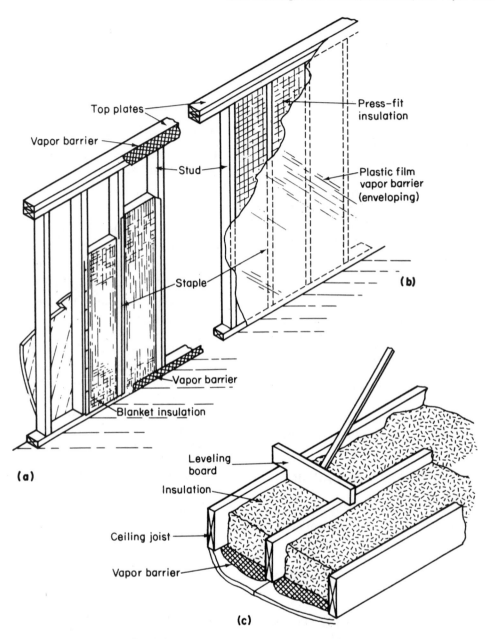

Fig. 20.12. Application of insulation: (a) wall section with blanket type, (b) wall section with "press-fit" insulation, (c) ceiling with full insulation. (*Courtesy of the Forestry Products Laboratory, U.S. Department of Agriculture.*)

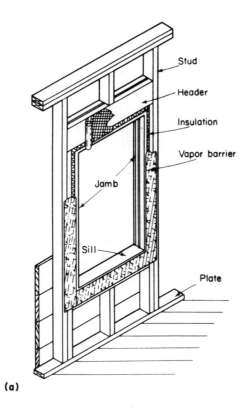

Stud

Header

Insulation

Vapor barrier

Jamb

Sill

Plate

(a)

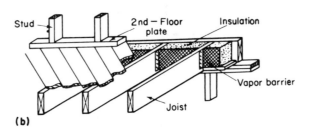

Stud

2nd – Floor plate

Insulation

Vapor barrier

Joist

(b)

Fig. 20.13. Precautions in insulating: (a) around openings, and (b) joist space in outside walls. *(Courtesy of the Forestry Products Laboratory, U.S. Department of Agriculture.)*

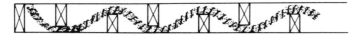

Fig. 20.14. Staggered stud partition with blanket roll insulation.

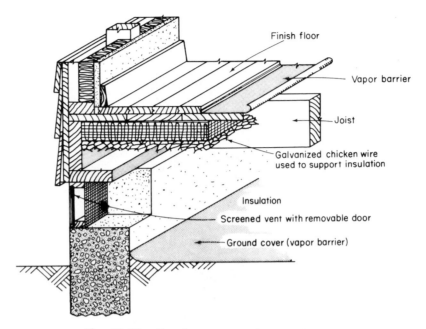

Fig. 20.15. Crawl space ventilator and vapor barrier ground cover. *(Courtesy of the Department of Forestry and Rural Development and the Central Mortgage and Housing Corporation, Ottawa.)*

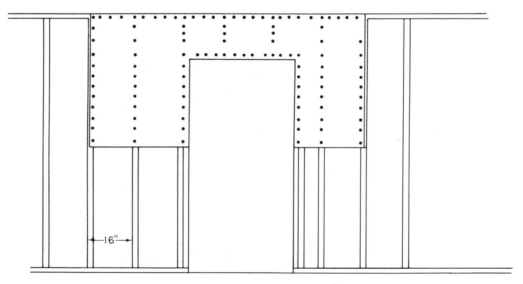

Fig. 20.16. To prevent checking, apply drywall without jointing over doorways.

Fiberglas building insulation

The following material has been excerpted from one of the publications of Owens–Corning Fiberglas Corporation and is published here with permission.

Where to insulate

To achieve full thermal benefits from building insulation, the insulation must form a complete thermal blanket around the living portion of the house, with no gaps. Install insulation in all walls, ceilings, and floors that separate heated from unheated space. The drawing represents a composite house, showing the places in a building where insulation is required.

- Insulate all exterior walls completely.
- Insulate all ceilings having cold space above.
- Insulate dormer ceilings and walls.
- Where attic is finished as living space or in 1½-story houses, insulate knee walls, sloping roof section and ceiling, leaving open space above for ventilation. Caution: make sure that insulation at the knee wall butts snugly to the ceiling insulation.
- Insulate floor over unheated spaces such as garages, open porches, or vented crawl spaces.
- When a crawl space is enclosed as a plenum, insulate crawl space walls instead of the floor above.
- If the second level of a 2-story house extends beyond the first story, insulate the overhanging floor area.
- Insulate basement walls when basement space is finished for living purposes.
- Insulate between floor joists at the top of foundation walls in

every house, with or without basement.
- Insulate the perimeter of a slab on grade.
- For protection against dirt and air, use sill sealer between sill plate and foundation masonry.

Insulating apartment buildings

The general rule for insulating single-family houses also applies to insulating apartment buildings: install insulation between heated and unheated spaces. When each apartment has a separate heating/cooling system, insulation in floors and walls between apartments for thermal reasons should be considered. This insulation may function as a part of sound control treatment. (See Owens-Corning Fiberglas publication, "Solutions to Noise Control Problems.")

Insulation in remodeling

A house being remodeled ideally should be insulated to the same extent as a new house. Blanket insulation can be applied where

interior finish has been removed in the course of renovation. For upgrading existing insulation in ceilings, use Fiberglas* Unfaced Friction Fit Insulation. Simply lay it in place from above. Since Friction Fit has no attached vapor-resistant facing, it will not interfere with attic ventilation nor will it cause condensation problems.

How much insulation

Owens-Corning Fiberglas Corporation recommends the installation of R-19 (6″) of insulation in ceilings and R-11 (3½″) in walls and floors. The thermal protection afforded by this insulation prevents excessive heat loss in winter and excessive heat gain in summer, maximizing comfort and operational savings.

Installing insulation in walls

General procedure

When applying insulation in walls, start at the top of each stud space and work down. Be sure to butt insulation firmly against both top and bottom plates.

Cutting insulation. All types of Fiberglas Insulation cut easily

with a sharp knife. Place the insulation on a piece of scrap plywood or wallboard, compress the material with one hand, and cut with the other. When cutting faced insulation, keep the facing up.

Installing Friction Fit

Friction Fit batts come in 15″ and 23″ widths, to fit 16″ and 24″ o.c. framing. Friction Fit usually requires a separate vapor-resistant film. Wedge Friction Fit batts into place between studs, butting them snugly against top and bottom plates. Fill spaces around doors and windows with insulation. Unroll polyethylene film across entire wall area, including window and door openings. Staple securely to top and bottom plates, studs, and door and window framing. When polyethylene has been securely fastened, cut out window and door openings. (It is sometimes left in place until after painting and finishing to act as masking, thereby reducing cleanup.) Duplex-laminated kraft vapor barrier may be used instead of polyethylene and applied in the same way.
Foil-backed gypsum board may also serve as a vapor-resistant material. It is applied in the same manner as ordinary drywall, with

the foil side facing the insulation. To seal window and door framing, staple a 6″ wide strip of polyethylene connecting that framing and the structural framing of the building, prior to the drywall application.

Installing faced insulation

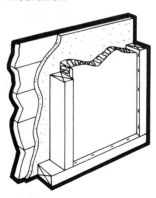

Inset stapling. Fiberglas Kraft-Faced and Foil-Faced Insulations may be inset stapled. Insulation comes in 15″ and 23″ widths to fit 16″ and 24″ o.c. framing.
Place insulation between studs. Staple both flanges snugly to the sides of the studs.
Where the insulation meets the top and bottom plates, peel back about 1″ of the facing, butt the blanket snugly against the plate, and staple the facing to the framing.

Installing insulation in ceilings

General procedure

Fiberglas Kraft-Faced and Foil-Faced Insulations may be inset stapled or face stapled to exposed ceiling joists. Friction Fit insulation is held in place between joists by its own resiliency until finish surface is applied.

If ceiling finish is already in place, faced insulation may be laid in from above with the facing down.

Owens-Corning recommends the installation of 6" of insulation (R-19) in ceilings for maximum comfort and economy.

Installing Friction Fit

Unfaced Friction Fit insulation is applied in a ceiling by placing it between joists. The insulation should overlap the wall plate slightly, but not enough to block eave vents. The insulation should touch the top of the plate along its full width to reduce air infiltration and consequent heat loss. If the

attic space is ventilated to meet applicable FHA requirements, a separate vapor barrier is not needed to prevent condensation damage. A separate vapor-resistant film will, however, help maintain controlled humidity levels within the house.

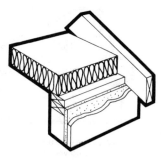

While insulation in a ceiling should always extend over the top wall plate, it is important that it is not allowed to block ventilation if eave vents exist.

Installing faced insulation

Inset stapling. In order to close the gap between inset stapled insulation and the plate at the end of a joist space and reduce air infiltration, pull the insulation

down slightly to lie snugly against the top of the top plate. Peel the facing back and staple to the edge of the plate as shown. Provide excess facing to accommodate finish application without rupturing facing.

Use sufficient staples to hold facing snug to the framing member. If the interior wall finish is to be drywall, caution the drywall contractor not to tear the flaps that are stapled to the top plate.

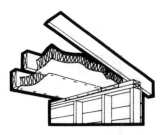

Face stapling. Insulation that has been face stapled to joists should be carried over the top of the top plate, as shown, to reduce air infiltration.

Installing insulation in floors

Reverse flange insulation

For insulating between floor joists from below, Owens-Corning provides a special Kraft-Faced insulation with the nailing flange attached to a special breather paper layer on the side opposite the kraft facing. This allows standard inset stapling techniques to be used, while keeping the vapor-resistant facing toward the warm-in-winter side.

Other methods

Ordinary Kraft-Faced or Foil-Faced insulation may be installed in floors with the facing up and supported by one of the following techniques:

1. Heavy-gauge wire pointed at both ends is bowed and wedged in place under insulation.

3. Chicken wire nailed to the bottom of floor joists will support the insulation.

2. Nails are located at intervals along the joists and insulation is supported by wire laced back and forth on the nails.

watt (W), which is equal to one unit of energy (joule) per second. The coefficient of heat transfer (U) is a measure of conductive heat loss through a material(s). The opposite of U is R, thermal resistance, where R = 1/U.

U is measured by heat flow (watts) per square meter of material(s) per degree Celsius temperature difference across the material thickness (W/m² • °C); the units of R are m² • °C/W.

Materials having one or two standard thicknesses are assigned R values for those thicknesses (Table 20.1). R values for other materials may be defined in terms of thickness and composition. Building assemblies (walls, roofs and floors) have R values that are sums of each component material's R value.

Table 20.1 which follows provides thermal and vapor resistant metric data for common building materials: insulation, structural, air, flooring, sheathing, cladding, exterior finish, and roofing. Comparisons of data are useful to possibly change pre-conceived ideas one may have with respect to thermal or vapor resistance. One example is cedar logs versus heavy concrete.

Careful examination of data in Table 20.1 may influence one to design buildings not only for strength and aesthetic values but for energy conservation.

Review

1. Define the term *cladding* as used in wood frame construction.

2. List five inside and five outside types of wall cladding.

3. Define the term *decibel,* and give an extract from your local building code concerning it.

4. List five different building materials used for sound control.

5. What considerations regarding noise should be taken into account before purchasing a building site for the erection of houses?

6. What is the function of a vapor barrier?

7. Make a freehand sketch of the plan of a staggered stud wall partition with blanket roll insulation.

8. Give three qualities of styrofoam T & G (tongue and groove) insulation.

9. Make a freehand sketch of a perimeter insulation detail for a heating duct and arrow and name the parts.

10. List eight characteristics of foamed-in-place insulation.

11. Make three neat freehand sketches of outside corner treatments of wood-wall siding.

12. Describe *Styrofoam* and state two advantages of using it.

Table 20.1   Thermal and Vapor Resistance of Common Building Materials

Building Material			Thickness (mm)	Thermal Resistance R(m²·°C/W)	Vapour Resistance r [(Pa·s·m²)/ng]
Insulation Materials		Flexible (Mineral Wool and Glass Fibre) Low Density High Density	89 89	1.8 2.0	2
		Loose Fill Macerated, Treated Paper Wood Shavings Vermiculite, Mica, Zonolite, Perlite	100 100 100	2.5 1.7 1.4	Variable
	Rigid	Structural		See Sheathing	
		Nonstructural Expanded Bead Polystyrene Type 1 Type 2 Extruded Polystyrene Foam Type 3 Type 4 Polyurethane or Isocyanurate Board Corkboard Glass Fibre Roof Board	100 100 100 100 100 100 100	2.6 2.8 3.0 3.5 4.2 2.6 2.8	10 - 30 48 36 — —
Structural Materials		Softwood Lumber (except cedar) Cedar Logs and Lumber	100 100	0.87 0.92	10 - 150 10 - 150
		Concrete 2400 kg/m³ 1760 kg/m³ 480 kg/m³	100 100 100	0.045 0.13 0.69	72
		Concrete Block (3 Oval Core) Sand and Gravel Cinder Aggregate Lightweight Aggregate	100 300 100 300 100 300	0.12 0.22 0.20 0.33 0.26 0.40	24
		Common Brick Clay or Shale Concrete Mix Face Brick (see Cladding)	100 100	0.07 0.05	72
		Stone (Lime or Sand)	100	0.06	Variable
		Steel	100	0.002 2	Variable
		Aluminum	100	0.000 49	Variable
Air		Enclosed Air Space (Nonreflective) Heat Flow Up Heat Flow Down Heat Flow Horizontal	20-190 20-100 20-100	0.15 0.18 0.17	None
		Air Surface Films Still air — Heat Flow Up — Heat Flow Down — Heat Flow Horizontal Moving Air	— — — —	0.11 0.16 0.12 0.03	None
Flooring		Asphalt Roll Roofing	Typical	0.026	Variable
		Asphalt Shingles	Typical	0.078	10 - 50
		Wood Shingles	Typical	0.17	10 - 50
		Built-Up Membrane (Hot-Mopped)	Typical	0.058	Impermeable
		Crushed Stone (Not Dried)	100	0.055	Variable

Table 20.1 (Continued)

	Building Material	Thickness (mm)	Thermal Resistance R($m^2 \cdot °C/W$)	Vapour Resistance r [(Pa·s·m^2)/ng]
Sheathing	Softwood Plywood	9.5	0.08	82
	Mat-Formed Particleboard, Waferboard	9.5	0.08	—
	Insulating Fibreboard Sheathing	25	0.4 - 0.5	1
	Vapour Barriers	Typical	—	>50
	Sheathing Paper	Typical	0.011	None
Cladding	Softwood Siding (Lapped)			Vapour resistance depends on finishing detail, materials and workmanship
	Drop (18 by 184 mm)	18	0.14	
	Bevel (12 by 184 mm)	12	0.14	
	Bevel (19 by 235 mm)	19	0.18	
	Plywood	9	0.10	
	Shingles	Typical	0.17	
	Fibreboard			
	Medium-Density Hardboard			
	(Panel or Lapped)	9.5	0.10	—
	High-Density Hardboard			
	(Tempered Service)	9.5	0.08	11
	Brick (Clay or Shale)	100	0.074	72
	Stucco (Metal Lath)	25	0.035	—
	Metal (Clapboard or Vertical V-Groove)	Typical	0.12	—
Interior Finish	Gypsum Board, Gypsum Lath	13	0.08	1
	Gypsum Plaster			3 - 5
	Sand Aggregate	13	0.018	
	Lightweight Aggregate	13	0.056	
	Wood Lath	Typical	0.05	—
	Metal Lath	Typical	—	—
	Hardboard (Standard)	6	0.032	5
	Insulating Fibreboard	25	0.42	—
	Plywood	7.5	0.07	—
Roofing	Maple or Oak (Hardwood)	19	0.12	Vapour resistance depends on finishing detail, materials and workmanship
	Pine or Fir (Softwood)	19	0.17	
	Plywood	16	0.14	
	Mat-Formed Particleboard	16	0.14	
	Linoleum or Tile (Resilient)	3	0.014	
	Terrazzo	25	0.014	
	Wood Fibre Tiles	13	0.21	
	Carpet			
	Fibrous Underlay	Typical	0.37	
	Rubber Underlay	Typical	0.23	

21

Subtrades and Job Safety

In this chapter, we shall discuss the persons involved in residential construction, the relationships between the GC (general contractor) and his subcontractors, and insurances.

The number of individual entrepreneurs compared to large organizations in the construction industry is decreasing, similar to that of the corner store and the supermarket. The pattern is set for this drift to continue. At this time, more and more individuals are specializing in fewer and fewer specific areas, but are becoming more skillful in their own fields. This demands ever better organizing ability by the GC, who must become efficient at having different subtrades and suppliers of materials of service units move onto, and from, the buildings at predetermined times. It also requires a wider, and up to date, knowledge of construction techniques on the part of the GC who also must be capable in the handling of men, finance, machine usage, and in anticipating future trends in the industry. See CPM (Critical Path Method) Chapter 6.

21.1 THE PROPOSAL TO BUILD

The concept of the erection of every building originates in the mind of one individual who, on his own, or in company with others, may exploit the idea. Immediate considerations involve such questions as: where to build residences, what design and price range of completed units, what financial requirements will be necessary, what types of service units (such as refrigerators and so on) should be installed; what building codes must be complied with. The GC should also keep in mind the prospect of building to meet the requirements of the "leisure industry" in such areas as lake or seaside homes or making one time logging camps into modern summer (or permanent) homes and so on. He should also take a close look at the prefabrication industry for home building. This is a fast developing area in residential construction.

As a rule of thumb, a family can afford to buy a house at roughly 2.5 times its annual income. Assume that a family income is $25,000.00; the family can afford to buy a house in the $65,000.00 range. *It is important for the GC to keep in mind that he build suitable residences, in appealing areas, to meet the demands of people earning specific salaries.*

21.2 THE APPRAISER

Before finalizing a design for a residence, it is useful to consider how an appraiser might value the proposed residence. Among other things, he uses a Measure-Master. This is an odometer wheel attached to the bottom of a long handle, which clicks off the footage as it is wheeled along the floor; it saves using a tape measure. This instrument is also used to check the traffic flow pattern, say, from the center of the kitchen to the front and back doors, to the laundry room, the garage, and so on. Assuming that it is 37'-0" from the central point in the kitchen to the laundry room, then it is 74'-0" for the round trip.

It is said that in a well-planned house one ought not to have to walk into the living room unless one wishes to do so; it should be a self-contained room to be used only for its specific role in the home and should not afford means of passage to any other area.

It is also considered by many people that the number of outside corners to a residence is one indication of its appeal. Four makes a house rectangular, six adds a recessed area, and anything over ten outside corners in a home may be considered as excellent. But the more corners, the greater the expense in concrete formwork, framing, roofing, and so on. From the underpinning to the chimney cap, the proposed residence should be assessed as to construction costs and sales appeal.

To remain competitive, a contractor must be adaptive to modern techniques and innovations, and be prepared to install many services such as:

(a) Air conditioning.

(b) Automatic pushbutton self-cleaning oven.

(c) Gas ranges and refrigerators.

(d) Automatic rotisserie and electrically operated thermometer.

(e) Double stainless steel kitchen sink with government approved waste disposal unit (sometimes called a garburetor).

(f) Automatic electric dishwasher.

(g) Fully formed formica counter tops and breakfast bars.

(h) Quick recovery large capacity water heater.

(i) Laundry room with installed washer and dryer, and an ironing area with ample

electric outlets including a 220 volt out-
let for dryer; outlets in this area for
telephone and television; and ample
storage for linen.

(j)   Total electric or other heating.

(k)   Door chimes.

(l)   Chandeliers.

(m)   The whole residence to be prewired for
      cable television, telephone in strategic
      areas, door chimes, and thermostatic
      controls.

(n)   All rooms and areas to be provided with
      vacuum cleaner outlets to carry dust
      direct to one large bag located in the
      garage; the bag may only require emp-
      tying every six months.

(o)   Silent switches.

(p)   Good plumbing fixtures, architectural
      metalware.

(q)   Ample mirrors and cabinets in the bath-
      room.

(r)   The latest and most attractive in metal
      ironwork and carpets.

(s)   Burglar alarm.

(t)   Smoke and fire alarms.

*Try drafting a newspaper advertisement
for your houses before you build them.* Then
compare it for value, appeal, and location
with current advertising for similar houses.
This will fix in your mind the type of competition you are to face.

21.3 RESPONSIBILITIES OF THE GENERAL CONTRACTOR TO THE SUBCONTRACTOR

It is usual in residential construction for the
GC to employ his own men for erecting and
removing concrete forms, for all wall and

roof framing, and in some cases to complete
the outside and inside trim.

The GC should provide each subcontractor with a pertinent extract of the progress
schedule and should endeavor to have the
dates for starting and completing each portion of work complied with. It requires great
organizing ability on the part of the GC to
arrange to have his own work crew advanced in their work, at each stage of production, so that the subtrades may commence their operations. As an example, once
a residence is closed, i.e., the walls roughed
in and the the roof framing and roofing
completed, the building may then be fitted
with temporary doors. The plumbers, electrician, air-conditioning contractors, telephone and cable television technicians, and
the sheetmetal workers may all run in their
lines.

Remember that all these lines must be
inspected by the local authority having jurisdiction before they may be covered with
insulation, wall boards or any other covering. Failure to have such work inspected
may result in the walls having to be opened
up for inspection.

Remember that, if any of the subtra-
despeople is late in completing his or her
work, every other operation may be equally
delayed. The longer it takes to complete a
unit, the greater the delay in the sale of the
project, and the longer it will have to be
financed by the GC. In addition, the prime
months for selling units may have passed.

It is important that the GC check that
all his subcontractors are bondable because
the GC may be held responsible for completing the work and financing the work of
a defaulting subcontractor.

All subcontractors should sign a subcontractor's form of agreement, and the GC
should make a practice of consulting with
his attorney before, *not after,* signing any
such legal document.

Some subcontractors work with the same GC, year in and year out, with amicable relations. It once came to my notice that a GC had placed a successful proposal bid for a project and had forgotten to include one page of an estimate sheet which amounted to more than $18,000.00. He called a meeting of all hs subcontractors, explained the situation, and they mutually agreed to cut their prices proportionately to the total contract price. They all made a profit, and they all respected each other. The memory is refreshing.

The GC should see that the area of operations for the subcontractors is always clear of debris and ready for them to start their work; also he must arrange that they each have an allotted place to store their materials.

21.4 THE EXCAVATOR

On small projects, the general contractor may use his own men, equipment, and knowledge of local ground conditions to clear a building site, grade the land to correct level, excavate, and take care of the water table, if necessary, by pumping, shoring or other means. But the GC must be aware that if he employs a subcontractor to do this work for him, such contractor must cover himself and his work crew by workmen's compensation and any other mandatory insurances. If this is not done, the responsibility for body or property damage is that of the GC.

Heavy construction equipment is expensive and requires continuous expert maintenance, accounting procedures, and a knowledge of allowable depreciation for income tax purposes. The GC must decide how much work to do himself, and how much to subcontract to others in their spec-

ialized fields. Although it is undesirable that the GC become merely the purveyor of other men's work, nevertheless it is usual for the GC to do no more than, say, 15% to 20% of all the work involved; this, in turn, means that he is only financing about that proportion of the total cost, but he may be held responsible for the safety of men, the public, adjoining property, and so on in case of default of any of his subcontractors.

Irrespective of who does the earthwork, the GC or his supervisor should be on the job from the turning of the sod to completion of the project. *A new building project that is correctly located on its legal location, with the first floor at its correct elevation in space is off to a good start.* Be careful with all preliminary building operations.

21.5 CONCRETE SUBCONTRACTORS

On most small residential projects, it is usual for the GC to use his own work crew to erect the concrete forms, place the reinforcing steel and the concrete, and remove the forms after use. These operations require the services of a supervisor who can interpret drawings, understand concrete form construction and know the reason why reinforcing steel must be placed as specified. Also, the supervisor must understand the design and control of concrete mixes.

While you are reading this, somewhere there has been a failure in the formwork for concrete, resulting in a loss of life, injuries to workmen, and presenting a very difficult job of cleaning up the mess and starting all over again. This delays the work and is an avoidable error. *Be doubly sure about the strength of the formwork.* Many companies specialize in this field, and for an inclusive price will erect and dismantle their own concrete forms, place the reinforcing steel and the concrete.

In rural districts of North America, and especially in developing countries, it is often necessary to mix concrete in the field, in which case the supervisor must be very competent and obtain the specified designed strength of concrete for every individual batch.

21.6 A GUIDELIST OF SUBTRADES

The following list is presented as a guide to the different specializing substrades. The list should be kept up to date and may be referred to when designing residential units. Remember that firm legal bids must be obtained from every subtrade before work is commenced. *Under no circumstances, should word-of-mouth agreements be accepted.*

1. land leveling and grading
2. water drainage and control
3. excavating
4. ditching and trenching
5. concrete contractors and finishers
6. concrete: prestressed, and post tensioned
7. concrete forms
8. concrete block
9. reinforced steel erectors
10. septic tank and field specialists
11. plumbing
12. electric and power
13. heating
14. air conditioning
15. telephone and television linesmen
16. sheetmetal workers
17. masons
18. swimming pool installers
19. roofing specialists
20. metalwork
21. drywallers
22. plastering and stucco wire
23. acoustic ceiling
24. chimney builder
25. doors and windows
26. glass block, glass and glazing
27. mirrors
28. chandeliers
29. tiles; earthenware, ceramic, plastic
30. insulators
31. beams "I"; wood solid, wood built up
32. flooring: hardwood, linoleum, tiles, broadloom, indoor-outdoor carpeting
33. hardware suppliers
34. painting and decorating
35. black top, gravel, and other drives
36. janitorial services
37. landscapers
38. sale and closing procedures

In addition to the foregoing, builders, supply houses and suppliers of units such as refrigerators should be regarded similarly to the subtrades, in that it is imperative that they make their deliveries at predetermined times, so that the progress schedule may be complied with. It is only in this manner that display homes may be opened for public inspection, and the advertising campaign be instituted to take advantage of the best selling seasons of the year.

21.7 WORKERS' COMPENSATION AGENCIES

All workers' compensation agencies publish general information, regulations, booklets, posters, films, notices, warning signs, signal cards, clues to accident protection, safety literature for inclusion in workers' pay checks, first-aid service requirements, and methods of artificial respiration. You must become familiar with them!

Prominently display by each telephone the numbers to call in an emergency for such services as: doctors, ambulance, fire, police, power and gas companies, city engineer, sanitation department, building inspectors, and the workers' compensation agency.

The supervisor or a senior assistant of the local workers' compensation board would make an ideal guest speaker at one of your association meetings. He will also show you some very impressive films. The board issues some very striking posters which should be prominently displayed around your jobs. They have the right to come onto your project at any time to check that all safety precautions are being observed, and that your medical kit or first-aid center is adequate for the job. Minimum standard kits are required according to the number of employees.

The question often arises with both workers and employers as to how serious an injury must be before a report is made and first-aid care is sought. *All accidents should be reported.* Many workers' compensation boards will honor any claim up to three years providing that an entry has been made at the time of accident in the accident report book or the builder's diary. Assume that a person slips and hurts the lower part of his back. No one knows whether or not this will develop into a serious malignant growth. It would be very difficult for the individual to register a claim unless a record was made at the time of the mishap. In the case of a married man with children (unless he could register a successful claim), it would be a tragedy. **All accidents, however minor, should be reported at the time of accident; check with the local workers' compensation board.**

The charges of the board for workers' compensation is about two per cent of the wage bill for ordinary construction. Do not start to work on a building site until you have covered every worker by this insurance. If the subcontractor has not legally covered his own people, he and his people are in your employ and you will be held responsible. Check that each subcontractor has insurance for his own people. (See sample form: Employer's Report of Injury or Industrial Disease, on page 279.)

Field First-Aid Rooms. The minimum requirement for any building operation *however small* is a first-aid kit. The agency for workers' compensation and employers' liability has information on the minimum first-aid requirements for any job, *however large.*

It is most important for you as an employer to be fully cognizant of your duties and responsibilities for accident prevention and for the administration of first-aid procedures to the sick and/or injured on your job site. You should get to know the officers of your insurance agency and have them give a talk to your staff.

First-aid notices (similar to the following) should be prominently displayed on the job near the first-aid room:

NOTICE

"When a qualified first aid attendant is engaged to render first-aid to injured workers, he/she shall be in complete charge of all

WORKMEN'S COMPENSATION BOARD OF BRITISH COLUMBIA

707 West 37th Avenue, Vancouver 13, B.C.   Telephone 266-0211   Telex 04-507765

Claim No.			
Firm No.	Loc.	Class & Sub.	Coded by

Employer's Report of Injury or Industrial Disease

FORM 7 REVISED 1969

SIGN HERE

Answer all questions, SIGN and mail to: Workmen's Compensation Board, 707 West 37th Avenue, Vancouver 13, B.C.

EMPLOYER'S NAME (please print)

WORKMAN'S LAST NAME (please print)
Mr.
Mrs.
Miss

Mailing Address

First Name(s)

Full Address

CITY   ZONE

NO.   STREET/R R   CITY & ZONE

Location of Plant or Project

Date of Birth
MONTH   DAY   YEAR

Social Insurance No.

Type of Business   Employer's Telephone No.

Occupation

Marital Status
MARRIED ☐   SINGLE ☐   OTHER

1. Date and time of injury   OR Period of Exposure Resulting in Industrial Disease:

19   , at   A.M./P.M.   FROM   19   TO   19

2. Injury was first reported to employer on
   19   , at   A.M./P.M.

IF EXPLANATIONS TO THE FOLLOWING QUESTIONS ARE REQUIRED, USE SPACE PROVIDED BELOW. USE SEPARATE NOTE OR LETTER IF NECESSARY.

3. Describe fully what happened to cause the injury and mention all contributing factors: description of machinery, weight and size of objects involved, etc.

OR In cases of industrial disease, describe fully how exposure occurred, mentioning any gases, vapours, dusts, chemicals, radiation, noise, source of infection or other causes.

8. Were workman's actions at time of injury for the purpose of your business? If NO, explain.   ☐ YES ☐ NO

9. Were they part of workman's regular work? If NO, explain.   ☐ YES ☐ NO

10. Are you satisfied injury occurred as stated by workman? If NO, explain.   ☐ YES ☐ NO

11. Have witnesses been interviewed?   ☐ YES ☐ NO
    If YES, do witnesses confirm workman's statement?   ☐ YES ☐ NO

12. Did workman receive first aid? If YES, attach form 7A.   ☐ YES ☐ NO

13. Is workman a relative of employer or a partner or principal in firm? If YES, specify.   ☐ YES ☐ NO

14. Was any person not in your employ to blame for this injury? If YES, give details and name and address of such person.   ☐ YES ☐ NO

State ALL injuries reported, indicating right or left if applicable.

4. City, town, or place where injury occurred.

5. How long has workman been employed by you?

15. Medical Insurance No. (MSA) or (BCMP)

6. How long at this particular job?

16. Name and address of physician or qualified practitioner.

7A. Was there any layoff beyond the day of injury?   ☐ YES ☐ NO
7B. Was layoff for three working days or more?   ☐ YES ☐ NO
    If YES, to part B, complete section below

1. Workman's gross earnings (enter one rate only) at time of injury
   per day $ per week $ per month $

7. Date and time he last worked.

2. If free room and/or meals were supplied in addition to above
   earnings indicate daily value. $

8. Enter normal working hours on day of lay off.
   From   A.M./P.M., to   A.M./P.M.

3. Do these earnings include rental of equipment? If YES, specify.   ☐ YES ☐ NO

9. Enter normal working days and hours per day   Sun. Mon. Tue. Wed. Thu. Fri. Sat.

4. Enter particulars of any payment, allowance or benefit made or to be made for period of disability.

10. Wages paid on day of lay off   Normal days pay
    $ $

5. Workman's gross earnings with you prior to injury
   3 mos $ 12 mos. $

11. Is he working now? If YES, give date and time of return.   ☐ YES ☐ NO

6. Duration of lay off, if any, from sickness during these periods.

12. If he worked after first lay off enter dates.
    From   19   to   19

Date	TITLE	SIGNED BY

Courtesy of the Workmen's Compensation Board, B.C.

first-aid treatments required. No person shall interfere while he/she is thus discharging proper first-aid duties, or while he/she is getting an injured worker to the nearest doctor or hospital to obtain treatment appropriate to the case.

Your cooperation is requested." *To be kept posted in all first-aid rooms.*

The following material has been excerpted from the fourth edition of *Insurance For Contractors* by Walter T. Derk, published by Fred S. James & Company, 230 West Monroe, Chicago, Illinois, 60606. The material is reproduced with permission.

21.8 INSURANCES

Some forms of insurance such as workmen's compensation and automobile insurance are (by law) mandatory. Some others for builders are obligatory upon and after signing a building contract; these may include a performance bond, lien bonds, and so on. Still others such as fire and public liability are imperative for the builder.

The complete loss of a business or its survival may often be ascribed to adequate insurance coverage or a lack thereof.

New contractors pay much higher insurance charges than experienced ones. The contracting business is a high risk industry; insurance is also a higher risk for newcomers into the field, and building supply houses are also less prone to accept new accounts without reserve.

It is very important for the contractor to remember that if a member of the general public wanders onto a building site (even out of curiosity) and is injured, the contractor is liable for such injury. Open excavations subject to flooding have often been the cause of a child's death from drowning, and the owner is culpable. You should fence!

It is prudent to make sure the insurance is adequate, but unnecessary insurance is a charge against successfully bidding, profits, or both. It is recommended that the contractor build a good business association with reputable bonding and insurance companies so that they can work together with mutual confidence.

Insurance companies have formulae to assess their risk with each contractor. One method used is the loss ratio. This is the ratio of premiums paid by the contractor to the company and losses paid out by the insurance company to the contractor. Another method is the experience modification formula, by which the actual experience of the contractor over a period of time (say five years) is assessed, affording good reading. The contractor should discuss these points with his broker and ask for an annual report about himself. As with many insurances, it may be more profitable to the contractor to absorb small material losses so that he may maintain a good record with minimum future premium charges.

Workers' compensation rates vary from state to state and in the provinces of Canada; they are also rated against the experience of the contractor.

Obviously it is only by progressing from simple, light construction to heavy construction that a contractor can build up his experience and reputation. Like everything else, success breeds success, and the more experience a contractor has with a minimum of claims, the cheaper the insurance.

Builder's Risk Insurance/Installation Floaters/Contractor's Equipment Floaters

The special problems of providing adequate property insurance during the course of construction are dealt with under Builder's Risk policy forms designed for that purpose. A good many variables tend to surround the subject, including not only the degree of coverage contemplated by several different policy forms but often who is covered and even what the coverage is called. In a limited space, we shall try to simplify matters a bit.

We shall concern oursleves here with the recommended Completed Value Builder's Risk policy and its Inland Marine counterpart, the Installation Floater. They may be written in the name of both the owner and the general contractor, either of them, or any of several variations; coverage may also apply to the work of subcontractors.

The prudent contractor, therefore, must review contract specifications to determine his obligation for this form of coverage.

He should guard against an outright duplication of coverage, however, since in many cases the owner or general contractor may have already purchased a policy protecting the entire venture.

Equipment and machinery, including electrical, plumbing, heating, and air-conditioning systems, should be insured as required while in transit from manufacturer to job site and during the period of actual installation or testing until fully released.

Coverage generally terminates when the insured's interest in the property terminates, when it is accepted, or when it is occupied by the owner. Covered building materials, such as bricks, steel, and lumber, are insured until actual installation into the real structure or until the insured's interest terminates, whichever happens first.

In some states, similar coverage is afforded the contractor under Special Builder's Risk Reporting Form, Contractor's Automatic Builder's Risk, or Contractor's Builder's Completed Value Reporting Form policies. What is available in your area should be determined by your insurance representative, who should make known what options

you have and determine which is recommended for you.

Even the perils covered by Builder's Risk and Installation Floater policies vary; they may insure against fire, lightning, the perils of Extended Coverage (windstorm, hail, explosion, riot, civil commotion, aircraft, vehicles, smoke), Vandalism and Malicous Mischief, or may be so-called "all-risk" floater policies designed to include still other risks. The latter are usually subject to variable deductible amounts, normally not applicable to the basic fire policy perils (This is probably as good a time as any to stress that "all-risk" is a relative, not an absolute term; there are still exclusions applicable, although the coverage is decidedly broad.)

The Inland Marine policy form applicable to contractor's equipment, other than vehicles designed for use on public highways, is called an Equipment Floater because it applies to things of a mobile or "floating" nature. Almost anything movable can be insured, whether a large crane, power shovel, caterpillar tractor, lift truck, or small tool. Most large units carrying high values are specifically scheduled on such policies and a blanket amount takes care of smaller items. Coverage can be made to automatically apply to new or replacement equipment. Note that automatic coverage for leased equipment requires a specific policy statement or endorsement to that effect.

Coverage is largely tailored to suit the exposure. It may apply to named perils or be written "all-risk," or sometimes a combination of the two. To provide protection against meaningful losses at a reasonable premium level, your insurance representative should arrive at a suitable deductible amount. If the exposures can be clearly separated, there is no reason why differing deductibles cannot be selected.

Premium rates are largely negotiated but based upon prior loss history; in general, elimination of petty pilferage claims is preferred to ground-up coverage on the presumption that any insurance company is going to want more than a dollar of premium for every dollar of routine loss they are called upon to pay. The small ones are best chalked up as a business expense.

The task of proper arrangement of coverage, deductibles, and premiums demands imagination as well as the experience of a skilled professional.

Contract and Other Bonds

A necessary adjunct to administration of a contractor's insurance program is the performance of similar services with regard to his contract bond requirements. One complements the other because a close working knowledge of work in progress, projects being bid or completed helps to enhance the close relationship which should exist between the contractor and his insurance/bond counselor. Obviously, it is a relationship dependent upon confidence, in many respects parallel to a good banking connection.

We shall limit ourselves here to naming some of the bonds required of contractors and briefly stating what they do:

Bid Bonds: Given by the contractor to the owner, guaranteeing that if awarded the contract, he will accept it and furnish final Performance or Payment Bonds as required.

Performance Bonds: Given by the contractor to the owner, guaranteeing that he will complete the contract as specified.

Labor and Material Payment Bonds: Given by the contractor to the owner, guaranteeing that he will pay all labor and material bills arising out of the contract.

Maintenance Bonds: Given by the contractor to the owner, guaranteeing to rectify defects in workmanship or materials for a specified time following completion. A one year maintenance bond is normally included in the performance bond without additional charge.

Completion Bonds: Given by the contractor to the owner and lending institution guaranteeing that the work will be completed and that funds will be provided for that purpose.

Supply Bonds: Given by the manufacturer or supply distributor to the owner guaranteeing that materials contracted for will be delivered as specified in the contract.

Subcontractor Bonds: Given by the subcontractor to the contractor guaranteeing performance of his contract and payment of all labor and material bills.

Such bonds are required by statute for federal, state, and local government work and, of course, specified for a great deal of private construction. They are the best form of guarantee that construction will be finished as required and that all bills will be paid. Amounts of bond required many vary from 10% to 100% of the total price of the contract, but are normally 100%.

Any undue delay or outright failure to secure a required contract bond could cost the contractor the job, so performance of the bond agent is all-important to success of the contractor/counselor partnership. You can help by promptly supplying all financial information requested and, in general, keeping him posted about the status of your present and future work program. Those who are relatively new to the contracting business should strive to establish a strong working relationship with such an insurance/bond source.

Other bonds you may encounter include:

License or Permit Bonds: Given by the contractor/licensee to a public body, guaranteeing compliance with statutes or ordinances, sometimes holding the public body harmless.

Sub-Division Bonds: Given by the developer to a public body, guaranteeing construction of all necessary improvements and utilities; similar to a completion bond.

Union Wage Bonds: Given by the contractor to a union, guaranteeing that the contractor will pay union scale wages to employees and remit to the union any welfare funds withheld.

Self-Insurers' Workers' Compensation Bonds: Given by a self-insured employer to the state, guaranteeing payment of statutory benefits to injured employees.

Others falling into the broad categories of Court Bonds and Fidelity Bonds will not be dwelled upon here; need for the former will be made known to you when and if the time comes, while the best method for protection against employee dishonesty will be brought to your attention by the professional charged with responsibility for your insurance/surety account.

Prompt Reports of Accident

Sprinkled throughout liability policies is a requirement that the insured give formal notice of claim to the insurance carrier as soon as practicable, an obvious requisite to efficient claim investigation and handling. By implication, this means promptly after the insured first has knowledge of a claim, although this could conceivably be a long time after the claimed occurrence itself.

Failure to do so may seriously inhibit your carrier's ability to investigate at all and further jeopardize their chances of arriving at a reasonable settlement. The company has a right to deny coverage under such circumstances.

It is always best in this respect to err on the side of reporting too much rather than too little. Notify your insurance representative at the first knowledge of any potential claim, leaving to to his judgment whether it is the opportune time to file a formal report, under which policies, etc. This will tend to convey a healthy feeling of loss control, professionalism in recognition of possible claims, and give your carrier a big jump on investigation while all the evidence is available, the facts fresh in everyone's mind.

21.9 EXPERIENCE RATING

Contractors and others become eligible for experience rating, that is, calculation of individual credits or debits applied to manual rates, dependent upon the ratio of premiums to losses over a given number of years. These rating plans vary a good deal with the kind of coverage involved. In principle, they are similar, however; all are closely scrutinized by state insurance departments, intrastate and interstate rating authorities, and independent rating organizations.

Manual rates contemplate a certain average level of losses and, by mathematical formula, a comparison is made of actual losses reported over roughly three years compared with expected levels. Weights or credibility factors are allowed to minimize the effect of single catastrophe losses so that the small contractor who reports just one serious case does not pay an astronomical premium for eternity. In general, a frequency of claims will count more in experience rating than will severity, but this effect decreases as premium volume increases.

Review

1. List ten important installations (such as a dishwasher or door chimes) that a competitive housebuilder should install to promote the sale of his houses.

2. List fifteen subtrades that may be involved in housebuilding.

3. List four professional persons who may be engaged by a housebuilder.

4. Define:

   (a) Bid bonds

   (b) Performance bonds

   (c) Labor and materials bonds

   (d) Maintenance bonds

   (e) Completion bonds

   (f) Supply bonds

   (g) Subcontractors' bonds

22

Stairs, Fireplaces, and Interior Trim

In effect, a stairway may be considered to be an inclined hall leading to other areas of a building. Remember that a good house is designed around the stairway. Stairs are provided for the purpose of passage of *persons of all ages in varying degrees of health,* and should be easy of ascent, and constructed strong enough to carry the weight of any predetermined load, such as persons carrying heavy pieces of furniture or equipment.

22.1 A GLOSSARY OF STAIR BUILDING TERMS

Stairwell opening: The opening in a floor through which ascent is gained to an upper floor.

Fascia board: The finished trim around the inside of a stairwell which covers the rough flooring assembly.

Total rise of a stair: The perpendicular height from the *finished* lower floor to the top of the *finished* floor above.

Riser: The perpendicular height from the top of one tread to the top of the next tread above. Note that there is one more riser than tread to every staircase because the top riser leads to a floor, not a tread.

Run of stairs: The horizontal distance from the front of the first riser at the foot of a stairway to the front of the top riser.

Run of stair tread: The horizontal distance from the front of one riser to the front of the next riser above. The nosing is additional to this. See Fig. 22.1.

Angle of Flight: The incline (slope) of a stair.

Headroom: The minimum allowable perpendicular height from a point on the angle of flight to the finished underside

of the floor, or stair soffit above. See Fig. 22.5.

Stair soffit: The finished underside of a stair.

Story rod: A straight wooden measuring rod which is placed perpendicular from the finish of one floor to the finish of the floor above on which is marked the total height of the stairs. It is used by stair builders. See Fig. 22.2.

Stringers: (a) The sides of stairs into which the treads and risers are secured.
(b) A mitered stringer is one into which the risers are mitered to an open stringer, i.e., a stringer that is not covered by a wall. See Fig. 22.1.
(c) A notched stringer is one from which (on the upper side) the profile of

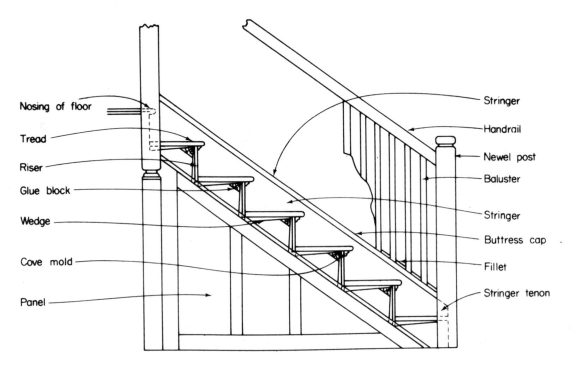

Fig. 22.1. Wooden stair with open stringer.

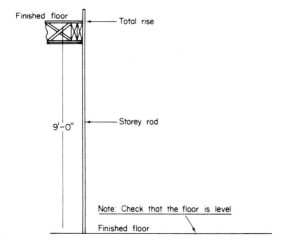

Finished floor — Total rise

9'-0" — Storey rod

Note: Check that the floor is level

Finished floor

Fig. 22.2. The story rod in position for measuring the total rise from finished floor to finished level floor.

the tread and riser is cut away. It is similar in some respects to a stair carriage. See Fig. 22.4.

(d) A housed stringer has grooves (trenches) cut into the stringer to receive the risers and treads. They are called housings in wood stringers and are usually half an inch deep. See Fig. 22.3.

Glue blocks: Triangular pieces of wood about three inches long and two inches wide on each side of a 90° angle. They are glued to the underside of wooden stairs. See Fig. 22.3.

Handrail: This is what its name implies. It should be placed thirty-two inches perpendicular above the face of the risers. At landings it should be placed thirty-six inches above the level of the floor.

Landings: Horizontal platforms between flights of stairs (usually to change the direction of the flight). They should be provided with a handrail.

Newel post: A post on a stair to which is secured the stringer. (See Fig. 22.1.)

Balusters: Vertical members placed between the tops of stringers (or treads) and the underneath side of the handrail. They must be close enough together to prevent children from falling between them. (See Fig. 22.1.)

Stairhorse: A rough lumber carriage supporting a staircase between stringers. (See Fig. 22.4.)

It is important that the local building code be studied and complied with, especially in such areas as:

(a) Maximum allowable (unvarying) heights of risers and widths of treads in any one flight.

(b) Minimum widths of stairs.

(c) Minimum allowable perpendicular headroom clearance between a point on the angle of flight to the underneath side of the floor, (or soffit of another stair) above.

(d) All stairs in residentail construction must be supplied with handrails. Stairs with less than three risers are a hazard and should be avoided if possible.

22.2 RISERS AND TREADS

There are several rules for determining the ratio-measurements between risers and treads. Some authorities assert that the sum of any two reasonable measurements for a riser and a tread, which together equal 17",

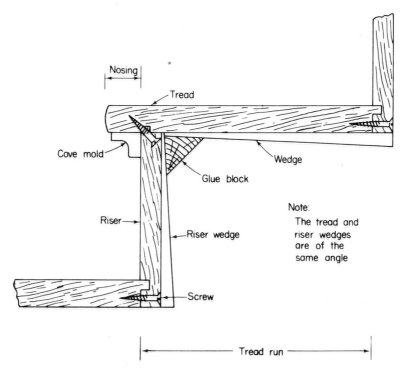

Fig. 22.3. Tread and riser assembly for a housed stringer staircase.

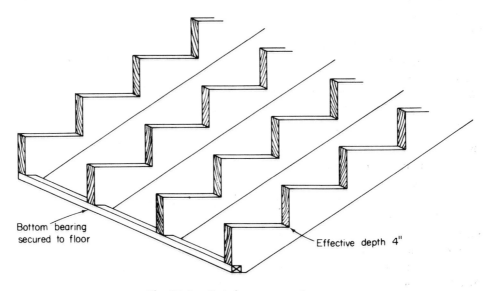

Fig. 22.4. Stair horse or carriage.

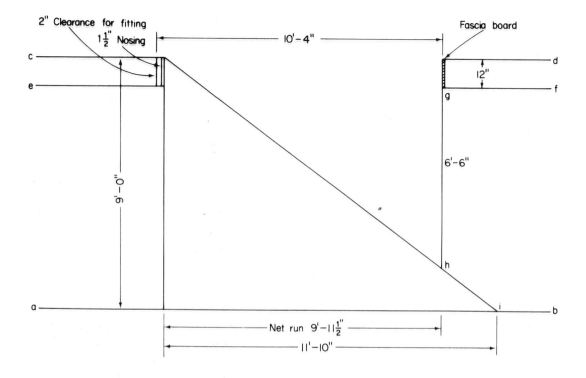

Fig. 22.5. Establishing the headroom clearance
and the line of flight for a stair.

will give an acceptable ratio, and provide a stair that is easy of ascent. A classic example may be seen at the Heliopolis at Baalbek in Lebanon built about 2,000 years ago.

Example

Rise	Tread	Inches
6	11	17
6¼	10¾	17
7³/₁₆	9¹³/₁₆	17
8	9	17 and so on.

The stairways for apartment buildings and new housing developments may be pre-fabricated either on or off the job, and they may be of wood, metal, or concrete construction, and all measurements are taken direct from the drawings and specifications.

22.3 FINDING THE LINE OF FLIGHT FOR A STAIRWAY

Assume that a stair builder has to design and build a staircase from the following references:

(a) rough stairwell openings 3'-3" × 10'-4"
(b) height from finished floor to
    finished floor   9'-0"
(c) total thickness of floor assembly   12"

(d) headroom clearance (check local
    code)   6'-6"
(e) clearance allowance for fitting the
    stair to the upper level   2"
(f) allowance at upper level for tread
    nosing   1¼"
(g) allowance for fascia board to
    rough floor opening   1"

Solution

Make a single-line scaled drawing as follows:

Step 1: Draw two parallel construction lines 9'-0" apart representing the two finished floors as at a-b and c-d, Fig. 22.5.

Step 2: Draw in the total thickness of the floor assembly. (12") as at e-f.

Step 3: Above line a-b lay off the length of the rough opening 10'-4".

Step 4: At the right hand end of the rough opening make an allowance for the thickness of the fascia board.

Step 5: Allow 2" at the upper left hand level for fitting the stair, and allow 1" for the thickness of the riser.

Step 6: Allow a further 1½" at the upper level for the stair nosing.

Step 7: From the bottom of the outside edge of the fascia board (right side of opening) project a 6'-6" perpendicular line as at g-h. This line represents the headroom clearance.

Step 8: From the top edge of the top riser at the upper floor level, draw a line of flight to

intersect with -h- (for headroom), and continue the line to the lower floor as -i-.

Step 9: Examine the drawing; this line of flight gives the best proportioned stairway from all the references given in this exercise.

22.4 RATIO OF RISE TO TREAD

To find an acceptable ratio for the rise and tread for the stairway shown in the foregoing exercise and assuming that the local building code states that no riser for this stairway may exceed 8" in depth, take the following steps:

Step 1: Arithmetically divide the total rise of 108" by 8, which equals 13½.

Step 2: Since 13½ risers are not permitted, divide 108 by 14. Using the rule of 17 for the ratio of riser to tread, this gives a rise of 7.71" and a tread of 9.29"; the sum of these figures equals 17". On one side of the story rod, mark with dividers all the riser positions. Adjust the dividers until exact measurements are obtained and recorded on the rod.

Geometrical Division of a Parallelogram into Equal Width Parts

Now let us have a bit of fun. To find the center line of a piece of 2 × 4 stock, (note that 2" × 4" is the sawn size of the lumber, and the finished size is 1⅝ × 3⅝") place a tape, square across the 3⅝" face of the stock. Traverse the tape until the 4" mark may be read on the top edge of the stock. Spot the 2" mark which is the center. Set an adjustable square to the center spot and draw in the center line ₵. See Fig. 22.6.

To divide a blank piece of 8½" × 11"

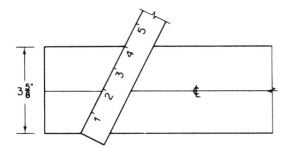

Fig. 22.6. Finding the center line ₵ of a piece of wood 3⅝″ wide.

typing paper into seven equal width columns, place a rule square across the paper as shown in Fig. 22.7 and traverse it until the 10½″ mark may be read on the opposite edge of the paper as shown. Spot mark every 1½″ unit onto the paper; note that 1½″ goes into 10½″ seven times. Now draw parallel lines to the lengthwise edge of the paper intersecting each spot mark. **Now ask yourself the question, what units would you use on a diagonally placed rule to divide the same paper into nine equal width columns?**

Now let us revert back to the stairs with step three:

Step 3: Figure 22.8 is drawn to the same scale as that of Fig. 22.5. To divide geometrically the total scaled rise of 108″ into 14 equal units, use as a focal point -b-, and traverse the scale rule to any convenient measure of 14 equal spaces and spot mark them (with a pin prick) as shown by the dotted line a-d.

Step 4: Draw horizontal lines parallel to the base line and intersecting the 108″ perpendicular, the pricked spots, and the line of flight. These lines at the intersection with the line of flight represent the treads. Drop perpendiculars to show the rise to each successive tread.

Problem: Re-do this exercise for a stair with similar specifications but with 15 risers.

Remember that stairs have one more riser than treads; this is because the top riser leads to a floor and not to another tread.

Handrails should be placed 32″ perpendicular *above the front* of the risers; and they should be placed 36″ above landings.

Mark the difference in headroom. **Question:** Do the headroom measurements meet local requirements?

Mark the headroom on the story rod.

22.5 CHIMNEYS AND FIREPLACES

In the whole field of residential construction, there are few things that will discredit a builder more than selling a house with an inefficient chimney which causes smoke in the room where the fireplace for solid fuel is provided. Apart from the nuisance, there is the risk of fire. For this reason, so that simple construction of a safe and efficient chimney and fireplace may be built, several authoritative sources of information are here given:

1. The Structural Clay Products Institute of America.

2. "Clay Masonry Manual," published by the Brick and Tile Institute of Ontario, Canada.

3. "Wood Frame House Construction," obtainable from the U.S. Government Printing Office.

4. "Wood Frame House Construction," obtainable from any office of the Canada Mortgage and Housing Corporation.

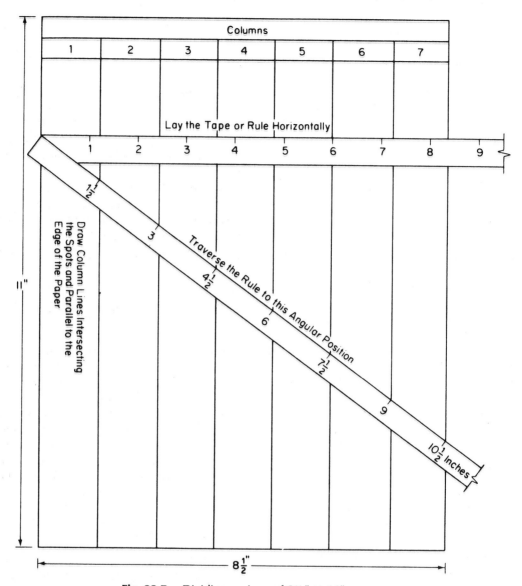

Fig. 22.7. Dividing a piece of 8½″ × 11″ paper
into seven equal width columns.

5. "The Canadian Code for Residential Construction," obtainable from the National Research Council of Canada.

6. "Book of Successful Fireplaces—How to Build Them!" by Donley.

7. The National Code as recommended by the National Board of Fire Underwriters.

8. Your local building code. Study it!

While there is nothing intricate nor

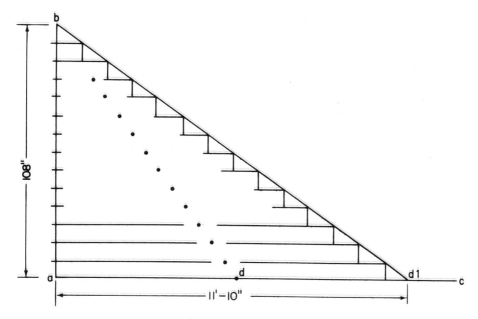

Fig. 22.8. The geometrical method of establishing the ratio between risers and treads.

difficult in the construction of a chimney and a fireplace, it is important that the contractor have knowledge sufficient to supervise his own men (or specializing subcontractors) in this field.

The following features are especially important:

1. The foundations for a chimney should be specially designed to support the heavy load.

2. All chimney flues serving solid fuel fires for any one stack shall be kept separate.

3. A metal cleanout opening with a tight fitting metal door shall be provided near the base of the chimney flue.

4. Chimney flues shall not be inclined more than 45° to the vertical.

5. Wood framing or other combustible material shall not be placed less than 2"

from the walls of a chimney, and 4" shall be allowed at the backs of fireplaces.

6. The space between the masonry of a chimney and any combustible material shall be firestopped with metal supported incombustible material.

7. Chimney flashing shall be provided at the uppermost point of the roofing at its intersection with the chimney.

8. The chimney shall be built at least 3'-0" above its intersection with the roofing, and it shall be not less than 2'-0" above the ridge or any other obstruction within 10'-0" of the chimney.

9. Chimney caps shall be designed to shed water away from the flue; they shall extend at least 1½" from all faces of the chimney; and be provided with a drip-

cap to prevent water from running down the face of the chimney walls.

22.6 A GLOSSARY OF CHIMNEY AND FIREPLACE TERMS

Fireplaces

ash dump; (see Fig. 22.9);
ash pit with metal door;

brick arch under finished hearth;
cleanout;
concrete slab under finished hearth;
damper;
flat concrete arch supporting chimney
     breast;
flue lining;
hearth, tiled;
mantle shelf;
metal arch supporting chimney breast;
mortar, cement above roof level and
     fireclay for enclosed brickwork;

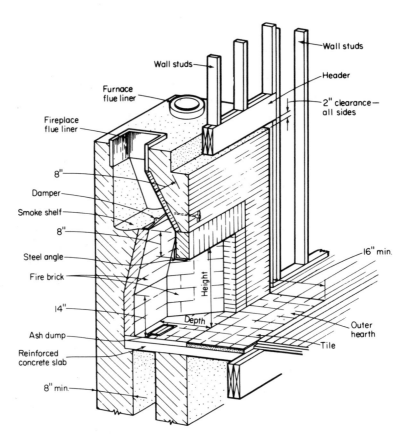

Fig. 22.9. Masonry fireplace *(Courtesy of the Forest Products Laboratory, U.S. Department of Agriculture.)*

smoke dome;
smoke shelf.

Chimneys

bricks, common, decorative, fireclay;
concrete cap over brick chimney;

cowl over chimney top;
cricket, small roof structure between the back of the chimney and the sloping roof;
flashing at chimney level;
flue lining;
height of chimney over roof line; See local bylaws;

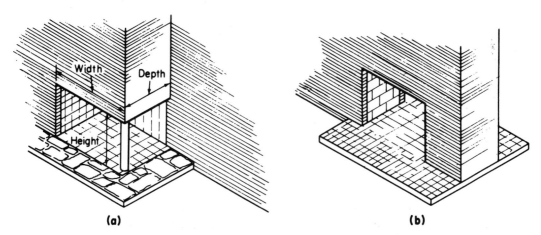

Fig. 22.10. Dual opening fireplace: (a) adjacent opening, and (b) through fireplace. *(Courtesy of the Forest Products Laboratory, U.S. Department of Agriculture.)*

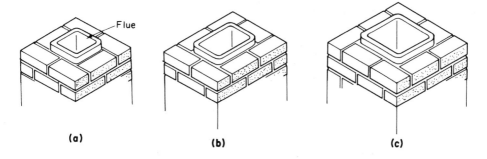

Fig. 22.11. Brick and flue combination: (a) 8 × 8 inch flue lining, (b) 8 × 12 inch flue lining, and (c) 12 × 12 inch flue lining. *(Courtesy of the Forest Products Laboratory, U.S. Department of Agriculture.)*

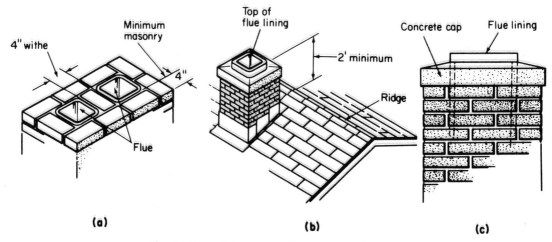

Fig. 22.12. Chimney details: (a) spacer between flues, (b) height of chimneys, and (c) chimney cap. *(Courtesy of the Forest Products Laboratory, U.S. Department of Agriculture.)*

independent concrete reinforced footings;

insulation between masonry and woodwork;

parging; lime, cement and sand mortar; pots;

revolving metal ventilators over the chimney cap.

22.7. CHIMNEY ILLUSTRATIONS

The following drawings are presented as graphic illustrations of chimney and fireplace construction; *but, study your local building code, and some of the publications mentioned in this section.*

22.8 THE METRIC "STANDARD" BRICK FORMAT

Although brick sizes may vary locally, the metric "Standard" brick format is 200 by 100 by 67 mm, when a 10 mm mortar joint is included. The brick itself measures 190 × 90 × 57 mm. The dimension of 67 mm is a rounded dimension and is such that 3 courses equals 200 mm. It takes 75 bricks to build 1 m² of wall. Nine courses, with mortar, are 600 mm high. (Reference: Housing and Urban Development Association of Canada. Information is compiled with permission.)

22.9. INTERIOR TRIM

The following material has been excerpted from a booklet published by Western Mouldings and Millwork Producers and is here reproduced by permission. Many of the mouldings are used when finishing stairs and fireplaces.

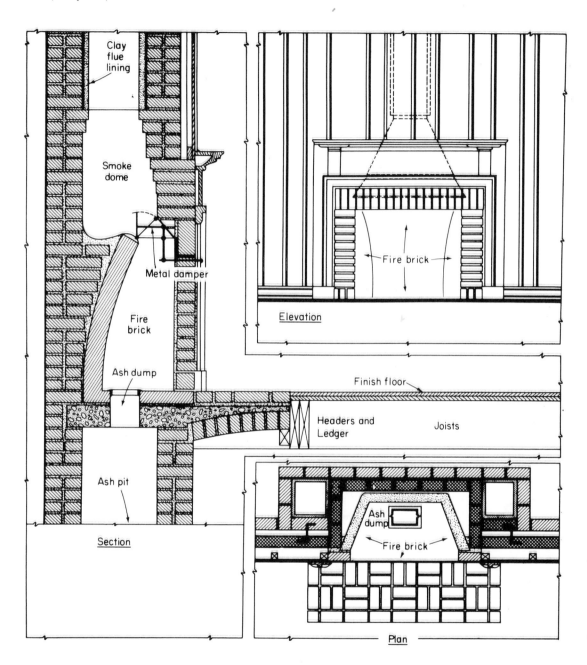

Fig. 22.13. Construction details of a typical fireplace. *(Courtesy of the Brick and Tile Institute of Ontario.)*

western wood moulding and millwork

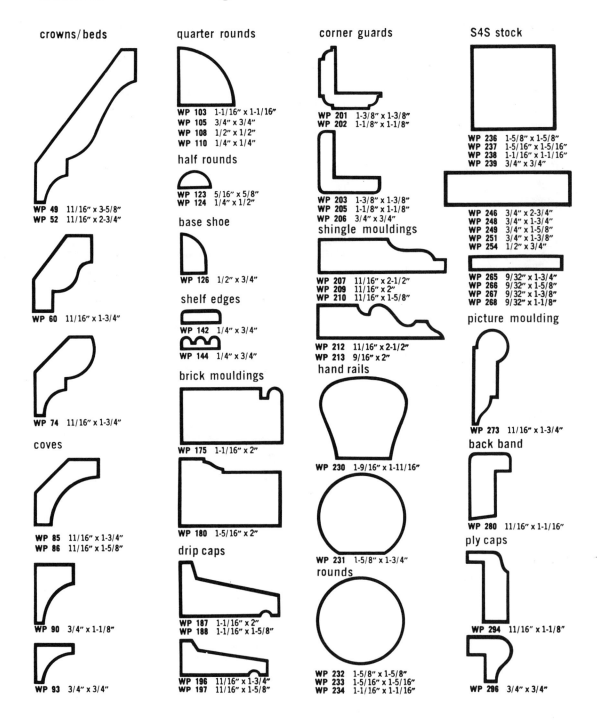

crowns/beds

WP 49   11/16" x 3-5/8"
WP 52   11/16" x 2-3/4"

WP 60   11/16" x 1-3/4"

WP 74   11/16" x 1-3/4"

coves

WP 85   11/16" x 1-3/4"
WP 86   11/16" x 1-5/8"

WP 90   3/4" x 1-1/8"

WP 93   3/4" x 3/4"

quarter rounds

WP 103   1-1/16" x 1-1/16"
WP 105   3/4" x 3/4"
WP 108   1/2" x 1/2"
WP 110   1/4" x 1/4"

half rounds

WP 123   5/16" x 5/8"
WP 124   1/4" x 1/2"

base shoe

WP 126   1/2" x 3/4"

shelf edges

WP 142   1/4" x 3/4"

WP 144   1/4" x 3/4"

brick mouldings

WP 175   1-1/16" x 2"

WP 180   1-5/16" x 2"

drip caps

WP 187   1-1/16" x 2"
WP 188   1-1/16" x 1-5/8"

WP 196   11/16" x 1-3/4"
WP 197   11/16" x 1-5/8"

corner guards

WP 201   1-3/8" x 1-3/8"
WP 202   1-1/8" x 1-1/8"

WP 203   1-3/8" x 1-3/8"
WP 205   1-1/8" x 1-1/8"
WP 206   3/4" x 3/4"

shingle mouldings

WP 207   11/16" x 2-1/2"
WP 209   11/16" x 2"
WP 210   11/16" x 1-5/8"

WP 212   11/16" x 2-1/2"
WP 213   9/16" x 2"

hand rails

WP 230   1-9/16" x 1-11/16"

WP 231   1-5/8" x 1-3/4"

rounds

WP 232   1-5/8" x 1-5/8"
WP 233   1-5/16" x 1-5/16"
WP 234   1-1/16" x 1-1/16"

S4S stock

WP 236   1-5/8" x 1-5/8"
WP 237   1-5/16" x 1-5/16"
WP 238   1-1/16" x 1-1/16"
WP 239   3/4" x 3/4"

WP 246   3/4" x 2-3/4"
WP 248   3/4" x 1-3/4"
WP 249   3/4" x 1-5/8"
WP 251   3/4" x 1-3/8"
WP 254   1/2" x 3/4"

WP 265   9/32" x 1-3/4"
WP 266   9/32" x 1-5/8"
WP 267   9/32" x 1-3/8"
WP 268   9/32" x 1-1/8"

picture moulding

WP 273   11/16" x 1-3/4"

back band

WP 280   11/16" x 1-1/16"

ply caps

WP 294   11/16" x 1-1/8"

WP 296   3/4" x 3/4"

Western Wood Moulding & Millwork
mouldings

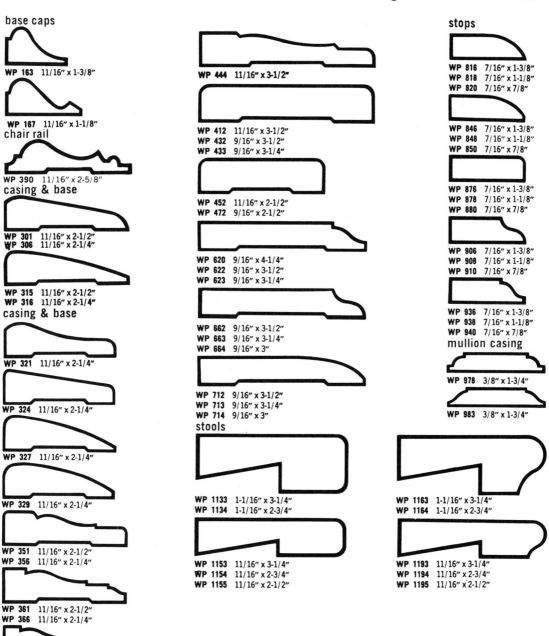

base caps

WP 163 11/16" x 1-3/8"

WP 167 11/16" x 1-1/8"

chair rail

WP 390 11/16" x 2-5/8"

casing & base

WP 301 11/16" x 2-1/2"
WP 306 11/16" x 2-1/4"

WP 315 11/16" x 2-1/2"
WP 316 11/16" x 2-1/4"

casing & base

WP 321 11/16" x 2-1/4"

WP 324 11/16" x 2-1/4"

WP 327 11/16" x 2-1/4"

WP 329 11/16" x 2-1/4"

WP 351 11/16" x 2-1/2"
WP 356 11/16" x 2-1/4"

WP 361 11/16" x 2-1/2"
WP 366 11/16" x 2-1/4"

WP 376 11/16" x 2-1/4"

WP 444 11/16" x 3-1/2"

WP 412 11/16" x 3-1/2"
WP 432 9/16" x 3-1/2"
WP 433 9/16" x 3-1/4"

WP 452 11/16" x 2-1/2"
WP 472 9/16" x 2-1/2"

WP 620 9/16" x 4-1/4"
WP 622 9/16" x 3-1/2"
WP 623 9/16" x 3-1/4"

WP 662 9/16" x 3-1/2"
WP 663 9/16" x 3-1/4"
WP 664 9/16" x 3"

WP 712 9/16" x 3-1/2"
WP 713 9/16" x 3-1/4"
WP 714 9/16" x 3"

stools

WP 1133 1-1/16" x 3-1/4"
WP 1134 1-1/16" x 2-3/4"

WP 1153 11/16" x 3-1/4"
WP 1154 11/16" x 2-3/4"
WP 1155 11/16" x 2-1/2"

stops

WP 816 7/16" x 1-3/8"
WP 818 7/16" x 1-1/8"
WP 820 7/16" x 7/8"

WP 846 7/16" x 1-3/8"
WP 848 7/16" x 1-1/8"
WP 850 7/16" x 7/8"

WP 876 7/16" x 1-3/8"
WP 878 7/16" x 1-1/8"
WP 880 7/16" x 7/8"

WP 906 7/16" x 1-3/8"
WP 908 7/16" x 1-1/8"
WP 910 7/16" x 7/8"

WP 936 7/16" x 1-3/8"
WP 938 7/16" x 1-1/8"
WP 940 7/16" x 7/8"

mullion casing

WP 978 3/8" x 1-3/4"

WP 983 3/8" x 1-3/4"

WP 1163 1-1/16" x 3-1/4"
WP 1164 1-1/16" x 2-3/4"

WP 1193 11/16" x 3-1/4"
WP 1194 11/16" x 2-3/4"
WP 1195 11/16" x 2-1/2"

Review

1. Define the following stair building terms:

   (a) stairwell opening

   (b) fascia board

   (c) run of stairs

   (d) angle of flight

   (e) story rod

   (f) newelpost

   (g) landing

   (h) stairhorse or carriage

   (i) baluster

   (j) stringer

2. State a rule for determining the relationship of the height of a riser to the width of a tread in stair building.

3. According to your local building code, what is the maximum height for a riser and the minimum width of a tread for basement stairs?

4. How many risers has a stair with twelve treads?

5. List three authorities from whom information may be obtained on how to erect a simple, safe and efficient chimney for a solid fuel fireplace.

6. List eight important features to observe when constructing a chimney for a solid fuel fireplace.

7. How would you estimate the total number of bricks required for any given residential chimney? Answer in not more than 120 words.

8. What is the minimum allowable height for a residential chimney above the highest point of the roof-line in your area?

9. Divide a piece of blank writing paper into 12 equal width columns.

10. Make a neat freehand sketch of each of the following traditional wood moulds: (a) a quarter round; (b) a shelf mould; (c) a brick mould; (d) a window stool; (e) a mullion casing.

23

Masonry Units, Glass Blocks, and Gliding Doors

In this chapter is presented a selection of excerpts from manufacturers' literature on the subject of masonry units, their types and methods of construction. This is followed with information about glass block construction and gliding doors.

23.1 INTRODUCTION TO MASONRY UNITS

During the last few years great progress has been made in the manufacture of masonry units in varying sizes, shapes, weights, textures and colors. They may be:

1. Manufactured for bearing walls, curtain or partition walls. (A curtain wall supports no compressive load other than its own weight. It is built between framing members of the building of which it forms part.)

2. Light or heavy weight, with two or three cores, and in different sizes, shapes and colors to meet specific needs.

3. Textured, natural concrete color, or glazed finish, also with a different color finish on opposite faces.

4. Cut on the job for fitting around other fixtures.

5. Filled with insulation.

6. Rodent free.

7. Easy for subtrades to chase for wiring such as electric, telephone, and television wiring. (To chase is to cut into the face of a structure to accommodate conduit and so on.)

8. Fire resisting.

9. Used for outside basement walls which may be water or dampproofed.

10. Plastered or furred out to receive decorative wood or other panels. (Furring strips of wood may be applied to a surface in order to secure another material such as tiles to a ceiling or wood panels to a concrete block wall.)

11. Used for wythes which may be anchored to each other.

12. Used in inclement or hot weather to build the outside faces of curtain walls; the masons may then work under weather controlled conditions to build the inner wythes, or back-ups.

13. Used for walls to be reinforced and bonded into any design, and be provided with control joints to prevent fracturing of walls due to settlement or small earth tremors.

14. Used ideally for modular construction.

15. Used (when suitably reinforced) to form piers for framing.

Where ground conditions are favorable, masonry units may be used to build basement walls, affording a saving in time and material for the construction, erection, removing, and reconditioning of concrete forms. Each concrete block when layed-up becomes an immediate integral part of the structure. A well designed basement may also be provided with party walls separating different areas, and some of the faces of such walls may be built with texture faced blocks with a different color on opposite faces. The outside walls of crawl spaces may be insulated against cold penetration from the outside and as a means of conserving heat within the walled enclosed area.

23.2 ADJUSTABLE WALL TIES, REINFORCING, AND CONTROL JOINTS

The material for this section has been excerpted from bulletins published by Dur-O-Wal National Inc., and is here reproduced with permission.

23.3 GLAZED MASONRY WALLS

The material for this section has been excerpted from literature supplied by The Burns & Russell Company and is here reproduced with the permission of the copyright holder. It may not be further reproduced or copied without the written permission of the Burns & Russell Company.

23.4 GLASS BLOCKS, AND GLASS BLOCK PANEL CONSTRUCTION

The material for this section has been excerpted from booklets supplied by the Pittsburgh Corning Corporation, and is here reproduced with permission.

DUR-O-waL®
TRUSS INSTALLATION AND PLACEMENT

PLACEMENT
Out to out spacing of side rods shall be approximately 2 inches less than the nominal thickness of the wall or wythe and shall be placed to insure a minimum of ⅝" mortar cover on exterior face of walls and ½" on the interior face.

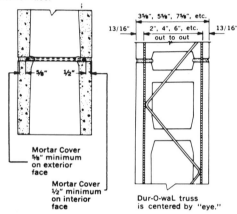

Mortar Cover ⅝" minimum on exterior face

Mortar Cover ½" minimum on interior face

Dur-O-waL truss is centered by "eye."

CORNERS AND TEES
Prefabricated or job fabricated corner and tee sections shall be used to form continuous reinforcement around corners, and for anchoring abutting walls and partitions. Material in corner and tee sections shall correspond to type and design of reinforcement used.

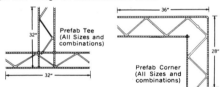

Prefab Tee (All Sizes and combinations)

Prefab Corner (All Sizes and combinations)

SPLICES
Side rods shall be lapped at least 6 inches at splices.

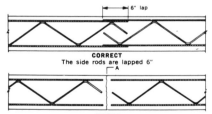

CORRECT
The side rods are lapped 6"

WRONG
The side rods are not lapped. Reinforcement is ineffective in preventing a crack from starting and opening up at A.
Proper lapping of rods at splices is essential to the continuity of the reinforcement so that tensile stress will be transmitted from one rod to the other across the splice.

FACED AND COMPOSITE WALLS
Dur-O-waL shall be centered over both wythes and the galvanized diagonal cross rods shall serve as ties. Dur-O-waL shall be spaced 16" o.c. vertically and the collar joint shall be filled solidly with mortar.

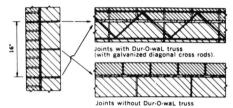

Joints with Dur-O-waL truss (with galvanized diagonal cross rods).

Joints without Dur-O-waL truss

WALLS NOT TIED WITH DUR-O-WAL TRUSS CROSS RODS
Place Dur-O-waL in (each wythe) (backing wythe) 16" o.c. of all faced, cavity or veneered wall not otherwise noted as being tied with the cross rods of Dur-O-waL.

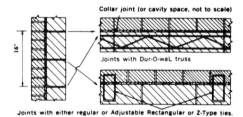

Collar joint (or cavity space, not to scale)

Joints with Dur-O-waL truss

Joints with either regular or Adjustable Rectangular or Z-Type ties.

EXTRA TIES
Provide extra ties at all openings in masonry walls by bending and hooking side rod or cross rod of Dur-O-waL or by adding either regular or adjustable wall ties in alternate courses with Dur-O-waL.

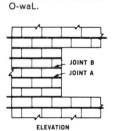

JOINT B
JOINT A

ELEVATION

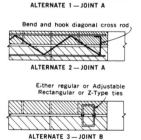

Bend and hook side rod
ALTERNATE 1 — JOINT A

Bend and hook diagonal cross rod
ALTERNATE 2 — JOINT A

Either regular or Adjustable Rectangular or Z-Type ties
ALTERNATE 3 — JOINT B

DUR-O-WAL®
TRUSS INSTALLATION AND PLACEMENT

PLACEMENT
Out to out spacing of side rods shall be approximately 2 inches less than the nominal thickness of the wall or wythe and shall be placed to insure a minimum of ⅝″ mortar cover on exterior face of walls and ½″ on the interior face.

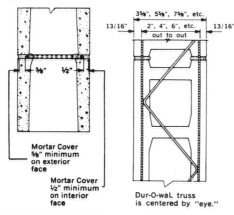

Mortar Cover
⅝″ minimum
on exterior
face

Mortar Cover
½″ minimum
on interior
face

Dur-O-waL truss
is centered by "eye."

CORNERS AND TEES
Prefabricated or job fabricated corner and tee sections shall be used to form continuous reinforcement around corners, and for anchoring abutting walls and partitions. Material in corner and tee sections shall correspond to type and design of reinforcement used.

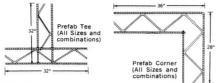

Prefab Tee
(All Sizes and
combinations)

Prefab Corner
(All Sizes and
combinations)

SPLICES
Side rods shall be lapped at least 6 inches at splices.

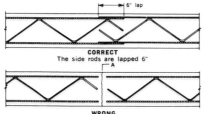

6″ lap

CORRECT
The side rods are lapped 6″

WRONG
The side rods are not lapped. Reinforcement is ineffective in preventing a crack from starting and opening up at A.

Proper lapping of rods at splices is essential to the continuity of the reinforcement so that tensile stress will be transmitted from one rod to the other across the splice.

FACED AND COMPOSITE WALLS
Dur-O-waL shall be centered over both wythes and the galvanized diagonal cross rods shall serve as ties. Dur-O-waL shall be spaced 16″ o.c. vertically and the collar joint shall be filled solidly with mortar.

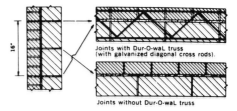

Joints with Dur-O-waL truss
(with galvanized diagonal cross rods).

Joints without Dur-O-waL truss

WALLS NOT TIED WITH DUR-O-WAL TRUSS CROSS RODS
Place Dur-O-waL in (each wythe) (backing wythe) 16″ o.c. of all faced, cavity or veneered wall not otherwise noted as being tied with the cross rods of Dur-O-waL.

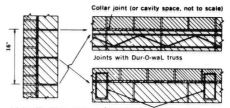

Collar joint (or cavity space, not to scale)

Joints with Dur-O-waL truss

Joints with either regular or Adjustable Rectangular or Z-Type ties.

EXTRA TIES
Provide extra ties at all openings in masonry walls by bending and hooking side rod or cross rod of Dur-O-waL or by adding either regular or adjustable wall ties in alternate courses with Dur-O-waL.

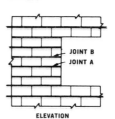

JOINT B
JOINT A

ELEVATION

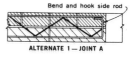

Bend and hook side rod

ALTERNATE 1 — JOINT A

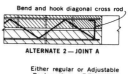

Bend and hook diagonal cross rod

ALTERNATE 2 — JOINT A

Either regular or Adjustable
Rectangular or Z-Type ties

ALTERNATE 3 — JOINT B

DUR-O-waL®

TYPICAL TRUSS INSTALLATIONS AND SPECIFICATIONS

COMPOSITE WALLS

12″ Tied Wall No. 12 Dur-O-waL
16″ c. to c.

12″ Tied Wall with Stack Bond
Facing No. 12 Dur-O-waL 16″ c. to c.

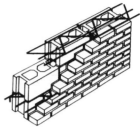

12″ Tied Wall Stack Bond Backup
No. 12 Dur-O-waL Trirod 16″ c. to c.

CAVITY WALLS

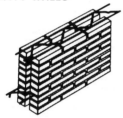

10″ Cavity Wall No. 10 Dur-O-waL
With Drip 16″ c. to c.

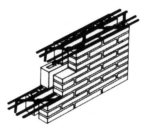

10″ Cavity Wall No. 10 Dur-O-waL
Double With Drip 16″ c. to c.

12″ Cavity Wall No. 12 Dur-O-waL
Trirod with Drip 16″ c. to c.

SINGLE WYTHE WALLS

Stack Bond Load Bearing Walls.
Dur-O-waL—8″ c. to c. Top 3
Courses. 16″ c. to c. Remainder of
Wall. Non Load Bearing Walls.
Dur-O-waL—16″ c. to c.

8″ Wall showing Corner No. 8
Dur-O-waL 16″ c. to c.

8″ Wall with Pilaster No. 8
Dur-O-waL 16″ c. to c.

WALL OPENINGS—Unless otherwise noted, Dur-O-waL shall be installed in the first and second bed joints, 8 inches apart immediately above lintels and below sills at openings and in bed joints at 16-inch vertical intervals elsewhere. Reinforcement in the second bed joint above or below openings shall extend two feet beyond the jambs. All other reinforcement shall be continuous except it shall not pass through vertical masonry control joints.

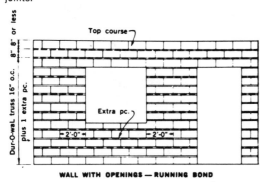

WALL WITH OPENINGS — RUNNING BOND

SINGLE WYTHE WALLS—Exterior and interior. Place Dur-O-waL 16″ o.c. and in bed joint of the top course.

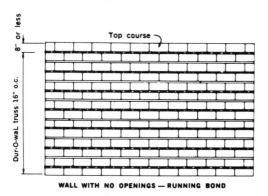

WALL WITH NO OPENINGS — RUNNING BOND

FOUNDATION WALLS—Place Dur-O-waL 8″ o.c. in upper half to two-thirds of wall.

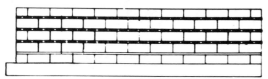

Foundation Wall

BASEMENT WALLS—Place Dur-O-waL in first joint below top of wall and 8″ o.c. in the top 5 bed joints below openings.

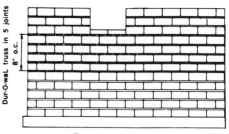

Basement Wall

STACK BOND—Dur-O-waL shall be placed 16″ o.c. vertically in walls laid in stack bond except it shall be placed 8″ o.c. for the top 3 courses in load bearing walls.

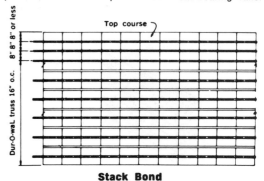

Stack Bond

CONTROL JOINTS—Unless as otherwise noted, all reinforcement shall be continuous except it shall not pass through vertical masonry control joints.

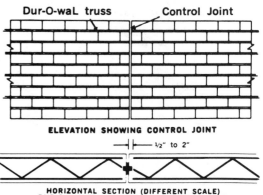

ELEVATION SHOWING CONTROL JOINT

HORIZONTAL SECTION (DIFFERENT SCALE)
DUR-O-WAL TRUSS SHOULD NOT CROSS OVER CONTROL JOINT

DUR-O-WAL ADJUSTABLE WALL TIES, THEIR STRUCTURAL PROPERTIES AND RECOMMENDED USE*

DESCRIPTION

As shown in Fig. 1 the ties consist of two pieces, a double eye unit and a double pintle unit. They are made of 3/16 in. diameter cold drawn steel wire complying with ASTM A82. The wire is galvanized to retard corrosion of portions of the tie which are not embedded in mortar and thereby protected.

Adjustable ties are designed for use in double wythe masonry walls in which the facing and backing do not course-out at proper intervals as to permit tying with masonry headers or straight metal ties. Where this situation is met by bending straight ties to fit or by using flexible metal strips the results are not satisfactory from either a structural or economic standpoint.

The ties will accommodate variations in joint levels up to $1\frac{1}{2}$ in. Practice in installation is to set the eye units in the wythe which is built up first, it being more convenient to engage the pintles in the eyes rather than vice versa. Generally the pintles are installed downward through the eyes although if necessary they can be installed in the reverse position. As indicated in Fig. 1 the looped portion or shank of each unit is embedded in the horizontal mortar joint.

STRENGTH OF TIES

The strength of the ties was investigated in a program of tests performed by the Armour Research Foundation of the Illinois Institute of Technology. Specimens consisting of single eyes and single pintles were loaded as shown schematically in Fig. 2. The average results of three or more tests are given in Table 1.

TABLE 1

Unit (3/16 in. diam. wire)	Load Position	y (Exposed Shank) in.	e (Eccentricity) in.	Yield Load, lb.
Single eye	—	—	—	550
Single pintle	1	$1\frac{3}{4}$	0	490
do	2	1	$1\frac{1}{2}$	50
do	2	$1\frac{3}{4}$	$1\frac{1}{2}$	40

The results indicate that the double pintle-eye tie will resist a compressive or tensile load of at least 80 lb. where applied at the maximum eccentricity ($1\frac{1}{2}$ in.) and greater loads up to about 980 lb. as the load eccentricity decreases to zero.

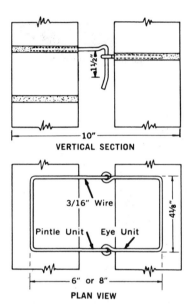

FIGURE 1. DUR-O-WAL ADJUSTABLE WALL TIE

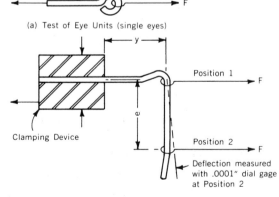

(a) Test of Eye Units (single eyes)

(b) Test of Pintle Units (single pintles)
Note: y = 1" & $1\frac{3}{4}$"
e = 0 (Position 1) & $1\frac{1}{2}$" (Position 2)

FIGURE 2. SCHEMATIC OF TESTS OF EYE AND PINTLE UNITS

DUR-O-WAL®

RAPID® CONTROL JOINT

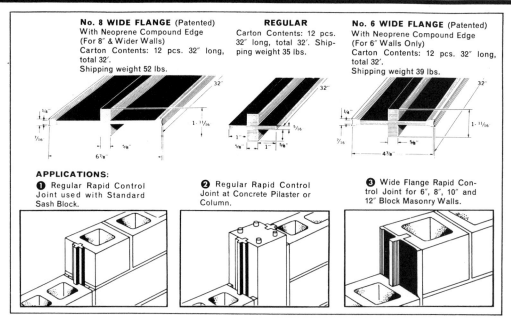

No. 8 WIDE FLANGE (Patented)
With Neoprene Compound Edge
(For 8" & Wider Walls)
Carton Contents: 12 pcs. 32" long,
total 32'.
Shipping weight 52 lbs.

REGULAR
Carton Contents: 12 pcs.
32" long, total 32'. Shipping weight 35 lbs.

No. 6 WIDE FLANGE (Patented)
With Neoprene Compound Edge
(For 6" Walls Only)
Carton Contents: 12 pcs. 32" long,
total 32'.
Shipping weight 39 lbs.

APPLICATIONS:

❶ Regular Rapid Control Joint used with Standard Sash Block.

❷ Regular Rapid Control Joint at Concrete Pilaster or Column.

❸ Wide Flange Rapid Control Joint for 6", 8", 10" and 12" Block Masonry Walls.

PRODUCT DESCRIPTION

Rapid Control Joint is preformed gasket designed to be used with standard concrete sash block to provide a vertical joint of stress relief in concrete masonry walls.

Types—The two basic types of the Rapid Control Joint are the Regular and the Wide Flange. The Wide Flange utilizes a concave neoprene compound edge that can be compressed tightly in the joint.

Regular Rapid Control Joint is a factory-extruded solid section of rubber conforming to ASTM D-2000 2AA-805 with a durometer hardness of approximately 80 when tested in conformance with ASTM D-2240. The shear section is ⅝-inch in thickness. The 5/16-inch flange thickness is designed to provide a control-joint width of approximately ⅜-inch.

Wide Flange Rapid Control Joint is a factory molded product of rubber conforming to ASTM D-2000 2AA-805 with a compressible neoprene compound edge conforming to ASTM 2BC-310C12 with a durometer hardness of 30.

BASIC USES AND FUNCTIONS

To provide a vertical stress relieving joint in concrete masonry walls while providing adequate shear strength for lateral stability of the wall.

For control joints to perform adequately, the following three principles should be considered:

1. *Stress Relief:* The joint must cut the masonry wall completely from top to bottom, so as to form a truly stress relieving joint.

2. *Shear Strength:* The joint must be structurally sound in that sufficient strength is developed to provide for lateral stability.

3. *Weather Tight:* The joint must be either self-sealing or one that can be easily caulked to prevent moisture penetration.

RESEARCH

Shear tests were conducted on the two types of Rapid Control Joint at IIT Research Institute (Formerly Armour Research Foundation). Results in Table 1 indicate a large factor of safety for recommended control joint spacing. For example, with control joint spacing of 20' a 20 psf wind load would result in a shear stress in the key of about 27 psi. This is significantly less than the shear strength of the material developed in the tests.

TABLE 14: SHEAR STRENGTH

Control Joint Type	Average Load per 8" of Joint (lbs)	Shear Strength (psi)
Wide Flange	2350	470
Regular	2706	541

SPECIFICATION FOR RAPID CONTROL JOINT.

(Regular) (Wide Flange) Rapid Control Joint, a product of Dur-O-waL, or approved rubber material of equal shear strength shall be placed in masonry walls as noted on plans.

 glazed masonry units   4uni / BU

The Economy of Block . . . The Performance of Glaze. Build and Finish in One Operation

Wide variety of structural shapes (See pgs. 4 & 5)

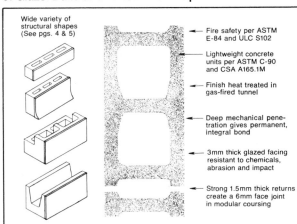

← Fire safety per ASTM E-84 and ULC S102

← Lightweight concrete units per ASTM C-90 and CSA A165.1M

← Finish heat treated in gas-fired tunnel

← Deep mechanical penetration gives permanent, integral bond

← 3mm thick glazed facing resistant to chemicals, abrasion and impact

← Strong 1.5mm thick returns create a 6mm face joint in modular coursing

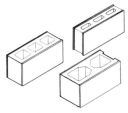

Double-glazed units provide the economy of two-face walls in a single operation, where precise bed-depth tolerances are not mandatory. For double-glazed units, bed-depth tolerances conform to ASTM C-90 and CSA A165.1M.

93mm units for partitions save 50mm of valuable floor space

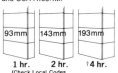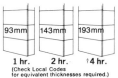

93mm	143mm	193mm
1 hr.	2 hr.	†4 hr.

(Check Local Codes for equivalent thicknesses required.)

SPECTRA-GLAZE® units provide fire rating of the block, certification upon request. Facing exceeds national code requirements as tested per ASTM E-84 and ULC S102.

Eliminate back-up wall by use of thru-wall units 143, 193 or 293mm thick

† With 75% solid block. In some states with expanded insulating fill in standard 193mm block.

Standard Series

NOTE: All dimensions shown are in millimeters (mm).

Units supplied will be 2 or 3 core, open or closed end, depending upon local block manufacturing practices.

Double-glazed units provide the economy of two-face walls in a single operation, where precise bed-depth tolerances are not mandatory. For double-glazed units, bed-depth tolerances conform to ASTM C-90 and CSA A165.1M.

Consult your nearest Manufacturer for availability in heights other than those shown.

*Specify right or left (right shown).
†Also in other standard thicknesses.
**Consult your nearest Manufacturer for availability (see page 12).

Cove Base

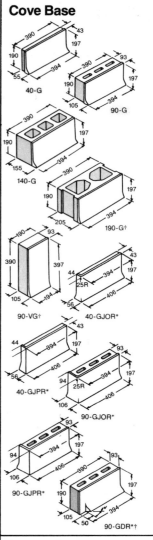

Field

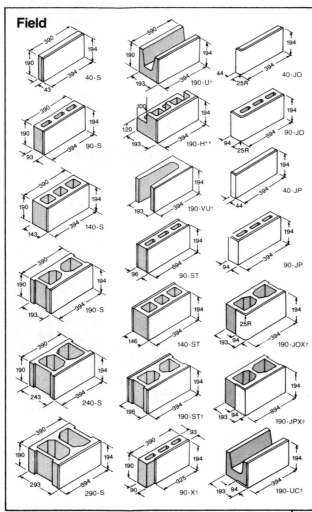

Straight Base

(94mm high, glazed 2 sides)

190/90-ST†

Specta-Glaze II ® | glazed masonry units | 4uni / BU

Greater design flexibility . . . Cleaner, subtler detailing . . . Elimination of unsightly joints.

25mm block thickness — 28mm glazed block thickness; 40mm block thickness — 43mm glazed block thickness.

Not all Manufacturers make both the 25mm and the 40mm Series. Please check with your nearest Manufacturer for units available.

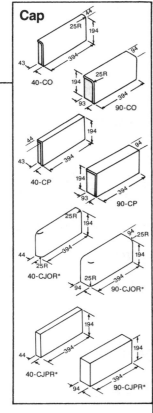

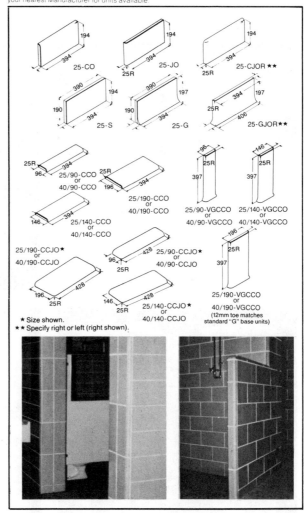

★ Size shown.
★★ Specify right or left (right shown).

The Cove Base provides a modularly dimensioned sanitary base unit installed without a floor recess. Meets OSHA requirements.

Glare and Heat Reducing Inserts

As indicated below, many of the PC glass units are available with fibrous inserts for medium control of brightness, solar heat gain and light transmission.

"LX" Insert—white fibrous insert for use where medium control is desired. SUNTROL® Insert—green fibrous insert for use where maximum control is desired.

Non-Light Directing Units

DECORA

ARGUS

Sculptured Glass Modules

These basic geometric shapes are pressed into the glass to a depth of approximately 1½ inches on both sides of the unit. All patterns are available in clear glass. Each unit is 12" square and weighs about 17 pounds. They are installed on the same proportionate module and in the same manner as all Pittsburgh Corning Glass Units. Modules like other Pittsburgh Corning glass units offer light, insulation value and a finished job in one operation.

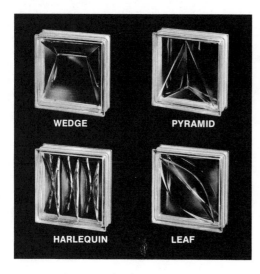

WEDGE   **PYRAMID**

HARLEQUIN   **LEAF**

Non-Light Directing Units

DECORA®—The Decora unit gives high light transmission and can be installed in any position. Design is pressed into the inner faces, and the outer faces of the unit are smooth. This unit is almost transparent and is not recommended for sun exposures. Available in 6, 8, and 12-inch squares and with "LX" or Suntrol® insert.

ARGUS®—The outer faces of this unit are smooth. Rounded flutes on inner faces are at right angles to each other. Laid with flutes on one side either horizontal or vertical. 6, 8, and 12-inch squares.

ARGUS PARALLEL FLUTES—High light transmission is available with this unit. It is the same basic unit as the Argus, except flutes are parallel. This unit can be laid with flutes horizontal or vertical. Available in 6, 8, and 12-inch squares plain and 8 and 12-inch squares with the "LX" insert.

VUE®—Here is a glass unit that provides high light transmission and good visibility. It is frequently used in panels of other patterns to provide a vision area where desired. It can be laid without regard to which edge is side or top. Both the outer and the inner faces are smooth and clear. 8 and 12-inch squares.

ARGUS PARALLEL FLUTES   **VUE**

4 x 12 Glass Blocks

This striking rectangular block is smooth on the outer faces, textured on the inner surfaces. In clear glass, it is offered in three degrees of light control. Plain (normal), "LX" (medium), or Suntrol (maximum). They can be integrated with standard blocks, Sculptured Glass Modules, or any number of other masonry building materials.

Light-Diffusing Units

ESSEX®—Diffuses sunlight in all directions. For sun or non-sun exposures. Give maximum light transmission; moderate brightness and solar heat control. 8 and 12-inch squares. Available with "LX" or Suntrol inserts, 8 and 12-inch squares.

Light-Directing Units

PRISM B—Recommended on sun or non-sun exposures for maximum light transmission; moderate brightness and solar heat control. Available in 8 and 12-inch squares. Available with "LX" or Suntrol inserts in 8 and 12-inch squares.
NOTE: Do not use light-directing blocks BELOW eye-level because they will direct light up into your eyes. EYE-LEVEL is considered to be 6 feet above the finish floor.

Glass Building Units

Details
(scale 1″ = 1′-0″)

These pages show elevations and sections of typical glass block panels. The large scale sections are typical head, jamb and sill details to show the architect principles of construction only.

Any structural members must be calculated for safe loading, and local building codes checked for any possible restrictions on panel sizes or detail. While single panels of glass block are limited to a maximum of 144 square feet, panel and curtain wall sections up to a maximum area of 250 square feet may be erected if properly braced to limit movement and settlement.

If chase construction as shown on page 9 cannot be used, substitute the panel anchor construction that is shown on page 10. Panel anchors are used to give lateral support for glass block panels.

Any glass block installation that is made in a frame construction shall have the wood adjacent to the mortar properly primed with Pittsburgh Corning Asphalt Emulsion.

For Underwriters' Listings refer to Underwriters Guide Cards R-2556A, R-2556B and R-2556C, Guide Number 120 IW7.

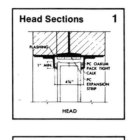

Head Sections 1

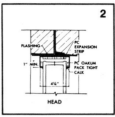

2

3

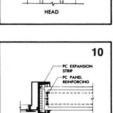

9

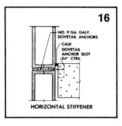

10

Sill Sections 11

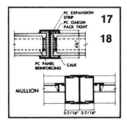
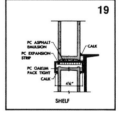

16

17
18

19

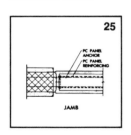
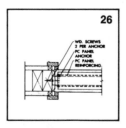
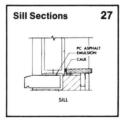
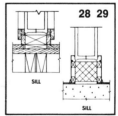
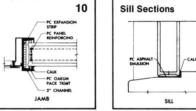

25

26

Sill Sections 27

28 29

Exterior Panels up to 250 sq. ft.

Individual Panels **Continuous Panels** **Ribbon Windows**

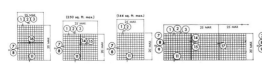
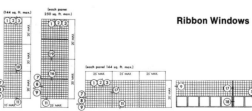

23.5 MASONRY UNIT LINTELS

The material for this section has been excerpted from 'The Clay Masonry Manual',
and is published with the permission of the
Canadian Structural Clay Association.

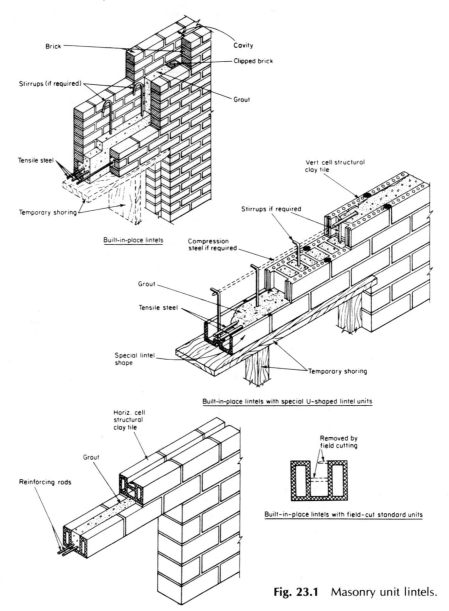

Fig. 23.1 Masonry unit lintels.

23.6 GLIDING DOORS

The material for this section has been excerpted from booklets published by the Andersen Corporation and is here reproduced with the permission of the copyright holder.

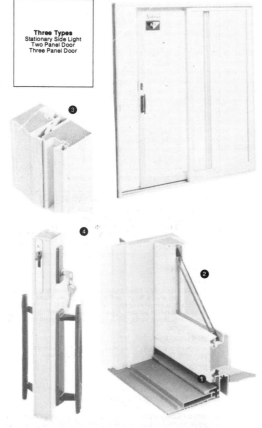

Three Types
Stationary Side Light
Two Panel Door
Three Panel Door

Andersen® Windowalls

AW

GLIDING DOORS

PP/Product Presentation

■ Perma-Shield® Special Size

A special size gliding door to replace problem doors available with white, low-maintenance rigid vinyl sheath.

■ Perma-Shield®

Low-maintenance rigid vinyl sheath in white on all surfaces.

■ Prefinished

Prefinished inside and out with a polyester urethane factory finishing process in Terratone color.

■ Primed Wood

Treated wood with exterior surfaces factory primed and natural wood interior.

FEATURES:

BASE UNIT

❶ **SILL.** Dual rollers provide smooth operation with self-contained leveling adjusters. Anodized aluminum sill track with stainless steel track cap resists stain, rust and denting. Thermal barrier reduces conductive heat loss and checks condensation on inside.

❷ **GLAZING.** Select quality ⅝" safety insulating glass designed to withstand an impact ordinary glass can't take. But if it does break under severe impact, it crumbles into small pieces that reduce the chance of serious injury.

❸ **MEETING STILE WEATHERSTRIP (PERMA-SHIELD®).** Full length vinyl covered urethane foam weather strip. Provides flexible seal at meeting stiles.

❹ **INTERLOCK** Full length with rigid vinyl spring tension type weatherstripping, pulls meeting stiles together for a weathertight seal (Prefinished and Primed Wood).

HARDWARE. Custom designed, operating handle and locking hardware. Operating handle is separated from locking mechanism. Stone color decorator finish.

OPTIONAL ACCESSORIES

ROLLING INSECT SCREEN. Delrin extruded, top and bottom, self-contained leveling adjusters. Aluminum frame with Perma-Clean® decorator finish. Specify white or Terratone color screen.

NOTE: For information, cautions and procedures see pages 42-51.

PERMA-SHIELD®
GLIDING DOOR II

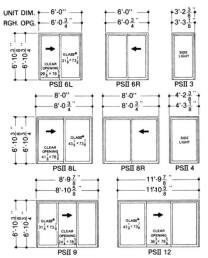

PERMA-SHIELD® GLIDING DOOR II SIZES

| UNIT DIM. | 6'-0'' | 6'-0'' | 3'-2 3/8'' |
| RGH. OPG. | 6'-0 3/4'' | 6'-0 3/4'' | 3'-3 1/8'' |

CLEAR OPENING 29 1/8 x 78 7/8	GLASS* 31 1/8 x 73 7/8		SIDE LIGHT
PSII 6L	PSII 6R	PSII 3

	8'-0''	8'-0''	4'-2 3/8''
	8'-0 3/4''	8'-0 3/4''	4'-3 1/8''
CLEAR OPENING 41 1/8 x 78 7/8	GLASS* 43 1/8 x 73 7/8		SIDE LIGHT
PSII 8L	PSII 8R	PSII 4

	8'-9 7/8''	11'-9 7/8''
	8'-10 5/8''	11'-10 5/8''
GLASS* 31 1/8 x 73 7/8 CLEAR OPENING 24 1/2 x 78 7/8	GLASS* 43 1/8 x 73 7/8 CLEAR OPENING 36 3/8 x 78 7/8
PSII 9	PSII 12

*Unobstructed glass sizes shown in inches.

NUMBERING SYSTEM
6L & 8L-left-hand operating panel
6R & 8R-right-hand operating panel
9 & 12-center panel operates to right only.
      (All handing as viewed from outside)
Door operation may be specified either left or right-hand as viewed from outside.

FEATURES:

BASE UNIT

Includes frame, door panel glazed safety insulating glass, weatherstripped, and wood core treated with a water repellent preservative. Entire surface of head jamb, side jambs, and door panel covered with white rigid vinyl (PVC). Stone color finish on interior and exterior handles, keyed exterior lock and interior locking lever furnished. Oak threshold and flashing included. Metal sill support for extended portion of metal sill furnished.

SIDE LIGHT UNIT

A stationary unit with white rigid vinyl covered frame and panel to match operating door unit. Sill support is furnished with side light unit.

OPTIONAL ACCESSORIES

GLAZING

3/16" Single Safety Float glass.
5/8" Grey safety insulating glass.
5/8" Bronze safety insulating glass.

INSECT SCREEN/Strong aluminum frame with Perma-Clean® white decorator finish, glass fiber cloth, gun-metal finish, 18 x 16 mesh. Interior and exterior door pulls integral with frame.

EXTERIOR CASING/Auxiliary casing is a treated wood core covered with white rigid vinyl. Used when a wider casing effect is desired.

Andersen Corporation reserves the right to change details, specifications or sizes without notice.

AVAILABLE IN WHITE

U.S. Patent No. 2,926,729 and 3,432,885
Canadian Patent No. 758-928
Other patents applied for.

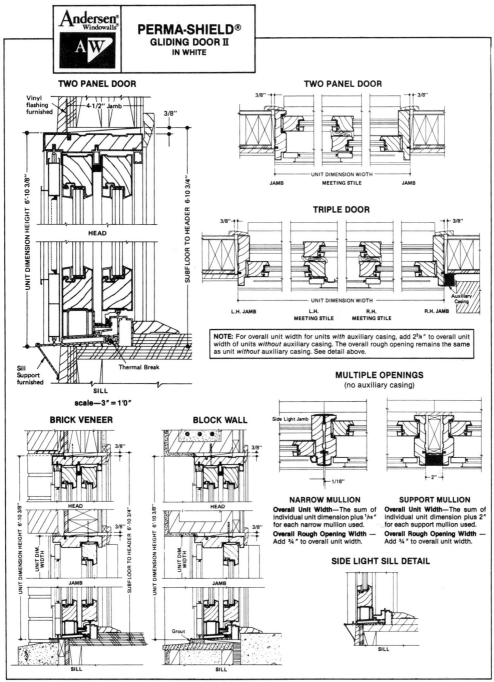

PERMA-SHIELD®
GLIDING DOOR II
IN WHITE

Andersen® Windowalls®

TWO PANEL DOOR

Vinyl flashing furnished
4-1/2" Jamb
3/8"

UNIT DIMENSION HEIGHT 6'-10 3/8"

SUBFLOOR TO HEADER 6'-10 3/4"

HEAD

Sill Support furnished

Thermal Break

SILL

scale—3" = 1'0"

TWO PANEL DOOR

3/8"   3/8"

UNIT DIMENSION WIDTH
JAMB   MEETING STILE   JAMB

TRIPLE DOOR

3/8"   3/8"

UNIT DIMENSION WIDTH
L.H. JAMB   L.H. MEETING STILE   R.H. MEETING STILE   R.H. JAMB

Auxiliary Casing

NOTE: For overall unit width for units *with* auxiliary casing, add 2³⁄₈" to overall unit width of units *without* auxiliary casing. The overall rough opening remains the same as unit *without* auxiliary casing. See detail above.

BRICK VENEER

3/8"

UNIT DIMENSION HEIGHT 6'-10 3/8"

UNIT DIM. WIDTH

HEAD

3/8"

JAMB

SILL

BLOCK WALL

3/8"

SUBFLOOR TO HEADER 6'-10 3/4"

UNIT DIMENSION HEIGHT 6'-10 3/8"

HEAD

3/8"

UNIT DIM. WIDTH

JAMB

Grout

SILL

MULTIPLE OPENINGS
(no auxiliary casing)

Side Light Jamb

1/16"   2"

NARROW MULLION

Overall Unit Width—The sum of individual unit dimension plus ¹⁄₁₆" for each narrow mullion used.

Overall Rough Opening Width — Add ¾" to overall unit width.

SUPPORT MULLION

Overall Unit Width—The sum of individual unit dimension plus 2" for each support mullion used.

Overall Rough Opening Width — Add ¾" to overall unit width.

SIDE LIGHT SILL DETAIL

SILL

NOTE: Light colored areas are basic parts furnished by Andersen. Dark colored areas are recommended parts to complete unit assembly.

PERMA-SHIELD®
SPECIAL SIZE GLIDING DOOR

PERMA-SHIELD® SPECIAL SIZE GLIDING DOOR
New size to replace problem doors

UNIT DIM. ⊢—5'-10½"—⊣
RGH. OPG. ⊢—5'-11¼"—⊣

PSR 510L

NUMBERING SYSTEM
510L-Left hand operating panel as viewed from outside.

* Unobstructed glass sizes shown in inches.

AVAILABLE IN WHITE

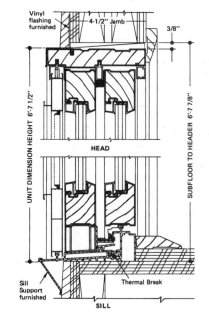

HEAD

SILL

scale: 3" = 1'0"

FEATURES:

BASE UNIT

Includes frame, door panel glazed safety insulating glass, weatherstripped, and wood core treated with a water repellent preservative. Entire surface of head jamb, side jambs, and door panel covered with white rigid vinyl (PVC). Stone color finish on interior and exterior handles, keyed exterior lock and interior locking lever furnished. Oak threshold and flashing included. Metal sill support for extended portion of metal sill furnished.

OPTIONAL ACCESSORIES

GLAZING

³/₁₆" Single Safety Float glass.
⁵/₈" Grey safety insulating glass.
⁵/₈" Bronze safety insulating glass.

INSECT SCREEN / Strong extruded aluminum frame with Perma-Clean® white decorator finish, glass fiber cloth, gun-metal finish, 18 x 16 mesh. Interior and exterior door pulls integral with frame.

EXTERIOR CASING / Auxiliary casing is a treated wood core covered with white rigid vinyl. Used when a wider casing effect is desired.

TWO PANEL DOOR

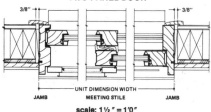

JAMB   MEETING STILE   JAMB
⊢————UNIT DIMENSION WIDTH————⊣

scale: 1½" = 1'0"

NOTE: Light colored areas are basic parts furnished by Andersen. Dark colored areas are recommended parts to complete unit assembly.

PREFINISHED WOOD GLIDING DOOR IN TERRATONE COLOR

PREFINISHED GLIDING DOOR SIZES

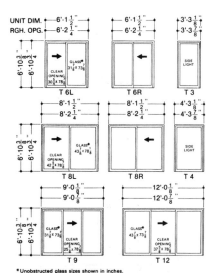

* Unobstructed glass sizes shown in inches.

NUMBERING SYSTEM

6L & 8L left-hand operating panel
6R & 8R right-hand operating panel
9 & 12 center panel operates to right only.
(All handing as viewed from outside)
Door operation may be specified either left or right-hand as viewed from outside.

FEATURES:

BASE UNIT

Includes frame, door panels glazed safety insulating glass, weatherstripped and treated with water repellent preservative. All surfaces of frame and door panel members prefinished. Stone color interior and exterior handles, keyed exterior lock and interior locking lever furnished. Oak threshold and flashing included. Treated and primed sill support for extended portion of metal sill facing furnished.

SIDE LIGHT UNIT

A stationary unit with frame and panel milled to match operating door unit. Sill support not furnished with side light.

OPTIONAL ACCESSORIES

GLAZING

$3/16$" Single Safety Float glass.
$5/8$" Grey safety insulating glass.
$5/8$" Bronze safety insulating glass.

INSECT SCREEN / Strong aluminum frame with Perma-Clean® Terratone decorator finish, aluminum cloth, gun-metal finish, 18 x 16 mesh. Interior and exterior door pulls furnished.

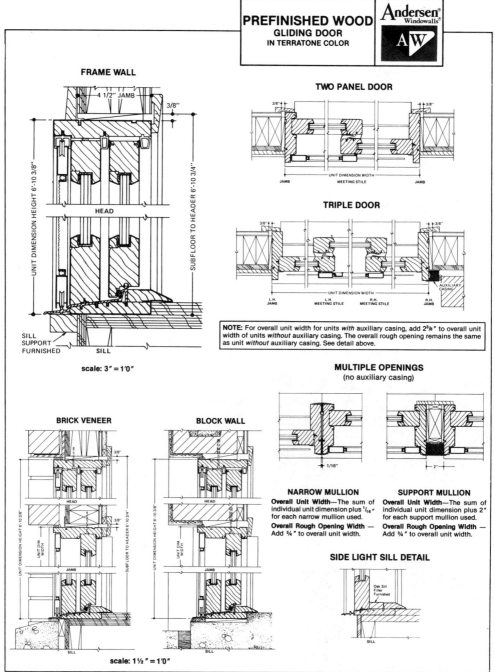

PREFINISHED WOOD
GLIDING DOOR
IN TERRATONE COLOR

Andersen Windowalls
AW

FRAME WALL

4 1/2" JAMB

3/8"

UNIT DIMENSION HEIGHT 6'-10 3/8"

SUBFLOOR TO HEADER 6'-10 3/4"

HEAD

SILL
SUPPORT
FURNISHED

SILL

scale: 3" = 1'0"

TWO PANEL DOOR

3/8"   3/8"

UNIT DIMENSION WIDTH
JAMB   MEETING STILE   JAMB

TRIPLE DOOR

3/8"   3/8"

UNIT DIMENSION WIDTH
L.H.   L.H.   R.H.   R.H.
JAMB   MEETING STILE   MEETING STILE   JAMB

AUXILIARY
CASING

NOTE: For overall unit width for units *with* auxiliary casing, add $2^3/8$" to overall unit width of units *without* auxiliary casing. The overall rough opening remains the same as unit *without* auxiliary casing. See detail above.

MULTIPLE OPENINGS
(no auxiliary casing)

1/16"   2"

NARROW MULLION
Overall Unit Width—The sum of individual unit dimension plus $1/16$" for each narrow mullion used.
Overall Rough Opening Width — Add ¾" to overall unit width.

SUPPORT MULLION
Overall Unit Width—The sum of individual unit dimension plus 2" for each support mullion used.
Overall Rough Opening Width — Add ¾" to overall unit width.

BRICK VENEER

3/8"

3/8"

HEAD

UNIT DIMENSION HEIGHT 6'-10 3/8"

UNIT DIM. WIDTH

SUBFLOOR TO HEADER 6'-10 3/4"

JAMB

SILL

BLOCK WALL

HEAD

UNIT DIMENSION HEIGHT 6'-10 3/8"

UNIT DIM. WIDTH

JAMB

SILL

scale: 1½" = 1'0"

SIDE LIGHT SILL DETAIL

Oak Sill
Filler
Furnished

SILL

NOTE: Light colored areas are basic parts furnished by Andersen. Dark colored areas are recommended parts to complete unit assembly.

PRIMED WOOD GLIDING DOOR

WOOD GLIDING DOOR SIZES

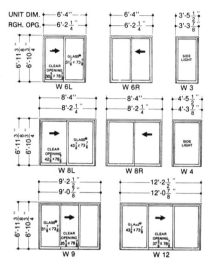

UNIT DIM. — 6'-4'' — | — 6'-4'' — | 3'-5 $\frac{1}{2}$ ''
RGH. OPG. — 6'-2 $\frac{1}{4}$ '' — | — 6'-2 $\frac{1}{4}$ '' — | 3'-3 $\frac{7}{8}$ ''

6'-11 $\frac{3}{8}$ '' / 6'-10 $\frac{3}{4}$ ''

GLASS* 31 $\frac{7}{8}$ x 73 $\frac{7}{8}$
CLEAR OPENING 30 $\frac{1}{8}$ x 78 $\frac{5}{8}$

SIDE LIGHT

W 6L | **W 6R** | **W 3**

— 8'-4'' — | — 8'-4'' — | 4'-5 $\frac{1}{2}$ ''
— 8'-2 $\frac{1}{4}$ '' — | — 8'-2 $\frac{1}{4}$ '' — | 4'-3 $\frac{7}{8}$ ''

GLASS* 43 $\frac{7}{8}$ x 73 $\frac{7}{8}$
CLEAR OPENING 42 $\frac{1}{8}$ x 78 $\frac{5}{8}$

SIDE LIGHT

W 8L | **W 8R** | **W 4**

— 9'-2 $\frac{1}{2}$ '' — | — 12'-2 $\frac{1}{2}$ '' —
— 9'-0 $\frac{7}{8}$ '' — | — 12'-0 $\frac{7}{8}$ '' —

GLASS* 31 $\frac{7}{8}$ x 73 $\frac{7}{8}$
CLEAR OPENING 25 $\frac{1}{8}$ x 78 $\frac{5}{8}$

GLASS* 43 $\frac{7}{8}$ x 73 $\frac{7}{8}$
CLEAR OPENING 37 $\frac{1}{8}$ x 78 $\frac{5}{8}$

W 9 | **W 12**

* Unobstructed glass sizes shown in inches.

NUMBERING SYSTEM

6L & 8L left-hand operating panel
6R & 8R right-hand operating panel
9 & 12 center panel operates to right only.
    (All handing as viewed from outside)
Door operation may be specified either left or right-hand as viewed from outside.

FEATURES

BASE UNIT

Includes frame, door panels glazed safety insulating glass, weatherstripped and treated with water repellent preservative. Exterior frame parts and exterior face of door panels are factory primed. Stone color interior and exterior handles, keyed exterior lock and interior locking lever furnished. Oak threshold and flashing included. Treated and primed sill support for extended portion of metal sill facing furnished.

SIDE LIGHT UNIT

A stationary unit with frame and panel milled to match operating door unit. Sill support not furnished with side light.

OPTIONAL ACCESSORIES

GLAZING

$\frac{3}{16}$ '' Single Safety Float glass.
$\frac{5}{8}$ '' Grey safety insulating glass.
$\frac{5}{8}$ '' Bronze safety insulating glass.

INSECT SCREEN / Strong aluminum frame with Perma-Clean® white decorator finish, aluminum cloth, gun-metal finish, 18 x 16 mesh. Interior and exterior door pulls furnished.

Andersen Corporation reserves the right to change details, specifications or sizes without notice.

23.7 METRIC MASONRY BLOCKS

The materials for this section are from the HUDAC booklet, ON-SITE METRIC: A Handbook for Construction Workers, published by the Housing and Urban Development Association of Canada, and is here compiled with permission.

The following drawing illustrates how the 10 mm joint is used to bring the actual size of block to a modular size. To reduce building costs, planning for full modular layout is necessary. The cutting of masonry blocks for non-modular construction is expensive in terms of time and equipment.

Typical Metric Block

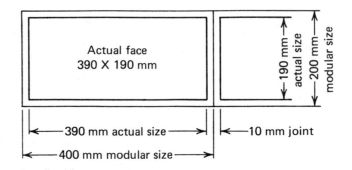

Metric Blocks

The metric modular block format, including a 10 mm mortar joint, is as follows:

Length	Width	Height
200 mm	100 mm	100 mm
300 mm	150 mm	*200 mm
*400 mm	200 mm	300 mm
	250 mm	
	300 mm	

*Indicates the most commonly used dimension

Masonry

Some effects of planning for non-modular
and fully modular layouts are indicated in
the drawings.

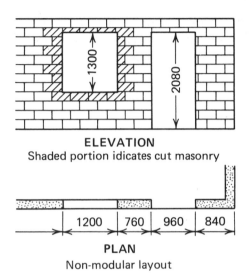

ELEVATION
Shaded portion idicates cut masonry

PLAN
Non-modular layout

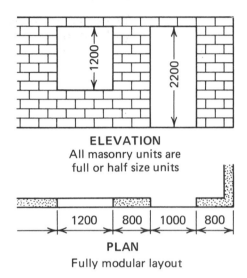

ELEVATION
All masonry units are
full or half size units

PLAN
Fully modular layout

Review

1. Define *curtain wall.*

2. List twelve characteristics of manufactured masonry units.

3. Why is it advantageous to build outside basement walls with concrete units where ground conditions permit their use?

4. Sketch an adjustable wall tie as used in building with manufactured masonry units.

5. List four distinct advantages of using adjustable wall ties in new concrete block wall construction.

6. Sketch and design a control joint as used in concrete unit built walls.

7. Draw a freehand plan of a concrete masonry wall built with a pilaster.

8. Sketch a built-in-place lintel with special U-shaped lintel units (reinforced), and name the parts.

9. Sketch and define the following wood members of a window or gliding door: (a) sill; (b) jamb; (c) meeting rail; (d) support mullion.

10. Define: (a) a bearing wall, (b) dampproofing; (c) waterproofing; (d) a wythe; (e) bonding; (f) modular construction; (g) a pier; and (h) chasing.

24

Painting, Decorating, Floor Finishing, and Extruded Metal Finishing Pieces

In this chapter we shall deal with some aspects of the above-mentioned subjects. It is important that speculatively built residences, both houses and apartment blocks, be painted, decorated and finished in the decor recommended by specialists. The builder cannot be all-knowing in every field of residential construction, and many suppliers give an inclusive service of decor advice for any materials that they supply.

24.1 PAINTING

Before any painting is commenced, the floors should be cleaned of all plaster droppings and other gritty materials, the ceilings and walls should be swept clear of dust and the floor swept clean.

When a builder is using his own work force for painting, it is advantageous to paint (from the bare subfloor) all the interior walls before the trim around doors, windows, other openings, and baseboards is applied. This method affords a great saving in time; the subfloor suffers no harm if it becomes splattered with paint. In addition, this method saves time in brush cutting-in around such places as door and baseboard trim (cutting-in is to paint up to, but without spotting paint onto, other fixed members of different color, such as baseboards). Some builders will spread a large piece of polyethylene in the middle of the subfloor, pour a gallon of paint onto it, propel the paint roller into it, and roll-paint the ceilings and the walls from a standing position. Without any impediment in the usage of the paint roller by fixed trim or different color, rooms are speedily and efficiently painted. To seal small cracks on surfaces to be painted, a paste filler may be made from plaster of Paris mixed with the actual paint with which the surface will be covered.

Wood trim may be stained or painted in another area of the house, but this presupposes that the finishing carpenters are clean, competent and careful workers; otherwise, they may scuff and scratch-mark the painted surfaces. When all the trim has been fixed, all countersunk nail holes should be stopped with matching colored putty, or with color matched nails. The rooms are then ready for the application of the finished flooring. After the flooring material is laid, all necessary touching up of paint, stain, and varnish work is completed.

There is a constant demand for paints of different quality for use in various conditions, and as a consequence, there is great competition among manufacturers for the market. It is a truism that one gets that which one pays for—this is particularly true of paint. It is recommended that purchases of paint be made from well-known and established dealers who have their reputations to maintain by the quality and price of their wares. Constant laboratory tests are made by manufacturers, and it is imperative that their instructions for application be complied with

rigidly. Some workmen may have their own pet ideas about painting, without realizing there are frequent changes in the composition of the paint they are to use. Where a customer adamantly wants a special color of paint, have him or her select the paint at the supplier's shop. Most people are amazed to find that the color of a painted wall is very different from the color they thought they had selected.

24.2 WALLPAPER, MIRRORS, AND CHANDELIERS

As with paint, there is a wide variety and quality in the types of wallpaper and chandeliers available. It requires an experienced person to hang wallpaper; the supplier will usually supply and fix the materials for an inclusive price.

The selection of the color and design of wallpapers should be left to experts, and the quality of the paper must be made against the funds allotted for the purchase. It is easy and cheap to change the color of a painted wall, but it is more expensive to change a wallpaper.

Large Mirrors and Chandeliers are now almost standard units supplied by speculation builders. Mirrors lend an added feeling of spaciousness, and they save the house purchaser the problem of buying them separately and of having to pay someone to fix them. The chandeliers contribute a feeling of elegance to a room. However, they may present a problem for the electrician to fix after the purchase of the house; when supplied by the builder, the electrical outlets are designed to receive them.

Some builders also include wrought ironwork in the halls and stairways. Remember that the framing for residential construction varies little per square foot from one project to another. It is the difference in the quality of the finish and in the supplying of units that makes the difference in the cost of the final product. Remember, a residence should be built in any given area to meet the needs of the persons for whom it is designed. Not one penny more than is necessary to meet these conditions should be expended. *It costs just as much to build a good house on a poor lot as a similar house on a good lot.*

24.3 RESILIENT FLOOR COVERINGS

Before any finished flooring is applied over a subfloor, it is imperative to check that all nail heads are sunk below the surface of the subfloor; that loose boards are securely nailed; and that all loose and gritty material such as knobs of dried plaster droppings, plumbers solder drippings, pieces of dry putty, clippings of electric wire be removed, and the floor swept clean. Unless the subfloor is clear and clean, resilient flooring (and carpeting) will reveal the underlying matter by sight, by foot, or both. The debris will cause the floor coverings to wear through more quickly and unevenly.

Resilient flooring includes: linoleum in either tiles or rolls; asphalt tile; vinyl asbestos; cushioned and self adhesive all purpose vinyl tiles, and some with rubber facings; cork; non spark and others. It is important to remember that no resilient flooring should be laid except on a subfloor underlay of fiber boards such as sheet plywood and so on.

24.4 CARPETED FLOORS

Most residential units are marketed with fitted wall to wall carpets in all areas except kitchens, bathrooms and work areas, and since the introduction of indoor-outdoor carpeting in rolls or tile form, there is no place in a modern home that need be without carpeted flooring. Types of carpeting range from exotic Indian and Arabian carpeting to those of manufactured fibers. Among manmade materials are nylon, viscose, polypropylene, acrilan, polyester/nylon; self adhesive carpet in tile form; and indoor-outdoor carpeting.

The speculative builder must be aware of the latest trends in all kinds of floor coverings, and study carefully the initial cost of the materials, *plus the cost to install them.* He must select the materials for quality, color, design, and appeal to the class of wage earners for whom he is building.

24.5 WOOD FLOORING

There is a wide selection of both hard and soft wood for finish flooring; the most commonly used T & G flooring is oak, birch, Douglas fir, hemlock, and southern pine. See Fig. 24.1 for side and end matched T & G flooring. Narrow boards are the most expensive because they require more handling, cut proportionately more to waste in the manufacturing process, and require more time to lay. As an example, there is just as much wood cut to waste in milling the tongues and grooves for 1½'' boards, as there is for 2'' boards; and the floor layer can place a piece of 2'' board just as quickly as he can place a 1½'' board. When estimating the number of square feet of floor to be covered with hardwood, first determine the face width of the boards required, and then consult a table of waste allowances. Add the percentage allowance for waste that is shown.

It is important that a good quality building paper be laid between the subfloor and the hardwood. This will help to eliminate a squeaky floor, and it will act as a dust barrier to unfinished floors below.

Study Figs. 24.1 through 24.5. Extra nailing of flooring should be made in hallways and doorways and anywhere that will have a heavy traffic flow. For minor bedrooms a cheaper softwood finish flooring will be adequate. This will make a saving in initial purchase of the material, especially in applying it.

Carefully study Fig. 24.3b which shows a spacing to be left at each longitudinal sidewall of the boards; this is to allow for the floor boards to expand if exposed to moisture. I have seen a hardwood floor raised three feet down the center of a room because provision was not made for expansion; such would be the consequence or else the force would displace one or both of the side walls.

The ancients used to quarry enormous stones by dressing them (on four sides) on their natural bed in the quarry, then applying dry wood between the back dressed side and the quarry face, and then applying a water treatment causing the wood to expand and cracking the stone at its base. Near the site of the Heliopolis at Baalbeck, in Lebanon, is the largest stone that was ever quarried by man. It is 14'-0'' in section and 64'-0'' long, and was quarried by this method two thousand years ago. It is still there for all to see. Be careful!

Another type of wood flooring is parquetry wood block flooring. These blocks are accurately machined for size, and some are made up (under quality controlled shop conditions) into panels which facilitate the final floor laying, especially for large areas.

Other types of wood flooring include 4'-0'' × 8'-0'' sheets of birch plywood; also aspenite. Such floors are usually finished with varethane which is a plastic (hard wearing) varnish. Other types of fiber boards are also used for flooring, in little used areas, such as basement storerooms; the fiber boards are then finished with quality enamel paint.

When planning the laying of a wood finished floor over a concrete base, it is

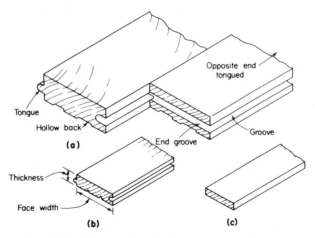

Fig. 24.1. Types of strip flooring: (a) side-and end-matched, (b) thin flooring strips, matched, and (c) thin flooring strips, square-edged.

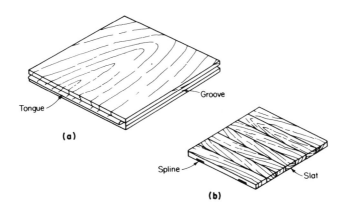

Fig. 24.2. Wood block flooring: (a) tongued and grooved, and (b) square edged, splined. *(Courtesy of the Forestry Service Products Laboratory, U.S. Department of Agriculture.)*

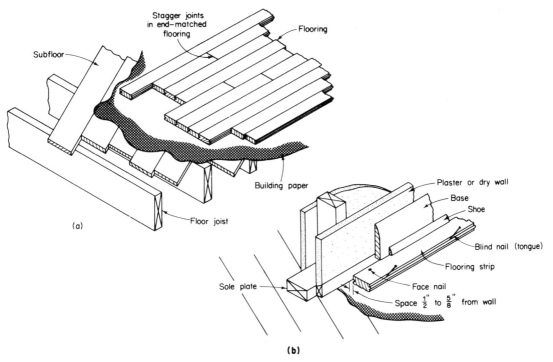

Fig. 24.3. Application of strip flooring: (a) general application, (b) starting strip. *(Courtesy of the Forestry Products Laboratory, U.S. Department of Agriculture.)*

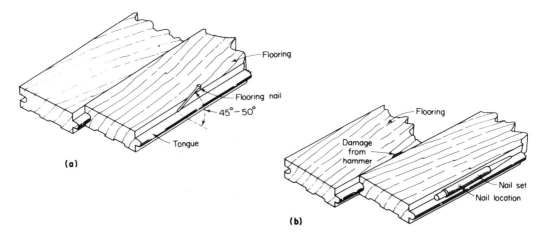

Fig. 24.4. Nailing of flooring: (a) nail angle, (b) setting of nail. *(Courtesy of Forestry Products Laboratory, U.S. Department of Agriculture.)*

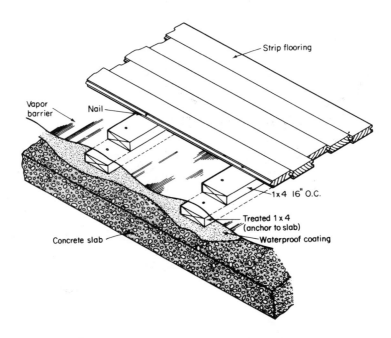

Fig. 24.5. Base for wood flooring on concrete slab (witbout an underlying vapor barrier). *(Courtesy of the Forestry Products Laboratory, U.S. Department of Agriculture.)*

imperative that the concrete surface be waterproofed, and that the sleepers (1 × 4 or 2 × 4) be treated and anchored to the slab with concrete nails, and that provision be made for air to circulate between the top of the concrete slab and the underside of the flooring, see Fig. 24.5.

24.6 ABRASIVE SAFETY STAIR AND WALKING PRODUCTS

The following material has been excerpted from a Wooster Products Inc. catalog, and is reproduced in Fig. 24.6 with permission.

STAIRMASTER SAFETY TREADS

Ideal for repairing worn and slippery stairs

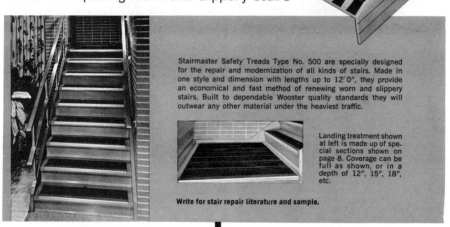

Stairmaster Safety Treads Type No. 500 are specially designed for the repair and modernization of all kinds of stairs. Made in one style and dimension with lengths up to 12' 0", they provide an economical and fast method of renewing worn and slippery stairs. Built to dependable Wooster quality standards they will outwear any other material under the heaviest traffic.

Landing treatment shown at left is made up of special sections shown on page 8. Coverage can be full as shown, or in a depth of 12", 15", 18", etc.

Write for stair repair literature and sample.

aluminum **SUPER-GRIT LADDER TREADS** INDUSTRIAL MARINE
TYPE 850

Treads are a complete unit, ready for bolting to stringers. The extruded aluminum base, alloy 6061-T6, is light weight with exceptional strength. Eight abrasive-filled ribs offer a non-slip walking surface even under wet or oily conditions. Standard 6" width. Other widths available in quantities sufficient for special set-up. Lengths to order to 2' 6". Standard hole spacing shown below for 3/8" bolts makes the tread reversible. Fasteners not included.

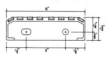

aluminum **SUPER-GRIT** Expansion Joint Cover

Uniform width, thickness, and smooth square edges makes it readily adaptable for use with various types of floor covering material. Flat abrasive surface eliminates smooth slippery surfaces in walking areas, providing a positive non-slip walk surface. Expansion joint covers available only in the widths shown — lengths up to 12'-0". Holes for fastening on approximate 12" centers factory drilled and ¼" machine screws for attaching to metal angles included.

ANGLES BY OTHERS

TYPE 645   TYPE 610

Fig. 24.6

Review

1. List four preliminary operations that should be completed before painting the inside of a newly built residence.

2. Why is it advisable that customers select their own paint colors from the suppliers?

3. What is meant by the term "cutting-in" as used by painters?

4. Define five types of resilient floor covering.

5. List five types of carpeting as used in modern residential construction. Indicate the characteristics of each. Be specific about fire and smoke ratings.

6. Why should hardwood floors have a building paper between them and the subfloors?

7. Draw a freehand sketch of the method to drive the nails of a hardwood floor above the tongue of the boards.

8. Why should the first and last strip of hardwood flooring be kept ½" to ⅝" from the walls?

9. Why is the wastage in the manufacture of hardwood flooring so great?

10. Give four places in residential construction where extruded thresholds may be used to advantage?

25

Landscaping, Final Inspection, Notarization of Documents, and Property Sale

In this chapter we shall discuss driveways, landscaping, the final inspection of the property, land titles, notarization of documents, advertising, and, finally, the sale of the property.

25.1 DRIVEWAYS, PATHS, AND OUTSIDE CONCRETE STEPS

As stated earlier, once a proposed building has been correctly located for its location and elevation on its legal lot, the builder is off to a good start; this also evidences itself in the final grading, drainage, landscaping, and in the building of driveways, paths, and outside concrete steps on the property. Any series of steps with three risers or more should be provided with a handrail.

The surfaces of all driveways, paths, and concrete steps should be fashioned to be non-skid, and to shed water quickly without leaving any low spots to form puddles of water or icy patches, either from rain, snow, or from a water sprinkler system. There are several methods to produce a non-skid surface to concrete such as:

1. Brooming, which will give a pleasing non-skid surface.

2. Finishing the surface with either a wood or cork float.

3. Sprinkling a fine particle abrasive over the surface such as emery, flint, or aluminum oxide, and finishing it lightly with a wood or cork float.

25.2 TYPES OF DRIVEWAYS

It is important that all driveways be provided with a level turnaround; this obviates the hazard of reversing a car onto a thoroughfare. The turnaround is also advantageous for the temporary parking of the cars of guests.

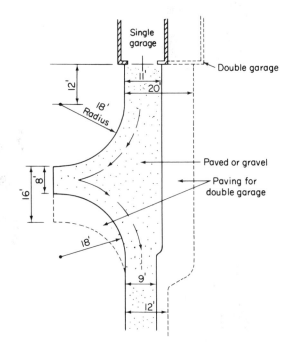

Fig. 25.1 Driveway turnaround. *(Courtesy of the Forestry Products Laboratory, U.S. Department of Agriculture.)*

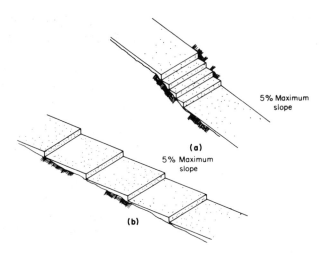

Fig. 25.2 Sidewalks on slopes: (a) stairs, (b) stepped ramp. *(Courtesy of Forestry Products Laboratory, U.S. Department of Agriculture.)*

Concrete Driveways in natural color or tinted should be placed on a well-tamped gravel base. To minimize cracking they should be stabilized with reinforcing rods, steel mesh, and/or temperature rods and be provided with control joints every eight or ten feet.

Flagstone Driveways (also ribbon type) should be set on a sand or gravel base topped with 2½" of concrete into which the flagstones are maneuvered into adjoining lineable positions. The concrete stabilizes the rocks and prevents weed growth between the joints. In some areas, this type of driveway is called "crazy paving."

25.3 LANDSCAPING

Among other preliminary building operations, the building site should have the topsoil stripped and stockpiled on the site, the surface brought to grade, and ultimately the soil dispersed over the lot after the driveways and paths have been built. Particular care should be taken wherever deep trenches have been dug, as these areas will subside unless the ground has been well compacted after the laying of service lines. Only then may the total area be landscaped.

Landscape gardening applies to leaving in position (whenever possible) some native trees, then making a pleasing arrangement of grassed (seeded or sodded) areas, plants, shrubs, other trees, rocks, water, hedges, decorative fences, wrought iron work, and so on, in such a manner that they will complement each other and their immediate surroundings. But, all this must be accomplished while having regard for the drainage of surface water from all sides of the building.

In some arid regions, the layout may be made attractive by the placing of several different colored gravels to form designs on either side of the driveway and paths. Monotony can be relieved by having several cactus plants set in complementary array.

The nature of any landscaping should lend charm, a feeling of restfulness, and sales appeal to the property. The builder must give careful thought to this subject. Some purchasers love gardening, others abhor it. In this age of leisure many people want to be off to their games, lakesides, or travels, and leave the chores of gardening to others. It is suggested that a minimum area be planted. Plants such as hedges which require continual trimming should be avoided. The choice to plant or not to plant should be left to the purchasers. Even the watering of lawns, unless done automatically by underground feeder lines to sprinklers, may be a chore to some people. For apartments, condominiums, and rented places, the care and upkeep of surroundings may be taken care of by private contract between owners and landscape gardeners.

25.4 THE FINAL INSPECTION

The critical path method (CPM) discussed in Chapter 6 made provision for the actual culmination or finishing of the building project. The planning, as indicated in Chapters 3 and 5, which was directed by the CPM, included recognition of those operations necessary to complete the work and to put the project on the market.

An outline of those operations is presented as a reminder to the builder with respect to what must be done to complete the project in readiness for responsible turnover to a client. Reference to earlier chapters should be made by the reader for details.

1.   Payments to the contractor

2. Progress schedule

3. Completion date

4. Correction of work after final payment

5. Landscaping contract

6. General Contractor's inspection

7. Window cleaning

8. Janitor services

9. Architect's final inspection

The maintenace of the building should also be considered.

25.5 MAINTENANCE

Many contracts state that after a period of six months the contractor will examine the building and ease all doors and windows and make good any settlement cracks in any of the walls. It is usual for buildings to settle; and the better the class of workmanship in the fitting of doors, the more likely it is that such doors will require a little easing after a few months. The actual maintenance period is shown in the contract. It is your duty as a builder to make a close study of the general conditions of the contract so that you will be in a position to allow for your company to make provision for the expense of maintenance.

Finally, use your schedules and remember that if any item is forgotten on the estimate, such item must still be purchased and installed.

As the project is completed, attention with respect to land title shifts from the builder to the buyer. Land title laws are the same for both parties.

25.6 LAND TITLE

As indicated in Chapter 3, the builder was obliged to give attention to land title. On

turnover, the new owner will probably be seeking counsel about:

1. Protection of title

2. Proof of execution

3. Examination of records

4. Title insurance

5. Encroachment on and by others

6. Registration of title

In the cycle of building and selling, land or space remains, and titles change.

25.7 FACTS TO ASCERTAIN BEFORE DRAWING CONTRACT OF SALE

1. Date of contract.

2. Name and address of seller.

3. Is seller a citizen, of full age, and competent?

4. Name of seller's spouse and whether he or she is of full age.

5. Name and residence of purchaser.

6. Description of the property.

7. The purchase price:

   a. Amount to be paid on signing contract;

   b. Amount to be paid on delivery of deed;

   c. Existing mortgage or mortgages and details thereof;

   d. Purchase money mortgage, if any, and details thereof.

8. What kind of deed is to be delivered: full covenant, quit claim, or bargain and sale?

9. What agreement has been made with reference to any specific personal prop-

erty, i.e., gas ranges, heaters, machinery, partitions, fixtures, coal, wood, window shades, screens, carpets, rugs, and hangings?

10. Is purchaser to assume the mortgage or take the property subject to it?

11. Are any exceptions or reservations to be inserted?

12. Are any special clauses to be inserted?

13. Stipulations and agreements with reference to tenancies and rights of persons in possession, including compliance with any governmental regulations in force.

14. Stipulations and agreements, if any, to be inserted with reference to the state of facts a survery would show; i.e., party walls, encroachments, easements, and so forth.

15. What items are to be adjusted on the closing of title?

16. Name of the broker who brought about the sale, his address, the amount of his commission and who is to pay it, and whether or not a clause covering the foregoing facts is to be inserted in the contract.

17. Are any alterations or changes being made, or have they been made, in street lines, name, or grade?

18. Are condemnations or assessment proceedings contemplated or pending, or has an award been made?

19. Who is to draw the purchase money mortgage and who is to pay the expense thereof?

20. Are there any covenants, restrictions, and consents affecting the title?

21. What stipulation or agreement is to be made with reference to Tenement

Building Department and other violations?

22. The place and date on which the title is to be closed.

23. Is time to be of the essence in the contract?

24. Are any alterations to be made in the premises between the date of the contract and the date of the closing?

25. Amount of fire and hazard insurance, payment of premium, and rights and obligations of parties in case of fire or damage to premises from other causes during the contract period.

Upon the Closing of Title, the Seller Should be Prepared with the Following

1. Seller's copy of the contract.

2. The latest tax, water, and assessment receipted bills.

3. Latest possible meter reading of water, gas, or electric utilities.

4. Receipts for last payment of interest on mortgages.

5. Originals and certificates of all fire, liability, and other insurance policies.

6. Estoppel certificates from the holder of any mortgage that has been reduced, showing the amount due and the date to which interest is paid.

7. Any subordination agreements that may be called for in the contract.

8. Satisfaction pieces of mechanics' liens, chattel mortgages, judgments, or mortgages that are to be paid at, or prior to the closing.

9. List of names of tenants, amounts of rents paid and unpaid, dates when

rents are due, and assignment of un-paid rents.

10. Assignment of leases.

11. Letters to tenants to pay all subsequent rent to the purchaser.

12. Affidavit of title.

13. Authority to execute deed if the seller is acting through an agent.

14. Bill of Sale of personal property covered by the contract.

15. Seller's last deed.

16. Any unrecorded instruments that affect the title, including extension agreements.

17. Deed and other instruments that the seller is to deliver or prepare.

25.8 ADVERTISING AND SELLING THE FINAL PRODUCT

A comprehensive list of selling methods was presented in Chapter 5. If, by the time the project building is finished, it is not sold then effective communication methods must be used. A priority-type list of methods selected from Chapter 5 might be:

1. Billboard

2. Open house or Show home

3. Newspaper advertisement

4. Real estate company

5. Radio or TV

After people have been told of the builder's desire to sell, the actual sale of the project may depend on how well the builder has planned and built and paid attention to the business of building.

Review

1. List three methods of producing non-skid surfaces to concrete walks and driveways.

2. What is the minimum allowable width for main walkways to private property in your area for serving a maximum of sixteen dwelling units?

3. What is the minimum number of steps allowable (in one place) in concrete walkways?

4. List six types of materials used in building residential driveways. State your preference with the reasons.

5. List seven methods of advertising (for sale) speculatively built residences.

6. Assuming that a private party wanted to purchase directly from you your first speculatively built home, what steps would you take to close the deal? *This is an important question!*

7. Define the duties of a title (deed to property) examiner in your area.

8. What is the reason for title insurance in some states?

9. From the buyer's point of view, briefly explain the implications of land title registration.

10. What is the address of the land title registration office in your area?

Appendix A

A Glossary of Common Building Terms*

Addenda: Statements or drawings that modify the basic contract documents after the latter have been issued to the bidders, but prior to the taking of bids.

Alternates: Proposals required of bidders reflecting amounts to be added to or subtracted from the basic proposal in the event that specific changes in the work are ordered.

Anchor Bolts: Bolts used to anchor structural members to concrete or the foundation.

Approved Equal Or: The term used to indicate that material or product finally supplied or installed must be equal to that specified and as approved by the architect (or engineer).

As-Built Drawings: Drawings made during the progress of construction, or subsequent thereto, illustrating how various elements of the project were actually installed.

Astragal: A closure between the two leafs of a double-swing or double-slide door to close the joint. This can also be a piece of molding.

Axial: Anything situated around, in the direction of, or along an axis.

Baseplate: A plate attached to the base of a column which rests on a concrete or masonry footing.

---

*Excerpted from *Estimating in Building Construction,* by Frank R. Dagostino, Reston Publishing Company, Inc., 1973.

Bay: The space between column center lines or primary supporting members, lengthwise in a building. Usually the crosswise dimension is considered the *span* or *width module,* and the lengthwise dimension is considered the *bay spacing.*

Beam: A structural member that is normally subjected to bending loads and is usually a horizontal member carrying vertical loads. (An exception to this is a purlin.)

There are three types of beams:

1. *continuous beam:* A beam that has more than two points of support.

2. *cantilevered beam:* A beam that is supported at only one end and is restrained against excessive rotation.

3. *simple beam:* A beam that is freely supported at both ends, theoretically with no restraint.

Beam and Column: A primary structural system consisting of a series of beams and columns; usually arranged as a continuous beam supported on several columns with or without continuity that is subjected to both bending and axial forces.

Beam-Bearing Plate: Steel plate with attached anchors that is set in top of a masonry wall so that a purlin or a beam can rest on it.

Bearing: The condition that exists whenever one member or component transmits load or stress to another by direct contact in compression.

Bench Mark: A fixed point used for construction purposes as a reference point in determining the various levels of floor, grade, etc.

Bill of Materials: A list of items or components used for fabrication, shipping, receiving, and accounting purposes.

Bid: Proposal prepared by prospective contractor specifying the charges to be made for doing the work in accordance to the contract documents.

Bid Bond: A surety bond guaranteeing that a bidder will sign a contract, if offered, in accordance with his proposal.

Bid Security: A bid bond, certified check, or other forfeitable security guaranteeing that a bidder will sign a contract, if offered, in accordance with his proposal.

Bird Screen: Wire mesh used to prevent birds from entering the building through ventilators or louvers.

Bond: Masonry units interlocked in the face of a wall by overlapping the units in such a manner as to break the continuity of vertical joints.

Bonded Roof: A roof that carries a printed or written warranty, usually with respect to weather-tightness, including repair and/or replacement on a prorated cost basis for a stipulated number of years.

Bonus and Penalty Clause: A provision in the proposal form for payment of a bonus for each day the project is completed prior to the time stated, and for a charge against the contractor for each day the project remains uncompleted after the time stipulated.

Brace Rods: Rods used in roofs and walls to transfer wind loads and/or seismic forces to the foundation (often used to plumb building but not designed to replace erection cables when required).

Bridging: The structural member used to give lateral support to the weak plane of a truss, joist, or purlin; provide sufficient stability to support the design loads, sag channels, or sag rods.

Built-Up Roofing: Roofing consisting of layers of rag felt or jute saturated with coal tar pitch, with each layer set in a mopping of hot tar or asphalt; ply designation as to the number of layers.

Camber: A permanent curvature designed into a structural member in a direction opposite to the deflection anticipated when loads are applied.

Canopy: Any overhanging or projecting structure with the extreme end unsupported. It may also be supported at the outer end.

Cantilever: A projecting beam supported and restrained only at one end.

Cap Plate: A horizontal plate located at the top of a column.

Cash Allowances: Sums that the contractor is required to include in his bid and contract sum for specific purposes.

Caulk: To seal and make weathertight the joints, seams, or voids by filling with a waterproofing compound or material.

Certificate of Occupancy: Statement issued by the governing authority granting permission to occupy a project for a specific use.

Certificate of Payment: Statement by an architect informing the owner of the amount due a contractor on account of work accomplished and/or materials suitably stored.

Change Order: A work order, usually prepared by the architect and signed by the owner or his agent, authorizing a change in the scope of the work and a change in the cost of the project.

Channel: A steel member whose formation is similar to that of a "C" section without return lips; may be used singularly or back-to-back.

Clip: A plate or angle used to fasten two or more members together.

Clip Angle: An angle used for fastening various members together.

Collateral Loads: A load, in addition to normal live, wind or dead loads, intended to cover loads that are either unknown or uncertain (sprinklers, lighting, etc.).

Column: A main structural member used in a vertical position on a building to transfer loads from main roof beams, trusses, or rafters to the foundation.

Contract Documents: Working Drawings, Specifications, General Conditions, Supplementary General Conditions, the Owner-Contractor Agreement and all Addenda (if issued).

Curb: A raised edge on a concrete floor slab.

Curtain Wall: Perimeter walls that carry only their own weight and wind load.

Datum: Any level surface to which elevations are referred (see *Bench Mark*).

Dead Load: The weight of the structure itself, such as floor, roof, framing and covering members, plus any permanent loads.

Deflection: The displacement of a loaded structural member or system in any direction, measured from its no-loan position, after loads have been applied.

Design Loads: Those loads specified by building codes, state or city agencies, or owner's or architect's specifications to be used in the design of the structural frame of a building. They are suited to local conditions and building use.

Door Guide: An angle or channel guide used to stabilize and keep plumb a sliding or rolling door during its operation.

Downspout: A hollow section such as a pipe used to carry water from the roof or gutter of a building to the ground or sewer connection.

Drain: Any pipe, channel, or trench for which waste water or other liquids are carried off; i.e., to a sewer pipe.

Eave: The line along the sidewall formed by the intersection of the inside faces of the roof and wall panels; the projecting lower edges of a roof, overhanging the walls of a building.

Erection: The assembly of components to form the completed portion of a job.

Equal, Or: (See *Approved Equal*.)

Expansion Joint: A connection used to allow for temperature-induced expansion and contraction of material.

Fabrication: The manufacturing process performed in the plant to convert raw material into finished metal building components. The main operations are cold forming, cutting, punching, welding, cleaning, and painting.

Fascia: A flat, broad trim projecting from the face of a wall, which may be part of the rake or the eave of the building.

Field: The jobsite or building site.

Field Fabrication: Fabrication performed by the erection crew or others in the field.

Field Welding: Welding performed at the jobsite, usually with gasoline-powered machines.

Filler Strip: Preformed neoprene material, resilient rubber or plastic used to close the ribs or corrugations of a panel.

Final Acceptance: The owner's acceptance of a completed project from a contractor.

Fixed Joint: A connection between two members in such a manner as to cause them to act as a single continuous member, provides for transmission of forces from one member to the other without any movement in the connection itself.

Flange: That portion of a structural member normally projecting from the edges of the web of a member.

Flashing: A sheet-metal closure that functions primarily to provide weathertightness in a structure and secondarily to enhance appearance; the metalwork that prevents leakage over windows, door, etc., around chimneys, and at other roof details.

Footing: That bottom portion at the base of a wall or column used to distribute the load into the supporting soil.

Foundation: The substructure that supports a building or other structure.

Framing: The structural steel members (columns, rafters, girts, purlines, brace rods, etc.) that go together to make up the skeleton of a structure ready for covering to be applied.

Furring: Leveling up or building out of a part of a wall or ceiling by wood, metal, or strips.

Glaze (Glazing):   The process of installing glass in window and door frames.

Grade: The term used when referring to the ground elevation around a building.

Grout: A mixture of cement, sand, and water used to solidly fill cracks and cavities; generally used under setting plates to obtain solid, uniform full bearing surface.

Gutter: A channel member installed at the eave of the roof for the purpose of carrying water from the roof to the drains or downspouts.

Head: The top of a door, window, or frame.

Impact Load: The assumed load resulting from the motion of machinery, elevators, cranes, vehicles, and other similar moving equipment.

Instructions to Bidders: A document stating the procedures to be followed by bidders.

Invitation to Bid: An invitation to a selected list of contractors furnishing information on the submission of bids on a subject.

Insulation: Any material used in building construction for the protection from heat or cold.

Jamb: The side of a door, window, or frame.

Joist: Closely-spaced beams supporting a floor or ceiling. They may be wood, steel, or concrete.

KIP: A unit of weight, force, or load equal to 1000 pounds.

Lavatory: A bathroom-type sink.

Liens: Legal claims against an owner for amounts due those engaged in or supplying materials for the construction of the building.

Lintel: The horizontal member placed over an opening to support the loads (weight) above it.

Live Load: The load exerted on a member or a structure due to all imposed loads except dead, wind, and seismic loads. Examples include snow, people, movable equipment, etc. This type of load is movable and does not necessarily exist on a given member or structure.

Liquidated Damages: An agreed-to sum chargeable against the contractor as reimbursement for damages suffered by the owner because of contractor's failure to fulfill his contractual obligations.

Loads: Anything that causes an external force to be exerted on a structural member. Examples of different types are:

1. *dead load:* in a building, the weight of all permanent constructions, such as floor, roof, framing, and covering members.

2. *impact load:* the assumed load resulting from the motion of machinery, elevators, craneways, vehicles, and other similar kinetic forces.

3. *roof live load:* all loads exerted on a roof (except dead, wind, and lateral loads) and applied to the horizontal projection of the building.

4. *seismic load:* the assumed lateral load due to the action of earthquakes and acting in any horizontal direction on the structural frame.

5. *wind load:* the load caused by wind blowing from any horizontal direction.

Louver: An opening provided with one or more slated, fixed, or movable fins to allow flow of air, but to exclude rain and sun or to provide privacy.

Mullion: The large vertical piece between windows. (It holds the window in place along the edge with which it makes contact.)

Nonbearing Partition: A partition which supports no weight except its own.

Parapet: That portion of the vertical wall of a building that extends above the roof line at the intersection of the wall and roof.

Partition: A material or combination of materials used to divide a space into smaller spaces.

Performance Bond: A bond that guarantees to the owner, within specified limits, that the contractor will perform the work in accordance with the contract documents.

Pier: A structure of masonry (concrete) used to support the bases of columns and bents. It carries the vertical load to a footing at the desired load-bearing soil.

Pilaster: A flat rectangular column attached to or built into a wall masonry or pier; structurally, a pier, but treated architecturally as a column with a capital, shaft, and base. It is used to provide strength for roof loads or support for the wall against lateral forces.

Precast Concrete: Concrete that is poured and cast in some position other than the one it will finally occupy; cast either on the jobsite and then put into place or away from the site to be transported to the site and erected.

Prestressed Concrete: Concrete in which the reinforcing cables, wires, or rods are tensioned before there is load on the member.

Progress Payments: Payments made during progress of the work, on account, for work completed and/or suitably stored.

Progress Schedule: A diagram showing proposed and actual times of starting and completion of the various operations in the project.

Punch List: A list prepared by the architect or engineer of the contractor's uncompleted work or work to be corrected.

Purlin: Secondary horizontal structural members located on the roof extending between rafters, used as (light) beams for supporting the roof covering.

Rafter: A primary roof support beam usually in an inclined position, running from the tops of the structural columns at the eave to the ridge or highest portion of the roof. It is used to support the purlins.

Recess: A notch or cut-out, usually referring to the blockout formed at the outside edge of a foundation, and providing support and serving as a closure at the bottom edge of wall panels.

Reinforcing Steel: The steel placed in concrete to carry the tension, compression, and shear stresses.

Retainage: A sum withheld from each payment to the contractor in accordance with the terms of the Owner-Contractor Agreement.

Roof Overhang: A roof extension beyond the end or side walls of a building.

Roof Pitch: The angle or degree of slope of a roof from the eave to the ridge. The pitch can be found by dividing the height, or rise, by the span; for example, if the height is eight feet and the span is sixteen feet, the pitch is 8/16 or ½ and the angle of pitch is 45° (See *Roof Slope*.)

Rolling Doors: Doors that are supported on wheels that run on a track.

Roof Slope: The angle that a roof surface makes with the horizontal. Usually expressed as a certain rise in 12 inches of run.

Sandwich Panel: An integrated structural covering and insulating component consisting of a core material with inner and outer metal or wood skins.

Schedule of Values: A statement furnished to the architect by the contractor reflecting the amounts to be allotted for the principal divisions of the work. It is to serve as a guide for reviewing the contractor's periodic application for payment.

Sealant: Any material that is used to close up cracks or joints.

Separate Contract: A contract between the owner and a contractor other than the general contractor for the construction of a portion of a project.

Sheathing: Rough boarding (usually plywood) on outside of a wall or roof over which is placed siding or shingles.

Shim: A piece of steel used to level or square beams or column baseplates.

Shipping List: A list that enumerates by part, number, or description each piece of material to be shipped.

Shop Drawings: Drawings that illustrate how specific portions of the work shall be fabricated and/or installed.

Sill: The lowest member beneath an opening such as a window or door; also, the horizontal framing members at floor level, such as sill girts or sill angles; the member at the bottom of a door or window opening.

Sill, Slip: A sill that is the same width as the opening—it will slip into place.

Sill, Lug: A sill that projects into the masonry at each end of the sill. It must be installed as the building is being erected.

Skylight: An opening in a roof or ceiling for admitting daylight; also, the reinforced plastic panel or window fitted into such an opening.

Snow Load: In locations subject to snow loads, as indicated by the average snow depth in the reports of the United States Weather Bureau, the design loads shall be modified accordingly.

Soffit: The underside of any subordinate member of a building, such as the undersurface of a roof overhang or canopy.

Soil Borings: A boring made on the site in the general location of the proposed building to determine soil type, depth of the various types of soils, and water table level.

Soil Pressure: The allowable soil pressure is the load per unit area a structure can safely exert on the substructure (soil) without exceeding reasonable values of footing settlements.

Spall: A chip or fragment of concrete that has chipped, weathered, or otherwise broken from the main mass of concrete.

Span: The clear distance between supports of beams, girders, or trusses.

Spandrel Beam: A beam from column to column carrying an exterior wall and/or the outermost edge of an upper floor.

Specifications: A statement of particulars of a given job as to size of building, quality and performance of men and materials to be used, and the terms of the contract. A set of specifications generally indicates the design loads and design criteria.

Stock: A unit that is standard to its manufacturer. It is not custommade.

Stool: A shelf across the inside bottom of a window.

Stud: A vertical wall member to which exterior or interior covering of collateral material may be attached. Load-bearing studs are those which carry a portion of the loads from the floor, roof, or ceiling above as well as the collateral material on one or both sides. Non-load-bearing studs are used to support only the attached collateral materials and carry no load from the floor, roof, or ceiling above.

Subcontractor: A separate contractor for a portion of the work (hired by the general contractor).

Substantial Completion: For a project or specified area of a project, the date when the construction is sufficiently completed in accordance with the contract documents, as modified by any change orders agreed to by the parties, so that the owner can occupy the project or specified area of the project for the use for which it was intended.

Supplementary General Conditions: One of the contract documents, prepared by the architect, that may modify provisions of the General Conditions of the contract.

Square: One hundred square feet.

Temperature Reinforcing: Lightweight deformed steel rods or wire mesh placed in concrete to resist possible cracks from expansion or contraction due to temperature changes.

Time of Completion: The number of days (calendar or working) or the actual date by which completion of the work is required.

Truss: A structure made up of three or more members, with each member designed to carry basically a tension or a compression force. The entire structure in turn acts as a beam.

Veneer: A thin covering of valuable material over a less expensive body; for example, brick on a wood frame building.

Wainscot: Protective or decorative covering applied or built into the lower portion of a wall.

Wall Bearing: In cases where a floor, roof, or ceiling rests on a wall, the wall is designed to carry the load exerted. These types of walls are also referred to as load-bearing walls.

Wall Covering: The exterior wall skin consisting of panels or sheets and including their attachment, trim, facia and weather sealants.

Wall Non-Bearing: Wall not relied upon to support a structural system.

Water Closet: More commonly known as a toilet.

Working Drawing: The actual plans (drawings and illustrations) from which the building will be built. They show how the building is to be built and are included in the contract documents.

Metric Conversion Tables*

Fractions of Inch to Millimeters and Centimeters

Conversion factor: 1 inch = 25.4 millimeters = 2.54 centimeters

Inches: in   millimeters:mm   centimeters:cm

in	mm	cm	in	mm	cm	in	mm	cm	in	mm	cm	in	mm	cm
1/64	.3969	.0397	1/4	6.3500	.6350	31/64	12.3031	1.2303	23/32	18.2563	1.8256	61/64	24.2094	2.4209
1/32	.7938	.0794	17/64	6.7469	.6747	1/2	12.7000	1.2700	47/64	18.6531	1.8653	31/32	24.6063	2.4606
3/64	1.1906	.1191	9/32	7.1438	.7144	33/64	13.0969	1.3097	3/4	19.0500	1.9050	63/64	25.0031	2.5003
1/16	1.5875	.1588	19/64	7.5406	.7541	17/32	13.4938	1.3494	49/64	19.4469	1.9447	1	25.4000	2.5400
5/64	1.9844	.1984	5/16	7.9375	.7938	35/64	13.8906	1.3891	25/32	19.8438	1.9844			
3/32	2.3813	.2381	21/64	8.3344	.8334	9/16	14.2875	1.4288	51/64	20.2406	2.0241			
7/64	2.7781	.2778	11/32	8.7313	.8731	37/64	14.6844	1.4684	13/16	20.6375	2.0638			
1/8	3.1750	.3175	23/64	9.1281	.9128	19/32	15.0813	1.5081	53/64	21.0344	2.1034			
9/64	3.5719	.3572	6/16	9.5250	.9525	39/64	15.4781	1.5478	27/32	21.4313	2.1431			
5/32	3.9688	.3969	25/64	9.9219	.9922	5/8	15.8750	1.5875	55/64	21.8281	2.1828			
11/64	4.3656	.4366	13/32	10.3188	1.0319	41/64	16.2719	1.6272	7/8	22.2250	2.2225			
3/16	4.7625	.4763	27/64	10.7156	1.0716	21/32	16.6688	1.6669	57/64	22.6219	2.2622			
13/64	5.1594	.5159	7/16	11.1125	1.1113	43/64	17.0656	1.7066	29/32	23.0188	2.3019			
7/32	5.5563	.5556	29/64	11.5094	1.1509	11/16	17.4625	1.7463	59/64	23.4156	2.3416			
15/64	5.9531	.5953	15/32	11.9063	1.1906	45/64	17.8594	1.7859	15/16	23.8125	2.3813			

*These tables have been taken from *Metric Conversion Tables,* published by Ottenheimer Publishers, Inc., and are reproduced with permission.

Feet and Inches to Centimeters and Meters
Conversion factor: 1 inch = 2.54 centimeters = .0254 meters
1 foot = 30.48 centimeters = .3048 meters
feet inches:ft in   centimeters:cm   meters:m

ft in	cm	m	ft in	cm	m	ft in	cm	m	ft in	cm	m	ft in	cm	m
1	2 54	0254	5 1	154 94	1 5494	10 1	307 34	3 0734	15 1	459 74	4 5974	20 1	612 14	6 1214
2	5 08	0508	5 2	157 48	1 5748	10 2	309 88	3 0988	15 2	462 28	4 6228	20 2	614 68	6 1468
3	7 62	0762	5 3	160 02	1 6002	10 3	312 42	3 1242	15 3	464 82	4 6482	20 3	617 22	6 1722
4	10 16	1016	5 4	162 56	1 6256	10 4	314 96	3 1496	15 4	467 36	4 6736	20 4	619 76	6 1976
5	12 70	1270	5 5	165 10	1 6510	10 5	317 50	3 1750	15 5	469 90	4 6990	20 5	622 30	6 2230
6	15 24	1524	5 6	167 64	1 6764	10 6	320 04	3 2004	15 6	472 44	4 7244	20 6	624 84	6 2484
7	17 78	1778	5 7	170 18	1 7018	10 7	322 58	3 2258	15 7	474 98	4 7498	20 7	627 38	6 2738
8	20 32	2032	5 8	172 72	1 7272	10 8	325 12	3 2512	15 8	477 52	4 7752	20 8	629 92	6 2992
9	22 86	2286	5 9	175 26	1 7526	10 9	327 66	3 2766	15 9	480 06	4 8006	20 9	632 46	6 3246
10	25 40	2540	5 10	177 80	1 7780	10 10	330 20	3 3020	15 10	482 60	4 8260	20 10	635 00	6 3500
11	27 94	2794	5 11	180 34	1 8034	10 11	332 74	3 3274	15 11	485 14	4 8514	20 11	637 54	6 3754
1 0	30 48	3048	6 0	182 88	1 8288	11 0	335 28	3 3528	16 0	487 68	4 8768	21 0	640 08	6 4008
1 1	33 02	3302	6 1	185 42	1 8542	11 1	337 82	3 3782	16 1	490 22	4 9022	21 1	642 62	6 4262
1 2	35 56	3556	6 2	187 96	1 8796	11 2	340 36	3 4036	16 2	492 76	4 9276	21 2	645 16	6 4516
1 3	38 10	3810	6 3	190 50	1 9050	11 3	342 90	3 4290	16 3	495 30	4 9530	21 3	647 70	6 4770
1 4	40 64	4064	6 4	193 04	1 9304	11 4	345 44	3 4544	16 4	497 84	4 9784	21 4	650 24	6 5024
1 5	43 18	4318	6 5	195 58	1 9558	11 5	347 98	3 4798	16 5	500 38	5 0038	21 5	652 78	6 5278
1 6	45 72	4572	6 6	198 12	1 9812	11 6	350 52	3 5052	16 6	502 92	5 0292	21 6	655 32	6 5532
1 7	48 26	4826	6 7	200 66	2 0066	11 7	353 06	3 5306	16 7	505 46	5 0546	21 7	657 86	6 5786
1 8	50 80	5080	6 8	203 20	2 0320	11 8	355 60	3 5560	16 8	508 00	5 0800	21 8	660 40	6 6040
1 9	53 34	5334	6 9	205 74	2 0574	11 9	358 14	3 5814	16 9	510 54	5 1054	21 9	662 94	6 6294
1 10	55 88	5588	6 10	208 28	2 0828	11 10	360 68	3 6068	16 10	513 08	5 1308	21 10	665 48	6 6548
1 11	58 42	5842	6 11	210 82	2 1082	11 11	363 22	3 6322	16 11	515 62	5 1562	21 11	668 02	6 6802
2 0	60 96	6096	7 0	213 36	2 1336	12 0	365 76	3 6576	17 0	518 16	5 1816	22 0	670 56	6 7056
2 1	63 50	6350	7 1	215 90	2 1590	12 1	368 30	3 6830	17 1	520 70	5 2070	22 1	673 10	6 7310
2 2	66 04	6604	7 2	218 44	2 1844	12 2	370 84	3 7084	17 2	523 24	5 2324	22 2	675 64	6 7564
2 3	68 58	6858	7 3	220 98	2 2098	12 3	373 38	3 7338	17 3	525 78	5 2578	22 3	678 18	6 7818
2 4	71 12	7112	7 4	223 52	2 2352	12 4	375 92	3 7592	17 4	528 32	5 2832	22 4	680 72	6 8072
2 5	73 66	7366	7 5	226 06	2 2606	12 5	378 46	3 7846	17 5	530 86	5 3086	22 5	683 26	6 8326
2 6	76 20	7620	7 6	228 60	2 2860	12 6	381 00	3 8100	17 6	533 40	5 3340	22 6	685 80	6 8580
2 7	78 74	7874	7 7	231 14	2 3114	12 7	383 54	3 8354	17 7	535 94	5 3594	22 7	688 34	6 8834
2 8	81 28	8128	7 8	233 68	2 3368	12 8	386 08	3 8608	17 8	538 48	5 3848	22 8	690 88	6 9088
2 9	83 82	8382	7 9	236 22	2 3622	12 9	388 62	3 8862	17 9	541 02	5 4102	22 9	693 42	6 9342
2 10	86 36	8636	7 10	238 76	2 3876	12 10	391 16	3 9116	17 10	543 56	5 4356	22 10	695 96	6 9596
2 11	88 90	8890	7 11	241 30	2 4130	12 11	393 70	3 9370	17 11	546 10	5 4610	22 11	698 50	6 9850
3 0	91 44	9144	8 0	243 84	2 4384	13 0	396 24	3 9624	18 0	548 64	5 4864	23 0	701 04	7 0104
3 1	93 98	9398	8 1	246 38	2 4638	13 1	398 78	3 9878	18 1	551 18	5 5118	23 1	703 58	7 0358
3 2	96 52	9652	8 2	248 92	2 4892	13 2	401 32	4 0132	18 2	553 72	5 5372	23 2	706 12	7 0612
3 3	99 06	9906	8 3	251 46	2 5146	13 3	403 86	4 0386	18 3	556 26	5 5626	23 3	708 66	7 0866
3 4	101 60	1 0160	8 4	254 00	2 5400	13 4	406 40	4 0640	18 4	558 80	5 5880	23 4	711 20	7 1120
3 5	104 14	1 0414	8 5	256 54	2 5654	13 5	408 94	4 0894	18 5	561 34	5 6134	23 5	713 74	7 1374
3 6	106 68	1 0668	8 6	259 08	2 5908	13 6	411 48	4 1148	18 6	563 88	5 6388	23 6	716 28	7 1628
3 7	109 22	1 0922	8 7	261 62	2 6162	13 7	414 02	4 1402	18 7	566 42	5 6642	23 7	718 82	7 1882
3 8	111 76	1 1176	8 8	264 16	2 6416	13 8	416 56	4 1656	18 8	568 96	5 6896	23 8	721 36	7 2136
3 9	114 30	1 1143	8 9	266 70	2 6670	13 9	419 10	4 1910	18 9	571 50	5 7150	23 9	723 90	7 2390
3 10	116 84	1 1684	8 10	269 24	2 6924	13 10	421 64	4 2164	18 10	574 04	5 7404	23 10	726 44	7 2644
3 11	119 38	1 1938	8 11	271 78	2 7178	13 11	424 18	4 2418	18 11	576 58	5 7658	23 11	728 98	7 2898
4 0	121 92	1 2192	9 0	274 32	2 7432	14 0	426 72	4 2672	19 0	579 12	5 7912	24 0	731 52	7 3152
4 1	124 46	1 2146	9 1	276 86	2 7686	14 1	429 26	4 2926	19 1	581 66	5 8166	24 1	734 06	7 3406
4 2	127 00	1 2700	9 2	279 40	2 7940	14 2	431 80	4 3180	19 2	584 20	5 8420	24 2	736 60	7 3660
4 3	129 54	1 2954	9 3	281 94	2 8194	14 3	434 34	4 3434	19 3	586 74	5 8674	24 3	739 14	7 3914
4 4	132 08	1 3208	9 4	284 48	2 8448	14 4	436 88	4 3688	19 4	589 28	5 8928	24 4	741 68	7 4168
4 5	134 62	1 3462	9 5	287 02	2 8702	14 5	439 42	4 3942	19 5	591 82	5 9182	24 5	744 22	7 4422
4 6	137 16	1 3716	9 6	289 56	2 8956	14 6	441 96	4 4196	19 6	594 36	5 9436	24 6	746 76	7 4676
4 7	139 70	1 3970	9 7	292 10	2 9210	14 7	444 50	4 4450	19 7	596 90	5 9690	24 7	749 30	7 4930
4 8	142 24	1 4224	9 8	294 64	2 9464	14 8	447 04	4 4704	19 8	599 44	5 9944	24 8	751 84	7 5184
4 9	144 78	1 4478	9 9	297 18	2 9718	14 9	449 58	4 4958	19 9	601 98	6 0198	24 9	754 38	7 5438
4 10	147 32	1 4732	9 10	299 72	2 9972	14 10	452 12	4 5212	19 10	604 52	6 0452	24 10	756 92	7 5692
4 11	149 86	1 4986	9 11	302 26	3 0226	14 11	454 66	4 5466	19 11	607 06	6 0706	24 11	759 46	7 5946
5 0	152 40	1 5240	10 0	304 80	3 0480	15 0	457 20	4 5720	20 0	609 60	6 0960	25 0	762 00	7 6200

Feet and Inches to Centimeters and Meters—CONTINUED

ft	in	cm	m	ft	in	cm	m	ft	in	cm	m	ft	in	cm	m	ft	in	cm	m
25	1	764 54	7 6454	30	1	916 94	9 1694	35	1	1069 34	10 6934	40	1	1221 74	12 2174	45	1	1374 14	13 7414
25	2	767 08	7 6708	30	2	919 48	9 1948	35	2	1071 88	10 7188	40	2	1224 28	12 2428	45	2	1376 68	13 7668
25	3	769 62	7 6962	30	3	922 02	9 2202	35	3	1074 42	10 7442	40	3	1226 82	12 2682	45	3	1379 22	13 7922
25	4	772 16	7 7216	30	4	924 56	9 2456	35	4	1076 96	10 7696	40	4	1229 36	12 2936	45	4	1381 76	13 8176
25	5	774 70	7 7470	30	5	927 10	9 2710	35	5	1079 50	10 7950	40	5	1231 90	12 3190	45	5	1384 30	13 8430
25	6	777 24	7 7724	30	6	929 64	9 2964	35	6	1082 04	10 8204	40	6	1234 44	12 3444	45	6	1386 84	13 8684
25	7	779 78	7 7978	30	7	932 18	9 3218	35	7	1084 58	10 8458	40	7	1236 98	12 3698	45	7	1389 38	13 8938
25	8	782 32	7 8232	30	8	934 72	9 3472	35	8	1087 12	10 8712	40	8	1239 52	12 3952	45	8	1391 92	13 9192
25	9	784 86	7 8486	30	9	937 26	9 3726	35	9	1089 66	10 8966	40	9	1242 06	12 4206	45	9	1394 46	13 9446
25	10	787 40	7 8740	30	10	939 80	9 3980	35	10	1092 20	10 9220	40	10	1244 60	12 4460	45	10	1397 00	13 9700
25	11	789 94	7 8994	30	11	942 34	9 4234	35	11	1094 74	10 9474	40	11	1247 14	12 4714	45	11	1399 54	13 9954
26	0	792 48	7 9248	31	0	944 88	9 4488	36	0	1097 28	10 9728	41	0	1249 68	12 4968	46	0	1402 08	14 0208
26	1	795 02	7 9502	31	1	947 42	9 4742	36	1	1099 82	10 9982	41	1	1252 22	12 5222	46	1	1404 62	14 0462
26	2	797 56	7 9756	31	2	949 96	9 4996	36	2	1102 36	11 0236	41	2	1254 76	12 5476	46	2	1407 16	14 0716
26	3	800 10	8 0010	31	3	952 50	9 5250	36	3	1104 90	11 0490	41	3	1257 30	12 5730	46	3	1409 70	14 0970
26	4	802 64	8 0264	31	4	955 04	9 5504	36	4	1107 44	11 0744	41	4	1259 84	12 5984	46	4	1412 24	14 1224
26	5	805 18	8 0518	31	5	957 58	9 5758	36	5	1109 98	11 0998	41	5	1262 38	12 6238	46	5	1414 78	14 1478
26	6	807 72	8 0772	31	6	960 12	9 6012	36	6	1112 52	11 1252	41	6	1264 92	12 6492	46	6	1417 32	14 1732
26	7	810 26	8 1026	31	7	962 66	9 6266	36	7	1115 06	11 1506	41	7	1267 46	12 6746	46	7	1419 86	14 1986
26	8	812 80	8 1280	31	8	965 20	9 6520	36	8	1117 60	11 1760	41	8	1270 00	12 7000	46	8	1422 40	14 2240
26	9	815 34	8 1534	31	9	967 74	9 6774	36	9	1120 14	11 2014	41	9	1272 54	12 7254	46	9	1424 94	14 2494
26	10	817 88	8 1788	31	10	970 28	9 7028	36	10	1122 68	11 2268	41	10	1275 08	12 7508	46	10	1427 48	14 2748
26	11	820 42	8 2042	31	11	972 82	9 7282	36	11	1125 22	11 2522	41	11	1277 62	12 7762	46	11	1430 02	14 3002
27	0	822 96	8 2296	32	0	975 36	9 7536	37	0	1127 76	11 2776	42	0	1280 16	12 8016	47	0	1432 56	14 3256
27	1	825 50	8 2550	32	1	977 90	9 7790	37	1	1130 30	11 3030	42	1	1282 70	12 8270	47	1	1435 10	14 3510
27	2	828 04	8 2804	32	2	980 44	9 8044	37	2	1132 84	11 3284	42	2	1285 24	12 8524	47	2	1437 64	14 3764
27	3	830 58	8 3058	32	3	982 98	9 8298	37	3	1135 38	11 3538	42	3	1287 78	12 8778	47	3	1440 18	14 4018
27	4	833 12	8 3312	32	4	985 52	9 8552	37	4	1137 92	11 3792	42	4	1290 32	12 9032	47	4	1442 72	14 4272
27	5	835 66	8 3566	32	5	988 06	9 8806	37	5	1140 46	11 4046	42	5	1292 86	12 9286	47	5	1445 26	14 4526
27	6	838 20	8 3820	32	6	990 60	9 9060	37	6	1143 00	11 4300	42	6	1295 40	12 9540	47	6	1447 80	14 4780
27	7	840 74	8 4074	32	7	993 14	9 9314	37	7	1145 54	11 4554	42	7	1297 94	12 9794	47	7	1450 34	14 5034
27	8	843 28	8 4328	32	8	995 68	9 9568	37	8	1148 08	11 4808	42	8	1300 48	13 0048	47	8	1452 88	14 5288
27	9	845 82	8 4582	32	9	998 22	9 9822	37	9	1150 62	11 5062	42	9	1303 02	13 0302	47	9	1455 42	14 5542
27	10	848 36	8 4836	32	10	1000 76	10 0076	37	10	1153 16	11 5316	42	10	1305 56	13 0556	47	10	1457 96	14 5796
27	11	850 90	8 5090	32	11	1003 30	10 0330	37	11	1155 70	11 5570	42	11	1308 10	13 0810	47	11	1460 50	14 6050
28	0	853 44	8 5344	33	0	1005 84	10 0584	38	0	1158 24	11 5824	43	0	1310 64	13 1064	48	0	1463 04	14 6304
28	1	855 98	8 5598	33	1	1008 38	10 0838	38	1	1160 78	11 6078	43	1	1313 18	13 1318	48	1	1465 58	14 6558
28	2	858 52	8 5852	33	2	1010 92	10 1092	38	2	1163 32	11 6332	43	2	1315 72	13 1572	48	2	1468 12	14 6812
28	3	861 06	8 6106	33	3	1013 46	10 1346	38	3	1165 86	11 6586	43	3	1318 26	13 1826	48	3	1470 66	14 7066
28	4	863 60	8 6360	33	4	1016 00	10 1600	38	4	1168 40	11 6840	43	4	1320 80	13 2080	48	4	1473 20	14 7320
28	5	866 14	8 6614	33	5	1018 54	10 1854	38	5	1170 94	11 7094	43	5	1323 34	13 2334	48	5	1475 74	14 7574
28	6	868 68	8 6868	33	6	1021 08	10 2108	38	6	1173 48	11 7348	43	6	1325 88	13 2588	48	6	1478 28	14 7828
28	7	871 22	8 7122	33	7	1023 62	10 2362	38	7	1176 02	11 7602	43	7	1328 42	13 2842	48	7	1480 82	14 8082
28	8	873 76	8 7376	33	8	1026 16	10 2616	38	8	1178 56	11 7856	43	8	1330 96	13 3096	48	8	1483 36	14 8336
28	9	876 30	8 7630	33	9	1028 70	10 2870	38	9	1181 10	11 8110	43	9	1333 50	13 3350	48	9	1485 90	14 8590
28	10	878 84	8 7884	33	10	1031 24	10 3124	38	10	1183 64	11 8364	43	10	1336 04	13 3604	48	10	1488 44	14 8844
28	11	881 38	8 8138	33	11	1033 78	10 3378	38	11	1186 18	11 8618	43	11	1338 58	13 3858	48	11	1490 98	14 9098
29	0	883 92	8 8392	34	0	1036 32	10 3632	39	0	1188 72	11 8872	44	0	1341 12	13 4112	49	0	1493 52	14 9352
29	1	886 46	8 8646	34	1	1038 86	10 3886	39	1	1191 26	11 9126	44	1	1343 66	13 4366	49	1	1496 06	14 9606
29	2	889 00	8 8900	34	2	1041 40	10 4140	39	2	1193 80	11 9380	44	2	1346 20	13 4620	49	2	1498 60	14 9860
29	3	891 54	8 9154	34	3	1043 94	10 4394	39	3	1196 34	11 9634	44	3	1348 74	13 4874	49	3	1501 14	15 0114
29	4	894 08	8 9408	34	4	1046 48	10 4648	39	4	1198 88	11 9888	44	4	1351 28	13 5128	49	4	1503 68	15 0368
29	5	896 62	8 9662	34	5	1049 02	10 4902	39	5	1201 42	12 0142	44	5	1353 82	13 5382	49	5	1506 22	15 0622
29	6	899 16	8 9916	34	6	1051 56	10 5156	39	6	1203 96	12 0396	44	6	1356 36	13 5636	49	6	1508 76	15 0876
29	7	901 70	9 0170	34	7	1054 10	10 5410	39	7	1206 50	12 0650	44	7	1358 90	13 5890	49	7	1511 30	15 1130
29	8	904 24	9 0424	34	8	1056 64	10 5664	39	8	1209 04	12 0904	44	8	1361 44	13 6144	49	8	1513 84	15 1384
29	9	906 78	9 0678	34	9	1059 18	10 5918	39	9	1211 58	12 1158	44	9	1363 98	13 6398	49	9	1516 38	15 1638
29	10	909 32	9 0932	34	10	1061 72	10 6172	39	10	1214 12	12 1412	44	10	1366 52	13 6652	49	10	1518 92	15 1892
29	11	911 86	9 1186	34	11	1064 26	10 6426	39	11	1216 66	12 1666	44	11	1369 06	13 6906	49	11	1521 46	15 2146
30	0	914 40	9 1440	35	0	1066 80	10 6680	40	0	1219 20	12 1920	45	0	1371 60	13 7160	50	0	1524 00	15 2400

Feet and Inches to Centimeters and Meters —CONTINUED

ft	in	cm	m	ft	in	cm	m	ft	in	cm	m	ft	in	cm	m	ft	in	cm	m
50	1	1526 54	15 2654	55	1	1678 94	16 7894	60	1	1831 34	18 3134	65	1	1983 74	19 8374	70	1	2136 14	21 3614
50	2	1529 08	15 2908	55	2	1681 48	16 8148	60	2	1833 88	18 3388	65	2	1986 28	19 8628	70	2	2138 68	21 3868
50	3	1531 62	15 3162	55	3	1684 02	16 8402	60	3	1836 42	18 3642	65	3	1988 82	19 8882	70	3	2141 22	21 4122
50	4	1534 16	15 3416	55	4	1686 56	16 8656	60	4	1838 96	18 3896	65	4	1991 36	19 9136	70	4	2143 76	21 4376
50	5	1536 70	15 3670	55	5	1689 10	16 8910	60	5	1841 50	18 4150	65	5	1993 90	19 9390	70	5	2146 30	21 4630
50	6	1539 24	15 3924	55	6	1691 64	16 9164	60	6	1844 04	18 4404	65	6	1996 44	19 9644	70	6	2148 84	21 4884
50	7	1541 78	15 4178	55	7	1694 18	16 9418	60	7	1846 58	18 4658	65	7	1998 98	19 9898	70	7	2151 38	21 5138
50	8	1544 32	15 4432	55	8	1696 72	16 9672	60	8	1849 12	18 4912	65	8	2001 52	20 0152	70	8	2153 92	21 5392
50	9	1546 86	15 4686	55	9	1699 26	16 9926	60	9	1851 66	18 5166	65	9	2004 06	20 0406	70	9	2156 46	21 5646
50	10	1549 40	15 4940	55	10	1701 80	17 0180	60	10	1854 20	18 5420	65	10	2006 60	20 0660	70	10	2159 00	21 5900
50	11	1551 94	15 5194	55	11	1704 34	17 0434	60	11	1856 74	18 5674	65	11	2009 14	20 0914	70	11	2161 54	21 6154
51	0	1554 48	15 5448	56	0	1706 88	17 0688	61	0	1859 28	18 5928	66	0	2011 68	20 1168	71	0	2164 08	21 6408
51	1	1557 02	15 5702	56	1	1709 42	17 0942	61	1	1861 82	18 6182	66	1	2014 22	20 1422	71	1	2166 62	21 6662
51	2	1559 56	15 5956	56	2	1711 96	17 1196	61	2	1864 36	18 6436	66	2	2016 76	20 1676	71	2	2169 16	21 6916
51	3	1562 10	15 6210	56	3	1714 50	17 1450	61	3	1866 90	18 6690	66	3	2019 30	20 1930	71	3	2171 70	21 7170
51	4	1564 64	15 6464	56	4	1717 04	17 1704	61	4	1869 44	18 6944	66	4	2021 84	20 2184	71	4	2174 24	21 7424
51	5	1567 18	15 6718	56	5	1719 58	17 1958	61	5	1871 98	18 7198	66	5	2024 38	20 2438	71	5	2176 78	21 7678
51	6	1569 72	15 6972	56	6	1722 12	17 2212	61	6	1874 52	18 7452	66	6	2026 92	20 2692	71	6	2179 32	21 7932
51	7	1572 26	15 7226	56	7	1724 66	17 2466	61	7	1877 06	18 7706	66	7	2029 46	20 2946	71	7	2181 86	21 8186
51	8	1574 80	15 7480	56	8	1727 20	17 2720	61	8	1879 60	18 7960	66	8	2032 00	20 3200	71	8	2184 40	21 8440
51	9	1577 34	15 7734	56	9	1729 74	17 2974	61	9	1882 14	18 8214	66	9	2034 54	20 3454	71	9	2186 94	21 8694
51	10	1579 88	15 7988	56	10	1732 28	17 3228	61	10	1884 68	18 8468	66	10	2037 08	20 3708	71	10	2189 48	21 8948
51	11	1582 42	15 8242	56	11	1734 82	17 3482	61	11	1887 22	18 8722	66	11	2039 62	20 3962	71	11	2192 02	21 9202
52	0	1584 96	15 8496	57	0	1737 36	17 3736	62	0	1889 76	18 8976	67	0	2042 16	20 4216	72	0	2194 56	21 9456
52	1	1587 50	15 8750	57	1	1739 90	17 3990	62	1	1892 30	18 9230	67	1	2044 70	20 4470	72	1	2197 10	21 9710
52	2	1590 04	15 9004	57	2	1742 44	17 4244	62	2	1894 84	18 9484	67	2	2047 24	20 4724	72	2	2199 64	21 9964
52	3	1592 58	15 9258	57	3	1744 98	17 4498	62	3	1897 38	18 9738	67	3	2049 78	20 4978	72	3	2202 18	22 0218
52	4	1595 12	15 9512	57	4	1747 52	17 4752	62	4	1899 92	18 9992	67	4	2052 32	20 5232	72	4	2204 72	22 0472
52	5	1597 66	15 9766	57	5	1750 06	17 5006	62	5	1902 46	19 0246	67	5	2054 86	20 5486	72	5	2207 26	22 0726
52	6	1600 20	16 0020	57	6	1752 60	17 5260	62	6	1905 00	19 0500	67	6	2057 40	20 5740	72	6	2209 80	22 0980
52	7	1602 74	16 0274	57	7	1755 14	17 5514	62	7	1907 54	19 0754	67	7	2059 94	20 5994	72	7	2212 34	22 1234
52	8	1605 28	16 0528	57	8	1757 68	17 5768	62	8	1910 08	19 1008	67	8	2062 48	20 6248	72	8	2214 88	22 1488
52	9	1607 82	16 0782	57	9	1760 22	17 6022	62	9	1912 62	19 1262	67	9	2065 02	20 6502	72	9	2217 42	22 1742
52	10	1610 36	16 1036	57	10	1762 76	17 6276	62	10	1915 16	19 1516	67	10	2067 56	20 6756	72	10	2219 96	22 1996
52	11	1612 90	16 1290	57	11	1765 30	17 6530	62	11	1917 70	19 1770	67	11	2070 10	20 7010	72	11	2222 50	22 2250
53	0	1615 44	16 1544	58	0	1767 84	17 6784	63	0	1920 24	19 2024	68	0	2072 64	20 7264	73	0	2225 04	22 2504
53	1	1617 98	16 1798	58	1	1770 38	17 7038	63	1	1922 78	19 2278	68	1	2075 18	20 7518	73	1	2227 58	22 2758
53	2	1620 52	16 2052	58	2	1772 92	17 7292	63	2	1925 32	19 2532	68	2	2077 72	20 7772	73	2	2230 12	22 3012
53	3	1623 06	16 2306	58	3	1775 46	17 7546	63	3	1927 86	19 2786	68	3	2080 26	20 8026	73	3	2232 66	22 3266
53	4	1625 60	16 2560	58	4	1778 00	17 7800	63	4	1930 40	19 3040	68	4	2082 80	20 8280	73	4	2235 20	22 3520
53	5	1628 14	16 2814	58	5	1780 54	17 8054	63	5	1932 94	19 3294	68	5	2085 34	20 8534	73	5	2237 74	22 3774
53	6	1630 68	16 3068	58	6	1783 08	17 8308	63	6	1935 48	19 3548	68	6	2087 88	20 8788	73	6	2240 28	22 4028
53	7	1633 22	16 3322	58	7	1785 62	17 8562	63	7	1938 02	19 3802	68	7	2090 42	20 9042	73	7	2242 82	22 4282
53	8	1635 76	16 3576	58	8	1788 16	17 8816	63	8	1940 56	19 4056	68	8	2092 96	20 9296	73	8	2245 36	22 4536
53	9	1638 30	16 3830	58	9	1790 70	17 9070	63	9	1943 10	19 4310	68	9	2095 50	20 9550	73	9	2247 90	22 4790
53	10	1640 84	16 4084	58	10	1793 24	17 9324	63	10	1945 64	19 4564	68	10	2098 04	20 9804	73	10	2250 44	22 5044
53	11	1643 38	16 4338	58	11	1795 78	17 9578	63	11	1948 18	19 4818	68	11	2100 58	21 0058	73	11	2252 98	22 5298
54	0	1645 92	16 4592	59	0	1798 32	17 9832	64	0	1950 72	19 5072	69	0	2103 12	21 0312	74	0	2255 52	22 5552
54	1	1648 46	16 4846	59	1	1800 86	18 0086	64	1	1953 26	19 5326	69	1	2105 66	21 0566	74	1	2258 06	22 5806
54	2	1651 00	16 5100	59	2	1803 40	18 0340	64	2	1955 80	19 5580	69	2	2108 20	21 0820	74	2	2260 60	22 6060
54	3	1653 54	16 5354	59	3	1805 94	18 0594	64	3	1958 34	19 5834	69	3	2110 74	21 1074	74	3	2263 14	22 6314
54	4	1656 08	16 5608	59	4	1808 48	18 0848	64	4	1960 88	19 6088	69	4	2113 28	21 1328	74	4	2265 68	22 6568
54	5	1658 62	16 5862	59	5	1811 02	18 1102	64	5	1963 42	19 6342	69	5	2115 82	21 1582	74	5	2268 22	22 6822
54	6	1661 16	16 6116	59	6	1813 56	18 1356	64	6	1965 96	19 6596	69	6	2118 36	21 1836	74	6	2270 76	22 7076
54	7	1663 70	16 6370	59	7	1816 10	18 1610	64	7	1968 50	19 6850	69	7	2120 90	21 2090	74	7	2273 30	22 7330
54	8	1666 24	16 6624	59	8	1818 64	18 1864	64	8	1971 04	19 7104	69	8	2123 44	21 2344	74	8	2275 84	22 7584
54	9	1668 78	16 6878	59	9	1821 18	18 2118	64	9	1973 58	19 7358	69	9	2125 98	21 2598	74	9	2278 38	22 7838
54	10	1671 32	16 7132	59	10	1823 72	18 2372	64	10	1976 12	19 7612	69	10	2128 52	21 2852	74	10	2280 92	22 8092
54	11	1673 86	16 7386	59	11	1826 26	18 2626	64	11	1978 66	19 7866	69	11	2131 06	21 3106	74	11	2283 46	22 8346
55	0	1676 40	16 7640	60	0	1828 80	18 2880	65	0	1981 20	19 8120	70	0	2133 60	21 3360	75	0	2286 00	22 8600

Feet and Inches to Centimeters and Meters —CONTINUED

ft	in	cm	m	ft	in	cm	m	ft	in	cm	m	ft	in	cm	m	ft	in	cm	m
75	1	2288 54	22 8854	80	1	2440 94	24 4094	85	1	2593 34	25 9334	90	1	2745 74	27 4574	95	1	2898 14	28 9814
75	2	2291 08	22 9108	80	2	2443 48	24 4348	85	2	2595 88	25 9588	90	2	2748 28	27 4828	95	2	2900 68	29 0068
75	3	2293 62	22 9362	80	3	2446 02	24 4602	85	3	2598 42	25 9842	90	3	2750 82	27 5082	95	3	2903 22	29 0322
75	4	2296 16	22 9616	80	4	2448 56	24 4856	85	4	2600 96	26 0096	90	4	2753 36	27 5336	95	4	2905 76	29 0576
75	5	2298 70	22 9870	80	5	2451 10	24 5110	85	5	2603 50	26 0350	90	5	2755 90	27 5590	95	5	2908 30	29 0830
75	6	2301 24	23 0124	80	6	2453 64	24 5364	85	6	2606 04	26 0604	90	6	2758 44	27 5844	95	6	2910 84	29 1084
75	7	2303 78	23 0378	80	7	2456 18	24 5618	85	7	2608 58	26 0858	90	7	2760 98	27 6098	95	7	2913 38	29 1338
75	8	2306 32	23 0632	80	8	2458 72	24 5872	85	8	2611 12	26 1112	90	8	2763 52	27 6352	95	8	2915 92	29 1592
75	9	2308 86	23 0886	80	9	2461 26	24 6126	85	9	2613 66	26 1366	90	9	2766 06	27 6606	95	9	2918 46	29 1846
75	10	2311 40	23 1140	80	10	2463 80	24 6380	85	10	2616 20	26 1620	90	10	2768 60	27 6860	95	10	2921 00	29 2100
75	11	2313 94	23 1394	80	11	2466 34	24 6634	85	11	2618 74	26 1874	90	11	2771 14	27 7114	95	11	2923 54	29 2354
76	0	2316 48	23 1648	81	0	2468 88	24 6888	86	0	2621 28	26 2128	91	0	2773 68	27 7368	96	0	2926 08	29 2608
76	1	2319 02	23 1902	81	1	2471 42	24 7142	86	1	2623 82	26 2382	91	1	2776 22	27 7622	96	1	2928 62	29 2862
76	2	2321 56	23 2156	81	2	2473 96	24 7396	86	2	2626 36	26 2636	91	2	2778 76	27 7876	96	2	2931 16	29 3116
76	3	2324 10	23 2410	81	3	2476 50	24 7650	86	3	2628 90	26 2890	91	3	2781 30	27 8130	96	3	2933 70	29 3370
76	4	2326 64	23 2664	81	4	2479 04	24 7904	86	4	2631 44	26 3144	91	4	2783 84	27 8384	96	4	2936 24	29 3624
76	5	2329 18	23 2918	81	5	2481 58	24 8158	86	5	2633 98	26 3398	91	5	2786 38	27 8638	96	5	2938 78	29 3878
76	6	2331 72	23 3172	81	6	2484 12	24 8412	86	6	2636 52	26 3652	91	6	2788 92	27 8892	96	6	2941 32	29 4132
76	7	2334 26	23 3426	81	7	2486 66	24 8666	86	7	2639 06	26 3906	91	7	2791 46	27 9146	96	7	2943 86	29 4386
76	8	2336 80	23 3680	81	8	2489 20	24 8920	86	8	2641 60	26 4160	91	8	2794 00	27 9400	96	8	2946 40	29 4640
76	9	2339 34	23 3934	81	9	2491 74	24 9174	86	9	2644 14	26 4414	91	9	2796 54	27 9654	96	9	2948 94	29 4894
76	10	2341 88	23 4188	81	10	2494 28	24 9428	86	10	2646 68	26 4668	91	10	2799 08	27 9908	96	10	2951 48	29 5148
76	11	2344 42	23 4442	81	11	2496 82	24 9682	86	11	2649 22	26 4922	91	11	2801 62	28 0162	96	11	2954 02	29 5402
77	0	2346 96	23 4696	82	0	2499 36	24 9936	87	0	2651 76	26 5176	92	0	2804 16	28 0416	97	0	2956 56	29 5656
77	1	2349 50	23 4950	82	1	2501 90	25 0190	87	1	2654 30	26 5430	92	1	2806 70	28 0670	97	1	2959 10	29 5910
77	2	2352 04	23 5204	82	2	2504 44	25 0444	87	2	2656 84	26 5684	92	2	2809 24	28 0924	97	2	2961 64	29 6164
77	3	2354 58	23 5458	82	3	2506 98	25 0698	87	3	2659 38	26 5938	92	3	2811 78	28 1178	97	3	2964 18	29 6418
77	4	2357 12	23 5712	82	4	2509 52	25 0952	87	4	2661 92	26 6192	92	4	2814 32	28 1432	97	4	2966 72	29 6672
77	5	2359 66	23 5966	82	5	2512 06	25 1206	87	5	2664 46	26 6446	92	5	2816 86	28 1686	97	5	2969 26	29 6926
77	6	2362 20	23 6220	82	6	2514 60	25 1460	87	6	2667 00	26 6700	92	6	2819 40	28 1940	97	6	2971 80	29 7180
77	7	2364 74	23 6474	82	7	2517 14	25 1714	87	7	2669 54	26 6954	92	7	2821 94	28 2194	97	7	2974 34	29 7434
77	8	2367 28	23 6728	82	8	2519 68	25 1968	87	8	2672 08	26 7208	92	8	2824 48	28 2448	97	8	2976 88	29 7688
77	9	2369 82	23 6982	82	9	2522 22	25 2222	87	9	2674 62	26 7462	92	9	2827 02	28 2702	97	9	2979 42	29 7942
77	10	2372 36	23 7236	82	10	2524 76	25 2476	87	10	2677 16	26 7716	92	10	2829 56	28 2956	97	10	2981 96	29 8196
77	11	2374 90	23 7490	82	11	2527 30	25 2730	87	11	2679 70	26 7970	92	11	2832 10	28 3210	97	11	2984 50	29 8450
78	0	2377 44	23 7744	83	0	2529 84	25 2984	88	0	2682 24	26 8224	93	0	2834 64	28 3464	98	0	2987 04	29 8704
78	1	2379 98	23 7998	83	1	2532 38	25 3238	88	1	2684 78	26 8478	93	1	2837 18	28 3718	98	1	2989 58	29 8958
78	2	2382 52	23 8252	83	2	2534 92	25 3492	88	2	2687 32	26 8732	93	2	2839 72	28 3972	98	2	2992 12	29 9212
78	3	2385 06	23 8506	83	3	2537 46	25 3746	88	3	2689 86	26 8986	93	3	2842 26	28 4226	98	3	2994 66	29 9466
78	4	2387 60	23 8760	83	4	2540 00	25 4000	88	4	2692 40	26 9240	93	4	2844 80	28 4480	98	4	2997 20	29 9720
78	5	2390 14	23 9014	83	5	2542 54	25 4254	88	5	2694 94	26 9494	93	5	2847 34	28 4734	98	5	2999 74	29 9974
78	6	2392 68	23 9268	83	6	2545 08	25 4508	88	6	2697 48	26 9748	93	6	2849 88	28 4988	98	6	3002 28	30 0228
78	7	2395 22	23 9522	83	7	2547 62	25 4762	88	7	2700 02	27 0002	93	7	2852 42	28 5242	98	7	3004 82	30 0482
78	8	2397 76	23 9776	83	8	2550 16	25 5016	88	8	2702 56	27 0256	93	8	2854 96	28 5496	98	8	3007 36	30 0736
78	9	2400 30	24 0030	83	9	2552 70	25 5270	88	9	2705 10	27 0510	93	9	2857 50	28 5750	98	9	3009 90	30 0990
78	10	2402 84	24 0284	83	10	2555 24	25 5524	88	10	2707 64	27 0764	93	10	2860 04	28 6004	98	10	3012 44	30 1244
78	11	2405 38	24 0538	83	11	2557 78	25 5778	88	11	2710 18	27 1018	93	11	2862 58	28 6258	98	11	3014 98	30 1498
79	0	2407 92	24 0792	84	0	2560 32	25 6032	89	0	2712 72	27 1272	94	0	2865 12	28 6512	99	0	3017 52	30 1752
79	1	2410 46	24 1046	84	1	2562 86	25 6286	89	1	2715 26	27 1526	94	1	2867 66	28 6766	99	1	3020 06	30 2006
79	2	2413 00	24 1300	84	2	2565 40	25 6540	89	2	2717 80	27 1780	94	2	2870 20	28 7020	99	2	3022 60	30 2260
79	3	2415 54	24 1554	84	3	2567 94	25 6794	89	3	2720 34	27 2034	94	3	2872 74	28 7274	99	3	3025 14	30 2514
79	4	2418 08	24 1808	84	4	2570 48	25 7048	89	4	2722 88	27 2288	94	4	2875 28	28 7528	99	4	3027 68	30 2768
79	5	2420 62	24 2062	84	5	2573 02	25 7302	89	5	2725 42	27 2542	94	5	2877 82	28 7782	99	5	3030 22	30 3022
79	6	2423 16	24 2316	84	6	2575 56	25 7556	89	6	2727 96	27 2796	94	6	2880 36	28 8036	99	6	3032 76	30 3276
79	7	2425 70	24 2570	84	7	2578 10	25 7810	89	7	2730 50	27 3050	94	7	2882 90	28 8290	99	7	3035 30	30 3530
79	8	2428 24	24 2824	84	8	2580 64	25 8064	89	8	2733 04	27 3304	94	8	2885 44	28 8544	99	8	3037 84	30 3784
79	9	2430 78	24 3078	84	9	2583 18	25 8318	89	9	2735 58	27 3558	94	9	2887 98	28 8798	99	9	3040 38	30 4038
79	10	2433 32	24 3332	84	10	2585 72	25 8572	89	10	2738 12	27 3812	94	10	2890 52	28 9052	99	10	3042 92	30 4292
79	11	2435 86	24 3586	84	11	2588 26	25 8826	89	11	2740 66	27 4066	94	11	2893 06	28 9306	99	11	3045 46	30 4546
80	0	2438 40	24 3840	85	0	2590 80	25 9080	90	0	2743 20	27 4320	95	0	2895 60	28 9560	100	0	3048 00	30 4800

Metric Conversion Tables, Barnes & Noble, 1975, pp. 3–16 (Ottenheimer Publishers, Inc.).

Index

A

Advertising new houses, 43, 338
Appraiser, 274

B

Bankruptcy, 11
Basement walls, 129
Building
    architect's final inspection, 42
    business failures, 1
    capital, 2
    final inspection, 41
    frigid conditions, 56
    lot survey, 2
    maintenance, 336
    permits, 5
    preliminary operations, 7
    site, 3

C

Carpenters, framing square, 163

Ceilings, 212
    flat roofs, 207–212
Chandeliers, 326
Chimney, 84
    courses, 87
    estimating fireplaces, 87
    fireplaces, 291
    openings, 145
Cladding, wall, 249
    bevel siding, 255
    crawl space, 264
    decibels, 261
    estimating, 257
    fiber boards, 249
    insulation, 261
    nailing techniques, 252, 253
    nail types, 254
    siding, 258
    sound control, 259
    tongue and groove siding, 254
    vapor barriers, 249, 250
Columns, 129
Concrete
    aggregate manufactured, 62

Concrete (*Contd.*)
  bank or pit-run, 103
  basement walls, 98
  consistency of mix, 157
  curing, 110
  dry materials per mix, 105
  embedding joists, 135
  floor slabs, 131
    insulation, 131
  forms, 149
    hardware, 153
  formwork, 97
    framed, 153
  ground slab, 135
  mixer sizes, 105
    mixing time, 105
  plywood forms, 153
    ready mix, 99
    release agent, 152
    repairing, 151
  slab and foundation, 132
  storage, 104
  stripping and reconditioning forms, 110
  subcontractors, 276
  surface area of aggregate, 101
  types of cement, 157
  types of plywood forms, 158
  vibration, 157
  weight, 99
  wood bucks, 106, 110
  work-up sheets, 107
Contract of sale, 336
Contractor
  general, 275
  subcontractor, 275
Critical path method, 43
  activity, 47, 48
  backward pass, 53
  computing CPM time, 50
  duration, 48
  event, 48
  forward pass, 48
  project, 47

D

Decibels, 261
Decorating, 325
Depreciation, 33
  book value, 33
  comparative depreciation value, 37
  declining balance, 35
  equipment schedules and industrial
    equipment maintenance, 38
  methods, 33
  salvage value, 34
  straight line method, 34
  sum-of-years digits, 36
Drawing, 6
Driveways, 334
Drywall, 264

E

Estimating, 104
  concrete floor, 104
  fire brick, 87
  land cut and fill, 61
  quantities of dry material for one cubic
    yard of wet concrete, 103
  runways, 105
  work-up sheets, 107
Estimator's guidelist for residential construction, 122

F

Fiberglass, 265, 268
Final inspection of new buildings, 42
  general contractor's inspection, 42
Fireplaces, 285, 296
  elevation, 297
  estimating, 87
Flat roofs tongue and groove decks, 213,
  215

Floor assembly, 129
   bridging, 114
   frame openings, 145, 146
   supports, 136
   typical sections, 140
Floor coverings, 327, 330
Foundations
   batter boards, 74
   builder's layout square, 70
   building lines, 70
   chimney, 84
   floor panel heating, 91
   grading, 70
   pier pads, 84
   piles and grade beams, 90
   right-angle triangle, 69
      slab on grade, 90
      step footings, 90
      underpinning, 83
      wall footings, 89
Framing
   anchors, 161
   balloon, 116, 117, 172
   brick veneer, 123
   conventional wall, 161
   corner layout, 164, 165
   corner studs, 162, 163
   door and window opening, 166
   platform and western, 113
   post and beam, 116, 118, 119
   prefabrication, 116
      semi-prefabrication, 167
      steel joist and studs, 184
   western, 115

G

Gallon, American/Canadian, 104
Glass blocks, 301, 312
   building units, 313
   gliding doors, 301, 321

Glossary
   chimney terms, 294
   common building terms, 341, 350
   stairs, 285
   underpinning terms, 130
Guidelist for residential constructors, 122

I

Inspection, buildings, 333
   final, 335
Insulation
   floor slab, 131
   types, 132, 133
Insurance, 280, 283
   experience rating, 283

J

Joists embedded in concrete, 135

L

Land, 59
   appraisal, 6
   benchmark, 60
   cut earth, 60
   estimating cut, 61
   grading terms, 59
   purchase, 3, 15
   registry office, 4
   restrictions, 23, 29
   swell percentage cut earth, 60
   title, 336
   title examiner, 25
   volumes, imperial, metric, 61
Landscaping, 333, 335

M

Masonry units, 301
    adjustable wall ties, 302
    Dur-O-Wall, 303, 308
    glass blocks, 302
    glazed, 302
    metric, 322, 323
    shapes, sizes, 309, 311
    unit lintels, 314
Mesh, steel welded, 92
Metal finishing, 325
Metric conversion tables, 351–355
    nomenclature for lumber products, 217,
        219
Mirrors, 326
Municipal planning department, 15
    zoning classifications, 17

N

Notarization, 333

O

Overhead expenses, 19

P

Painting, 325
Partnerships, 8
    advantages, 10
    disadvantages, 11
    general, 9
Post and beam construction, 197
    curtain walls, 198, 203
Preliminary building operations, 53
    datum and batter boards, 54
    inspecting the building site, 54
    residential units, 51
    test pits, 56

Preliminary building operations (*Contd.*)
    underground conditions, 55
Property sale, 338

R

Reinforcing, 92
Residential construction, 122
Roofs
    data for traditional and metric framing
        squares, 248
    definitions, 223
    elevation, 223
    framing squares, 234, 235
        applications, 226–244
    pitch, 227, 228, 229
    sawtooth, 223
    truss plates, 247

S

Sale
    closing of title, 45
    contracts, 44
Sanitary fill, 5
Scaffolding, 191
    half horse, 192, 193
    metal, 193–196
Specifications, 6
Stairs, 293
    floor openings, 145
    glossary of terms, 285
    illustrations, 147
    ratio, rise to tread, 291
    safety treads, 331
    story rod, 287, 289
    wooden, open stringer, 286
Story rods for carpenters, 77
    kitchen cabinets, 78, 79
    masons, 78
Subcontractors, 276
    concrete, 276
    excavating, 276

Subcontractors (*Contd.*)
    guidelist, 277
    subtrades, 273

T

Tables, thermal and vapor, 270, 271
Trim, interior, 296
Typical wall section, 114

W

Wall cladding, 249
Wallpaper, 325
Wall sections, 113
Wood moldings, 298

Z

Zone classifications, 17